A Fortress and a Legacy

From Lorela and Joe

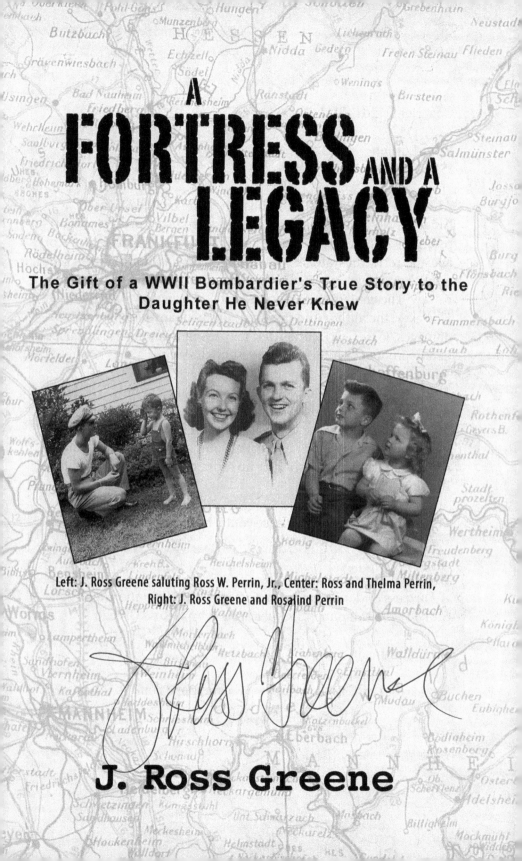

A FORTRESS AND A LEGACY

The Gift of a WWII Bombardier's True Story to the Daughter He Never Knew

Left: J. Ross Greene saluting Ross W. Perrin, Jr., Center: Ross and Thelma Perrin,
Right: J. Ross Greene and Rosalind Perrin

J. Ross Greene

Print Edition
ISBN: 978-1-5122-6230-8

For further information, please contact the author by email at rossgreene@afortressandalegacy.com.

Greene, J. Ross
A Fortress and a Legacy: The Gift of a WWII Bombardier's True Story to the Daughter He Never Knew by J. Ross Greene

First Printing in 2015.

Text layout by Clark Kenyon, www.camppope.com

Contents

Author's Note

THE CORE OF THE BOOK emanates from the cache of letters written to, from and about Ross W. Perrin during the period 1941-1947. Where quotations from these letters appear in the book, they are stated exactly as they were written, with only minor punctuation and word alterations for clarity.

A Fortress and a Legacy is written as a non-fiction historical novel. The events surrounding WWII, missions flown and made a part of this book are as accurate as I could make them from the multifaceted research used to assimilate data and facts. Where these letters, Air Force information and personal interview information are clear, the facts are related spot on. Where these sources are silent, I have linked all that I have gathered in my research with what I believe to be philosophically and materially correct and consistent with the intent, world-view and heart of Bud and the other characters, to create dialogue and action.

Dedication

To my wife, **Lynne**: Thanks for always believing in and loving me.

To my children and their spouses, **Dan** and **Ginger**, **David** and **Jackie**, and **Meredith** and **Michael**: I hope you will use this story to advance your understanding of the importance of WWII and help focus the attention of your children, our grandchildren, on the significance of this critical period of our history.

To my grandchildren **Lauren, Jack (John Ross II), David, Michael, Perrin, Avery, Walker and Griffin**: I pray you will use this book as a catalyst to learn more about how WWII affected the world; the contribution Ross Perrin made to keep our nation free, and the importance I place on his life, his story, and his legacy.

To Ross W. Perrin, Jr.'s daughter, **Rosalind**, and his granddaughters **Mary** and **Elizabeth**: I hope this provides a vibrant word picture of the man your Dad and Granddad was and the great daddy and granddaddy he would have been.

To each of you: Please keep my Uncle Bud's life story and legacy alive for generations to come.

Foreword

A Gift that Will Keep on Giving

IF EVER THERE WAS A gift that will keep on giving, it is *A Fortress and a Legacy*. My cousin, its author, wanted to give me my father. This book does and will continue to do just that.

I am among the many born during WWII who grew up knowing their fathers only from what others said. Dad was killed before he learned that "Junior" was indeed the "prissy little girl" who would have "hung on to him for life."

And in one sense, that is what I have done. Even with the love of my devoted mother, my stepfather, and other family members, I grew up with a longing for this good-looking, godly man who was loved by everyone who knew him.

While it may seem odd to grieve for someone I never met, I did. And I have to admit: sometimes I was jealous of J. Ross, as we called him, because *he* was the one who knew and was cherished by his Uncle Bud, my dad. Yet that relationship, brief as it was, has led to a six-year mission (some would say obsession) culminating in this tribute to my father, one I cherish more than words can ever express.

I experienced mixed emotions when in the spring of 2009, my sisters presented me with my parents' WWII correspondence. I knew that in those letters lay a beautiful but sad story about a loving couple who, along with many others, experienced the war's tragic impact. As much as I wanted to know more about their story, I was reluctant to reopen old wounds. Yet with my sisters' strong encouragement, I read a few letters. The tears came as anticipated, along with the fear that I could never make it through them all. But it became clear that the correspondence between my journalist mother and airman father brought these long-ago events and emotions to life. I also realized they represented a book that begged to be written.

In the meantime one of my sisters, Mom's fulltime caregiver

since her debilitating stroke, started reading the letters. Although Dad wasn't her father, she became engrossed. She, too, thought the letters should become the core of a book and urged me to find an experienced writer with an interest in WWII. I knew the task was beyond me but couldn't abide the thought of involving a stranger in something so personal.

During this time, I shared excerpts of the letters with J. Ross. Among them were detailed accounts of his own challenging but precocious behavior as the family's own "little rascal." He was clearly their bright spot during that fearful time. The more I read, the more I shared with him. When my sisters took on the enormous project of scanning every word, we began the cathartic experience of living through what our family—each one a hero—endured during those years.

And so this is how the experienced writer my sister suggested I find came to be my own beloved cousin. I believe God called him to write this book. When I think of the meticulous research; the extensive travel; and the people he has found, involved, and befriended—all in the midst of career, family vacations, health concerns, and countless frustrations, I'm amazed the project reached fruition. His perseverance proves his reliance on divine inspiration, guidance, and support. And I can't imagine anyone better equipped to carry out this calling than the grown-up, strong-willed little rascal who adored his "Palsy-Walsy."

Yet, as he shared with me the depth of his work, I sometimes wondered: Would this engineer turned financial wizard write the book I envisioned? I felt confident in his ability to create a thorough account of the events and surrounding details of the war. But would he include the romance, pathos, and humor of the people who lived them out? Would his story appeal to the heart as well as the head?

The day came when I received the first draft of *Fortress*. The more I read, the more I connected, to the point that I had to put my life on hold until I finished. There in those pages were the people I knew, portrayed in the essence of their true character and spirit—from my grandmother's strong faith, my mother's adjusting and supporting others, my sweet Aunt Evelyn's deep love, to my Uncle

Leonard's quick sense of humor and wisdom beyond his years, not to mention the antics of an adoring little J. Ross.

I am grateful to God and my family, most especially my cousin, for the gift of this book. It fulfills his desire to give me my father, and I know I will read it again and again. I am confident my extended family as well as many others—some friends and some strangers—will learn, laugh, and cry as they read the amazing culmination of his six-year journey.

I would love to have some of my cousin's energy and a small portion of his brain power, but I am grateful my grown-up J. Ross has such a wonderful amount of both. I wish my words could adequately express all the gratitude I have in my heart for this gift he has given me.

Rosalind Cannon Perrin Davis, aka "Junior"
Fort Lauderdale, Florida

CHAPTER 1

Introspection

After Three Months of Combat

Ridgewell, England: December 10, 1944

DARKNESS HUNG HEAVY AS BUD walked out through the double doors of the Officers Club and grabbed the cold handlebars of his bike. Swinging his leg over the wet, icy seat, he steadied himself and began pedaling. The tires played a monotonous crunching melody on the snow-covered gravel path during his ten-minute slog to his barracks.

He slowed to a stop and leaned his bike against the box-like corrugated metal hut that had been his home for the past three months. The biting cold of this sleet-laden night chilled him to the bone and matched the feeling deep in the pit of his stomach. The predictably bad English winter weather had shown up early and worsened as the day progressed.

The flashlight that illuminated his trip also guided his steps through the muddy snow and up the single step to the landing at the entrance. Shivering and wet, he grimaced as he twisted the doorknob. The door creaked open, revealing only darkness.

I'm alone. And I guess if I'm honest, afraid.

He remembered that the two other crews billeted with him were hoisting drinks at a pub in the nearby town of Halstead. *I've got no interest in joining 'em. And Glenn's* [Glenn Vaughn, his crew's co-pilot] *still at the Officers' Club (OC). But it's just as well; I don't want any company. I need some thinking time.*

The beam of Bud's flashlight scanned the eerily dark room, seeking the light switch. It stopped on his footlocker. "ROSS W. PERRIN, JR." adorned the front in white block letters with no rank indicated. Ranks changed often in wartime, and his would soon go from second to first lieutenant. *At least it should.*

His crew's pilot, Leo Belksis, had made first lieutenant earlier that day as had their squad's navigator, Jim Collett. Bud was happy for both, but their promotions, coupled with the delay of his own, punctuated his frustration.

He had been awakened much earlier on this morning, at 0330, for a mission to Mainz, Germany. "Take off at 0730," the CO said at briefing. They were parked on the hardstand with all four engines of their B-17G Flying Fortress at idle when, at 0700, red flares shot from the control tower indicated the mission had been scrubbed. *Frustrated again.*

As soon as he could, Bud swung his legs through the front hatch of the Fortress and plopped back onto the hardstand for a ride back to his hut and some more shut-eye. A long day to Mainz and back wasn't something to relish, but it would have helped end the war. *And it would have been my fifteenth mission, leaving twenty to go. Now my count still stands at fourteen.*

Bud and all the 381st crews headed back to their respective huts, hoping for a few more hours of sleep. Successful in his attempt, he awakened later that morning for the second time. After lunch at the officers' mess hall and hours of bridge at the OC, the darkness of winter again descended on the base.

So far, Bud had resisted the perpetual temptation of "just one more hand." Bridge helped numb the frustration and pass the otherwise monotonous hours between terrifying missions. On this night, his opponents tried to entice him to stay, as he was "into 'em for a couple of bucks," and they wanted it back.

"No dice," he said as he strode to the door at the back of the club.

Three months earlier, Bud had come to the air base at Ridgewell as the 532nd Bomb Squad's bombardier. He qualified as a navigator in his first month, and hoped that it would increase his opportunities to check off required missions.

Since Collett was the navigator assigned to the 532nd Squadron, Bud occasionally flew navigator with other crews. His proven expertise gave him the honor of flying with the lead crew on a number of missions. These assignments had brought more responsibility his way but also resulted in his not flying as often, so his mission count had slowed.

Vaughn had missed a few missions due to illness, so they both lagged behind the others in the original crew—just far enough behind to postpone their promotions. *Crap. I wonder if and when things will break my way.*

He plopped on his unmade bed and snapped off the flashlight. The hut was pitch-black. No moon. No truck or jeep lights. The lights of the Christmas decorations at the OC were too far away to be seen. Bud was alone with only his thoughts to keep him company, and not even the thought of Christmas could get him out of his funk.

I know I should write Thelma. But for some reason, I don't feel like it.

Thelma, his wife of two years and mother of his child due soon after Christmas, was the consummate scribe. As an advertising executive and amateur actress, her letters were long, detailed, and loving. *She sure knows how to turn a phrase,* he mused. Better yet, her letters could transport him the 4091 nautical miles (he knew the exact distance) back to Knoxville, the hometown he loved so much. *I wonder what my baby's doing right now?*

God alone witnessed his wistful smile.

In her letters, Thelma could tell him how she felt. She could also tell him what she did, in the minutest of detail. He liked that, but he couldn't come close to doing the same. *I can't tell her anything about missions and locations. I can tell her I've had a rough, long day. I can't tell her where I went. I can't say we were shot at by what seemed like bottle rockets zooming through our bomber stream, or that unseen flak kegs exploded and shot shards of metal through our ship. I can't tell the whole truth.*

The Air Force wouldn't let him, and officers censored outgoing mail to make sure details of the war effort didn't leak out. To make it more constraining, he was one of those chosen as a censor, and a rule-follower to boot. No skirting the edges for him.

Shackled. I'm shackled. And I can't let her know what we face on missions or that I'm terrified. But maybe that's for the best. She's scared, too. She just doesn't know what to be afraid of—except that I might not return home. That's something else we share. I just don't want to hold that thought too long and jinx things. Time to concentrate on something else.

At least we can write about our love. No censor will stop that. And that's a freedom to cherish.

These thoughts and more raced through his mind, colliding with the many emotions that held him captive. *This isn't like me. The guys know me as sensible, logical, cool under pressure, able to hold my emotions in check. Usually. But not tonight.*

A continuous movie of the previous day's Stuttgart mission was playing on a screen in his mind. *It was a tough day, but no worse than my first mission to Merseburg three months ago—or the two to Cologne, or the lead navigator mission to Magdeburg. What's the big deal with Stuttgart?*

No answer came. But the movie continued in all its terrifying clarity. *I can almost hear the clicking sound of the projector as the film slips from one reel to the other. Or is that flak?*

Bud had heard a rumor that there would be a mission to Mannheim the following day. Sometimes the grapevine was accurate, sometimes not. *If it's right, the crews will be in for another rough day.*

Mannheim was a collection and distribution point, a marshalling yard, for German war supplies destined to reinforce the Reich. It was also just across the Rhine from a major chemical plant, so protective German flak emplacements were heavily concentrated in the area. *Our crew will definitely fly this one, if it happens. Today's Mainz scrub just about assures that.*

Bud's mind hopscotched from combat to "Junior," his preliminary name for the child he looked forward to bouncing on his knee and spoiling like the dickens. *Girl, boy, it doesn't matter.*

His crewmates chided him unmercifully about his continual referring to his soon-to-be-born baby as "Junior." *It's easy, that's all. And "Juniorette" just doesn't have the same ring to it.*

Yep, a prissy little girl will hug on me for life. But a rambunctious boy will stop that hugging stuff someday and switch to shaking hands. A little girl sounds pretty good to me.

Still alone, he let the darkness envelope him with its soothing protection and silence. Eyes still closed, he smiled again. *I wonder if the glow from my smile lit up this room.*

He opened his eyes. It hadn't.

His mood lightening, Bud's heart beat faster at the exhilarating thought of fatherhood, of teaching his kids about the war and their dad's part in it. *I know I want a houseful of the little rascals. And if I can't tell them my story, who will? Lord, let that day come soon.*

After almost three years of US involvement, the tide in this grueling conflict seemed to be shifting ever so slightly the Allies' way. Guarded optimism was coursing through the base. Earlier that day, the 381st Bomb Group (BG) report for December 10 was posted: "The first ten days of the month were optimistic ones for the station personnel [at Ridgewell]. Our ground troops on the continent are making steady progress and speculation regarding the date of Germany's fold-up is rife."

Bud sighed. *Will all this optimism bear fruit? No one knows, but everyone hopes.*

Lost in his thoughts, he finally recognized the late hour. *Ten o'clock. I've got to get some sleep in case we fly tomorrow. I'll just have to deal with these frustrations later. But first, I'd better get busy and write Thelma.*

> *Dearest,*
> *I'm already in bed, but thought I'd like to say goodnight to my sweet little wife before going to sleep. I had to get up real early again this morning, but got back to bed earlier than I usually get up, so I got plenty of sack time. Didn't write yesterday because I was too tired after a rather tough day—it was long anyway ...still don't have any mail from you since last Monday. Now sweetheart, if you don't mind, I'll stop this letter short and try to get some shut-eye. I love you, baby, an awful lot—think of you constantly.*
> *Goodnight—Bud*

He folded the letter, sealed it, and put it in his Bible where he would find it the next morning. *I don't want to forget to post it on the way to mess.*

A deep sleep soon covered Bud like a blanket, obliterating his concerns—if only for the moment.

CHAPTER 2

Confusion and Change

More Than Three Years Earlier

Knoxville, Tennessee: September 1, 1941

IN THE SOUTH, LABOR DAY has long been a day of transition. In post-Depression Knoxville, Tennessee, the transition had multiple faces. The chill in the air during late August diminished the use of public swimming pools, and Labor Day marked their annual closing. Kids prepared for the dreaded opening of school a week or so later. On "The Hill," as locals called the University of Tennessee, the vaunted Volunteers began preparation for what everyone hoped would be another successful football season.

Labor Day had, for a few years, been UT's team picture day and open to the public. The hard, two-a-day practice sessions that began after that were closed to all but players, coaches, staff, and a few sportswriters. The Vols couldn't run the risk of opponent spies invading the hallowed Upper Hudson, the larger of two practice fields used by the football team.

With the season opener against the Furman Paladins a mere twenty days away, the town was abuzz with talk of the 1941 schedule. A stunning event a few weeks earlier heightened the intensity of the conversation as well as the concern over the success of the upcoming campaign. The athletic department had named a new coach, John Barnhill, to direct the 1941 team. Major Robert Reese Neyland, head coach for fourteen of the previous fifteen years and known by all as "The Major," would not be roaming the sidelines adorned with his ever-present John B. Stetson hat and stern expression. His departure from the coaching ranks stunned the city for two primary reasons.

First, Tennessee football was at the pinnacle of success after undefeated seasons the previous three years. The '38 and '40 teams

7

were national champs, and the 1939 team was unscored-on. Neyland's leadership in this unprecedented run had propelled him to
the status of football god not only in the hills of Tennessee, but also
among knowledgeable college football followers across the country.
With the departure of such a successful architect, Knoxville's football faithful waited with undeniable, understandable concern.

The other reason proved even more stunning. The Major was returning for a second time to military service after being called up by
the Army powers-that-be. Was this an ominous reflection of recent
world events, or a coincidental career reversal of a successful military officer determined to obtain the coveted general's stripes?

President Franklin D. Roosevelt had been reelected for a third
term in 1940 only after assuring voters he would not lead the country into a "foreign" war. Decisions and events after his election,
however, stood in sharp contrast to this assertion. Neyland's call-
up emphasized both this contrast and the country's growing uneasiness about the possibility of war. Both young men of military age
and their parents had personal reasons for fear.

Tennessee football, long the central topic of conversation among
Knoxvillians, was declining in importance as geopolitical issues
escalated. Coffee breaks, dinner tables, and group gatherings became common venues for discussions about what looked like the
imminent involvement of the U.S. in the European conflict. Despite
protests from the nation's staunch isolationists, such a step was beginning to seem more likely.

Big Ridge State Park, north of Knoxville, was a favorite getaway
location for families and young couples alike. The park had a large
natural swimming facility with a barge-like dock in the middle. The
surrounding shoreline resembled an ocean beach. Since the closest
real beach was four hundred miles away, Big Ridge was a cheap-
er alternative. Numerous areas near the water provided space for
softball and touch football games. Benches and pits for small camp-
fires afforded both a necessary respite from sporting activities and
needed picnic facilities. On this Labor Day, the temperature was

rising and would reach a comfortable eighty-five degrees with low humidity.

Bud Perrin had, on short notice, put together a day of fun and food at Big Ridge. His date that day was Thelma McGhee, a beautiful young girl two years his junior. Bud, no stranger to the Knoxville dating scene, had been linked for the past decade to many of the city's most attractive, intelligent, and available young ladies. But Thelma now seemed to be crowding out the others who vied for his attention.

This day marked the one-year anniversary of her winning the Miss Knoxville crown. The honor had earned Thelma a Knoxville *News Sentinel* front-page photo, taken on her way to Atlantic City to

Thelma McGhee and Ross "Bud" Perrin - Summer, 1941
Rosalind Perrin Davis Collection

compete in the 1940 Miss America Pageant. And her detailed dating calendar indicated a waning interest in other suitors and an accompanying focus on the square-jawed, 165-pound, five-foot-eleven-inch chiseled "catch" known as Bud.

The Perrins were a close-knit, patriarchal family that began with the marriage of Ross W. Perrin, Sr. and Maude Foster. They raised their three children, Evelyn, Bud, and Margie (born with Down syndrome), in a strongly religious Southern Baptist home.

Mr. Perrin (Southern tradition called for the head of the household to be addressed as mister) was a hard-working, soft-spoken, highly respected man. For more than two decades, he worked as a machinist at the Roundhouse, the repair shop for Southern Railway engines in John Sevier, northeast of Knoxville. The job proved physically demanding, but this quiet, wiry man didn't complain. The Depression from which his country had clawed and scratched its way out had taught him to be happy to have a job—any job.

Evelyn and J. Ross Greene;
Bud, Margie and
Maude Perrin - Spring, 1943;
Greene Family Collection

Ross W. Perrin, Sr.- circa 1939
Greene Family Collection

But on June 14, 1940, at age forty-nine, he had a heart attack at work. His fellow employees transported him by car to the family home on Scott Street, propping him up next to an oak tree in the front yard to await the family physician.

Dr. Trotter arrived and had Mr. Perrin moved inside to his bed, where he died a few hours later, Evelyn, Margie, and Maude by his side. His excruciating pain traumatized his family, who were helpless to lessen it. In one long day, Bud became the man of the house.

Finances were tight for almost everyone in post-Depression Knoxville. But despite these and other hardships, the Perrins' close family bond left them feeling rich and secure. Depression days included many dinners of fried meal cakes and little more. Conditions had improved in the decade since, but the residual strains of the national crisis were never far from the mind of the family's bread-winner or its bread-maker, Maude. And now she was alone, with neither job skills nor experience. The stress of losing a spouse, caring alone for a dependent daughter, and the accompanying financial burden ravaged both her health and her psyche.

Bud had always been the apple of his parents' collective eye. He knew it, and they didn't deny it. And his sisters not only accepted it but were, like the rest of the family, equally enamored with this man of character and kindness.

Bud graduated from Knoxville High School ("Knox Hi" to

townspeople) in the class of 1935. He was intelligent but certainly not a bookworm, to which his less than stellar grades attested. There were, he believed, other necessary segments of a well-rounded education, and well-rounded he became. His movie-star good looks and charismatic personality served him well. Active in basketball, baseball, softball, and football, he was a fixture in the training rooms at the YMCA on Clinch Avenue.

Bud's magnetism, however, went far beyond physical appearance. His smile was the gateway to a man who built instant friendships and had few, if any, enemies. He put others at ease, and his intense focus made them feel important because to him, they were.

After graduation he went to work at the Knoxville Electric Power & Water Board, the local electric utility. There, he carved out a decent path of advancement, and his future seemed promising and secure. But after five-plus years, he was growing restless. He wished he had withstood the temptation of solid employment after high school graduation in favor of the more difficult path of a college education. But at the time, he had no way to fund such an endeavor. Since he had saved some money, enrolling in UT was now a consideration. But at the advanced age of twenty-five, other factors made this drastic life change significantly more difficult.

In January of 1941, Bud took a Dale Carnegie course in an attempt to better himself and his employment opportunities. Later in May, he applied for but failed to get a sales job in Memphis. Although the rejection frustrated him, he didn't allow it to deter his search for something better. Only close friends and family knew of his restlessness, so the job search did not compromise his present job.

Bud's habit of playing the field of young, interesting ladies in Knoxville had also met an obstacle, if the affections of a stunning former Miss America contestant could be considered an obstacle. Of course, Thelma wasn't an impediment in the traditional sense. But their relationship did have him considering marriage, a family, and upward mobility, all of which caused him to reconsider his carefree lifestyle. This dilemma, coupled with a nation arguably on a collision course with another war, yielded a season of personal turmoil.

Bud was not the only young American male caught in such a conflicted maze of thinking. Issues surrounding the possibility of war now crept into the conversations of all age groups. Like others of his age and position in life, Bud wished he knew more about the history of WWI and what had happened in the twenty-plus years since its 1918 conclusion. Such knowledge might help him sort out the opposing views now in hot debate across the country.

Bud also, like many of his friends, had chosen to skate through two years of high school history. Miss Neubert, his history teacher in his senior year, made that skating possible. She had a benign and innocent fondness for male students and athletes, and Bud was both. That helped him slide through without too much study but placed him at a severe deficit when it came to a broad understanding of history. Current events made this lack of knowledge neither palatable nor acceptable. Something had to change.

More than a few families, anxious to wring the last bit of swimming out of a beautiful summer, had already staked out strategic spots along the recreation areas at Big Ridge. But the slightly more secluded areas favored by young couples in love remained wide open. Bud and Thelma were intent on arriving ahead of the others on that sun-drenched day to ensure a prime spot for an early afternoon supper and an evening of spirited conversation.

Bud's sister, Evelyn, and her husband, Leonard Greene, soon drove up with their six-month-old son, J. Ross. This little boy had captured Bud's heart, making him even more conscious of his strong desire for a family of his own.

"Hey Evie, got my 'Palsy Walsy' with ya?" Bud hollered as Leonard brought his car to a slow stop beside his Ford. The special nickname would stick, binding uncle and nephew together in the coming years.

"You may not want him. He's been a stinker today in more ways than one," she said, a slight frown replacing her usual smile. "Wanna change this muddy diaper?"

Bud responded with a twisted mouth and turned-up nose that silently shouted, "He's all yours."

Evelyn was a slightly built, beautiful, and gracious lady who loved her brother as much as he loved her. Bud was intensely protective without smothering, a perfect combination. Leonard and Evelyn had been married three years. At about the time they wed, Leonard left a job at Kern's Bakery for one at the Southern Railway, where his father-in-law had worked for over a decade. Ross, Sr. vouched for him, asking the company to "Give him a chance. He's a good man and a good worker." Mr. Perrin's word was his proven bond, and Leonard was hired on September 9, 1938.

Leonard was rail-thin, six feet tall and 135 pounds at most. He loved baseball and had played for a number of semi-pro teams in the Knoxville area. Bud, thrilled at his sister's choice of such a hard-working, easy-going man, had become one of Leonard's closest friends.

"Who else is coming today?" Leonard asked as he helped Evelyn pack away the dirty diaper for later laundering.

"Don't know," Bud replied. "Dusty Holder and Emma for sure." All three had been close friends during high school, and they now worked together at the Knoxville Power Board. Emma, a demure girl with silky blond hair, had eloped with Walter a year earlier. Her groom had always been called "Dusty," although no one seemed to know why.

Leonard and Evelyn Perrin Greene - circa 1939
Greene Family Collection

"Grover Blevins said he would have come, but Henry already promised her family they'd join them at the lake."

"Henry" was Henrietta Bowman, Grover's current girlfriend, although she didn't approve of either that designation or her single status. Much in demand as a date, she'd given Grover a recent ultimatum: "Shape up or ship out, bub!"

Grover knew she meant it and was making plans to put a ring on her finger. "You'd better hurry up, Grover, she's not waitin' much longer, and you're not the only boy in line," Bud told him.

"I invited Joe and Linda Mucke," Leonard said. Joe and Linda had "stood up" for Leonard and Evelyn at their wedding a few years earlier. Joe was a fellow railroader and Linda was, well, just Linda. No one, not even Joe or Linda herself, knew what she might say next. But what everyone did know was that her words would include plenty of salty expressions, each followed by Joe's admonishment, "Now, Linda." His correction never worked, but he never quit trying, and she rarely quit talking.

"I called Dick and asked him to bring Mickey," Bud's sister added. "I'm sure they'll show up." Their cousin Dick Foster was a gentle man, younger than the rest of the group, who graduated from Knox Hi's rival, Central Hi or "County," in 1940. Intelligent and knowledgeable in many subjects, including history, Dick had completed a year at UT as a civil engineering major. He and his fiancée, Mickey Halburnt, fit well in any crowd.

"Ty and Gertrude are sure to be here," Evelyn said. Ty McCloud had introduced Bud and Thelma in March of 1941. Since then, the four of them had double-dated dozens of times and had become quite close. Thelma and Ty both worked in advertising, Ty with WROL, the local NBC affiliate, and Thelma with J. C. Penney, the anchor department store on Gay Street in downtown Knoxville. Ty and "Truji" ("Don't you dare call me 'Gerti,' asserted his plain-spoken fiancée) were planning a November wedding

Over the next couple of hours, the couples all arrived. The girls first prepared the hot dogs, hamburgers, and "fixin's" for the supper to come. Evelyn brought the chocolate pie her brother loved, which had also become one of Leonard's favorites. Dick's fiancée, Mickey, brought a scrumptious chocolate cake. The guys suggested the group start the meal with desserts. The girls disagreed, and as usual, their decision carried the day.

The guys peeled away from the food preparation so they could throw a football around. This gave the girls, who didn't know each other as well as the boys, a little time to get acquainted. Thelma was somewhat of a celebrity because of articles in the newspaper about her Miss Knoxville victory. Evelyn, Emma, and Truji knew Thelma well, but Linda and Mickey didn't. Never one to hold back when

Linda and Joe Mucke -1941
Mary Evelyn Mucke Collection

Ty and Truji McCloud - November 7, 1941
Rosalind Perrin Davis Collection

Grover "Cleve" Blevins -1941
Blevins Family Collection

Henrietta Bowman (Blevins) - 1941
Blevins Family Collection

Walter "Dusty" & Emma Orben Holder-1941
Holder Family Collection

Dick Foster and Mickey Halburnt (Foster) -1940
Foster Family Collection

she had a thought or a question, Linda jumped headlong into the conversation.

"I read in the paper last year that you didn't think you had a chance of winning Miss America. How come?"

"I was dumbfounded when I won Miss Knoxville, thrilled but

very surprised. A little high school actress competing with all those talented, beautiful girls—I could hardly believe it."

"So the quote in the paper on the Sunday after the pageant was what you actually said?" Mickey asked.

"You mean, 'I don't have what it takes to be Miss America'?" Thelma asked (Knoxville Journal, September 1, 1940).

"Yes, that's the one."

"My exact words."

"So the paper got it right. That's unusual." Linda said with a wry smile. "I think FDR was in a parade down Gay Street right after the Miss Knoxville Contest. Did you see him?"

"I was getting ready to go to Atlantic City and missed the parade," Thelma said.

A few more questions about Thelma's time in Atlantic City and what it was like walking across the stage in a swimsuit, and conversation drifted back to meal prepara-

Thelma McGee, Miss Knoxville, 1940
Rosalind Perrin Davis Collection

tion. Thelma's self-deprecating manner had quickly captivated both Linda and Mickey, just as it had the others who already knew her.

Meanwhile, the boys were passing the football around, but a game of touch never materialized. By the time enough players arrived for a three-on-three game, serious conversations had already begun. Their first topic: the Tennessee football situation.

"Hey Ty, what's the word out of the football office about Neyland's departure?" Leonard asked, knowing that his advertising connections probably gave Ty the inside track.

Thelma McGhee, Miss America Pageant, Atlantic City - 1940
Rosalind Perrin Davis Collection

Even though the Vols were at the top of the college football world after the late thirties, they had yet to fill their expanded venue on any Saturday afternoon. Shields-Watkins Stadium, completed in 1921 and named for its prime benefactors, Colonel W. S. Shields and his wife, Alice Watkins-Shields, underwent a sixty-percent expansion in 1938. The addition of 12,030 seats on the east side of the field started a seventy-year enlargement that no one of that era could have anticipated. People feared that, with Neyland handing off the baton to Barnhill, both team and attendance might suffer.

Ty responded, "All I hear is upbeat. What else are they going to say, they have tickets to sell?"

"They gotta be concerned about losing Foxx, Molinski, and Suffridge [the team's three All-Americans from the previous two years]," Bud interjected, "but if I were Barnhill, I'd be excited about Johnny Butler and Walt Slater."

"I agree," Leonard said as he threw a perfect sidearm spiral to Joe, who muffed it. "I believe the only teams that have much of a chance against them are Alabama, Duke, and Boston College, and only the 'Bama game is at home."

His concerns would prove to be prophetic as the Vols would eventually lose to both the Blue Devils of Duke and the Crimson Tide of Alabama. So much for perfect seasons.

The afternoon autumn chill set in as the sun dropped below the trees on the west side of the lake. Thousands of crickets chirped their sharp, low-pitched, monotonous song as the couples enjoyed the last picnic of summer. Sitting by the fire crackling in the pit beneath the grill, the conversation turned from the delicious food to the political climate and the pervasive concern they all felt over world issues. The mood became somber.

"Did anyone see the Gary Cooper movie at the Tennessee?" asked Dusty.

"You mean *Sergeant York*?" asked Bud. "I did, and it was great. What a dilemma he faced!"

Sergeant York was the much-acclaimed movie about Alvin York, a young Tennessee hillbilly. A spiritual encounter transformed York's life from one of drinking and fighting to that of a conscientious objector. After a further transformation, he ended up as the most-decorated U.S. serviceman of World War I, whose life story became known nationwide. The Warner Brothers film was held over at the Riviera Theater after a long run at Knoxville's premier downtown theater, the Tennessee.

"Did you see those horrible trench conditions: mud, snow, and freezing temperatures?"

"I saw that, too," Joe interrupted Dick's question. "I've spent way too much time in the mud, and getting shot at to boot? Count me out."

"Hey, Joe, World War I was two decades ago," Bud said.

"Yeah, but with the way things are going, another one could be right around the corner." Joe slammed a stick to the ground in frustration.

The fear of war rolled around in everyone's minds, but Joe's words stunned them to silence.

After a minute that seemed like an hour, Dusty looked up from his unfocused, downward stare to ask, "How in the heck did Germany go from gettin' their butt whipped in World War I and havin' their hands tied by the Treaty of Versailles to the strength they obviously have today?"

Dick Foster was the only one present who had made an independent study of the war in Europe. He had also paid closer attention in high school history classes than the others. But as the youngest in the group, he was hesitant to assert his views until he saw their genuine interest in the topic. "There was a lot of turmoil in all of Europe after World War I, but especially in Germany," he said. "The invasion of Poland two years ago today wasn't really the beginning of the war. Under Hitler, the Nazis actually annexed Austria without firing a shot in March of 1938. Seven months later, in October, they took over the Sudetenland."

"Where exactly is that?" asked Leonard.

"That's the German term for the northern, southwestern, and western regions of Czechoslovakia, inhabited by ethnic Germans. And five months later, in March of 1939, Hitler took over the remainder of Czechoslovakia without military opposition," Dick added.

"And then Poland. Why didn't anyone stop him before that?" Evelyn asked.

"Yeah. Why not?" Thelma chimed in.

"Sounds like all the mouthy weaklings aren't just teenage punks. Some of them are lily-livered, wine-swilling national leaders," Linda offered. Joe, frowning his displeasure at her harsh comment, was in fact relieved. After all, she hadn't cursed. He breathed a sigh of relief.

"I think some tried, sort of half-heartedly, didn't they?" Joe asked before Linda could take a breath and start again.

"'Half-heartedly' is right. Plenty of nations stuck out their chests and played Billy Goat Gruff, trying to bluff Hitler out of his conquests, but no one would really go toe-to-toe with him," Dick explained. "Britain sent Neville Chamberlain to Munich in September of 1938 to negotiate with Hitler over the Sudetenland. He returned thinking he had secured peace, but that devious Hitler had him fooled."

"After Czechoslovakia and Austria, Hitler formed an alliance with the Soviet Union in the summer of 1939, and the shooting began with the invasion of Poland," added Ty.

"A year or so ago, I saw a Movietone News clip on last summer's bombing of Britain. It was devastating," Bud said. "They also showed the results of Nazi bombing in the city of Coventry in November, I think it was. I couldn't believe the way that place was leveled. How did they last through such shelling?"

To make extra money, Bud worked as an usher at the Tennessee, a job he had kept from his high school days. It provided him the privilege of seeing lots of movies and newsreels (current films of national and global events).

"Churchill actually has been a stalwart in keeping Great Britain in the game under incredible stress. The will of the Brits has been nothing short of phenomenal," Ty said.

"How did Chamberlain fit into the days before the war started?" Joe asked.

"He sorta gave away the British store when he agreed that Great Britain would not oppose Hitler's desire to take back the German territory in western Czechoslovakia," Dick Foster added.

"Was that the reason Churchill became prime minister? And wasn't he a senator in England at the time?" Leonard asked.

"Their representatives are called 'members of parliament'—MPs, I think," Bud responded.

"Right," Dick confirmed. "Churchill had a spotted career in the previous years but was considered an intelligent military man."

"I guess he knew the odds were stacked against him with the Germans shelling Britain as they were," Dusty said.

The English people needed a strong leader who could manage a war effort while giving the people a good dose of Guinness courage, as the Brits referred to the false strength brought on by imbibing the popular British ale.

It was well known on both sides of the pond that Churchill, while no stranger to Guinness and other similar beverages, did not need them to muster courage. He had proven many times over that he possessed a strong backbone and the willingness to apply it regardless of the doom that might exist. Roosevelt's lack of commitment to Churchill seemed to result in part from his concern over his British counterpart's leadership ability. Churchill, however, faced the situation with aplomb, relieving even his most ardent critics of their concerns. His skill in managing the battle with the better-financed and prepared Germany quickly became obvious.

As the months wore on, funds declined, nerves frayed, and the devastation increased in London and all across England. Roosevelt's ability to act prior to his closely contested presidential reelection victory over Republican Wendell Willkie added difficulty to Churchill's problem. But later, he had more freedom to provide assistance. The question on everyone's mind, including the picnic group, was: "Will Roosevelt finally get us into this war? And if not, why not?"

Edward R. Murrow's nightly report on CBS had escalated in popularity since early in 1940 after the narrow escape of the British from Dunkirk. His urging for US involvement in his early broadcasts had, by mid-1941, turned into a clarion call for intervention. As the fire snapped out its opinion, Bud added, "Murrow says the Brits can't go it alone."

The discussion about intervention or isolation continued well into the September evening. The fire that provided a warm, conversation-enhancing glow had started to sputter. As it did, an army of ravenous mosquitos began their buzzing and biting attack. Almost in unison, everyone began slapping at the pesky bloodsuckers. "I guess it's time to leave," said Thelma.

Before going home, they all recognized they had some work to do in order to learn more about the circumstances surrounding what might soon become their war. And not only did they need to learn more, but they needed to pray more as well.

Bud broke the silence brought about by the sober reflections. "My lack of understanding of the world situation embarrasses me. I want to know more. After all, we may all end up in this conflict before we know it. And I may have to explain all this to my children one day—if I'm blessed enough to have some, that is."

He winked at Thelma, whose coy smile confirmed her agreement. His heart beat faster as he continued. "I want them to know how the world got to this point and why. I need to play catch-up so I can decide what I think. Who's in?"

They stared at each other through the flickering light of the dying fire and agreed, still wondering what their assent meant. Bud put words to the consensus.

"Let's commit that by Christmas we'll be able to have a discussion with anyone about what the world faces today, why we face it, and what might be in store for us in the days ahead."

They nodded. After gathering their belongings and what little was left of the food, each couple ambled to the parking lot in silence, arm in arm. They drove into the chill of the September evening night with a newfound resolve—and a healthy fear of what the future might hold.

CHAPTER 3

Back to School

A Belated History Lesson

Knoxville, Tennessee: September 2, 1941

THE ALARM CLANGED ITS GET-UP message much too early and way too loudly. Never one to languish in bed, Bud rubbed his eyes as he bolted up to face the busy day. As he dropped off to sleep, the somewhat sobering discussions of the day's otherwise enjoyable picnic had filled his thoughts. And the same topic flooded his half-awake mind as he stumbled to the bathroom for a quick shave, shower, and polishing of the pearly whites that anchored his frequent smile.

As he readied himself for the work day, his mind raced with thoughts of how to fulfill his growing responsibilities to his employer and still sort out the issues surrounding the real possibility that the US would enter this war. And he had no choice but to consider the impact the conflict would have on most boys his age.

Why am I doing this? he mused. If war comes, it comes. *No amount of study to learn the hows and whys will make one iota of difference as to whether or not our nation gets involved.*

But the issue was not easy to dismiss. *Maybe I can't alter the future as it relates to war or my possible participation, but I need more insight,* he told himself. *Maybe then I'll know whether or not my viewpoint is correct. Or at least I'll know it's my own and not someone else's.*

In recent months, Bud had weighed the isolationist arguments for non-involvement. He had also considered the pugilistic stance for partnering with Great Britain against Nazi Germany. Both had merits. The isolationists didn't seem like pacifists who didn't believe in war under any circumstances but instead opposed this war in particular. After all, less than two decades had passed since the U.S. became entangled in the first pan-European war. *Our nation paid a tremendous financial and psychological price, and to what end? Bud wondered.*

The more aggressive interventionist posture is less palatable and more costly in every way, he thought, *at least in the short term. But, depending on the will and military strength of Western Europe, immediate participation in this war may end up costing less in the long run.* He continued his musing. *Would we simply be protecting Great Britain and France, or would this serve as pre-emptive protection from a possible Nazi plan to ultimately attack our own nation? It's confusing at best.*

Lunchtime came, but Bud took an uncharacteristic pass, choosing rather to take time for some research. He grabbed a cup of coffee and settled down in an empty office. After a quick flick of his pocketknife to sharpen his increasingly short yellow #2 pencil, he jotted notes on a company pad: "Hitler, Churchill, Poland, When?, How?, Lend-Lease." In no particular order, he listed the areas he wanted to research in putting this puzzle together.

But he still didn't know where to go to gather information. Knoxville's afternoon daily paper, the *Knoxville News Sentinel,* had a research room, and the Lawson McGee Library had a large number of periodicals. His thoughts trailed off as his high school history teacher, Miss Neubert, popped into his mind. *She'd make a great resource, but given my lackluster record in her class, I doubt she'll give me the time of day. Maybe she's forgotten me,* he thought with a twinge of hope. *Well, I'll give it a shot. What have I got to lose?"*

Bud turned right on Fifth, left on Lamar, parked next to the curb at the side of his former high school, and bolted from the car. Knox Hi was a stately building that had been *the* secondary school in the city since 1905.

As he scurried up the walkway, his eye caught sight of the familiar but often overlooked bronze statue of a WWI doughboy close to the street. He cut quite a foreboding figure with his left hand clutching a bayonet rifle and his right hand, fist clenched, stretched

Knoxville High School - circa 1940
Public Domain

up and forward in full victory stride. This memorial to the WWI 117th Infantry Division had stood guard over the school since John "Blackjack" Pershing spoke at its dedication in 1922.

Bud had passed this statue hundreds of times, but on this day he stopped to read the two inscriptions and consider each poignant message.

ERECTED
IN THE YEAR 1921
BY THE OFFICERS AND MEN
OF THE 117TH INFANTRY
59TH BGE. 30TH DIV.
THIRD TENNESSEE INFANTRY
TO OUR LIVING DEAD;
THAT COMPANY OF SHINING SOULS
WHO GAVE THEIR YOUTH THAT THE
WORLD MIGHT GROW OLD IN PEACE. . .

The message of the dedication statement that followed on the statue's inscription was piercing; "faithful to their father's teachings, love of country, endurance of suffering and heroism to death... but at home they would not be forgotten." These words were both sobering and frightening. *The current war in Europe has the potential to be just as devastating as the one this statue represents. I don't want to think about it, but I have to.*

Bud paused to reflect further on these men who paid the ultimate price for the freedom that was again being threatened. *I don't want to reach Miss Neubert's classroom too late to catch her,* he thought as he bounded up the stairs two at a time and strode toward the front door

At the top of the well-worn marble steps hung a sign that read, "Knox Hi. Home of the Trojans." The nickname had a unique and strong appeal: no Cats, Bears, Tigers, or Lions for the school's blue-and-white teams. *Trojans* signified warriors, and warriors they were. The success of their sports teams over the years had infused a confidence in each successive class since before WWI.

He opened the front door and bounded up the wooden steps that responded with the familiar creaking sound they had emitted for decades. He turned left, then took an immediate right at the first hallway to find himself in front of Miss Neubert's room. Almost

Doughboy Monument in front of Knoxville High School-circa 1937
Knoxville News Sentinel

seven years earlier, in his senior year, she had taught him history—or tried to. Although her last class had concluded almost two hours earlier, she was just putting on her coat.

"Miss Neubert?" he ventured.

"Yes. May I help you?"

"Yes, ma'am." Bud smiled and dipped his head forward in respect. "I'm Ross Perrin, one of your students from the class of '35."

She squinted, paused, smirked, and chortled, "Uh. . . Bud, right?"

Miss Jessie Lou, as Miss Neubert was affectionately known, was, in Bud's senior year, a thirty-eight-year-old unmarried "schoolmarm," still sporting a tight hairdo pulled back into a bun. The six years since 1935 had done little to change her appearance or her quirky mannerisms.

"Yes ma'am, 'Bud'."

"Well, I must admit, I'm surprised to see you. Surprised, but happy."

Also surprised—and a little chagrined, Bud said, "I need some assistance, and I think you're the perfect one to help. If you have the time, that is."

Miss Jessie Lou Neubert
KHS and EHS History Teacher
(b1896–d1964)circa 1958
1958 East High School Yearbook

She pursed her lips in what looked like an embarrassed smile. "Well, I'll try. Sit down, please, and tell me how I can help."

Bud pulled his notes from the inside pocket of his suit coat as, for the first time since graduation, he parked himself in a student chair across from Miss Neubert's desk. *I've never sat this close to the front,* he thought, as he glanced at the back of the classroom. As Bud explained his dilemma, her amused gaze indicated that the irony of the regression to the teacher-student relationship of years earlier seemed to escape neither.

Once he finished relating the discussion at the Labor Day picnic and the Geopolitical education the group had agreed to pursue, Miss Neubert asked, "Who's in this group of aspiring history professors, and what would you all like to learn?"

"Well, most of us are Knox Hi grads whom you may remember: Leonard Greene, who married my sister Evelyn; Joe Mucke and his wife, Linda; Dusty Holder and his wife, Emma—she was Emma Orban. Grover Blevins and his fiancée, Henrietta, are prospective students. Gertrude Meyer, I mean 'Truji,' wants to come, as does her fiancé, Ty McCloud. Dick Foster and his fiancée, Mickey—Central grads are also part of our group."

"I vaguely remember some of those names. Seems like most of them were here a few years before you, right? What about your wife—you are married, aren't you?"

"No ma'am, I'm still single, but I think I've met the one. She graduated in 1937, Thelma McGhee. She'll join us, too."

"I remember her. She was on the *Blue and White* newspaper staff, right?" And wasn't she Miss Knoxville last year?" she added before he could answer.

"Yes. You have a good memory."

"Now, what exactly do you all want to know?"

"Well, uh. . . " he gazed at the ceiling as he searched for a way to express what they really wanted to know: where this quagmire in Europe was leading and how it was going to affect the US, boys of military age, and—yes—themselves.

"We for sure want to know *what* the future holds with this problem in Europe. But we also know that to understand it, we have to connect the dots of history to *know why* and *how* we got to where we are today."

"You left out *who*, Bud, because we can't understand this multi-dimensional and deadly chess game without knowing all the major players."

"You mean Hitler, I guess."

"Yes, to be sure, Hitler's the catalyst and key adversary, but he has henchmen, and not all of them are in Germany. Mussolini and Stalin each play a role. Secondary, to be sure, but a role nonetheless. And don't forget Japan."

"What about Churchill? And FDR?

"First things first. Why don't you and your friends take a look at Hitler's role in the current world situation? That should provide some needed background. But if you all truly want to understand what's happening in Europe right now, you have to start at World War I. Maybe not its beginning, but at least at the end. The way it ended probably created the environment for the beginning of a second global conflict."

Bud had a strong desire to get caught up on the details of history, even as far back as WWI. *I know it was a catalyst that in some part led to the current situation, but I hope we don't get bogged down there. I can't—our group can't—afford to overlook what's happening on the ground right now.* He bit his lip as his thoughts ran over each other. *But I can research the situation between Churchill and FDR by myself and ask questions later. Guess we oughtta stick with her plan.*

Miss Neubert glanced at her watch and interrupted her pupil's reverie. "I've got to go. I'm meeting my brother for supper at the S & W at 6:00, and it's a thirty-minute walk. I don't want to be late.

Then I have a test to prepare for my new class." Bud cringed at the thought of taking a history test. *Maybe in a month or so, but not now.*

"I'll give you a lift if you like. I'm going right by there." *I wasn't planning to, but it's the least I can do to repay* her kindness.

"That's really nice of you, thanks. That'll give us a few more minutes together. Let's talk about how you can get the most out of this history journey," she said, pausing in her preparations. "But first, let me give you an assignment for the group's first meeting."

The knot in his stomach twisted at the prospect of a study assignment. But *I have to remember our* goal. *I'm just glad she didn't expel me—even though she's sending me to study hall again. Still, I was kind of hoping she'd pull out some books or articles to help get me up to speed without much effort. But I don't think she intends to.*

Her next words shocked him. "My guess is you want me to give you a shortcut: tell you about some *Life* magazine story or what articles to read from the *Sentinel* or the *New York Times* to speed up the process."

Can she read my mind? He was afraid to say yes but might have done just that if she hadn't continued.

"Sure, I could make it easy for you. But if you dig out the facts on your own, you'll learn more and reach better conclusions. One day, you'll be better able to teach your children. I bet you'll tell them to pay better attention in history class,"

S & W Cafeteria,
Knoxville, Tennessee, circa 1940s
Public Domain

she said with a wry smile and her customary cackle.

"So what do you want us to do?" Bud responded, attempting to slide under her obvious shot across his bow.

"I want you to learn as much as you can about the lasting effects of World War I on the world and then to frame the problem by listing ten defining words that best characterize Germany and its citizens. Also, consider how a country of very intelligent people could go from the Treaty of Versailles in 1919 to a point in 1933 and 1934 when they accepted Hitler as their leader. What national conditions and which attributes of ol' Shickelgruber were so compelling that the people of Germany suspended their disbelief about what was happening?"

Bud smiled as he remembered Miss Neubert's penchant for using unusual names to add interest to her teaching. She told his class in 1935 that Adolf's father was born as Alois Schicklgruber. Thirteen years before Adolf was born, his father jettisoned his surname in favor of Hitler, arguably the only thing he did of which his son approved. *I'll tell the others about that later,* Bud thought.

Looks like she's dead-set on the WWI starting point, Bud thought. *I wonder if this assignment has more parts, though.* He decided to risk another question. "That's it?"

"If you do it right, that'll be enough. It'll force you to think about the who, when, why, and how of the events and conditions that led to this war. That's what you said you wanted. No shortcuts now. Understanding this is critical," she emphasized. "It will clearly define the dilemma the German people faced as war was foisted upon them."

Miss Neubert took her coat from the hook on the back of the classroom door, and the unlikely duo headed down the dimly lit hall and out to Bud's car. Ever the gentleman, he opened the door and helped her into the front seat. Light conversation with no war talk filled the short drive to the restaurant.

Bud pulled his '39 Ford to a stop at Clinch and Gay Streets, and Miss Neubert got out. As she exited, she turned and issued a challenge. "I expect your best work. Come by Friday week, this time a little earlier, say 3:30. And bring your history class with you," she said with a smile. "See you then."

"Thanks," he responded, "I'll be there. I mean, we'll be there." *I don't know exactly who "we" is, but I'm going to make certain someone else joins me. I don't want to take on this project—or Miss Neubert's chiding —by myself.*

She was crossing the street before he realized that she said Friday week. *That's less than two weeks away,* he thought. *Gotta get with it.*

Bud continued driving south on Gay Street toward the river. He first thought about turning right and going to the library, but he let his heart rule his head. He turned left, then left again, and headed north toward Thelma's. *I could use some R and R*, he told himself.

The next few days passed in a blur. Bud related his conversation with Miss Neubert to the others from the Labor Day picnic group. It would be hard to get them all together before they were to meet with their mentor, so they would all have to work on their own or in small groups.

Thelma was a great help to Bud, as was Evelyn. But planning for their upcoming wedding kept Ty and Truji too occupied to help.

Dick knew quite a lot. At nineteen, he had studied high school history only a year or so earlier. *He's got a more current exposure to the war events than we do,* Bud thought. *I sure hope he'll take a key part.*

Since Bud, Dusty, and Emma worked at the same place, they lunched together on Wednesday to map out a plan. Being married made it easier for Dusty and Emma to be assigned specific parts of the research.

Bud and Dusty left work early on Thursday and met Leonard in the research section of Lawson McGhee Library at 4:30. Periodicals lined a display case to the left of the entrance to the research section. The current issues of *Life*, *Look*, *Time*, and *Sport* occupied the top of the magazine rack.

Ted Williams's photo on the cover of the current *Life* Magazine soon captured their attention, and they drifted off into baseball talk. "Can you believe Williams? Three homers in the Labor Day doubleheader against the Senators in DC?" Leonard asked in amazement. "He's hittin' 410. Unbelievable!"

"Not anymore. He was one for one today in Yankee Stadium, so he's hittin' .411, with two games coming up in Fenway on Saturday and Sunday," Bud added. "Reckon he'll go .400 for the season?"

"Yeah, and since the Sox lost to New York 6-3, the Yanks cinched the AL pennant," Leonard chimed in. "I wonder if Williams'll be AL

MVP? DiMaggio had a great year too. That fifty-six game hitting streak may never be broken."

"Hey guys, that's all well and good, but we've got some reading to do," interjected Dusty, bringing the others back to their goal for the day.

Whispers turned to loud exchanges as they discussed their reading. A few sharp glances from other researchers, along with the librarian's warning index finger in front of pursed lips, quieted their discussion. The give-and-take continued in subdued tones. After an intense hour, the group winnowed their list to the twenty words they thought best fulfilled their assignment. *It feels good to have our homework done, but we've already learned enough to scare every one of us,* Bud mused.

Bud had begun to listen to Edward R. Murrow's daily newscast, in which he painted a consistent and dim picture of the situation in London. "Where can I get some more information on Murrow's radio war reports?" he asked the head librarian.

"You might try some back issues of the *New York Times*," she suggested. Bud had no idea how much clarity Murrow's candid reporting would bring to his perspective in days to come

On Friday of the following week, Dusty, Dick, and Leonard met Bud and Thelma at the Doughboy statue in front of Knox Hi at 3:35. Classes had dismissed and students were pouring from the building, dispersing in all directions.

The Retread history bunch weaved their way through the energetic Trojan students as they jostled their way up the outside marble stairs, then the wooden ones and down the hall to Miss Neubert's classroom. They had chosen the "Retread" name for their ragtag research group, and *it sure seems to fit,* Bud thought. When they related it to their mentor, she chuckled. But the brief touch of humor would not interfere with her opportunity to instruct this eager group. "OK, where's the list?" she asked.

Thelma pulled a stack of paper from a large envelope. She passed everyone a single sheet, making sure Miss Neubert got the original and the Retreads each an onionskin carbon copy. The type on each successive sheet was fuzzier than the previous one because Thelma's office, where she had typed the report, used carbon paper multiple times. In this way, J.C. Penney was no different than most companies, constantly focused on reducing costs. "After all, another Depression could be on the way," was management's frequent admonition.

Without expression, Miss Neubert reviewed how the group characterized Germany's post-WWI plight, silently mouthing the words as she read: "*Humiliation, disgrace, poverty, anger, rage, unemployed, fear, revenge, weakness, unprotected, hungry, despondent.*"

The group, immersed in their studies, had cut their list from twenty but couldn't reduce it to the ten she had requested. Looking out over the tops of her glasses, she addressed them as a whole. "I might have used a few different words, but you captured the Germanic mood. Congratulations. Now, how did this situation come about, and what did you learn from it?"

Bud spoke up. "Germany was in a bad way and the people were despondent. That term encompasses several of the words on our list."

"And I'm not too sure I wouldn't have felt the same way," Leonard added. "I remember what it was like here in Knoxville during the Depression. I stuffed cardboard inside my shoes to cover the holes in the soles—and even had a hard time finding cardboard. My underwear was made out of flour sacks—Tube Rose Flour to make it worse—with the red roses adorning my rear end. I had no car or streetcar fare and had to walk to town. No job or prospects of one," he lamented. "Ten years ago, life wasn't pretty. Without the ROTC uniform I could wear three days a week, I couldn't have gone to school here. But food, a job, and some clothes have made a world of difference in my attitude today."

They all smiled and nodded in agreement. Everyone had stories of how the Depression affected their family. *Murrow talked about that last night,* Bud thought. *There are food shortages across Britain, especially in London.* He wanted to inject this situation into the discussion but held back. *We need to move past the past and talk about what's going on now*, he thought. *I guess she's making a point, and I hope it's soon.*

"It seems that the Treaty of Versailles may have solved some problems, but it sure created others," Dick Foster chimed in. "The arguments between President Wilson, Britain's Lloyd George, and economist John Maynard Keynes over reparations and the carving up of Europe were quite combative. The question was then, and still might be, whether the combination of reparations, military, and commerce restrictions and the loss of some of their land was more a punishment for Germany than a solution from which better world relations could emerge."

All eyes cut toward Foster. The insights that belied his youth seemed to impress everyone, including Miss Neubert.

"Why did you include Keynes?" their teacher asked.

"During the Paris negotiations in early 1919, Keynes argued for easier economic restrictions on Germany so they could have a chance to emerge from the ditch faster," Dick said. "He claimed that a weak Germany wasn't good for Europe or the rest of the world."

"Do you agree with him, Mr. Foster?" Miss Neubert prodded.

Dick hesitated, but then responded. "I'm not sure, but given the devastation and loss of life laid at Germany's feet, I think not." The teenager had, in the last sixty seconds, leaped to the head of the class with his well-thought-out contributions.

"These questions are good and germane to the world's condition, but they don't deal directly with the question you all are trying to answer, do they?" Neubert asked.

After their nodded affirmation, she proceeded before they spoke. "Now what about Adolf?" she asked, a note of derision in her voice. "He must have given the Germans something, or he wouldn't have been able to rise to power as quickly as he did. What was it? What were the skills, character traits, and strengths that aided him? How did he commandeer the position of Führer?"

She paused, giving her questions time to sink in. This was the assignment she had given Bud earlier in the week, and the group was at least somewhat prepared. But the combination of questions seemed to stymie them.

Leonard, ever the pragmatist, spoke up. "He seems to have come to power through a combination of charisma, ruthlessness, and fear—along with lots of lies."

"How so?"

"Well, in the early '20s—1923 I think—he got into that fight in a beer hall and was thrown in jail."

"How did being thrown in jail help him? And where does the charisma come into play?"

Bud responded to the teacher's pressing questions. "Well, the jail time took him out of commission. It isolated him and gave him an opportunity to write *Mein Kampf* (*My Struggle*)."

"Why was this an important piece of literature? Or was it?" Miss Neubert asked.

"Well—," Bud hesitated, then continued. "The book may have expressed Hitler's inner turmoil over the extreme penalties and restrictions of the Treaty of Versailles. It reduced Germany to a helpless nation." He looked around the room, but seeing no one else eager to respond, he continued.

"I saw a Movietone News clip not long ago that helped me better understand the thinking of Germans in the early '20s. It seems to me that Hitler's strident and commanding style of oratory, coupled with a nation hungry for jobs, food, and national pride, started his rise to prominence in the minds of the German people. Longing for a return to their lofty pre-WWI world position, they were more than willing to overlook his ruthless, sometimes-crazy ideas."

"Well put, Bud. Where was that insight when you were in my class seven years ago?"

Bud's impish grin showed a combination of pride in his newfound understanding of history and embarrassing recognition that Miss Neubert's little barb was spot-on. *Is this the time to discuss the growing necessity for US involvement in the War that Murrow keeps calling for?* Bud asked himself. But Miss Neubert interrupted his thoughts.

"OK. So how and when did he finally assume full power?"

"You could say it happened in September of 1933, eight years ago, when he became Chancellor," Leonard said.

"Or a year later when von Hindenburg died and Hitler declared himself Führer," Dusty chimed in.

"You're both correct. So what are some dynamic events that led up to these two pinnacles of Hitler's dominance?"

No one spoke, so Miss Neubert broke the silence.

"What disastrous event occurred in early 1933 that punctuated the upheaval in which the Reich found itself?" Since no one responded, she answered her own question.

"First, the Reichstag, the building housing the German Parliament, was burned. Next, the Nazis burned books all across Germany that did not adhere to their strict philosophy. In mid-1934, through the *Schutzstaffel* (SS), his personal protectors, Hitler imposed the devastating 'Night of Long Knives.' He ordered the execution on that night of all Nazi operatives thought to be disloyal to the Führer, including his close friend and head of the *Sturmabteilung* [SA, Hitler's group of storm troopers], Ernst Rohm." She looked around the room as if to gauge the response. "Through this harrowing act of cleansing, Hitler rid himself of potential internal opposition and at the same time injected additional fear into the Nazi party as well as all of Germany. These events accelerated his ruthless march toward dominance. At that point, no one would openly oppose him."

She paused again before her next question. "With Hitler firmly entrenched as Führer, leader, or maybe you could say dictator, then what?"

Bud jumped in. "Well, with control of both the government and the German people, he was able to continue rebuilding Germany. He ordered the construction of roads and other infrastructure with jobs, food, and promises of a future payoff to the workers: a car, the 'people's car,' or *Volkswagen*." He added, "Even though forbidden by the Treaty of Versailles, Hitler also began rebuilding Germany's military machine. And the Spanish Civil War gave him a chance to test out his new equipment, especially tanks and aircraft. So by the time of the Berlin Olympics in 1936, Germany was a far cry from the shambles that existed in 1918."

"Excellent, Bud. Why then did the US compete in those Olympics if we knew all that was going on under Hitler?" Miss Neubert prodded. "His philosophy and actions were in no way consistent with ours. Or were they?"

"We haven't given you our complete list of adjectives describing

Hitler, but I think the '36 Olympics clearly illustrate a key one: deceptive," Foster said. "He's a deceitful, deceptive, lying despot!"

"Exactly!" Leonard added. "As word of Hitler's treatment of his people began to leak out, many spoke out about their growing concern over Hitler's increasingly aggressive actions. "Avery Brundage, head of the USOC (United States Olympic Committee), realized both the public's backing of the US Olympic team and his own reputation were at stake," Leonard explained. "He had to soothe the fears of his adversaries. He also had to put his own nominal concerns about Hitler's repressive regime to rest. To assess the situation for himself, Brundage took a trip to Berlin. Hitler put on a real show and convinced Brundage that the world's view of his oppressive regime was false." Around the room, heads nodded in agreement.

Leonard continued, "Hitler was also intent on showing that, contrary to commonly-held world opinion, Jews were being allowed to compete openly for the German national team."

Bud broke in. "And Hitler tricked the world and Brundage with his charade during the USOC's visit. His deceptive guise was effective, and the US did compete. Jesse Owens smoked the field in the 100- and 200-meter races as well as the broad jump, and was on the winning four-by-one-hundred relay team. Hitler was irate and snubbed Owens by refusing to shake his hand."

"I agree with both of you." Miss Neubert responded with a slight smile. "So, Hitler is a deceptive, lying despot. But what else defines him?"

Adjectives flew from each of the eager students: "*Cunning, charismatic, malevolent, vengeful, devious, confident, insecure, powerful, lying, ruthless, megalomaniacal, deceptive. . .*"

"Confident and insecure. Hmmm. Interesting contrast, but I agree," Miss Neubert confirmed. "How did he further exhibit his deceitfulness?"

"Well, in 1937 he tricked both British Prime Minister Neville Chamberlain and his emissary, Lord Halifax, into continued appeasement of his land grab in Europe." Bud said.

"And in March of 1938 he tricked an unknowing, willing Austria into allowing him to take over their country without a shot being fired," Leonard added.

Miss Neubert again gazed at the group as she spoke. "Many of you heard this when you were in my classes a few years ago, but it bears repeating." With her characteristic chortle and the tight-lipped smile that accentuated her crookedly-applied lipstick, she added, ". . . as a refresher."

OK, this'll be short, Bud thought. *And then I'll inject some questions about the growing imperative for us to get in this thing in support of England. Am I the only one listening to Murrow?* he wondered as he gave Thelma a furtive glance. He knew she recognized his growing impatience.

Miss Neubert began a narrative that she had obviously used many times with her students. "In September of 1938, Hitler signed the Munich Agreement with Chamberlain, agreeing that if allowed to take over the Sudetenland, a German-speaking people whose land was ceded to Czechoslovakia by the Treaty of Versailles, they would seek no further territory." She looked around as if to make sure of everyone's attention. "Chamberlain, suckered in either by fear, an incorrect reading of Hitler, or both, acquiesced and returned to Britain holding high the pact he and his country's new ally had signed. With his smile indicating the victory he thought he had achieved, he told the British people and the world, 'There will be peace in our time.' A mere six months later, Germany took over additional Czech territory. So much for the perceived victory," she said with another of her wry smiles.

"Only two years ago, Hitler began World War II by invading Poland. This invasion arguably continued a war that began in his despotic mind in 1919. This became more and more evident to the world as early as 1937, even though few wanted to believe it." (Note: As early as 1932, Churchill is quoted by the counselor of the German embassy in London as saying in a dinner at the embassy that "Hitler declares he does not intend starting a world war but Churchill believes that Hitler and his followers will grasp the first chance to resort to arms again," John Lukacs, *The Duel: The Eighty-Day Struggle Between Churchill and Hitler* [New Haven: Yale University Press, 2001], 7.)

She continued. "Given the enthusiasm you've shown in your research and this discussion, it's obvious that you're ready to go further in your study. But this is a good stopping point. We've focused almost entirely on Hitler thus far, but there are certainly other key players in this multifaceted chess game. Let's discuss who they are and the magnitude of the roles they play, now and in days to come. First, who do you think they are?"

Finally we're getting to the here and now, Bud thought as he responded, "Certainly FDR and Churchill."

"What about Mussolini and Stalin?" Dusty asked.

"All are correct, but for our next meeting, let's focus on Churchill and FDR. We'll stick with the same study method. Be prepared to discuss traits for these two leaders, the role they play on the world stage now, and how you think they have influenced and will influence the future of World War II." She added, almost as an afterthought, "By the way, what was the Phony War?"

They looked at each other, but no one spoke.

"What happened in the war after Poland was defeated in September of 1939 and the first of May 1940?"

"Not much," Bud said, half-asking, half-asserting.

"Kinda phony when evaluated by war standards, isn't it? Think about it, and let's begin there. Let's get together on Monday, October 20. Tennessee plays Alabama the Saturday before, so we may have trouble keeping our discussion to the war, especially if the boys in orange win—but we'll try."

The group offered smiles and thanks all around and left the classroom, stopping in the vestibule to discuss preparations for their upcoming meeting.

"Given the perspective of how we may have been tricked into World War I and the direction World War II has taken in the last two years, I'm beginning to believe we have no good way of avoiding involvement," Bud said as he looked first into Leonard's eyes, then down at the ground and back.

"Me too," Leonard affirmed.

Thelma added quickly, "I'm covered up at work planning the fashion show at the *Tennessee* in three weeks. I just can't spend a lot of time reading. I think I'm going to have to leave this one to you boys."

"J. Ross is all I can handle right now, and Mother hasn't been well since Daddy died. I'm not sure I can be much help either," Evelyn said.

"Dick, I know you're carrying a full load at UT. Engineering is a tough discipline, so I'm sure you have a full plate. Dusty and Emma are busy at church. Ty and Truji are planning a wedding, And Henrietta and Grover are caring for ailing parents. So it looks like it's me and you, Leonard," Bud added. "Whaddya think?"

"I guess it doesn't matter what I think. If we need to do it, we'll just do it."

Leonard, raised as the youngest of four children of limited means in a strict Wesleyan Methodist home, was no stranger to diligence. He was always the first to "throw his heels," as he said, when there was work to be done. Although neither had actually seen combat duty, Bud considered him a true foxhole buddy.

"OK, Leonard and I will take the lead here," Bud advised. "But if you read or see something you think we need, please let us know. We may get together closer to the October meeting. We'll let you know. And if you can, start listening to Edward Murrow's daily broadcasts, and listen carefully. What he says is important to our discussion."

They nodded agreement, shook hands, and dispersed into the chill of the early fall night.

As he and Leonard walked to the car, Bud said, in a manner that seemed more a reminder to himself than to his brother-in-law, "We need to keep our eye on the ball in the next few weeks. Our initial goals were to know more about the history that got us here, figure out where 'here' is, and determine what we think our nation should and will do in this crappy conflict. And then to figure out what it mean for each of us." He paused as if to emphasize his point. "I think these are still intact, but I also believe the conditions in England plus the way Churchill and Roosevelt see this thing—and each other—are keys to our involvement. I'll tell you more after a do a little more reading."

His voice trailed off as he stopped, lost in his thoughts. *Our lives could all change by what happens over the next few months. This isn't just history. It's our future.*

CHAPTER 4

Study Hall

Research and Beyond

Knoxville, Tennessee: Later in the fall of 1941

THE PHONY WAR? I HAVE to find out what she meant, Bud thought. He began his research by seeking to understand just what this oddly-named conflict entailed. But parallel to this historical study was his commitment to clarifying for himself just what was happening in England. *Is the rising drumbeat of Murrow's warning real, and if so, what does it mean to our country? Pursuing both avenues of study will take more time, but I've gotta do it,* he told himself.

As he read accounts of Poland's surrender to Nazi troops in September of 1939, Bud soon realized that the Phony War was actually the period after the surrender and before the invasion of France by German Troops on May 10, 1940. The period was aptly referred to as *phony* because nothing happened, at least nothing outwardly visible. The British did nothing. The French did nothing. And the Nazis laid low, or seemed to.

Some called it the Reluctant War, Churchill called it the Twilight War, and other Brits deemed it the Boer War, an obvious play on the real Boar Wars of the late 1800s and early 1900s.

Extensive accounts of the invasion of France by Germany on May 10, 1940, an event that brought the Phony War to an abrupt halt, filled the various periodicals Bud examined. The date also marked the resignation of Neville Chamberlain as British Prime Minister with the mantle, or noose as some considered it, passed on to Sir Winston Churchill.

Hitler's abrupt halting of Nazi forces in hot pursuit of the French and the British Expeditionary Forces (BEF) and their left turn toward Paris puzzled military men and most who thought about such an uncharacteristic move. This change of plans allowed 338,226 men, more than half of whom were British soldiers, to be evacuated from Dunkirk and surrounding coastal towns between May 24 and June 4 of 1940. Within three weeks, France fell to the German war machine, and Hitler took his first trip to Paris, where he looked across the Seine to the Eiffel Tower, the iconic symbol of the country he had just conquered. At that time Hitler stood symbolically with Herman Goering, head of the Luftwaffe, on the legendary banks of the English Channel considering the prospect of invading and annihilating Great Britain.

Bud sat back in his chair, gazed up at the ceiling and thought, *If Hitler had the British in his sights with them having little chance of defeating the onrushing German Army, why did he relent? And how does that square with what was happening in England between the spring of 1940 and June of 1941? Does Britain need the US to protect them or to join forces in protecting the rest of Europe and the rest of the Western world?* The questions continued to swirl, but Bud trudged ahead in his quest for answers.

Much of the early part of the war from early May to mid-June of 1940 was well-chronicled in radio broadcasts, print media of all types, and military statements. However, Bud thought that a clandestine war of wills, emotions, and strategies must surely have been playing out among British politicians in late May of 1940. (Note: For years, few would know for sure about this crucial struggle. It was, nonetheless, one of the most critical battles of the entire war.)

Bud plunged further into his research to discover more about Churchill. Recognizing the difficulty the French were having with Nazi troops and not being confident of the resolve of French politicians and military leaders, the British leader seemed to feel that Britain might have to "go it alone" in the war with Nazi Germany. On May 15, he wrote President Roosevelt to that effect and further entreated him to enter the war as an active ally. FDR answered but was noncommittal as to the plans of the US.

In his own country, Roosevelt was in the midst of a hard-fought presidential campaign, one where those favoring isolationism by staying out of European affairs vigorously opposed any overtures of assistance given or promised by FDR. Fully cognizant of this tenuous position, FDR had to exercise caution regarding promises to

Churchill while believing that commitments, even costly ones, were inevitable.

Information was hard to come by, but Bud was intent on learning how Churchill intended to hold the Brits together in the midst of the devastation of German bombing. He learned that the British war effort was directed by a five-member War Cabinet comprised of Prime Minister Winston Churchill, Edward Wood, more commonly known as Lord Halifax (Note: Bud would later in 1943 be a part of a group of airmen who welcomed Halifax and his wife to America), former prime minister Neville Chamberlain, Clement Atlee, and Arthur Greenwood. The strategic and tactical viewpoints of committee members varied widely. With the future of the Commonwealth at stake, they each felt the weight of the shared burden. As Bud learned more about the political struggles Churchill faced, his estimation of the British leader escalated.

In the southern part of Continental Europe, Hitler made no attempt to hide his courtship of Mussolini. Although the British were not optimistic that this partnership of despots could be averted, they tried to prevent it nonetheless. Lord Halifax was an outspoken proponent of Britain negotiating with both Mussolini and Hitler in an attempt to prevent being invaded and overtaken by superior land forces. Chamberlain had become less willing to negotiate with Hitler than in 1937 and 1938 but was still not as strident in his willingness to "go it alone" as Churchill.

Bud learned that on Tuesday, May 28, 1940, the War Cabinet had reached unanimous agreement on a number of Churchill's assertions. The first related to Hitler's lack of veracity. Having lied many times before, he would certainly do so again. And any peace they might negotiate with Hitler would doubtless involve a loss of their sovereignty. If they fought on and lost, the terms of peace at that time would be no worse than a negotiated peace. The cabinet members agreed that they would rather fight valiantly and lose than resign themselves to a quiet defeat. They might not have the power to win the war alone, but if they held on long enough, they hoped to persuade Roosevelt, with his powerful US military backing, to enter the war.

These agreements meant the die was cast: Great Britain was fully committed—to what, they were not fully sure. They agreed, however, to follow Churchill's admonition that they "Stand up to him (Hitler) so that all of Europe may be free," regardless of the cost. (Winston Churchill, "Finest Hour" speech to the House of Commons, June 18, 1940).

As he read accounts of the war in France, Bud grew in his understanding of the tremendous odds faced by all of Western Europe. This message affirmed the assertions he heard on Murrow's nightly newscasts. *I need to see that movie Murrow wrote and narrated— what's it called?—"This is England." If I can't do that, I should at least try to get a printed copy of the narration,* Bud vowed. *And what did Jimmy Hines say at work the other day? That isolationist Joseph Kennedy lost his job as ambassador to Great Britain. I don't know if his replacement, Gilbert Winant, is a Nazi sympathizer, too, or if he'll do a better job of standing up to Hitler. I sure hope he will.*

Lawson McGhee Library kept copies of major newspapers for a year. Bud had heard that an article in the *Boston Globe* from nearly a year before contained a quote from Kennedy about England and the US. The librarian helped him find the article in the November 10, 1940 edition, where he read the stunning remark: "Democracy is finished in England. It may be here" (Ambassador Kennedy's statement to two reporters, Louis M. Lyons of the *Boston Globe* and Ralph Coghlan of the *St. Louis Post-Dispatch*, November 10, 1940). *Incredible,* he thought. *I'm sure glad he doesn't represent our country any longer. If what he said is even remotely true, we'll have to enter this war—not only to protect Britain but the world.*

Bud now found in the *New York Times* a portion of the speech Churchill made to Parliament and the British people on May 13, 1940, his first public speech after King George VI appointed him Prime Minister, defining the position finally agreed on by the War Cabinet at the end of that same month. *The Retreads need to read this one. I'll copy it out and have Thelma type it up for them.*

> We have before us an ordeal of the most grievous kind. We
> have before us many, many long months of struggle and
> of suffering. You ask, what is our policy? I will say: It is to

wage war, by sea, land and air, with all our might and with all the strength that God can give us; to wage war against a monstrous tyranny, never surpassed in the dark and lamentable catalogue of human crime. That is our policy. You ask, what is our aim? I can answer in one word: victory; victory at all costs, victory in spite of all terror, victory, however long and hard the road may be; for without victory, there is no survival. Let that be realized; no survival for the British Empire, no survival for all that the British Empire has stood for, no survival for the urge and impulse of the ages, that mankind will move forward towards its goal. But I take up my task with buoyancy and hope. I feel sure that our cause will not be suffered to fail among men. At this time I feel entitled to claim the aid of all, and I say, "Come then, let us go forward together with our united strength." (Winston Churchill, "Blood, Toil, Tears, and Sweat" speech to the House of Commons, May 13, 1940. The Churchill Centre, http://www.winstonchurchill.org/).

Bud also found a summary article in the *New York Times* reporting that on June 14, 1940, Paris fell, and three days later the French sought an Armistice with Nazi Germany. On June 18, Churchill gave a speech to the House of Commons in which he outlined the horrible events of the previous fortnight. He spoke with the stark realization that Great Britain stood alone and virtually defenseless against the might of the Third Reich. Realizing what was to come, he concluded with the following words that would define this magnificent call to arms: "Let us therefore brace ourselves to our duties, and so bear ourselves that if the British Empire and its Commonwealth last for a thousand years, men will still say, 'This was their finest hour'" (Churchill, "Finest Hour" speech).

Leonard found and copied this quotation, asking Thelma to type it up with the one Bud had already given her. (Note: In desperation Churchill scribbled a letter to Roosevelt in which he said; "I trust you realize, Mr. President, that the voice and force of the United States may count for nothing if they are withheld too long. You may have a completely subjugated, Nazified Europe established with

astonishing swiftness and the weight may be more than we can bear"
The note was written by Churchill to Roosevelt on May 15, 1940 and
sent through the US Embassy and marked "Most Secret and Personal." - (John Lukacs, *Five Days in London–May 1940* [New Haven,
Connecticut: Yale University Press, 1999], 72. This poignant and realistic view of the situation between the US and its ally Great Britain
was unknown to historians until almost five years later, after the end
of the war.)

Bud pieced together bits of information from various sources to
help him better understand the events of late 1940 and 1941. In mid-
1940 Hitler turned his ravenous sights toward Britain. He placed
World War I Nazi flying ace Hermann Goering at the head of the
Luftwaffe. Goering's charge was to have the Luftwaffe so devastate
the British Royal Air Force (RAF) that an invasion of the island
would be relatively easy. The onslaught by the Nazi air attack was
intense and horrific. The months that ensued proved that both Hitler and Goering had greatly overestimated Germany's strength and
vastly underestimated the British will. However, the RAF was both
undermanned and under armed. But the Brits had other weapons,
some of war and others of mind and will.

As Bud learned, the RAF's cadre of fighter aircraft, Spitfires and
Hurricanes, was much smaller than the Messerschmitt Bf-109s and
Focke Wulf Fw-190s of the Nazi Luftwaffe. However, the Brits had
been developing a secret weapon: radar, still in its infancy. Coupled
with the home guard, a network of civilian and military information
flow that gave early warning to Nazi air attacks, radar provided the
RAF with an equalizing defense system. Led by Commander "Bomber" Harris, they were able to use this primitive but effective arrangement to withstand the power of the stronger Luftwaffe.

As he was making notes in preparation for the next meeting with
the study group, Bud paused to reflect on a few confusing facts. *I
think we left off some key words that define Hitler: diabolical and
unpredictable. Why did he stop and let almost 400,000 men escape
at Dunkirk?* he wondered. *And why, just when the substantial loss
of RAF planes and the destruction of much of their early warning
system put Britain precariously close to defeat, did Hitler turn his
wrath and armed forces on Russia, the country that had until then*

been his ally in the conquest of Western Europe? Is Hitler a tactical genius or the consummate idiot?

Hitler's strategy, or lack of it, also baffled the best military minds of the day.

The Friday meeting with their mentor was fast approaching. Much of the research had been left to Bud and Leonard, who had, in their normal fashion, taken their responsibility seriously—perhaps too seriously, if that was possible. The operative questions of the future involvement of the US and men of fighting age remained unanswered. They had, however, assimilated a wealth of information about the events of the last few years. These facts and their interpretation seemed to indicate a clear path for their country, but how that direction might manifest itself still seemed unclear. *It's time to discuss how both go together: the critical situation in London and the imperative of US entrance into the war,* Bud told himself.

The Retread history bunch had not been together as a group since the September meeting with Miss Neubert. As expected, schedules and responsibilities had prevented the involvement of some, but Bud and Leonard had immersed themselves in the research effort. All agreed that they needed to convene before their next meeting with Miss Neubert. Friday, October 17, seemed to work for everyone, so they planned a dinner and cram session at the S & W.

The S & W serving lines stretched clear back to the entrance, the linen-covered drop leaf tables overflowed with hungry people, and the noisy chatter of excited football fans blended with the ever-present music from the Hammond organ at the base of the curved staircase. The Volunteer faithful coupled with a number of Crimson Tide fans gathered for the annual Tennessee-Alabama contest the following day reflected the intensity of the annual rivalry. Orange and white corsages on female Vol fans matched the crimson flowers of 'Bama ladies in both size and number.

In preparation for the meeting, Bud had outlined in detail the key points of his study, including the Churchill quotes he and Leonard had copied and Thelma had typed. He distributed these to the group once everyone finished eating. As he reviewed his thoughts, injecting some of his now-strong personal opinions, his fellow Retreads peppered him with questions.

Bud's admiration for Churchill was impossible to conceal, and he didn't try to do so. Grover, however, had a different opinion. "Churchill's just a drunk. He has little if any respect from the general public or even the politicians with whom he works closely," he said. "I wonder if FDR thinks the same way, and that's why he's not pushing the US into the conflict?"

Shifting forward in his chair, Bud responded with an uncharacteristic piercing look and an equally piercing opinion. "We have to remember that FDR was and still is on the horns of a dilemma. His actions seem to indicate that he realizes full well that the US can't remain uninvolved in the growing European War. But he would have had a hard time being re-elected last year if he revealed that position too soon. Our country still has plenty of isolationists, and vocal ones at that. And Wilkie [Wendell Wilkie, FDR's presidential opponent in the fall of 1940] made his strong belief in isolationism the focal point of his campaign."

Bud pulled newspaper clippings and notes from his folder. "Here are some things I got from a couple of sources that provide some perspective on the presidential election conflict." He began to read aloud: "As the war of words preceding the election waged on, Willkie said that FDR, ". . . has courted a war for which this country is hopelessly unprepared and which it emphatically does not want." (Wendell Wilkie, address when accepting the Republican presidential nomination, Elwood, Indiana, August 17, 1940).

He turned to another clipping and added, "In his speech for the signing of the Selective Service Bill in September of 1940, FDR countered with a telling statement of strength: 'We must and we will marshal our great potential strength to fend off war from our shores.' And on October 30 in a campaign speech in Boston, he added, 'I have said this before, but I shall say it again and again and again: Your boys are not going to be sent into any foreign wars'" (Franklin D. Roosevelt, "Campaign Address at Boston, Massachusetts," October 30, 1940 in Gerhard Peters and John T. Woolley, "The American Presidency Project," http://www.presidency.ucsb.edu/ws/?pid=15887).

Bud looked around at the group as he continued his explanation. "Six days later, on Election Day, November 5, 1940, the outcome was considered too close to call. FDR garnered 54.7% of the popular votes and carried thirty-eight states, eight less than in 1936. He got over two-thirds of the vote in Tennessee, one of the widest margins of all states" (Wikipedia Contributors, "United States Presidential Election 1940," *Wikipedia: The Free Encyclopedia,* http://en.wikipedia.org/wiki/United_States_presidential_election,_1940).

Bud then informed his fellow students of his parallel research on conditions in London and throughout England. He read the quote from the *Boston Globe* of a year earlier and quoted many phrases from Murrow's newscasts and the narrative from *This is England*. He related facts that portrayed the former British Ambassador, Joe Kennedy, as a self- serving defeatist and Nazi sympathizer, and how differently the British had received Kennedy's replacement, Gil Winant. By now, Bud's insights carried a preacher's fervor.

"Roosevelt can't help but realize that the capture or destruction of Europe would annihilate Britain and possibly put the whole of Western civilization in peril. Given the situation in Europe, I'm not sure we can stay out of the fray. The risk not only to the US but the whole world is too great. But FDR said he'd never send our boys—*us*—into a foreign war. If you can bring those two opposing forces together and make sense of them, you're much smarter than I am."

After Bud spoke, silence reigned for a few minutes. The group seemed stunned by his intensity and the clarity of his words although still perplexed by the overall situation. But they weren't alone. The paradox and accompanying risks had bewildered the entire country.

"Notwithstanding his promise regarding a 'foreign' war, FDR surely knows that Churchill needs help—and quickly," Bud asserted. "His actions then showed that Roosevelt had been hatching a plan to aid Britain in a circuitous manner. Because of Britain's need he arranged to meet their request for destroyers through a lending arrangement. The security for this debt would be British bases in the Caribbean. In addition he conceived of a way to assist further through the Lend-Lease Act, which he had proposed to Congress at the State of the Union address on January 6, 1941. Regarding the Brits, Roosevelt stated, 'They do not need manpower, they do need billions of dollars worth of the weapons of defense... we simply can't tell them that they must surrender merely because they can't pay for the weapons which we know they must have' (*Vital Speeches of the Day*, Vol. VII: 199). And after an acrimonious debate, Congress approved the bill on March 8, 1941.

"Wait a minute," Dusty Holder said. "Miss Neubert will ask us about our ten descriptive words for FDR and Churchill, and we haven't listed them."

"I think we're way beyond that with all our research—I mean *your* research," Evelyn offered. "But let's do it so she won't scold us. I still hate being taken to task by a teacher. Old habits die hard."

"Churchill: *bold, courageous, eloquent, principled, patient, insightful, intelligent, resourceful, learned, smart, witty, realistic, understood the times,*" came the descriptors in rapid-fire fashion from all over the group.

"For FDR: *political, narcissistic, elitist, calculating, pragmatic, courageous, stately, devious, social leaning, willing to take risk, risk averse.*"

Thelma dutifully wrote down the two lists and would later type them as additions to the sheet of Churchill quotations she had prepared. Now, the Retreads were ready for Miss Neubert.

"You all staying for breakfast?' the waitress asked, a tinge of sarcasm altering her otherwise inviting smile.

"If you're making biscuits," Linda groused. Joe frowned at her. It did no good.

"Sorry," Evelyn said, chagrined that they had imposed on the woman's time. "When do you close?"

"Forty-five minutes ago," came her reply. "But I've had a lot to do. Now I've got to go home to three kids—I mean four. I almost forgot my husband. He's the biggest kid I have."

"I know the feeling," Evelyn said, cutting her eyes toward Leonard and smiling.

"Thanks. The food and service were both great," Bud said, pulling his coat and scarf from the coat pole at the wall.

The group hurriedly gathered their belongings and exited, most through the S & W's trademark revolving door and into the nippy night air.

The sixth period bell had rung only minutes earlier, and Miss Neubert awaited the arrival of her newfound history enthusiasts, holding the door of her classroom open and welcoming each one in her shy, polite manner. *It's hard not to like this lady,* Bud thought. *Her willingness to help this bunch, none of whom distinguished ourselves as history scholars during our high school days, proves her dedication and kindness.*

"Who saw the Alabama game?" she asked. A few of the guys groaned, indicating their displeasure at the 9-2 loss the Vols had suffered at the hands of the Crimson Tide three days before. In recent years, Tennessee fans had grown unaccustomed to losing football games, and the sting of Saturday's loss was widely felt and much discussed in Knoxville.

"Barnhill's now two and one since he took over," Leonard said. "I'm not sure whether Neyland could have made a difference or not. The team seemed flat, and 'Bama played us tough."

The loss of Neyland to the Army was certainly on the minds of the Orange faithful, and for more reasons than the gridiron. The mention of Major Neyland again raised the specter of war. In fact, thoughts of war were everywhere. And even Tennessee football could not make them disappear.

"Well, enough of that. What have you learned since we last met?" asked Miss Neubert. "Do you have your list of descriptors for Winston and Franklin?"

She must know 'em pretty well, thought Bud. *She refers to both by their first names.*

Thelma handed her a copy of the list along with the Churchill quotations. She perused the paper, smiling and again mouthing the words as she read them.

"Interesting, and quite accurate, I might add," she said. "But how can FDR be both 'risk averse' and 'willing to take risks'?"

"He's a schizo," Linda blurted. Accustomed to her outbursts, the group let the caustic remark pass without comment.

"We saw examples of both traits," Dusty Holder responded. "So we thought both should be on the list."

"How so?" asked their teacher. "Do you think this represented an unwillingness to state his true view or pragmatism? Maybe he realized that a clear statement of his opinion would cost him the election and thus the opportunity to help Churchill. And he already knew Wilkie would have backed away from the war effort."

"That's why we deemed FDR political and calculating," Evelyn said. "And I'm not sure I like that in a leader."

"Is that why you said Churchill is principled but Roosevelt not? Or was that an error of omission?"

"It wasn't an error," Bud said. "We discussed it at length and came to the conclusion that Roosevelt is a mystery. We're not sure which predominates with him: principles or pragmatism." Bud looked around at his fellow group members, who responded with affirmative nods.

"Which do you think is the better leader?" Miss Neubert asked. "And why?

"It's way too soon to know," Leonard responded. "FDR's decision regarding involvement in the war and the ultimate outcome of that decision will probably tell the tale on him."

Bud then launched into a discussion of what he had learned from the past six weeks of exhaustive research. At the end of his five-minute impromptu presentation, Miss Neubert smiled and said. "Mr. Perrin, how would you like to come teach my class one day next week?"

That was certainly the last thing Bud expected to hear, but he smiled, half in appreciation and half in pride. *Since we started all this, the group and I have come a long way in our understanding of recent history. But is her invitation serious?*

"I must admit, I was skeptical when you first approached me, Mr. Perrin. But you and this Retread group have proven to be a refreshing gift. I wish I could make your enthusiasm and dedication to learning into a pill and give it to all my students. But I do realize you had two goals in this project, the first of which was to learn so you could later teach. As I remember, the other was to help each of you develop a position on the war and to determine whether or not you boys would be called on to serve in the military. What's your position? And do you think you will be called to serve?"

An eerie silence fell over the group. For almost a minute, no one spoke. Leonard broke the silence at last. "Yes, I've decided we should come to the aid of Great Britain, Churchill, and the US. We're all at risk. The Brits held off the Third Reich, hoping against hope that we'd eventually provide the assistance they need to win." He sighed as he added, "And even with our help, they may not be able to do so."

"I want to add a reluctant but resounding *yes,* we have absolutely no choice. We must act, and quickly," Bud asserted with fervor.

The group agreed, despite some reluctance on the women's part. "But will FDR and Congress get us involved?" came Miss Neubert's next question. Joe and Linda Muck thought no. The others thought yes.

"Remember, we may be geographically isolated, but are we immune? How will the adamant isolationists be convinced?" Miss Neubert asked. No one seemed to have an adequate answer.

"Maybe there will be an incident, a catalyst," Dick Foster interjected. "We've already seen a number of skirmishes in the Atlantic between German troops and our naval protectors. Maybe one will be too big to overlook."

"I think you may be right, Mr. Foster. Do you think the incident will occur in the Atlantic?"

"It sure seems so, if our involvement requires an inciting incident. Do you agree?" Dick asked.

"Yes, but there sure is a lot of hostile activity between China and Japan," Miss Neubert responded. "But every day, we increase our assistance to the Brits. Hitler surely won't overlook this. What do you all think he wants?"

Before anyone offered an opinion, she added the operative question. "And what's to stop him?"

"I think we know." Bud's tone was somber.

In an equally pensive inflection, Leonard added, "Where do we go from here? We know what this probably means."

After a long silence, Miss Neubert responded, "I'm not sure a graduation ceremony is proper, but we have reached a milestone in our quest for understanding this segment of history."

"What about a pre-Christmas dinner to celebrate, if not our enthusiasm for the conclusion, at least for the education?" Thelma asked. "Say on Monday night, December 22, at the S & W?"

"Sounds perfect!" said Bud as each of them, including Miss Neubert, nodded, confirming the date.

The group dispersed. Bud felt the pride of accomplishment coupled with the lasting impact of the previous three months of study, a bittersweet moment.

"We need to get Miss Neubert a gift of thanks to commemorate our graduation," Thelma said. "I'll take care of that at Penney's.

"Even with the consensus pointing toward war, this has been a wonderful experience," Evelyn told her husband, Thelma, and Bud as the four walked together. "Maybe J. Ross will be interested in history someday and I'll be able to help him with my newfound knowledge, if I don't forget it in the next dozen years."

On October 31, a German U-boat torpedoed and sank the destroyer USS Reuben James, sending 115 of the 159 on board to a watery grave. The ship was a part of the US escort force established to promote the safe arrival of war material to the United Kingdom. Was this the catalyst the group anticipated? No. Underreported, the event was taken in relative stride by a nation with its collective head firmly in the sand.

On December 2, Edward R. Murrow, back on US soil for the first time in more than three years, spoke to an enthusiastic crowd at a banquet in his honor at the Waldorf-Astoria in New York. After a prolonged standing ovation, he spoke passionately about his long-held conviction that for Britain to survive and Hitler to be stopped, America had no choice but to enter the conflict. He further laid the outcome at the feet of the US government by saying that the war "would be decided on the banks of the Potomac. General headquarters for the forces of decency is now on Pennsylvania Avenue" (Lynne Olson, *Citizens of London: The Americans Who Stood with Britain in its Finest Hour* [New York: Random House, 2011], 142).

The answer may have seemed unclear, but clarity lay only days away.

CHAPTER 5

Some Questions Answered

Pearl Harbor

Knoxville, Tennessee: December 7, 1941

THIS FIRST SUNDAY IN DECEMBER was a typical early winter day in East Tennessee. A light dusting of overnight snow melted in the warming sun of late morning. The snow, however, did little to diminish the attendance at Knoxville's predominately Protestant churches.

Shortly after noon, most parishioners returned home and began discussing the Sunday sermon while eating what was traditionally the week's largest meal. Discussion of the war in Europe had also become a common lunch topic, and football was never far from the minds and lips of the Volunteer faithful.

The Vols had not won a New Year's Day bowl spot following the '41 season. This failure added to the rumblings resulting from the two-loss campaign. The loss to Duke hurt, but the one to traditional rival Alabama proved a crushing blow.

UT football was the biggest industry in Knoxville, and this atypical Vol season disturbed the corporate psyche of East Tennesseans. Football discussions invariably led to questions about Major Neyland's return to military service, which led to discussions about the war in Europe, completing the conversational loop.

Those present in the Perrin home at 331 East Scott Street on this lazy Sunday afternoon engaged in the ritual no different from most. Leonard, Evelyn, and J. Ross dined with Bud, Thelma, Mrs. Perrin, and Margie. As had become his habit since his father's death, Bud helped his mother with the dishes. Thelma lovingly tied an apron around his waist and kissed him as he turned his head to the side. He turned his head over the other shoulder, anticipating a repeat performance. With a coy smile, she moved out of his reach, and the family laughed. She was rapidly endearing herself to the Perrin clan.

Leonard, Evelyn, and a fussy J. Ross, now approaching his first birthday, had eased down the steep back steps and loaded into their 1934 Hudson Terraplane. Leonard then began the process of starting the fickle engine, hoping to make the short trip to visit his family. The Green place on Isabella Circle stood on a craggy cliff overlooking the Tennessee River a few miles away. The decades-old home was a traditional Sunday afternoon gathering spot for the close-knit Green kinfolk.

As the engine coughed and rumbled to a start, Leonard told his wife, "All right, we're off." As he looked to his left before pulling from the curb, Dusty Holder's A-model Ford screeched to a halt beside him. In a voice mixed with excitement and fear, Dusty hollered, his words drowned out by the rumble of the Terraplane's idling engine. J. Ross and his limited but demanding vocabulary added to the confusion.

Leonard rolled down his window and heard Dusty excitedly repeat, "Have you heard? The Japs attacked us at Pearl Harbor!"

"When?" Leonard asked, his tone revealing shock and disbelief.

"At 7:55 this morning, their time" came the reply from Dusty's wife, Emma.

It was now 3:45 p.m. on December 7, 1941, in Knoxville. The attack on the critically important US naval base had begun more than two hours earlier.

Leonard bolted from the car, running up a small hill and back up the steps to give the news to Bud and the rest. "Come on, honey," he called back to Evelyn. He ran into the house, breathlessly repeating, "The Japs bombed us at the base in Pearl Harbor."

"Oh no," groaned Mrs. Perrin, voicing the hurt that follows a heavy blow.

Bud was unprepared but not surprised. He now knew the answer to the question that had haunted him for more than three months. *We're going to war*, he thought to himself as he turned a loving but solemn gaze toward the bewildered face of his sweetheart. She wrapped her arms around his waist and nestled her head to his chest. Realizing what this news meant, the two clung to each other as never before.

"1500 KILLED IN HAWAII!" screamed the *Sentinel's* bold, black headline the next Monday afternoon.

That day's paper contained only ten pages. Each held articles relating to the attack on Pearl Harbor. Above the fold on page two another headline read, "Sen. Wheeler Says Isolationists Will Support War."

Montana's influential and outspoken Senator Burton K. Wheeler was a Democrat-Progressive and consummate opponent of US involvement in the growing European war. Only months before, on February 28, 1941, Senator Wheeler again declared to the Congress his strong opposition to the Lend-Lease Act in an impassioned speech that included these words:

"If the American people want a dictatorship—if they want a totalitarian form of government and if they want war—this bill should be steam-rollered through Congress, as is the wont of President Roosevelt. Approval of this legislation means war, open and complete warfare. I, therefore, ask the American people before they supinely accept it—Was the last World War worthwhile?

If it were, then we should lend and lease war materials. If it were, then we should lend and lease American boys. President Roosevelt has said we would be repaid by England. We will be. We will be repaid, just as England repaid her war debts of the First World War—repaid those dollars wrung from the sweat of labor and the toil of farmers with cries of "Uncle Shylock." Our boys will be returned—returned in caskets, maybe; returned with bodies maimed; returned with minds warped and twisted by sights of horrors and the scream and shriek of high-powered shells." (Senator Burton K. Wheeler, Speech to Congress [Washington, D.C.: Congressional Record Appendix, Washington, 77 Cong. 1 Session, February 28, 1941], A178-A179).

Notwithstanding this and other objections, the bill, later passed on March 11 of 1941, enabled Roosevelt to provide financial and military aid to Great Britain without going to war, as he had promised in his reelection campaign.

On the day following the attack, Senator Wheeler was quoted as saying: "That [the attack on Pearl Harbor] means war and we will see it through" (*Knoxville News Sentinel*, Issue #18260, December 8, 1941, p2).

Given the intensity of Wheeler's position on both isolationism and the Lend-Lease Act, his statement of support so soon after to the vicious attack in Hawaii seemed no small concession. It later proved to reflect the collective heart of a people rallying behind their leader.

Little work was accomplished on Monday following the attack. Thelma slipped away from her job at Penney's and joined Bud at the Power Board, where people were gathered around numerous radios on desks throughout the building. President Roosevelt's speech that morning was sure to define how the US would respond to the previous day's attack. Thelma first clutched Bud's hand, and he then wrapped his arms around her. Dusty and Emma stood beside them, also clinging to each other. The President's moving speech exuded the clear resolve of a nation destined to carry the fight to its enemies. He stirred the hearts and will of interventionists and isolationists alike with these words:

"Yesterday, December seventh, 1941—a date which will live in infamy—the United States of America was suddenly and deliberately attacked by naval and air forces of the Empire of Japan. . . . No matter how long it may take us to overcome this premeditated invasion, the American people in their righteous might will win through to absolute victory. . . . I ask that the Congress declare that since the unprovoked and dastardly attack by Japan on Sunday, December seventh, a state of war has existed between the United States and the Japanese Empire" (Franklin Delano Roosevelt, Speech before a joint session of Congress, December 8, 1941).

That day, the *Sentinel* issued an extra. Common at the time, this supplemental newspaper edition was printed to update readers on an event of extreme importance prior to the next day's scheduled publication. In bold type, the terse headline stated: "U.S. DECLARES WAR."

FDR's speech to the nation had occurred prior to the first edition of the *Sentinel*. The extra added the definitive results of the Congressional vote taken thirty-three minutes after its conclusion. Other headlines drew further attention to House and Senate activities, including those about member of Congress, Janet (Jeannette) Rankin of Montana. Miss Rankin was a lifetime pacifist and the only member of the Congress who also voted against WWI a quarter-century earlier. ("Jeannette Rankin Biography," http://www.biography.com/people/jeannette-rankin-9451806.)

As at no other time in the history of the United States, people of all faiths, races, ideologies, political parties, and socio-economic segments came together with one purpose. The *Sentinel's* new slogan, found at the bottom of page one, expressed it well: "Our Cause Is Just–All Together For Victory–Work, Save. Fight!"

That evening, as Bud and Thelma snuggled and drank coffee in her living room, they reread Roosevelt's stirring speech, looking into each other's eyes as they smiled knowing but forlorn smiles.

The Pearl Harbor attack not only stunned the nation but brought the Retreads' question about possible military service close to the hearts and minds of many. If anyone realized what the Japanese attack meant, it was young men of military age and their families. Considerations of career, future, school, marriage, family, military service, fear, and responsibility blended to form a diabolical mess. And no one knew just how to sort it out.

The issue of whether or not the US would enter the war was settled, as was the fact that able-bodied boys of fighting age would be required to serve. But what service and when to enter remained unclear to most draft-eligible men.

On September 16, 1940, Congress had signed into law the Selective Training and Service Act, the first conscription in United States history. It required all men between the ages of twenty-one and forty-five to register with local draft boards. Pearl Harbor had made it clear that the US would need many more soldiers than previously thought. On December 19, FDR extended the mandatory registration ages to include those men between eighteen and sixty-five, with only those forty-five and younger eligible for immediate conscription. The truth seemed clear: If you could fog a mirror, you would ship out.

The requirement of military service lifted some confusion. Instead of "Will I go?" able-bodied young men asked, "How and when will I go?" And they all faced the question of whether to wait for the inevitable draft notice or pick a service branch and enlist.

At thirty, Leonard was at the upper end of the age range for the draft. Because trains were an absolutely essential transportation source for moving vast amounts of troops across the US for training, railroad jobs could also protect men from an immediate military call-up. His friends joked that Leonard would be taken when the women and children got back. He didn't appreciate the attempt at humor but didn't object to serving his time with the Southern Railroad, either.

Others in the study group would doubtless go unless they failed the physical. Only Bud and Dick were unmarried, but as far as the US was concerned, marriage had no effect on potential military status.

If I enlist, I'll have a chance to be an officer. Qualifying could be tricky, but the pay's better, Bud thought. *And it could help me build toward a career. After all, I'm not getting anywhere at the Power Board. I've got time to think this through*, he mused. *But I need to make it snappy. I don't want to wait too long.*

With Thelma's help, Bud sorted through his options. Despite the brevity of their relationship, they seemed to share an unspoken understanding that their futures were moving toward marriage.

The S & W Cafeteria was located in the geographic center of Knoxville, nestled between the city's two main theaters, the *Riviera* and the *Tennessee*, and just north of the bustling Farragut Hotel. Serving both a mainstay clientele and the occasional transient businessman, it was more than a mere place to eat. The light atmosphere and outgoing staff made mealtime at the S & W akin to entertainment.

On prominent display in the center left of the main dining area stood a Hammond B-3 organ. Organist Lois Harris kept the air filled with upbeat tunes designed to keep the patrons happy and inclined to return often. A curved staircase flowed elegantly from the upper-level eating area to the center of the main dining room. The wait staff, in starched waistcoats, remained in constant motion, carrying trays, chatting up the customers, and generally keeping things moving.

No one arrived late for the appointed December 22 dinner. Miss Neubert showed up first, enjoying the organist's repertoire of bouncy Christmas carols as she waited for her students. Despite the heaviness of the impending build-up to war, the joy of the Christmas season overtook the Retreads. They laughed and chattered as they made their way through the right side cafeteria line, choosing from the tantalizing options that had helped make the S & W famous. They were soon seated in a room designed for small groups but within earshot of the music. Dick prayed a blessing on his study partners as he gave thanks for the meal.

The mealtime conversation was upbeat and Christmas-focused. But the discussion that followed dealt directly with the war. "In our study, we discussed Japan only in passing," Leonard said. "I was shocked at their attack at Pearl Harbor."

"Definitely."

"Right."

"Me, too," came a litany of agreement.

"We did question whether or not the catalyst, if one occurred, would come from the Atlantic or the Pacific," Miss Neubert reminded them. "But you're right. We did focus primarily on Europe. I thought that would be the hot spot that would precipitate our involvement. But I was wrong—and so were many others."

Since the invasion of Manchuria by the Japanese in the early 1930s, a continuing conflict had existed in China. In the months leading up to the attack on Pearl Harbor, negotiations took place between the US and Japan arising from US opposition to the second Sino-Japanese conflict. Secretary of State Cordell Hull, a former Tennessee senator, played a part in the failed communication between FDR and Japanese Ambassador Nomura that immediately preceded the December 7 attack.

The group spoke briefly about the Japanese attack, but soon

realized the fruitlessness of such an after-the-fact discussion. The girls, not wanting to add to the angst, nestled closer to the boys as they discussed their plans. Thelma smiled slightly as she slid her hand into Bud's and squeezed it as once again, they shared looks of longing.

"We'll make it through all of this," Bud whispered, followed by a loving peck on Thelma's cheek.

"I know we will," she responded as she laid her head on his shoulder.

The organ music died down and the crowd began to disperse. Taking their cue from the wait staff bussing their table, the Retreads retrieved their coats, scarves, and gloves, prepared to face the biting wind and spitting snow.

Miss Neubert walked ahead of the group. As she came to the revolving door, she stopped and turned toward her students. "I pray for you all a very Merry Christmas, wisdom in your decisions, and safety in the coming months. I have grown quite fond of each of you."

Touched by her uncharacteristic expression of personal thoughts, the group crowded closer to their mentor.

In a likewise uncharacteristic response, Bud hugged his longtime teacher.

"Thank you so much. We'll never forget your kindness and re-instruction. When we send our kids to your class in a few years, we'll make sure they pay better attention than we did."

The group smiled and nodded. Miss Neubert cocked her head, pursed her lips, and offered her familiar smile.

"We'll let you know what decisions we make, or what decisions the War Department makes for us," Bud said.

Following their teacher one last time, each couple then slipped arm in arm into the December chill.

The Christmas season passed quickly for Bud and Thelma. They attended the service on Thursday, Christmas Day, at Broadway Baptist and the Sunday service at the Presbyterian Church three days later. The message at each church tied the coming of Christ to the comfort of a relationship with him, a welcome balm to the consternation of war and the looming decisions the young couple faced.

On the day following New Year's, Bud and Thelma had seen the movie *Johnny Eager*, with Robert Taylor and Lana Turner, at the *Tennessee*. Before the movie, a Movietone News film clip showed some of the burning of US ships on battleship row during the Japanese attack on Pearl Harbor: the *Utah*, the *Oklahoma*, the *Arizona*, and others, all destroyed. The narrator stated that the *Arizona* took a bomb down one of its gunnels, a lucky drop by a Zero's [Japan's attack fighter-bomber] pilot. (Note: Years later, analysts cross-referenced film and still photographs and concluded that the bomb did not descend through the gunnel, but instead penetrated the ship into a lower deck, igniting black powder and ammunition stored there. The explosion caused smoke to be expelled through the adjacent stack, thus making it seem as though the bomb descended down through the gunnel.)

Japan had followed the lead of Hitler in Europe, attacking first and declaring war afterward, the narrator said. This was a clear violation of the protocol of war.

Holding hands, the couple strolled through the vestibule behind the theater and down the long and ornate terrazzo-covered entrance into the biting chill of the evening. As they neared Bud's car, parked a block away, Thelma broke the long silence. "Chilling," she said, referring to the devastation portrayed in the news film.

"And maddening," added Bud as he opened the passenger door. "Makes me want to take 'em on hand to hand."

"Not so fast now. We need more time together first," Thelma pleaded.

On the way back to Thelma's home on Chicago Avenue, they stopped at a local diner for a warming cup of coffee and conversation. "This may be the last Christmas season we have together for a few years," he observed as they snuggled close.

She gazed into the brownish-green eyes she had grown to cherish and whispered, "I know. And no more trips to the Smokies [the nearby Smoky Mountains] for a while. It's hard to think about."

Bud had a couple of extra nickels to feed the jukebox in the corner of the diner. As the first tune played, the two pulled even closer together, oblivious to other conversations or the din of clanking dishes. The smooth rendition of the song sung by the vocalist for the Harry James orchestra flowed over them: ". . . 'cause I only have eyes for you."

Their silence said more than either could voice.

Thelma had for years used her diary to record dutiful entries of important events: dates, play practice, thespian performances, church, movies, and more. Early entries about her new suitor in late '40 and into early '41 included, "Ross Perrin," then "RWP," then "Bud." Even her diary revealed the way he had pushed out all others who sought the favor of a date with Thelma.

As spring slid rapidly into summer, Bud and Thelma began to talk of marriage and family. As he considered his future, a little girl who was a mix of his sister Evelyn and the one he hoped was his future bride, and a little Junior, spunky like his nephew, filled his thoughts.

By this time Thelma's daily diary entries had waned, then stopped. The need to chronicle her life had come to a halt. But in early October, another noteworthy event occurred when Bud popped the long-awaited question. And much to Bud's relief, she said yes, yes, yes!

Plans for marriage developed as determinations about his military future followed a parallel course. A decision must come soon.

Bud considered the enlistment opportunities. *Navy: too claustrophobic riding around on a ship in tight quarters. Army: slogging around in the cold, rain, and snow holds little appeal. Army Air Corps: Now, there's a possibility.*

He talked with an Air Corps recruiter and liked what he heard. *Flying seems exciting,* he thought. *And a post-war career in aviation sounds pretty good, too. But first things first.*

For Bud, first things involved one Thelma McGhee. Deciding that preparation for a large wedding was a waste of time and money, both in short supply, the pair eloped. On September 5, 1942, they stood for a brief ceremony before Reverend Reed Rushing in Lake City, Tennessee, north of Knoxville, and honeymooned in Kentucky.

A month and five days later, Bud enlisted. The recruitment office at 518 Union Avenue stood just around the corner from the local YMCA, where he had spent many lunch hours over the past few years playing basketball, swimming, and lifting weights. *If I make it to the level of first lieutenant*, Bud mused, *I'll be making $34.61 a week, $4.38 less than at the Power Company. So much for career advancement.*

A terse induction notice arrived seventeen days later. "Report to Room 5 in the New Post Office Building at 6:45 a.m. on November 7, 1942," it read. "Have breakfast at home."

On the appointed Saturday, Bud stood in the first of many lines he would encounter over the next two years in the Army Air Corps. Along with over a hundred other boys, he swore to ". . . support and defend the Constitution of the United States against all enemies, foreign and domestic. . . so help me God." Realizing what lay at stake, he took the oath seriously.

Later that day and only blocks away at Shields Watkins Stadium, the Tennessee Vols beat the Cincinnati Bearcats 34-12. But this game didn't mean as much to Bud as in previous weeks or years. A much bigger conflict was being played out across the globe, and he was excited and fearful about the role he would play in it.

CHAPTER 6

Thinking, Wondering, and Worrying

Riding the Rails to Miami

Knoxville, Tennessee: January 30, 1943

"THERE'S A PARKING SPACE," EVELYN said as she saw a car pulling away from the curb in front of the Southern Railway terminal at the corner of Depot and Gay Streets.

Grinning at their good fortune, Bud wheeled his sister's ten-year-old Hudson Terraplane into the just-vacated space. "I thought we'd have to park blocks away and traipse through the snow. What luck," he commented.

"And you didn't have to parallel park," Evelyn teased her brother, knowing how he hated that aspect of driving. "You must have paid the preacher this week."

Bud's pursed lips showed his mild displeasure at her all-too-frequent but loving barb.

It wasn't that thousands of cars filled the streets of Knoxville in 1943. They didn't. But the Depot, as Knoxvillians called the Southern Terminal, was the central point from which numerous troop trains departed to carry new military inductees to the various training sites throughout the country. The few area parking spots were infrequently vacant.

Escaping from the jam-packed car, Bud, Evelyn, Thelma, Bud's mother, Margie, and a rambunctious J. Ross slogged across the slush on the pedestrian bridge that connected the terminal with Depot Street. The now two-year-old J. Ross's incessant chatter broke the family's nervous anxiety about seeing Bud off to Miami but didn't bring calm. The job that Bud and hundreds of thousands of other young men were called to do was both filled with faraway

Southern Railway Terminal-circa 1940s
Public Domain

travel and fraught with danger. Like families all across America, each member of the Perrin clan faced this reality in his or her own way.

Bud opened the ornate oak door at the upper entrance to the terminal and held it as the family entered. All but he started down the traditional staircase that led to the lower-level waiting room and boarding area.

Noticing Bud had not followed the group, Mrs. Perrin turned to see her only son immersed in thought, his small suitcase on the marble floor at his side. The faraway look on his face confirmed his immersion in an intense reverie evoked by the familiar scene.

His father's family had owned a news and cigar stand on the level below, and for more than a decade, Bud and his father had entered this door together. He had enjoyed being by his father's side on Saturday mornings as Ross Sr. helped service the rail-traveling crowds weekends always brought.

Bud's gaze caught his mother's, and her lip quivered as tears trickled down her cheeks. The emotions evoked by memories of Ross Sr. and the realization of what the ensuing wartime might bring gripped them both as they embraced. But it didn't take long for little J. Ross to break the calm of the poignant moment with an impetuous tug at his hero's coat sleeve and an urgent demand.

"Choo-choo coming, Uncle Bud. Let's go!"

"Come on, knothead." Big hand holding tiny one, Bud and his namesake bounded down the steps.

The overflow mob in the first-floor waiting room and on the loading platform was abuzz with excitement. Through the smoky cigarette haze and din of noise, the short blasts from the steam whistle of the inbound engine captured the crowd's attention. J. Ross flinched at the first one, but his wide-eyed look of fear soon morphed to a smile as the family laughed first at and then with him.

"Looks like he's not quite as tough as he likes to act," Evelyn said.

"Oh, yes he is. He and his daddy are going to be the men around here till I get back," Bud asserted as he held his nephew close. "Take care of these girls, Palsy Walsy." J. Ross clasped his hands, squeezing Bud's neck one final time.

The recruits were easy to pick out in the massive crowd. The soon-to-be fighting men had entire families hanging onto them and were the only ones not shedding tears. After all, crying didn't seem to fit the persona of a soldier. So even if they felt like it, they didn't show it.

The Perrin family had said their emotional good-byes the night before. Bud and Thelma had already begun to plan when she might visit him in Miami. But neither knew whether or not the Army would accommodate their desire.

All too soon, Bud and Grover Blevins boarded the train and scrambled through three coach cars before finding two seats together. They placed their suitcases in the rack above the grimy window and plopped down on the wooden cane seat. Thelma and Henrietta Bowman, Grover's girlfriend, had both graduated from Knox High in 1937 and worked together at J.C. Penney for three years. The two couples often double-dated and had become close friends. *I know it's a long shot, but I hope we can go through training together*, Bud thought. *At least Miami should make a good start*.

Groaning under the added weight of hundreds of new passengers, the train crept from the station as smoke and steam belched from the engine's stack. The soon-to-be-flyers inside the passing coaches strained to catch a last glimpse of family as tears flowed and hands waved.

Bud, Grover, and hundreds of their fellow inductees settled in for the long, uncomfortable ride. Miami was almost nine hundred miles away—nine hundred miles in a crowded, smoke-filled coach surrounded by raucous aviator wannabes. With a little liquor added in, a tedious trip was not a possibility but a guarantee.

Steam Engine at Southern Terminal-
circa 1943
Public Domain

Their first stop: Chattanooga, then Atlanta, Macon, and more until they arrived in Miami more than twenty-four hours later.

"We might as well get used to this," Bud lamented. "Betcha there'll be many more just like it."

"Plus long lines, waiting, and bad food, no doubt," Grover added with a frown. They would both be proven right, and soon.

Dressed in his navy blue uniform and distinctive hat, the conductor entered the passenger car with the announcement, "Tickets! Have your tickets and passes ready." He punched a hole in each printed card as he shuffled his way down the aisle between the huddled recruits, who were talking, engrossed in card games, or both.

He reached Bud, who looked up and asked, "Sir, do you know Leonard Greene? He's also a Southern conductor."

"Sure do. Fine man. We're good friends."

"He's my brother-in-law." Bud stood, stuck out his hand, and smiled.

"So you're Bud. Thin talks about you all the time. He also says his son thinks you're something special. I'm Bert Waldrop," the conductor said, pumping Bud's hand.

"*Thin*?" Bud frowned, indicating his confusion.

"Yeah, *Thin Man*. I call Leonard *Thin* for short," Bert responded with a laugh. "What's he weigh, 140 tops?"

They both laughed as Bert slapped Bud on the shoulder. "We'll pray for you son. Be safe," Bert said as he pushed through the wall of men who had also stood to stretch their kinks out.

The train slowed and screeched to a stop in the Chattanooga terminal. The crew changed in Chattanooga, but the troop train remained the same, as did the cramped quarters and monotony: hour after hour of noise, smoke, dry sandwiches, and bad coffee. After leaving Chattanooga, the raucous laughter, bawdy jokes, and occasional challenging conversation over meaningless differences of opinion slowly subsided. The repetitive clickety-clack of the train wheels on the steel rails took over. Soon, the sound became restful, and quiet conversations broke out throughout the coach.

"Did you see in the *Journal* [Knoxville's morning paper, the *Knoxville Journal*] this morning where Nazi General Paulus surrendered his troops to Russia at Stalingrad yesterday?" Bud said.

"That shocked me. I didn't think Germany had the word *surrender* in her vocabulary."

"They'd been getting their butts handed to 'em for months. I guess he finally saw that the light at the end of the tunnel was actually a freight train," Grover responded.

"The reporter on *Movietone News* at the show on Saturday said the Germans lost a half-million men on the Eastern front, and Russia even more," Bud added as he squirmed in his seat in an attempt to get comfortable. "I bet Hitler's rethinking his decision to stop bombing Britain and turn on Russia."

Grover stood up and rolled his shoulders first clockwise and then counterclockwise in an attempt to stretch the kinks out of his six-foot-two-inch frame. "Are we there yet?" he said in a derisive tone.

Back in their seats, Bud and Grover fell into a fitful sleep. An hour passed before their rest came to a halt when the conductor walked through the car announcing, "Atlanta, five minutes."

"Can we get off?" came a loud response from a boy across the aisle. Laughter echoed from all corners.

Bud and Grover played conversational ping pong, their topics batting back and forth between Tennessee football and the war. Tennessee had just completed a 9-1-1 pigskin season that included a 14-7 win over Tulsa in the Sugar Bowl led by Walter Slater. (Note: Slater later flew five missions as a navigator on a B-24. His plane was shot down over Sweden in 1944 on his fifth mission. He later returned to Tennessee and played in the 1946 season for General Neyland, who coached the team that year in his first year back at the helm after WWII.)

Talk about the possibility of the Vols not fielding a team for the 1943 season had already begun to swirl throughout the city. The war had an impact on every facet of life, including college football. Most institutions of higher learning had lost players to the service. Able-bodied young men of college age had volunteered or been drafted into the armed forces. Many of these were paired with professional players to create "service teams" that played against college teams. These included Georgia Pre-Flight, the Great Lakes Naval Station, Iowa Pre-Flight, Jacksonville NAS, and St. Mary's Preflight.

"I guess most colleges won't be able to field teams if this war doesn't end soon," Bud said.

"I'm not as big a fan as you, but let's try to do all we can to whip the Krauts and win this thing. Then we can get home and see a UT game together. How 'bout it?" Grover said, slapping Bud's knee.

"Deal."

South of Atlanta and after more hot but not-too-tasty coffee, the conversation returned to the war. A recruit sitting across from Bud had been thumbing through a *Yank* magazine, which Bud had never seen before. "Can I take a look?" he inquired.

"Sure," the stranger replied, smiling as he handed his prize across the aisle to Bud. "They put 'em out every week. This one's the January sixth edition. My brother brought it back a week ago from his last training stop. Pretty good read. Take a look at the article on the Battle of Midway," he said, sticking out his hand. "By the way, I'm Billy Rhodes from Straw Plains."

Billy's strong grip and calluses were a dead giveaway that he was the product of a farm family and accustomed to hard work. Bud liked him right away.

"Ross Perrin, and this is Grover—Grover Blevins, both from Knoxville. Thanks, I'll give it back," Bud said, returning Billy's infectious smile.

"I remember seeing a story about Midway back in the late summer in *Life, Look,* or *Collier's,* I can't remember which. Seems like there was a Navy officer's picture on the cover. I think he was in the battle," Bud commented. (Note: The magazine was the August 31, 1942 issue of *Life* magazine. The cover picture was of Ensign George H. Gay, who was shot multiple times on the last day of the three-day Battle of Midway from June 3–7, 1942.)

Over the next hour, Bud devoured the periodical, stopping only to give Grover some facts, especially from the Midway article.

"I saw some newsreel accounts of the Midway Battle back during the summer," Bud said, slapping the paper with the back of his right hand for emphasis. "But this gives some details they didn't show in the film."

"They can't exactly put a three-day battle into a three-minute newsreel," Grover reminded Bud, his sarcasm no doubt enhanced by the monotony of the ride and the ever-thickening haze emanating from a mixture of Camels, Lucky Strikes, and Chesterfields. "How can doctors say those things are good for you?" the agitated Grover asked, casting a furtive glance at his friend.

Against his mother's repeated protests, Bud was an occasional cigarette smoker, so he couldn't in good conscience agree. "Quit bellyaching and look at this," Bud responded as he thrust the *Yank* diagram of the Midway battle in front of his friend. "The losses Japan took at Midway may have been as important in the Pacific War as Stalingrad was in Europe."

Bud continued. "The article says, 'The Japs lost at least four carriers, along with at least 275 planes, three destroyers, two cruisers, and one transport.' Sounds like it would be crippling, but who knows what they have in reserve?"

"What'd we lose?" Grover asked.

"Not sure."

From across the aisle, Billy broke into the conversation. "If it's OK with you guys, I can give you some of what I learned from my brother. He's quite a military brain, especially about the Navy. Our Dad was in the Navy in World War I. It's in our blood."

"Hey, do you realize you're on the wrong train?" Grover asked. "Did your family break your plate at the table when you chose the Air Corps?"

"Naw," Billy chuckled. "I've always been independent. Always loved airplanes. Hope to be a pilot. They all encouraged me, and here I am," he said from across the aisle. From his window seat, Grover leaned across in front of Bud so he could hear.

"We had three carriers in the Midway fight," Billy said. "The *Yorktown* was lost on June 7, the last day of the battle. The *Hornet* and *Enterprise* made it all the way through. We also lost a number of other ships and about 150 airplanes. We got hurt pretty bad but ended up winning."

"I guess Midway is critical in reaching Japan, which it seems we'll eventually have to do. Do you agree?" Bud asked. "And the *Hornet* is the same ship Doolittle and his Raiders took off from earlier in '42, isn't it?"

"Right on both counts," Billy responded. "The Japs had to protect their homeland. They thought they couldn't be reached—that is, till Doolittle and his sixteen B-25s and eighty men bombed Tokyo in April of last year. Pretty gutsy move by FDR."

"Not to mention Doolittle and his men," Grover added as he sipped his last few drops of tepid coffee. "It seems they weren't sure they could actually carry enough fuel to make it."

"The Japs thought they were unreachable by the US, but Doolittle disagreed," Bud added. "By the way, did you guys know the B-25's Doolittle used were stripped bare of extra weight so they had a better chance of bombing Tokyo and then being able to land in China? The mechanics cut out the tail guns and the gunner. To make it look like they still had the protective guns in the tail position, they replaced them with two broomsticks painted black. And the guy who thought of that brilliant move was named—drum roll, please—Captain *Ross* Greening," Bud trumpeted with a feigned sense of pride in their shared given names. "Commit that fact to memory, boys."

"Yeah, the Doolittle raid was obviously a wake-up call for the Japs," Billy continued. "And it probably made the protection of Midway all that more important. "It's still a critical spot for them and for us, halfway between the Pacific coast of the US and the island of Japan. And we have it. At least for now."

"The Japs had been capturing Asian territory ever since they invaded Manchuria in 1931," Bud asserted. They didn't have enough natural resources to fuel their increasing population, so they needed resource-rich territories in the surrounding Pacific areas."

Bud handed the *Yank* back to its owner. "Thanks for helping us learn more about the Pacific part of this war. We probably know somewhat more about Europe, but very little about North Africa. I guess we'll learn soon enough, though," Bud said, sighing as he slid back down in the seat in an unsuccessful attempt to get comfortable.

The conversation of the last half-hour caused Bud to reflect on last year's study time with Miss Neubert and his heightened interest in keeping up with the war ever since. Like most young men, he had mixed emotions about its escalation.

"Five minutes to Waycross, last stop in Georgia. Ten-minute stop. Hustle back. This train waits for no one," came the voice of the conductor.

The train screeched to a halting stop. Bud scrambled down the steps at the end of the car and hurried to the newsstand. Flipping through the postcards, he found one with a picture of Waycross on the front. He plopped down a nickel, thanked the proprietor, and rushed back to the train."All aboooard," came the conductor's call. Three blasts on the steam whistle, and the train, straining and clanking as the slack between cars was taken up, chugged away from the station.

Not enough time to write and mail the card, Bud thought. *I'll do it at the next stop.*

"Dear Thelma, Greetings from Waycross, Georgia. Feeling fine considering its now 12:30 a.m. Sunday and we are just now in Waycross, Ga. If we make it to Miami by midnight we'll all be surprised. This train beats walking but not much. Love, Bud." After Waycross came Jacksonville, where he mailed the postcard.

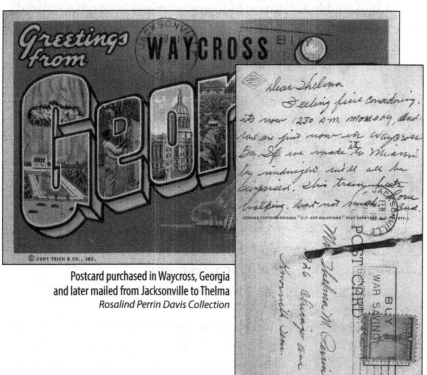

Postcard purchased in Waycross, Georgia
and later mailed from Jacksonville to Thelma
Rosalind Perrin Davis Collection

The chatter subsided as fatigue gave way to sporadic sleep throughout the coach. But Bud was still mulling over some thoughts that had gnawed at him since he enlisted: *Many of these boys have had at least some college. I haven't. Will I be able to keep up with the academics? Do I have the skills to be a pilot? And I'm twenty-six. Can I keep up with these eighteen- and nineteen-year-old kids? Are my eyes good enough for pilot training? I hear they only want those with twenty/twenty vision.* He hadn't shared these concerns with anyone, even Thelma. Ever the optimist, Bud's thoughts surprised even himself. But his uneasiness had intensified as the day of departure loomed.

He stuck his right elbow in Grover's unprotected rib. Blevins flinched but didn't respond. So Bud punched him again and hit the emotional nerve. "What?" Grover responded with sleep-deprived consternation. "Get to sleep."

But Bud couldn't. "Do you have any worries about what's ahead?" he whispered.

"You mean other than getting some sleep?"

"Yeah. Like washing out for some reason. Does the possibility bother you?"

The question hit home. Wiping his just-opened eyes, he murmured, "Well, a little bit, I guess."

"What bothers you the most?" Bud asked.

"Cuttin' the mustard, handling an airplane. I want to fly one, and I'm a little anxious about how complex it's gonna be. Can I learn to react like a pilot? And what about you?"

"Pretty much the same. The no-college thing bothers me the most. And my eyes. Sometimes I have blurry vision. I had a collision playing baseball, and I think it started then," Bud said in a low voice, not wanting to broadcast his concerns.

"You passed the induction physical, didn't you?" Grover asked, his voice tinged in sarcasm.

"Yeah, but I understand we have a more rigid one coming up in Miami. Maybe my eyes are good enough to operate a radio but not fly the ship. Or shoot a gun out of the side of a bomber but not command a fighter," Bud grimaced as he whispered. "Man, would I hate to wash out!"

Look, we've got plenty of time to deal with this stuff, but not to-night," his friend shot back with a frown. "Get some shut-eye."

Grover turned his head toward the window and again curled up as much as he could. Bud shut his eyes in a futile attempt to catch at least a few winks, his mind continuing to chase his concerns in a circle. Finally, emotional and physical exhaustion caught up with him, and he slept once again.

Over the next six hours, other Florida cities came and went. The first of many monotonous train treks was nearing its destination, and none too soon. Most boys had lapsed into a stupor brought on by thirty hours in a hard passenger seat. To the left of the train, the moon shone just above the eastern horizon.

"We're comin' up on Miami," came a voice from the middle of the car. It was just past midnight on Sunday, the last day of January, and the message spread. Stirring and stretching, the groggy passengers wiped sleep from their eyes to meet the day, their first as real soldiers at last.

US Army Air Forces Training during WWII

Myriad difficulties impeded the US Army throughout WWII as it faced the daunting task of structuring efficient and effective training for its Air Corps component. Before the war, the majority of the USAAF recruits knew little or nothing about aviation. Most had never even seen an airplane up close. Some had never driven an automobile. Coming from widely divergent backgrounds, they had to be trained as individual professionals and molded into cohesive teams that could synchronize to carry the bombing fight to an equally well-trained and equipped enemy.

To accomplish this monumental task, facilities had to be purchased, leased, built, or converted from one use to something entirely different. Hotels became barracks. Colleges became aviation training centers. Factories were converted from automobile assembly to aircraft production and their shops to technical training classrooms. Airfields were expanded, constructed, and adapted for use by military aircraft.

The two decades between WWI and WWII had compromised the military readiness of US forces. Coming from a standing start in many of the training and production areas, the mission was one beyond any ever attempted by the collective US military. Gunnery training didn't exist in the USAAC, so it was initiated and enhanced throughout the war. Not only were soldiers trained for the specific gunner position, but bombardiers, navigators, and radio operators added this skill to their other technical expertise.

Qualifying officer candidates were offered basic college courses either to begin or add to their education. The government created flight schools that focused on both existing aircraft and the new equipment just coming online. Bombardiers and navigators trained on advanced equipment and techniques needed to move beyond any developments the enemy made. Supporting technical professionals, crafts, and equipment without which no aircraft could be kept in the air were developed and improved even before the first mission could be considered.

In direct conflict with the restrictions of the Treaty of Versailles of 1919, Germany had developed a formidable fighting force and much advanced equipment. The Spanish Civil War during 1936-1937, in which Hitler aided nationalist Francisco Franco, provided a real-time laboratory in which to battle-test both equipment and fighting forces. So the enemy of the US and Western Europe was both well-prepared and itching for a fight.

Training for all in the flying cadet program was intense and demanding. For each neophyte inductee, it began with basic training, where young men endured thorough physicals, short haircuts, numerous inoculations, skill-specific aptitude tests, and multiple opportunities to march in unison with their fellow recruits. Rounding out their development were guard duty and both the instruction in and opportunity to practice kitchen patrol (KP) in all its glory, including potato-peeling.

Neither Bud's months of research and study nor his long train ride to Miami prepared him for all he would face in the days ahead.

CHAPTER 7

You're in the Army Now

Hurry Up and Wait in Line

Miami, Florida: Basic Training, Winter 1943

Wednesday, February 3, 1943
Dearest Thelma,
We got here at 1:05 Monday morning. Uncle Harry and
Aunt Inas [Bud's maternal aunt and her husband] *were at*
the train, and also our [new] *good friend, "the Sergeant,"*
who tucks us in bed every night. After standing around
for about an hour and a half, they brought us over to the
beach, and let us stand around over here for a couple
hours longer. Then the real fun began. We were assigned
to a tent, and then to a hotel, but no room. We arrived just
in time for chow call. So we went down and stood in line
there for 2 more hours (without sleep for 2 nights). After
chow they let us rest 5 minutes, then we fell in again for a
little close order drill.

We are up every morning at 5:00 a.m. I'm now waiting
for chow call, and I hope it will be soon. The food here is
fair but I eat it, every bit.

Last night was the first time in several months that
I had to sleep without my little wife. If I hadn't been so
dog-tired I would have probably stayed awake for some
time, but after staying up all night Sunday [1/31/1943]
and Monday nights, and also a pretty tough first day's
drilling I went to sleep before I hit the bed.

After that, chow again, which always takes a lot of
standing around. This time there was no rest period. We
fell in for what we thought was to go watch some of the

older boys do a little parading, but it ended up with us doing most of it. Some of the fellows had to drop out for first aid by this time.

The above was just a small sample of our first day. And probably even a smaller sample of what's to come, but I can take it if the rest of these fellows can. Even though we spent two sleepless nights we had a lot of fun. Someone always cracks a joke to keep everybody in good spirits. We met a soldier on the train from Knoxville who kept us going by his jokes and wisecracks.

So far, we have no uniforms. Some say they are out and others say we'll get them today, but that's the army for you. Nothing's very different. This is not pre-flight training, but pre-aviation, they call it. They say we'll only be here 30 days, then off to some classification center, if we're all good boys and do everything the sergeant tells us to.

So far Grover and I have been together. We're in the same flight command, but do not room together. I was in a room last night with 3 fellows from Savannah, Ga. They seem to be OK. They are all asleep right now.

I'm not going to tell you how much I think of you— would take too long, but you know that anyway. In case I don't find time to write Mother today. Please call her and tell her I'm OK. Chow call now. –All My Love, Ross

A couple of days later on Friday, February 5, Bud wrote, "*I am now a soldier at last—uniform and all. Our uniforms were issued last night about 9:30.*"

Bud's group was frustrated by the repetitive monotony of basic training, typical of training throughout the nation. He related, "*You've probably heard it said before that most of your time in the army is spent standing in line. Well it's certainly true. Everything we do, with the exception of going to bed, we wait in line for sometimes as long as two hours at a time.*"

Bud's group endured other mundane activities, which were hated but necessary for discipline, uniformity, unity, and classification. These included:

Constant Changes: On February 7, Bud wrote: *I believe I mentioned that we were to be moved to another hotel. Well, we moved Friday from the Ocean Grande to the President Madison. We were combined with another incomplete outfit. The set-up here suits me much better. Grover and I have a room with two fellows from Atlanta. Their names are Jay Pyles and Dick Wilber. They are really swell fellows. Jay is as smart as a whip. He made 129 out of possible 150 on the exam like I took in Knoxville that I made 81 on. Can't imagine why he'd have anything to do with a dumb lug like me. He saw your picture and wants to know how a good-looking girl like you ever fell for a big ugly so-and-so like me. I wonder that too.*

Medical Exams: On February 8, he added: *Today we got our first shots: typhus, smallpox, and tetanus. My arms are both a little sore tonight. All three shots you get in one time, two in the left arm and one in the right. Several boys from our outfit fainted. The rest of the shots we get one at a time, ten days apart, which will take a month. So we may be here longer than I expected.*

Haircuts, or better said, "buzz cuts": as Bud wrote on February 8: *You should see my haircut, cadet style. I look like a peeled onion, but it feels good, and I don't have to comb it. I believe I got the best haircut of anybody in our room at that. Grover's wasn't cut quite short enough, and slightly resembles a mop.*

Exercise: *We had a pretty tough day today—that is physically. The exercises are getting more rigid every day. So far, I've been taking it better than the majority of these other fellows. No one believes I am an old man of 26 years. They say I look like I'm about 20, but I suppose they are just trying to make me feel good. It works.*

Sick Bay: On February 11, Bud wrote: *These big army shoes have done things to my feet. Today I had to answer to the sick call because of blisters on my feet after standing in line from 7:30 a.m. to 12:30 p.m. The doctor put a little patch on my blisters* *and told me to go on back and drill. The next time I'm sick they will have to come and get me. This afternoon we had a parade of all the cadets here, which is quite fun, or maybe more than that. I limped thru OK but my feet are plenty sore now.*

Inspections: Bud lamented in his letter of February 12: *We were required to work on our rooms all afternoon. With Jay Pyles out of commission temporarily, and Dick Wilber sick with the flu, it was up to Grover and [me] to do the work. You should see our room. If they find any dust here, I don't know where it could be. We scrubbed the floor, washed the windows, cleaned the screens, cleaned up the bathroom, etc. Tell Henrietta Grover should make some girl a good househusband. He's a pretty good housekeeper—and I'm learning more about it every day, but don't you get any ideas. I'll need a rest after all this.*

Study and Examinations: Bud had a hard time adjusting to the classroom work and tests, exacerbating his concern about his lack of college experience. On February 18, he wrote:

I can't offer any alibis if I did flunk that examine (Note: "examine" was a common way to refer to an exam in the WWII period) *today. It was really tough. I've talked to guys that have had six years of college, and they say it was the toughest examine they have ever had. I probably made 50 out of 150. It was about 4 times as hard as the one I took in Knoxville.*

The following day, he wrote:

We haven't heard from our exam. A lot depends on the outcome of that. I'm expecting to be one of those that failed, but who knows. I might have been lucky and passed. I hope so. I gotta shine my shoes right. I wish J. Ross was here to help me—his birthday is in three days. I sent an airmail card, while we were out. I hope it gets there.

On February 20, he seemed encouraged when he wrote:

. . . feel somewhat better today after an interview with

the army classification men. I qualified for OCS on the ex-
amination we took last week. All but about 10 percent of
our squadron qualified. But still I'm in doubts about re-
maining a cadet. We haven't heard from the exam we took
yesterday.

His family's financial situation was never far from Bud's mind. Since his father's death in 1940, his mother had suffered a decline in finances and health, both physical and emotional. No doubt her disabled daughter, Margie, added to her concern. Evelyn and Leonard had graciously taken on the care of both Margie and Mrs. Perrin, but the physical and mental strain were taking a toll on the young family. Fully accepting of his role as his mother's primary financial support, Bud wrote:

I just learned that as long as we're aviation cadet can-
didates, we won't be allowed allotments and [will] only
make 50 bucks a month. I probably won't have to worry
about that much longer anyway. So if I do wash out I'll be
better from a financial standpoint. You mentioned about
the money mother needs. I'll be able to send her that much
and more even if I don't get the allotment. If I do get an al-
lotment I can get $50 for you; I don't know how much for
her. Would you fix it so she could get about $40 anyway?

In an attempt to keep his mother's spirits up in his absence, even though his own were somewhat low, he wrote to her:

I can't believe it's still just February. This has been the
prettiest day since we have been here. I kinda hate to
leave, but probably will in a few days. It's rumored those
that passed their examine will be sent to college. I know
my grade on one examine, which I passed, and qualified
for officer's training school, but have my doubts about the
other one. It can be a pretty tough test.

Bud wanted to know what was happening back home, and Thelma wanted to know everything he was doing. After only five months of marriage, they both loathed the separation brought about by the war. But Bud didn't miss the opportunity to remind his bride of a postal fact that eluded many who thought they could speed up the mail: *"By the way, the next time you send mail, just put one air-mail stamp on it. The last air-mail letter had two air-mail stamps. They don't get here a bit faster that way. I believe it was the letter where you were telling me off."*

On February 8, Thelma wrote in one of her regular letters,

> *Oh darling—I do wish it was all over! But I know our love will last through it all, and we'll have the rest of our lives together afterwards. Maybe later Uncle Sam will send you closer home and I can see you on weekends or maybe I'll become a "camp follower" —I'm tempted! At least we can get letters to each other quickly. That's a lot. Night before last I slept in your bed and last night in your PAJA-MAS. It makes me feel so close to you.*
>
> *I'm anxious to hear how you make out in your exams, etc. Write as often and as long as you can, sweetheart. Your letters are my main diet now, you know they mean whether or not I keep smiling! —All My Love, Your wife*

Thelma often spent time with Bud's family, a camaraderie that seemed to bring closeness both to Bud and to each other. In his letter of February 8, Bud made a request: *"Let me know how J. Ross is. I'd like to see that little rascal."*

As confirmation to the characterization of his nephew, Thelma responded a week later:

> *During supper (we ate in Evelyn's apt.), he wouldn't eat his vegetables, kept wanting GRAVY! And then the little scamp began talking about shining shoes. So I shined shoes with him while Evelyn and Mrs. Perrin washed dishes. Then he yelled, "Let's shave!" Of course, always before, that was a privilege he denied me, but he was willing to accept me as a substitute since you were not here. He took me in "daddy's" bathroom and we "shaved" and*

of course, finished with "poo poo" water [Leonard's term for aftershave lotion]. *But no sooner had we gotten back to the kitchen than he yelled "Let's shave AGAIN!" I gave up! At this point, I decided that Evelyn was the one who would miss you most!"*

Later that day, Thelma added to the characterization:

J. Ross said as he was getting mad tonight. . . "go see Bud a Choo-Choo!" I told him I wouldn't mind a bit for myself! Incidentally, he still says he is going to name his new dog, "Mr. What" and later J. Ross said he wanted Bud to hurry back and "play football." I want Bud to hurry back PERIOD! That boy is one rambunctious character.

On February 24, Thelma wrote, "*Evelyn said J. Ross's card came this morning—said he really seemed to enjoy it, and carried it around all day. He'd look at your card and say, 'Hey Kid, shine shoes, shave.' He never forgets anything, the little scalawag!*"

Some letters compared the weather in both places: eighty-five degrees in south Florida and sub-freezing temperatures with snow in Knoxville. Another common topic was Bud's upcoming departure from Miami and the location of his next posting.

Later in February, Bud wrote:

I got hold of a clipping from the [Knoxville] *News Sentinel about the classes for cadets starting at UT March 1. Looks like we'll be leaving here by the 1st of March, but who knows? I thought at first I wouldn't want to be there. But now I feel different. If I was there I could be with you every Sunday anyway. Would you like that? It's a happy thought for me anyway.*

On February 26, he added:

Jay Pyles came rushing in just now with some good news. We are leaving here tomorrow night but without Grover, which I don't like at all. This is on the QT. We don't know where, but I'll let you know as soon as possible by wire. The way they picked us was alphabetically, and 'B' [Blevins] and 'P' [Perrin] are pretty far apart. Maybe we'll run into each other later, but the chances are slim.

That Saturday night at 9:45p.m., a troop train headed north, with hundreds of cadets destined for higher education somewhere in Tennessee

Dearest,
Well here I am on the choo-choo again, but this time I don't know where I'm headed for. We were notified at 4:00 a.m. this morning to be ready to leave at 5 a.m. All of our old 440 Flight (our 47 men we started with in Miami) with the exception of the first 12 on the list, which is arranged alphabetically. Sorry to say we left without Grover. He was the best-liked guy in our outfit. Every few minutes someone, speaks up with "if only Blevins was along." Grover will probably leave tomorrow, but I doubt if we'll see him at our destination. I wish we could be lucky enough to be together again. I'll sure miss him. We're really great pals.

As they made their way through the training maze, Bud and Grover had also shared some private fears about their fate over the next two years. For some reason, the specter of combat evoked less concern than climbing the training ladder. *I wonder if I'll find another pal I can open up with,* Bud thought. *But Jay Pyles seems like a good guy. Maybe the two of us can talk—if he's got anything to talk about, that is.* He continued his letter:

We have fifty men on our car headed for the same place. I was selected to be commander of the men in our car. It's my job to keep them in good behavior and see that they keep the car clean. We have breaks quite often lasting about 15 or 20 minutes. The Major says for us to call the men off the train and drill them around to keep this blood circulating. It's not such a bad job since we all know one another. They cooperate very well.

*Jay Pyles and Dick Wilber, my other roommates, are
still with me, which makes not having Grover along a little better, but we still miss him an awful lot. I don't have
the slightest idea where we are headed for and if I knew
I couldn't say. It may be west, north, or east. You know I
hope it's near home more than anything in the world. I
hope I get to see you before so very long.*

*Sort of an unusual feeling riding along not knowing
where we are headed for. But we are all in the same boat
or I should say on the same train.*

*I've never seen as many blackjack games at one time.
There's about ten on this car. Tell Garland [Thelma's
brother] I think of him every time I get in one. This is some
job trying to write on the train. I have a hard enough time
as it is. I hope you can read this.*

*Up-to-date news—I did have hope of going to UT. On
the train several rumors got started that we were headed for there, but after we left Atlanta and started west,
I started hoping it was Memphis. On our car, 25 out of
the 50 were Memphis boys. We were told after leaving
Birmingham that Memphis was our destination. There is
where the celebration really started. —All my love, Bud*

Memphis, Tennessee: Southwestern College, March 1– May 16, 1943

For military recruits, each training stop served two purposes.
First, it educated and trained the men for the conditions they would
face and the duties they would perform in combat. It also served
as a weeding-out process to separate those the officers believed
could "cut the mustard" from those perceived as too great a risk to
continue.

Some of the culling factors were precise. For pilot training, eyesight was critical. Near-perfect vision was required to operate the
costly aircraft and to protect the crew under the pilot's command.
Some positions also required innate intelligence in specific areas, so
the authorities evaluated test scores in both math and physics. Age,

Bud Perrin and Grover Blevins
Basic Training - February, 1943
Greene Family Collection

Julius W. "Jay" Pyles and Bud Perrin
1944
Rosalind Perrin Davis Collection

maturity, and physical conditioning were also evaluated, but more subjectively.

Maintaining his focus on becoming an officer and possibly a pilot, Bud decided to concentrate on his studies and move forward as best he could. On March 1, he wrote: *"We were issued a set of 24 textbooks today. They consist of Math, English, Physics, History, and Geography. I plan to study in all my spare time and take advantage of every opportunity. . ."*

Feeling a little overwhelmed with the intensity of the instruction, he wrote six days later, *"I expect any day to be placed in one of the other groups who are studying the first steps in Math and English."*

The next day he penned this message:

> *I got to study Math and History but don't know when. I'll make a deal with Jay Pyles. I'll teach him the Manual of Arms and let him tell me what he read for our History lesson tomorrow. Being in the smart class kinda puts the pressure on me. We start in Math [soon]—something I know nothing about. Maybe I can learn.*

His wasted days at Knox High kept coming back to haunt him.

More study time and less sports seem like the smart thing. I should've figured that out sooner, he thought. *Too late now. I gotta get with it.*

On March 12, he wrote, somewhat encouraged:

> *With the help of Jay Pyles, I've been doing fairly well in my studies. He's almost as good a teacher as Newell An-derson* [a teacher at Knox High] *and has about the same amount of patience too. Trigonometry, the subject I ex-pected to be the hardest for me, so far has been the eas-iest. The others, airplane identification, history, and ge-ography have been giving me most of the trouble. We are supposed to be able to identify about sixty different planes up to now by seeing a silhouette of the plane flashed on the screen. Somehow I haven't found the secret of how it should be done, but I'm not the only one that has this trou-ble. Out of our class of fifty men, only 5–10 are making passing grades in that subject.*

On March 18, Bud wrote:

> *We had our history test today. You know that's one I've been dreading. I believe I made a pretty good grade, though. I was never able to get anything out of our text-book but kept notes on everything said in class. Every question asked was one that I had taken note of and stud-ied last night. I hope this luck stays with me so I can get away from here in a few weeks. Some of the history ma-terial was on things we covered in our study group with Miss Neubert. If you have a chance, go by and tell her thanks.*

A stickler for proper grammar and spelling, Thelma chided her husband on his more than occasional butchering of the English lan-guage. She also sent him a dictionary.

In a not-too-cryptic response, Bud wrote:

> *I'm glad your husband is not too sensitive about his poor*

spelling and grammatical errors or else he might have been a little offended from the general hint thrown at him. However since he has been fully aware of that fact for a little over twenty years now, I believe he'll take it as constructive criticism. No kidding, honey, I've been needing a dictionary for a long time, especially since we have been here. I appreciate all the trouble you went to fixing the tabs. They are a big help. In the future I'll try to make use of them. And I'm sure that will be quite often. In fact, I have both books before me right now trying to make sure and spell every word correctly. However if I do misspell several words don't criticize me now. Give me a little time to get use to the ideas of being careful about my spelling.

It didn't take long before Bud's studies were looking up. With some excitement, he reported to Thelma: *"Our last month's averages were posted this afternoon. Mine looks some better. Math 75, Geography 97, Civil Air Regulation 81, Airplane Identification 94. . . averaged almost 87. I've got to get that math grade up."*

Whether through hard work, the tutoring of Jay Pyles, the gentle persuasion of Thelma, or the combination of all three, Bud passed all the required subjects. But other hurdles loomed. Bud knew that, at twenty-six, he was one of the oldest recruits in his training group at Southwestern and possibly among the entire Army Air Corps. Officers at both Miami and Memphis recognized his maturity and rewarded him with leadership responsibilities. *Sometimes these responsibilities seem more like constraints, but that's life*, he mused.

His lifelong penchant for physical conditioning and participation in sports also placed him in the top groups in almost all physical tests. *"I did more pull ups than anybody in our class but wasn't so hot on the 300-yard run. We then played baseball. I hit two home runs with the bases loaded both times. After the baseball game we had a cross country run (about 2 miles),"* Bud reported proudly to Thelma. *"We stopped long enough to eat, then took the new boys outside. Drilled them for an hour. All of this sorta got me tired. A couple of the boys said they couldn't believe I am 26. What is this— do they think I am over the hill at 26?"*

The Army wondered the same thing. Bud may have been an anomaly, in better physical shape than those who were years younger, but at twenty-six, he was on the bubble. Would his age alone cause him to wash out? No one knew—especially not Bud. A few weeks earlier, he wrote to Thelma: *"One boy was shipped out today after they learned he was 27 years old. Keep your fingers crossed for me. You know I'm getting older every day."*

Not long after that, he wrote: *"I just learned that the boy that left yesterday was 26 years and 11 months [old]. Just 6 weeks older than me. Maybe I'll [only] be here a month. I was wrong about his going to OCS. He went to Nashville classification center. From there he'll go to pre-flight school. Doesn't sound bad, but I still like it here."*

On April 22, Bud shared more of his concern:

> *It looks like that old thing called fate might be against us again. The Sgt. and I went to see the commanding officer about an overnight pass for Saturday and found out that the CO had just wired Maxwell Field about me. He had just been checking our ages and saw that I would be 27 in May. It seems that I must be classified before I reach 27 and it takes three or four weeks, or sometimes more, at Nashville before you can be classified. An answer to the wire should be here tomorrow so the CO says they might order me to leave immediately or I might be here another week. I am up a tree—don't know what to tell you to do now* [about coming to Memphis to see him]. *I hope to know something before you call Thursday.*

The end result? Officers felt Bud's record and physical conditioning superseded the rules, so the age issue was either waived or ignored. He would be classified at his next training stop and receive a position assignment sometime after that. *Another hurdle cleared,* he thought. *I can breathe again.*

Whether by intent or accident, Bud and Thelma kept parts of each letter they wrote lighthearted. Bud wanted his wife to know what he was doing other than soldiering, so he wrote about sports, food, movies, radio shows, and music. She shared details of mutual friends she had seen and the normal activities that occupied her day. And they both made sure each letter expressed the intensity and faithfulness of their love for each other.

Bud sent Thelma this typical remembrance of home:

> *I caught a ride back from the airport with a civilian. He gave us a nice long, roundabout ride home so we could see the city. I enjoyed the ride a lot. The way we came back looked like the road between Knoxville and Sevierville. I kept thinking of all the times me and my baby had gone riding out that highway and how nice it would be if we could be together again soon. I thought of how we use to take our lunch and ride out this way to eat. It was a lot of fun, wasn't it?*

In a time of extreme loneliness, he penned the following:

> *I enjoy getting a little lonesome every now and then. It makes me realize more and more how nice it was to be with you and how much nicer it will be after I become a civilian once more. It would be so very long before we can be together and then we have our whole lives to be together. We'll raise a dozen kids, and I hope they all look like you."*

In some further comments about military haircuts, Bud wrote:

> *I had to get another one of these GI haircuts last night. The barbershop is about four blocks from the campus. I was put in charge of the barbershop detachment (about 25 men). So I spent about 3 hours in the barbershop. There was a radio, so for the first time since we left Knoxville I heard Fibber McGee [and Molly], Bob Hope, and Red Skelton.*
>
> *The Memphis boys figured out a pretty good system on seeing their wives. They had their wives meet them at the barbershop. I never saw so much courting in all*

my life. Made me wish I could call my wife and have her
come down to the barbershop. All my love, Your faithful
husband.

His bride responded: *"The barber shop thing sounded like fun.*
Wish I could have been there—I'd show those Memphis (folks) what
'COURTING' really is! At that time [during Fibber's program] *I was*
writing a letter to my baby."

The intensity of training (and a bit of laziness) often kept Bud
from his Sunday church regimen. But the officers recognized the
need for a spiritual component to the recruits' lives and set forth
rules intended to alter this behavior, common among new officer
candidates.

On the topic of church attendance, Bud wrote:

> *We are all required to attend church here in the chapel*
> *at 10:45 this morning. Until then our time is our own, as*
> *long as we stay on the campus. Getting back to church,*
> *as you probably know this is a Presbyterian College so,*
> *therefore, we had a Presbyterian sermon conducted by*
> *the president. He was all right but doesn't compare with*
> *Dr. Barbour. We are to go to church every Sunday, and*
> *I'm glad. Maybe I'll get back in the habit again.*
>
> *By the way,* [afterward] *we three "old men" came up*
> *to the room and did a little singing for our own enter-*
> *tainment. We are pretty good. You should hear Jay Pyles*
> *sing. Nelson Eddy doesn't have a thing on him. He sang*
> *in his church choir back in Atlanta, and also at special*
> *occasions.*

Later, he wrote: *"The preacher we heard today was almost as*
good as Dr. Barbour. He held my attention every minute of the time
he spoke. He talked like Cary Grant. He talked along the same lines
as Dr. Barbour. All during the service I was wishing you were there
to help me enjoy his wonderful talk."

In another letter, he wrote: *"We were allowed out yesterday*
from 7 a.m. until 2 p.m. to attend any church we liked. I enjoyed
the service very much. The minister was the best I've heard since

last Easter but still doesn't come close to Dr. Barbour. The choir was good."

"The men's brotherhood class of the Broadway Baptist Church sent me a nice little New Testament. Practically every soldier has one. They are mighty nice to have. I also received a copy of the church's reminder. I noticed my name was on the church's honor roll. They have a pretty good memory don't they?" Bud wrote later that spring.

Jay Pyles and Bud had similar worldviews and lifestyles, so during their time in Memphis, they became quite close. They both missed Grover but made the best of his absence. After one evening mess, Bud was engrossed in a long letter to Thelma. In the bunk next to him, Jay was propped up in bed, half-heartedly scanning an Atlanta paper his wife had sent a few days earlier.

In the style of a nosy kid, Pyles asked, loud enough for all to hear, "Hey Perrin, how 'bout letting me write a note to that beautiful wife of yours?"

"I'll let you if I get to read it before you send it," Bud said with a toothy grin. "OK, here's the deal. Write the note on the back of this page of my letter, and I'll send it—if you say nice things about me."

"It'll be hard, but I think I can make that work," Jay responding, reaching for the still-incomplete letter. He wrote:

> *Dear Thelma, I've never met you and you, you lucky girl, have never met me. But by this time I feel as though we are close friends. This big lug you call a husband has drilled all of your fine points to me at every waking moment. Not that it's unpleasant—mind you—because in addition to seeing your picture (a very nice picture by the way) Bud has said enough nice things to make a very sweet gal out of you. Of course I wouldn't take Bud's word for it. He's prejudiced. But Grover Blevins also had a word for you—nice. We try to take of care of this lug, and he's doing OK and being a very nice boy—which you knew all the time—of course. I understand you'll be down here pretty soon [a* planned trip for the next weekend] *and I hope I get*

a chance to say "Hello." Anyway if I don't, "Hello." Jay
Pyles

Bud added: *"Hi, sweetheart. Jay Pyles said to tell you he thought*
you were wonderful, but not to get conceited. We just opened up
that big box with all the 'goodies' in it. More and more I'm thinking
you are the most wonderful wife in the world. How I ever managed
to hook you is beyond me."

After all the physical and scholastic training, the boys were anxious to get to the main reason they joined the Air Corps rather than
another branch of service: flying. Bud wrote on April 3, *"According*
to the latest rumors we are to start taking flying lessons April 5th.
That is, our group of 50 men are. I'm looking forward to that. It
will be a change of scenery from the four walls that have been star-
ing us in the face for almost two months now."

On April 6, Bud added some information about his initiation to
aircraft: *"Right after breakfast I just told you about going out to*
the airport was a lot of fun. We climbed up in a P-47 Thunderbolt
(tell Garland about it, it's his favorite plane) and a Lockheed Vega
Vultee, P-38 Lightning, P-51 Mustang. . . all sorts of planes. They
are all to be shipped to combat duty."

"I got in two flying lessons yesterday. My first was OK. We did
stalls and several other maneuvers. I felt good, and did them all
as well as could be expected. My next lesson wasn't so good," Bud
wrote to Thelma on April 16.

The next day, he added:

> *We went up in a different plane and I couldn't get used*
> *to it. I did take offs and landings. I do both of them fairly*
> *well, but can stand plenty of improvement.*
>
> *I go up tomorrow for a check ride with Oscar Brabson.*
> *I hope I do all right. I'm so tired right now I can hardly*
> *hold up my head up after all that flying yesterday. I was*
> *plenty tired last night and was still tired this morning. To*
> *start things off this morning I had a math test. Then the*
> *next period a final in airplane identification, after that a*
> *test in our physical ability.*

On April 18, Bud wrote:

I enjoyed my flying a lot today. I went up for a check ride with one of the other instructors. Oscar Brabson wasn't there today. The fellow who took me up is really a swell fellow. We did spins and stalls and all of the other things I had already learned. He said I was ok. A spin is a lot of fun. You pull the stick back until the nose climbs so high the ship stalls. Then you kick left rudder when the ship starts to drop. It starts spinning the earth look like its coming up and turning around all at the same time. When we pulled out is when I got the funniest sensation. I felt like someone was pulling me down hanging on back of my jawbone. It was funny I tried to laugh but couldn't because of that pulling force on my face.

As I told you I was having trouble with airplane identification, only made 39 on the examination which was about average for the class. We took another examination on which I made 84. That was very above the average mark made by the entire group. In fact only fifteen out our fifty men made as high as 80. I still have a lot to learn about this subject we are expected to know 150 different planes before we leave here (this doesn't mean I won't leave if I don't, though).

In late April, Bud reported to Thelma: *"I'm finished my flying now. I flew three hours yesterday but was only given credit for two. The highest grade made ever was 86. I made 83. I believe I could have done better if I had been feeling better."*

Knoxville news was always welcomed. But one note in a letter from Thelma about a mutual friend was not. On April 22, Bud wrote: *"I saw where Bill Luttrell is a German prisoner. That's better than being lost but still pretty bad."*

Also in April, Thelma shared: *"They [the church] gave us forms to send to our local newspaper here. I sent one to the Journal several days ago. Today I saw the report in yesterday's paper."*

But Bud's responsibilities at home were never far from his mind.

Earlier in April, he wrote his mother: *"About money—it may be soon time before it will come thru $54 has already been taken out of my pay for the past two months' allotment. I hope you can get along OK until it comes thru. We may not be here very much longer, and then if I become a cadet I'll get $75 a month—then I can send it to you and Thelma myself."*

Being in a leadership position on base had its perks. A precious letter had informed Thelma: *"The Lord and Lady Halifax are coming to Southwestern, we were told yesterday."* (Note: Lord Halifax, Edward F. L. Wood, was a key figure in Great Britain and one of the five-man War Cabinet working directly with Prime Minister Winston Churchill since May of 1940 to direct British war efforts.) Regarding this visit, Bud received the following notice:

APRIL 2, 1943 FRIDAY

CADET CAPTAIN ROSS W. PERRIN, JR., 13TH COLLEGE TRAINING DETACHMENT, SOUTHWESTERN, IS CORDIALLY INVITED TO ATTEND A TEA IN HONOR OF THE BRITISH AMBASSADOR AND LADY HALIFAX ON MONDAY, APRIL FIFTH, FROM FOUR-FIFTEEN TO FIVE-FIFTEEN O'CLOCK, IN THE CLOISTER OF PALMER HALL.

FOR THE COMMITTEE, CHAS. E. DIEHL

Bud continued in his note to Thelma:

Bill Monday, the Squadron Commander, and I will be part of the guard of Honor. Our commanding officer [will] make up the rest of the guard. We will meet them at the train or someplace and escort them out here. Our men are to form a single file on either side of the road leading up to Palmer Hall. Each man will be about 10 feet apart. I'll tell you all about it later. They will be here next Tuesday.

News of the meeting with Lord and Lady Halifax leaked back to Knoxville and found its way to Bud's former employer, the Knoxville

Power and Water Board. In the April 6 edition of its internal paper, *The Kilo-Water Account,* pictures of Dusty Holder, stationed in Ohio, and Bud Perrin were printed on page three. Under Bud's photo was a comment he sent in jest to a former co-worker, *"Lord and Lady Halifax are going to have the high honor of having tea with me."*

Bud remained fond of his namesake, J. Ross. Letters from his sister, Evelyn, his mother, and of course Thelma made it quite clear that the two-and-a-half-year-old was becoming quite a handful. In one letter to Thelma, Bud wrote: *"I received Evelyn's letter yesterday along with two from you. From what she says, J. Ross must be picking up a lot of meanness, or maybe it's just coming out. Sure would like to see that little rascal. Wonder if he would know me now? I really haven't changed much except I don't wear the same sort of clothes and my hair is a little shorter."*

And later, after a phone call home, he added: *"Wasn't it luck that mother and J. Ross were there? J. Ross sounds grown up. The scamp talks so plain."*

He wasn't quite prepared for an Easter card he received from his nephew, however. Realizing his "Palsy Walsy" loved Teaberry chewing gum, J. Ross insisted on sending his uncle a couple of sticks of his tasty treat. Bud opened the card to find two sticks of Teaberry with a note penned by Evelyn with the determined help of J. Ross. It read: *"Dear Unca Bud, Here is your Easter present, Kid. I got some new shoes. Love, J. Ross."*

This precocious nephew remembered shining shoes with his uncle. To her son's words, Evelyn added: *"We wish you a Happy Easter—We were down at the Power & Water Board yesterday. Andy, Emma, Mr. Van D. all send regards."*

On April 25, Bud wrote: *"I was almost a sissy* [almost cried] *after reading the card from J. Ross and then the letter from your mother. I got that old choked-up feeling for the first time since January 31, 1943. . . . I'm so glad Leonard and Evelyn got into their Cherry Street house. I can't wait to see it. Evelyn drew me a sketch of it, and it seems great.*

On May 13, Bud lamented his birthday separation from his bride: *". . . well, I'm absent from you on my 27th birthday, and am officially*

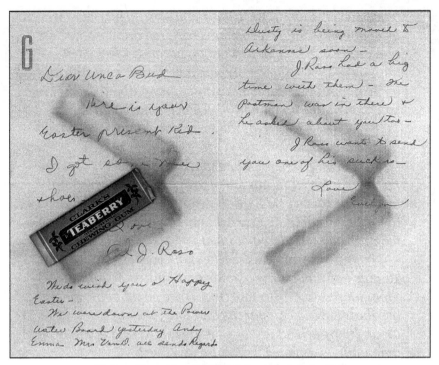

"Teaberry Chewing Gum Card" from J. Ross to Bud - Easter, 1943
Rosalind Perrin Davis Collection

an old man now, at least in the eyes of the AAC. I hope I don't get pulled out of formation and put in a rolling chair. I hope to spend my 28th with you, sweetheart."

Thelma had sent her birthday greetings on the appropriate day:

> *My Dear, I wish I could say "happy birthday" and knew that you WOULD have a happy feeling this 13th of May, 1943. But I know with things as they are, with the uncertainty of your life right now, it is hard to keep in good spirits. But, my baby, it will be easier, I'm sure, when you are moved into a new place and begin new studies there. Looking ahead to happier times is about all any of us can do now, sweetheart. Your wife stays in a rosy dream, whenever possible; filled with pictures of us together again, leading the life we want to live.*
>
> *I've tried hard, sweetheart, not to get into those ole*

blues spells! Funny my telling you that, when I've been weeping like a silly ole woman every ten minutes the past two days! But I know it is partly because I feel your un-happiness–your unrest. When you sound cheerful and write about your baseball team winning about the home runs you made, about how well you enjoyed your flying — THEN it isn't so hard for me to keep smiling, despite how much I miss you!

But darling, when I know you are lonesome, I feel like I've failed, failed in my job of keeping you cheered up! I feel like I haven't written the right things–haven't done the little things that might have made the difference in whether you felt happy or blue!

I hope by the time this reaches you, you will be out of the 'dumps'– if not, do me a favor and jump out right quick! I'm going to try to do that, too. If we could only remem-ber that nothing can part us and that nothing can take us away from each other. And sweetheart, it isn't going to be long until I see you–I'll promise you that!

I know you would enjoy coming home and seeing your family. But they are well and will write you soon I know. Your mother is better in spirits (and physically) than I've ever seen her. She wears those wings as if her son was the only one who ever saw an airplane—she is that proud of you, and I am too.

By the way—J. Ross is a little ole mean rascal now— and I mean it! He is smart enough to figure out how to get whatever he wants and poor little Evelyn really has a time with him.

You'd be surprised at how slim Evelyn is now—she looks so pretty. She's been taking her last year's dresses up inches! —All my love, your wife.

But change again loomed on the horizon. In his last letter from Memphis, Bud wrote, *"Looks like I'm going to Texas, not Nashville."*

CHAPTER 8

The Making of a Soldier

Preparing for Action

San Antonio, Texas: Cadet Classification
Spring and Summer 1943

RANDOLPH FIELD, NAMED AFTER CAPTAIN William Millican Randolph, lay fifteen miles northeast of downtown San Antonio. Building 100, the nerve center for base operations, could be seen down a long straight drive from the tightly guarded entrance to the base. This building was also a well-known but seemingly misplaced symbol for the base itself.

The center of the structure was a water tower resembling a giant antique salt-shaker, its eight filigreed sides topped with a rounded dome. To say this section of the building seemed out of place would be a gross understatement, since anyone who saw it felt sure it belonged in India. The structure built around it did little to alter its unusual appearance. Hence, it came to carry the slightly derisive moniker of "The Taj," short for the real Taj Mahal in Agra, India.

Near the Taj on the left and nestled among a clump of trees stood a chapel, completed nine years earlier. Like all the other buildings on base, it was constructed in the traditional Spanish Colonial Revival style. Barracks and buildings housing classrooms dotted the vast expanse of land leading to the airfield to the west of the entrance.

Upon arrival at the base in San Antonio, each cadet was required to write the same precisely-worded letter home. It said:

> *I'm sending this from the Army Air Force's Classification Center here at San Antonio, Texas...I'm here with the rest of the future Army aircrews and am assigned to squadron 109 where I will remain until I am ready to enter a preflight school. During this time I will have my physical*

*examinations and tests, to determine whether I become
a bombardier, navigator, or pilot. If I am classified as a
bombardier, navigator, or pilot, I will then be appointed an aviation cadet and will receive free, a $10,000 na-
tional service life insurance policy. After being classified
and transferred to preflight school, I will commence my
actual preflight training, which will last for about nine
weeks.*

On Monday, May 17, Bud added some words of his own to the
required letter:

*We left at about ten o'clock Saturday night (5/15/43). I
went right to bed. We had a fairly good trip down except
for our Pullman car being so hot. Bill, Jay and I had us a
nice stateroom but right at the last minute they took one
of our cars away from us. I slept in an upper berth so I
could sleep alone. I don't care about sleeping with anyone
other than my wife. I slept real good even though it was
a hot car.*

Bud and Thelma's correspondence often included references
to Knoxville. He was always looking for a cadet from back home,
and she was constantly telling him about mutual friends she saw in
town. On May 18, he wrote:

*I didn't get to write last night—was busy meeting, for-
mations, and talking to the brother of one of your old
boyfriends. Tom Evans came up to our barracks looking
for someone from Tennessee. I spoke up that I was from
Knoxville. We talked a long time about our training up to
date. After a while he mentioned his brother, Dick, and
asked if I knew him. I told him I thought he used to go
with the girl I married. Then he started talking about
how pretty you were and invited me down to see some
of the pictures he had of you in his scrapbook. I didn't go
last nite but I think I'll go and see his collection in a few
days."* [Note: Tom and Dick Evans's father, W. E. Evans,

was principal of Knoxville High School from 1917 until the school closed in 1951.]

Bud thought he had left many of the dreaded military hurdles back in Memphis. Although not a candidate for valedictorian of his cadet class, he was comfortably in the upper quarter in all subjects and near the top in two of them. Flying, although not easy, had proven to be something he caught onto quite well. When he reached San Antonio, he thought he was home free. But a few of the words in the required letter jumped out at him: "physical examinations and tests," and "If I am classified as a bombardier, navigator, or pilot." *What if I don't make it?* he couldn't help but wonder.

Reeling from a day of dizzying tests on May 19, he wrote from a combination of frustration and humor:

The tests we took today would drive a man crazy, if he would just let 'em. Some of 'em were fun though. The first one was a nerve test. We had to hold a small rod with a lever in one hand (with the arm perfectly straight). This rod was placed in a small circle. The idea was to keep the rod from touching the side of the hole. Each time it touched, a red light flashed and registered a mistake. At the same time a man was standing behind us shouting code numbers and letters and asking questions. After the test we had to write down all the numbers he had given in 10 seconds. And also remember the number of times the red light flashed. The next six tests weren't hardly so bad but bad enough to give me one of the worst head-aches I've ever had. My headache was cured after I got back and found such a nice letter waiting for me. You did an awful lot of bragging on your husband in that letter. Makes me feel good to know you love me almost as much as I love you.

I won't take another test until 12:30 tomorrow. It's probably the most important of all: the physical. I hope I'm OK. The next one I take is where the man tries to talk you out of wanting to fly. You always said I was stubborn.

I bet he'll have a hard time with me. I told Jay about all the nice things you said about him and his wife. He said to tell you he thought you were tops. That's to you for me, too, only more so. I think I'll get to bed before long and rest up for that physical tomorrow. Be as sweet as you always are. —Love, your husband.

The tests on the following day were both puzzling and personal. In reporting his consternation to Thelma, Bud said:

...went over for half of our physical and the talk with a psychiatrist. All we had was a blood test and another X-ray of our chest. Then came the talk with the big fellow. It wasn't bad—as bad as I had been told I would be. I got by with my fingernails OK. He asked personal questions about my family—If my father ever beat my mother—If there was any member of the family [who was] insane and some [other] very personal questions about me. Sometime I'll tell you all about them. One [other] thing he tried to cross me up on but didn't succeed. He asked me if I was to be put off to myself, with only one other person, would I rather it be a woman or man. I told him I would rather go with a woman—then he asked me why. I told him why. Then he asked what I thought my wife would do about me making a choice to go with a woman. I said I had figured on her being the woman. He laughed and said, "Well, you got me there." He asked what you and mother thought about my wanting to fly. I told him both of you were very much in favor of it. Then he got up and said, "OK, if you want to fly." I take the other half of the test tomorrow—the part when they check our eyes, ears, nose, throat, teeth, heart—in fact everything we've got.

Two days later, he wrote:

This afternoon Hank and I got a baseball from this Detroit ballplayer and played a little catch. I was worried because we scarred the new ball up on the rocks. When I took it back I told him we would replace it, he said, "That's okay, keep it and when that one wears out come and get another. I've got plenty." It was funny though, Hank and I sat outside his barracks for about ten minutes trying to get up courage to take it back.

Frustrated and somewhat resigned to the foreboding results of yet another test of his physical abilities, Bud related some bad news to Thelma on May 21:

I'll take time out now to tell you my troubles. Right at the present it looks as though your husband is going to be in the walking army. I got thru everything they gave except for one better test. It was an eye test where they put a pair of glasses on you with one red lens and no lens at all in the other side. Something like the pair I wore on our honeymoon. Then the doctor turns off all the lights and flashes a small light in front of you. You see two lights while in front because your eyes cross. Then he places the light to your right left up and down. I still saw two lights. I was supposed to only see one. He called in another doctor and had him look at me. He discovered that my right eye turns at a greater angle than my left. I have to go back tomorrow for a recheck. I don't know what good it will do. I can't do anything about the way my eyes work. It may be that a muscle was injured when I got that blow over my right eye several years ago. I hope something will cause my eyes to correct themselves before 8 o'clock in the morning. I would like to able to pass and be classified as a pilot, but I don't want to worry too much about it. There is nothing I can do. Being so far away from you is enough for me to have to worry about.

Jay got thru OK with his bum knee. He was lucky that there were so many of us in the same room when we took our examination requiring knee bends. Jim Harrison made the grade too. That is he wasn't required to take a recheck on any of his tests. Bill Monday made it

too—went thru with flying colors. Maybe I'll make it yet.
I still hope so.

   Baby, my love for you and knowing that you love me
means more to me than anything else in the world. If I
can't fly I'll have to do something else worthwhile. I want
to be somebody you can be proud of. I hope you get this
Sunday. I'll send it airmail special. —All My Love, Your
"cockeyed" husband

The next day brought both relief from that frustration—and an
additional physical impediment. He wrote:

   I feel a little bit better about the washing out situation
now. I went over for my check on my eyes at eight this
morning after waiting a couple of hours to see the doc-
tor. I made that part of it OK. But I have another check
coming up next Friday. My record shows that mother has
diabetes. They call the test we take a Glucose Tolerance
Curve. I don't know what it means, but it will probably
determine whether or not I have any trace of the disease
or not. If this test has anything to do with it I will either
be a flying cadet or a civilian. Under these conditions I
would rather be a flying cadet.

   Jay and Jim got their official classification today. They
both made pilots. Bill hasn't heard anything more. I was
beginning to think it never rained here until last nite. The
rain really came down and the wind blew so hard & I
thought sure these barracks were coming down.

   Baby I want you to think about me and when you're
thinking, remember that I'm trying my best just because
I love you. Tomorrow is Sunday—no "Sugar Report" on
Sunday. Gotta wait 'till Monday. I love you baby—Bud

The follow-up medical tests might have been amusing if they
hadn't been so critical in determining Bud's future as an airman.
About these tests he wrote on May 26:

   I went once for my recheck this morning. It wasn't what

*I had expected. I haven't completed my eye examine yet.
Got to go back again in the morning for what will probably be the last check. I was in a little dark room surrounded by four Army doctors, all of them watching my eyes
do tricks for them. They put a card in front of me and
switched it from eye to eye while I'm looking at a small
light at the other end of the room. They say my right eye
goes down and my left eye goes up. You didn't know you
had such a freak of a husband did you? After watching
me for a few minutes the Captain in charge said, "Come
back in the morning, Sonny." I'm going to quit worrying
about it all. If I make it, OK and if I don't, there's nothing
I can do about it.*

Seeking solace, on Thursday of the same week, he added:

*I went back for my eye recheck today—didn't do any bet-
ter. They say that they will reexamine me for a bombardier. It has to go before the board and I won't know for
a few days. I didn't act too happy when they said I was
disqualified as a pilot and my only chance in the aircrew
was [as a] bombardier. They may not give me that since I
acted like I didn't care if I did or didn't. Since I've thought
about it, I'm kinda anxious to try it. It doesn't take near
as long to get a commission as pilot training. Only takes
four or five months. What do you think about it? I can
always back out if I don't like it or you don't like it.*

*Jay and I will be split up here since he qualified as a
pilot. He'll stay here more than likely. Preflight for pilots
is just across the road from us. If they do happen to go
someplace else, they'll probably go to Santa Ana, Calif.
I've got a few of my buddies who asked for bombardier
and made it. Maybe I'll get to stay with them if I happen
to make it.*

But the last day of May didn't bring Bud any resolution. He wrote,
"Haven't found out anything further about my classification a few

more names were posted today. But mine wasn't there. I suppose
they are having a hard time trying to make out my mental test."

Each day added to Bud's frustration and disappointment. He felt
detached from everything: the cadets who had been classified and
moved on, home, his future, and most of all, Thelma. On June 2, he
was notified that he was assigned to ground duty, GDOD. About the
assignment, he wrote:

> *I was expecting it all along after I talked to the board*
> *members the other day about being a bombardier. I told*
> *you how I acted. I made a mistake asking about OCS and*
> *showing how little I wanted to be a bombardier. I also*
> *rated bombardier last as what I would rather be in the*
> *aircrew. I can't say that I'm not disappointed because I*
> *am. I only hope you aren't as disappointed as I am.*
>
> *I found out that I qualified on my mental test. It's one*
> *consolation to know that the reason I didn't make the*
> *grade was something I couldn't help* [his eye condition].
> *I ship out of this Squadron tomorrow and go over to*
> *Squadron 114 not far from here. I hate to leave all the*
> *fellows here. We knew it was coming sooner or later. I*
> *believe Jay hates it worse than I do. He has been running*
> *around cussing the Army for a few days.*
>
> *I'd like to stay in San Antonio long enough to know*
> *what options I have on the ground to compare with being*
> *a bombardier. But I think we will ship out soon—before*
> *that happens.*

Bud knew some of the decisions the AAC had made about him,
but not his all-important classification. Frustrated to the point of
action, he asked if he could speak to the area CO, Captain Brown:

> *...a swell fellow. The best man I believe I've met since I've*
> *been in the army. I told him my whole story so he went*
> *to work on the phone to find out more from the classifi-*
> *cation board.*
>
> *After about thirty minutes he called me over and said,*
> *"Well, I have some good or bad news for you." He says,*

"You are 27 years old aren't you?" I said, "Yes, sir." He said, "Well, I must say you don't look it." And I said, "Thank you, sir." Then he explained that in my case being 27, that they were certainly giving me a rough check. He said, "You know when a man reaches your age he loses most of his value as a member of the aircrew. However," he said, "The GDO [ground duty officer] has been removed for the present." I will either be called back before the board, probably to see how bad I want to be a bombardier, and be classified as a bombardier or be GDOD for sure. The Captain said, "I can assure you that whatever decision they make as to what you'll be will be the best for you."

As a whole, the morale of most of the fellows here is very low. The fact that most of us feel as though the past four months have been wasted and now we have to start all over again is enough to discourage most people.

There are several former glider pilots here. They were within two weeks of getting their commission when glider pilot's school was closed. They joined the Air Corps as a Cadet and didn't make it. You can imagine how they feel?

I don't have any hopes of being reclassified since they tell me it just doesn't happen. After a man has been grounded, it's almost impossible to get back in—so some of the fellows say. I don't want to build my hopes up about having another chance and then be let down again. I'll just consider myself out and then if I do make it I'll have a surprise. Since Captain Brown told me that whatever they decided on would be best for me I've felt better about the whole thing.

On June 5, Bud wrote about a fellow who admired the family photos on his footlocker:

I showed him the picture of you and J. Ross—I said they were my wife and boy.

He said, "I see! No wonder you don't look at the girls in the PX twice." I told him later [that] J. Ross was my nephew. He said he still didn't blame me. Everybody thinks I've got the prettiest wife of anybody. So do I. The pictures [you sent] are all good. I sure can tell a difference in J. Ross. He looks much taller and more filled out also has a look of understanding out of his eyes. I'd give anything to come home for just a couple of days. Mother looks better than she has in four or five years. Evelyn looks prettier than ever, and Margie's permanent shows up well in the picture. She's getting kinda prissy lately isn't she?

Bud was fearful that his family would be disappointed if he were not able to fly in some capacity. Reflecting his uneasiness, he wrote on June 9:

Knowing that you aren't disappointed about my being on ground duty is all it takes to keep me from being disappointed. As long as I love you nothing else really matters anyway. If you were only here to tell me you love me so I could hear it, everything would be OK again. Baby, I realize more and more how much you mean to me. I get a little down in the dumps and you can pick me up so easy. You sure know what it takes to keep your husband happy or [as] happy as possible under the present circumstances.

He still had no word on classification, so much of his letter covered other topics: "*...some boys are getting discharges because their families are short of help back on the farm...a boy went AWOL last night—said someone slipped him a mickey in a bar—I don't believe it. Just heard Al Jolson, George Burns, and Gracie Allen are coming on the air—think I'll listen.*"

On Thursday evening, June 10, Bud was able to talk with Thelma by phone. After the multitude of emotional highs and lows brought on by numerous tests, delays, medical hurdles, and other frustrations, he could hardly contain his excitement as he told her he had made bombardier at last.

After the call, he wrote her the following heartfelt words:

Baby, about this bombardiering business, any time I want to, I can ask them to ground me and if you would be happier if I do, that's exactly what I want to do. Happiness with you means more than all the airplanes in the world to me. One of the big reasons I took it was to have the satisfaction that I could make it, and all the fellows I came down with seemed so happy when I got it. You see there are only two out of the fifty that didn't get something. So please write me and let me know exactly how you feel, and don't tell me to do what I want to. I want to do what you want me to.

In his second letter of June 11, he filled his wife in on some of the details of how he learned about his classification:

I didn't tell you how I happened to find out I was a bombardier. I got tired of waiting around here until they notified me. So I went over to the office of the classification board and ask to see the board. The boys tell me it is usual to go before a board of five men and they ask questions of every nature. When it was my turn to go in, there was only one officer in there, a First Lt. with wings.

He had my records there before him. When I walked in (and) reported, he told me to sit down. Then he said, "What are you doing here?" I told him to find out why I was GDOD [grounded]. He said, "Have you been in any trouble since you've been here?" I told him no (the only thing I've done is not do anything). Then he said, "Do you want to be a bombardier?" Since I hadn't gotten your letter, I told him yes. Then he said, "OK, you're a bombardier." That's all there was to it.

That afternoon I went over to my old squadron and told the boys what had happened. They all seemed happier than I was. They certainly are a good bunch of boys as far as sticking up for one another is concerned.

Bud's strong sense of right and wrong and his disdain for marital cheating prompted him to add:

> *I was sorta disillusioned a while ago after talking to one of the boys who came down with me. He's married and has a little girl. Yet he went to town yesterday, ran into a married girl whose husband is in the Army and had himself a big time. I can't imagine you or me doing anything like that. I'm so proud to have such a wonderful wife as you that I never look at a girl twice. It's a nice feeling knowing that even though we are so far apart we are closer together than any other two people I know of.*

Still bothered by the fellow's infidelity, Bud added in a letter on June 21:

> *...don't you ever worry about my being tempted to do any of those things some of these fellows have done. You know I love you too much to even think about anyone else. I know you do, but just thought I'd remind you. I like for you to keep reminding me quite often that you feel the same way—also got a nice Father's Day card to "Uncle" from J. Ross. Tell Mother and Evelyn I'll write them this weekend. –All my love, Bud*

News also came from Grover, so on July 4, Bud wrote to Thelma:

> *...think I'll write mother tonight. After I come back from the PX also may go over to Squadron 109 to tell Jay and the boys about Grover being classified bombardier. It would sure be swell if we did happen to be sent to the same place. Maybe I could get in on some of his good luck, like coming home every now and then. I received Wednesday, Thursday, and Friday's Journal today. The ad [for Penney's department store] you made up was in my paper. Baby, you don't know how proud I am of the wonderful work you've done. You are just about the best I've ever known at anything you try. Only one thing you*

overlooked. You should have had your husband's pictures in that group, don't you think?

On July 7, he wrote, *"...looks now like I'll be leaving either to-morrow or Friday and from all indications will go to Ellington Field at Houston, Texas."*

Ellington Field, Texas; Pre-flight Training

Some level of anxiety accompanied each move to a new training lo-cation. Each stop had a defined objective and a probable length of time to reach it. After navigating the classification maze at San Antonio, Bud was excited about Ellington, the next stepping stone to real combat. He knew pre-flight was the crucial introduction to the specific individual skills essential in creating a cohesive air combat team.

Bud would soon learn that his time at Ellington would only es-calate the intense classroom work he encountered at both South-western and San Antonio. He would also be introduced to bombar-dier-specific equipment, mechanics, protocol, and tactics. And the question of his ability to withstand the avalanche of physical and emotional strain every airman faced in combat would take up per-manent residence in his mind.

Still, military leaders threw a healthy dose of marching, mouth-ing, and monotony into the training mix, looking upon them as es-sential to melding discipline and unity. Cadets, who saw them as unnecessary distractions, groused. But the AAC and its officers won any argument that arose.

In his first letter to Thelma from Ellington, Bud wrote on July 10:

Hello baby, You've got a tired Poppy tonight. These boys here sorta put us on the ball this morning and kept us that way all day. We left San Antonio last night at 5:00 and after a miserable trip we arrived here around 6:30 this morning. We were met at the train by some very "eager beavers" who had their hearts set on putting us thru the paces—and they did a pretty good job of it. They keep us so busy from the time we arrived until 4:30 this afternoon that not a one of us has had a chance to even wash our hands. We stood at attention most of the day with one of these so-called eager beavers, upper-class-men, or student officers shouting down our throats. If you saw that OCS short [film] with Clark Gable telling the story, then you'll have a pretty good idea of what it's like. It's going to be plenty rough for a while I'm sure but it's good for all us I believe—after all the loafing we did at SAACC.

I was chosen as temporary guide sergeant of my flight. This is the only job, or highest job a new man can hold—it'll get me out of all details and also walking guard duty.

Roscoe Ates, the former movie actor, is our command-ing officer. He gave us a little talk today—was funny in places and pretty tough in others. He looks just the same as he did in the movies. He says there ain't no such a thing as one-night passes here. That doesn't sound any too good—or would you come down here for just one day and night? I don't like the idea of not getting overnight passes at all. What do you think about it? Do you think it's worth going thru all this to be a flying officer? Please let me know exactly how you feel about the thing.

We stay here nine weeks. That would probably mean nine weeks more that I wouldn't get to see you—sounds like an awful long time. We'll be way up in September and past our anniversary too. I sure hope we can be together on September 5, 1943 [their first anniversary]. *Don't you?*

We start classes tomorrow. We are only about two blocks from the airfield. About every two or three min-utes a "big ole bomber," as J. Ross says, comes zooming over the top of our barracks.

Feeling the classroom pressure, Bud soon scribbled a hurried note to Thelma:

"Classes started—moving fast—don't ever let anyone tell you pre-flight for bombardier is not tough. They start

cramming knowledge down you as soon as you get to this place—saying, 'If you drop your pencil will lose 2 years of college physics.'" He added: *"We've been wearing our gas masks most of the morning. It seems that we are supposed to wear them most of the time here."*

In baseball, basketball, football, golf, running, or calisthenics, Bud could easily compete with any of his peers. Success had removed any concerns he had about his advanced age. But with a test pencil in his hand and the clock ticking down to the closing classroom bell, he didn't feel so sure of himself. The next day, he added a few anxiety-filled phrases to his note: *"...never been so rushed in my life—hardly any time to study—always have some (trivial) duty for us—like cleaning the street in front of the barracks—makes no sense...I probably won't be a cadet for long."*

But on July 20, his letter took a different tone:

I got back my examine papers from the two examines I had in Memphis and math. (Note: "examine" was commonly used by service branches in WWII for "examination.") *Made 100 in navigation and 90 on math. Should have made 100 on the math test but misread two problems and therefore made two very careless mistakes. I have another test coming up tomorrow in navigation may not have much time to study. So don't expect to do so well. Better stop now and do a little work. These guys around me make me feel rather silly working so hard while I'm sitting here writing my baby.*

But the next day, more success came his way. *"This has been a tough day. We were on the go all day as usual. I took another examine in navigation made 90."*

With the pressure off, at least momentarily, Bud's thoughts turned to home, as his letter reflected:

Good morning, baby. It seems more like afternoon to me though. I suppose along about now—you are on your way to work. Sure wish I was riding along with you this morning. I'm supposed to be out working with the boys on our new squadron area. I gave an excuse that I had some reports to make out which I have already done. Only took one about five minutes. What I really had in mind was writing you.

So Grover was home again. I don't see how he does it. His luck just won't let up, will it? If he is leaving Friday, I hardly think he will be coming down here, since classes come in here about every three weeks. However he could be coming here. I hope so. Sure would like to see him.

Seven months away from family made Bud even more focused on home and starting a family of his own. And when one of the boys in the cadet corps became a father, the homing instinct grew even stronger. On July 22, he expressed this longing to Thelma.

I saw with my own eyes today a cadet from air squadron going home for a fifteen-day furlough. His wife had a baby the other day. This boy was the happiest boy I've seen since I was been in the army. Everybody gathered around him so they could get a good look at a man going on furlough.

"Why don't you come down right away, baby? Let's get things started!

Three days later, a trip into town again reminded him of home. "...*I was behind the wheel of a car for first time since the day I drove to the depot to catch the train to Miami.*"

But on Sunday, August 1, Bud was able to relax, as he wrote to Thelma:

...I've enjoyed today—got a lot of rest—written several people, my wife twice. The one I wrote this morning you should receive tomorrow I gave it to a boy going to town to mail.

I walked down on the field to look at the planes. I got in several of them. One B-24 and a B-26. The bombardier of the B-26 was there, and showed around, pointing out the

*things he had to take care of on the ship. On the B-26 he
is both bombardier and navigator. The rest of the crew
came along while I was there and [then] they took off.
They didn't know where they were going when they left.
Sorta a crazy bunch. Didn't seem to care much for anything, but were all having a good time.*

On August 11, the base informed the cadets that all leaves had
been cancelled and they would all be confined to base until further
notice. Thelma's scheduled visit had to be cancelled—again. Bud
used his pen to vent his anger:

*This is one time I'm really good and mad; in fact, too
mad to even be writing this letter. I keep wondering now
if you'll get to come down before I leave here. Why does
something always have to happen to ruin our plans? I
know you must be pretty unhappy after working so hard
getting things in shape to come down—I'm really burned
up. I always hate the letters I get written before our plans
had to be broken. You always sound so happy because
you are coming to see me. And then I have to stop and
realize that you aren't coming. I know you must go thru
the same thing. Wasn't it awful?*

*I found out this afternoon that the reason we were
confined was a little different from what I told you this
morning. A boy who had just come back from furlough
developed Infantile Paralysis [polio]. They say we have
all been in close contact with him, so they confine all cadets, bombardiers, and navigators. The same thing happened at Southwestern. The civilian workers go back and
forth, but we stay here. It doesn't make sense, but it's a
regulation, and they say a regulation doesn't have to
make sense.*

*There is a possibility of the confinement being lifted
within a week, but you know how those possibilities always work. If another man comes down with it [polio],
chances are it will last longer than two weeks, but if you*

will make plans to come in two weeks, if possible, also pending confinement being lifted, I'll have something to look forward to and to keep fighting for—Tell J. Ross to keep including me in his prayers and to put something in there about Thelma going to see Uncle Bud—I've thought several times about getting some little wings for J. Ross and Margie—I'll do that right away. All my love, Bud

The days dragged on with no cessation of the confinement. Finally, on Tuesday, August 24, Bud smiled as he scribbled a quick note to Thelma:

Great news—I just returned from the base movie, a corny musical comedy, Fred Astaire & Rita Hayworth in "You Were Never Lovelier." When I got to my room I heard that the quarantine would probably be lifted before the weekend but haven't been able to find out anything definite as yet. The tea for the new men is being planned for Sunday, so I've been told this may mean something. However I've been in the Army long enough not to jump to conclusions. If I only knew for sure, I'd call you and ask you to come at once—if possible. Don't be surprised if I call you sometime Thursday and ask you to leave Thursday night.

Oh yes—I passed my final NAVAL examine today with about a 90 or 95. What's worrying me now is airplane identification. I know the planes okay but can't do so well on the Renshaw System. I did okay for the first few days but haven't even been able to see the planes lately in the time we are allowed (1/10 sec). (Note: The Renshaw Training System for Aircraft and Ship Recognition, developed by psychologist Samuel Renshaw, was a method of training the mind to rapidly identify enemy aircraft. The American Psychological Association reported that it was "generally considered to have "saved untold lives during World War II" [American Psychological Association, March 2010, Vol.41, No. 3: 24]).

The emotional roller coaster of the cadets' confinement to base continued without resolution. Once again, Bud wrote to his bride.

This army life is pretty hard to take under the present condition. They build you up one day and then the next they let you down. Yesterday we had some hopes of getting out this weekend but the hopes were not to be. Today at one cadet officer meeting plans for the pilots' graduation dance have been cancelled. So that must mean that we will still be confined—got a nice letter from you written Monday night. Letters like that are what keep me going as well as I do. Had one from mother too. She sounds so happy. Sounded like a young girl.

In the midst of the base lockdown, cadet training went on as usual.

...was on the pistol range from 7:30 this morning until almost noon. Fired 85 rounds. Didn't do so hot but had a lot of fire. My ears are still ringing—I can hardly hear. I take my final physics examine tomorrow so I suppose I should do some reviewing. Wouldn't want to fail to make that 21 and not pass the course.

Grover came over for about an hour tonight. We had a long chat and you should be able to guess what or who we talked about most of the time. He said T.G. Brown [a Knoxville friend whose father owned Kern's Bakery, a large regional bakery south of the river in Knoxville] *was among the new bunch of boys here. I haven't seen him. He's in another squad. They are assigned to Squadrons alphabetically. Ours is from the L's to R's. Don't have a Tennessee man in the other outfit—couldn't be a very good squadron, could it?*

I showed him the note you sent about the comment in the Kilo-Water account about me: "Things we miss around the office—Ross Perrin cracking jokes—Dusty Holder's infectious laugh." I sure do wish I could join in that fun again for a few days. Well—maybe soon if we can get this training over and get on with winning this thing.

By Thursday, August 26, Bud could write:

I got by my physics with a 94. Should have had a 100 but made a careless mistake just like I made on my math examine. All I have now is that airplane identification to get by. It gets worse all the time. I'll be lucky if get a 70 but I'm not worrying about it. All of us are in the same boat. No one can catch on to the planes in the length of time we have.

The following day the cadets were tested to determine their ability to withstand high elevations. Both the B-17 and B-24 flew at elevations approaching 30,000 feet, so this was a critical test.

Our class went to the pressure chamber this morning, but your old man couldn't take it very long. We are supposed to go up to 30,000 ft. I had to come out at 5,000. They told us anyone who had trouble with their ears at that attitude to go and be examined by the doctor. I took their advice, and the doc told them not to let me go back in. He used some long medical terms about my ears. All I know is that they were hurting pretty much and felt like my eardrums were swollen. They still feel a little funny. I'll probably have to go back for another trip. It was probably due to me having a slight cold. I'm not worrying about it though. I think I'll make it okay.

Realizing his letter reflected a bogus confidence, he wondered, *Is this the medical problem that will prevent me from flying?* Two weeks later, he repeated the test and wrote home, *"...this time I didn't have so much trouble. Only one ear, my right one, gave me trouble. That's the one I had trouble with about two years ago. I may be able to make it the next time 'cause it looks like I'm improving."*

The Ellington Field rumor mill first confirmed a "definite end to base confinement," only to have it summarily reversed in less than two hours. On his first anniversary, Bud thus found himself alone. In a vain attempt to overcome his sadness, he went to the base movie, *Heaven Can Wait,* with Don Ameche and Gene Tierney. "*...was fantastic in parts but I always like that kind* [of picture show]," he wrote.

If open base had been declared, and I had told Thelma not to come to Houston, I'd have been miserable, he thought. As a result, he was only in a slight funk on this important day. In his letter to Thelma that Sunday, Bud wrote:

> *Grover came over this afternoon and brought two other Knoxville boys along, J. S. Brown and a boy named Brooks.*
>
> *From all indications, we will probably be allowed out this weekend. As soon as I find out something definite I'll either call or wire you. Oh yeah, almost forgot. I passed airplane identification with 82 1/2. Was glad to get that though—25% of our squadron failed, and will have to take a re-examination. Until tomorrow I'll have to sign off and say I love you—and HAPPY ANNIVERSARY—it'll be happier when we are together. Good night, your loving husband*

The base confinement was finally lifted, and the couple confirmed their plans for Thelma to visit on September 18. An excited Bud wrote five days before the visit,

> *Baby—all I can think about is this coming week end. I'll do my best to be at the station by 3:05 Saturday. If by chance I can't meet the train you take a taxi to the Red Hotel. I'm getting more excited every minute. Sure hope you can get reservations so you won't be so tired when you get here, but if you are I'll rest with you. Can't think of anything else except I love you more and more—will write again tonight.*
>
> *Baby, I'll be thinking of you every minute, but hurry up and come on down here. Oh yes—I'm sending a money*

order for $50. You can give some of it to mother if you think she needs it and do whatever you want to with the rest. Use your own judgment about how much mother needs. Good night, Your happy husband

An excited Bud met Thelma's thirty-minute late train at the station. A long, loving embrace and multiple kisses were only a prelude to a week of revisiting their honeymoon of a year earlier. The eight days of Thelma's visit seemed to fly by.

"I hope to be home before Christmas, at least for a week or so," Bud said, fighting back tears as the two said good-bye at the station. Thelma's own tears flowed as she rested her head on her husband's chest. They embraced for what seemed like hours, their dream world invaded only by the shrill whistle announcing the train's impending departure.

"All aboard," came the conductor's call as he checked his pocket watch, snugly attached to his belt with a leather loop. Thelma climbed the two steps at the back of the Pullman car in the middle of a ten-car passenger train, turned her head over her left shoulder, and whispered a teary "I love you," to Bud. He blew her a final kiss. The conductor followed her up the steps and held the vertical grab-iron on the side of the steps as he made sure no one was in danger from the moving train.

Before Bud's bride could reach an empty seat, the train whistle bleated its good-bye. The train shuddered and began its halting march eastward. Thelma found an open chair and tumbled into it in time to catch a final view of her sweetheart waving goodbye.

Bud stood on the platform until the train was out of sight, then turned and trudged back to his borrowed car. As he opened the door, he turned back toward the station in a vain attempt for one more glimpse of the departing train. But all he could see were the clouds of smoke belching from the engine.

His drive back to Ellington Field was long, lonely, and more silent than ever.

CHAPTER 9

Refining An Aviator's Skills

Equipping a Bomber Boy

Laredo, Texas: Gunnery School
September 27, 1943–December 7, 1943

AFTER SEVEN MONTHS APART THAT seemed like seven years, the week he and Thelma spent together seemed to Bud like a second honeymoon. *It'll be tough to refocus and concentrate on the training I've got left,* he thought. *But I've got to do it. I have no choice.*

The imperative, however, did little to ease the frustration he felt after the train carrying his love chugged away from the station. *I know how Thelma must have felt watching my train pull away from the Southern Station. And without her, it feels as cold in September as it did that January day.*

The next evening, Bud wrote Thelma for the first time in a week and a half.

> *I was a little sad last night going back to the field.... I thought of you all the way back and tried to imagine you weren't on that train back to Houston and I could see you again that night.*
>
> *Seems funny writing my little wife again. I almost called Hadley 8085* [the phone number at Thelma's hotel room for the past week] *this morning. I sure hated to put you on that ole train last night. When I walked away I felt like I left part of me on that train. Maybe I did. I guess I'll know in a little while.*
>
> *I pulled a trick this morning that I haven't fully convinced myself if it was the thing to do. We were given a chance to go back to aviation students and take advantage of our allotments if we wanted. I took the chance*

and signed to go back as a student. Several of the fellows seem to think it wasn't exactly the thing to do.

They gave us about ten minutes to make a final decision and I usually have to have more time than that to study things over. The way the Captain explains it, I believe it'll work out ok. I'll wear the same uniform as a cadet, eat the same food, and live in the same barracks. It looks to me like a plan to get more men with dependents to come into the cadets. Also while flying I'll get $25 a month flying pay. With your $50 a month, mother's $20, my $23 and $25 while flying, it will all total to $118 a month, $43 more than I make as a cadet. This all sounds good to me. I only hope there isn't a catch to it. Let me know what you think about it. Hope you think it's okay.

I guess we'll be leaving here in a very short while, in a day or two. Bob Owen left today to drive to the place we'll go next. It's Gunnery, I'm sorry, but couldn't say exactly where [it will be] right now, 'cause I'm not supposed to know. Baby I guess you are getting pretty close to that ole Tennessee line about now—wouldn't mind being on that train with you.

Guess I'd better go and see if any late rumors are put out. I'll write again tonight. Don't forget who loves you baby, that's me—Your husband

Early-morning letter-writing was quite unusual for Bud. It was either stay in the sack or answer the bugle call. But on this morning, September 28, shortly before nine, he wanted to share a new connection to their hometown with Thelma. Stopping the dreaded packing of his belongings for the trip to gunnery school, he wrote:

Good morning, baby,

I suppose by now you are back to that place I'd like to be. Hope you aren't too tired and had a good trip home.

This morning about 5:45 we were listening to the radio we acquired when the boys slipped out yesterday. I was fussing about having to listen to such stuff, especially at that time of the morning. About that time the fellow said, "This is WNOX Knoxville." Didn't know that station was so strong—maybe it's just that hillbilly music looking for its family down here in Texas.

I had to make new applications for the allotments and will also have to furnish the justifying evidence six months from Oct 1, 1943. That means another marriage certificate and also an affidavit for mother, I put down she was 75 per cent dependent—did I tell an untruth? Don't bother about it right away—we got plenty of time to get them in. The checks should start coming around Nov. 5, so the Sgt. who took my application said. I just put on my gas mask. We have to wear them from 9:00 until 9:30—that's every Tuesday. It's not so bad now but was a big bother during hot weather.

Baby, I guess I'd better quit now and get ready to go hear that list read off. May not get to write tonight, could be on the train. You know who loves you—Your husband

Laredo, Texas – September 29–October 12, 1943

Laredo, Texas was 350 miles of desert sand, sagebrush, and monotony southwest of Ellington Field in Houston. Bud's late September trip to Laredo was a scorcher.

It's cool in Knoxville, with the leaves turning their vibrant fall hues of yellow, red, and orange—the beautiful orange of the Vols' jerseys, he thought. A blast of hot air through the open window of the car in which he was riding brought this reverie to an abrupt halt, reminding him that he was not in East Tennessee but in Southwest "by God" Texas, as he'd heard it called. *But I don't want to use that sacrilegious term,* he thought. *Wish I could wipe it from my brain.*

Almost the southernmost city in Texas, Laredo sat only three miles from the Mexican border. It was slightly north of Miami's latitude but light-years away from its appeal.

The base at Laredo had opened just over a year before on September 23. Dedicated as an aerial gunnery site for new cadets in the effective use of the 30- and 50-caliber Browning machine guns used on the B-17 and B-24, it formed an important cog in the Army Air Corps machinery.

On Wednesday, September 29, Bud wrote:

> *Dearest, Well, here I am in Laredo, almost in Mexico and to think, so many people said I would never see foreign service. Ha!*
>
> *We had a fair trip down—left yesterday at six o'clock p.m. —arrived in San Antonio at six this morning. They marched us to the Gunter Hotel where a real good breakfast was waiting for me. We left there at 9:30 and arrived here at 2:30 this afternoon. I was in a model 1902 (train) car—-had gaslights— but I slept better than I have so far on the other trips. Most of the fellows, especially the cadet officers are pretty sore about being sent to Gunnery. I wasn't too happy myself but realize that I have to take what the army puts out.*
>
> *This place doesn't look too bad. In fact I like the post better than Ellington. It has a swell swimming pool open until ten at night and a large PX [Post Exchange]. It's real hot here, almost as hot as Houston was about two months ago—so the pool sounds nice. I understand it never gets very cold here—so looks like I'm here at a good time—if there is such a thing as a good time in Laredo.*
>
> *Our barracks are just as nice as the ones at Ellington, but the food doesn't come close. The town isn't any place for a fellow's wife to be, so the veterans tell us. The cheapest room is sixty a month and they say a girl can't get a job unless she speaks Spanish. However, if a fellow was lucky enough to be able to afford the price, he'd have a pretty good setup. Anyone can come on the post all day long and we get weekend passes from Saturday afternoon until Sunday night—or so we hear.*

Bud thought that after a year and a half, he had finally escaped the pressure of physicals and intense academics. But once again, he was wrong. On October 1, he wrote to Thelma, "*I was called out at one o'clock this morning and put in a dark room where I remained until three-thirty taking various eye tests. I passed them, I guess, but was too sleepy to care if I did or not."* Other tests were sure to come, but he chose not to worry.

The travails of academia also persisted in gunnery school. He wrote again to Thelma on Monday October 4:

> *I thought we were busy the first three weeks at Ellington, but I believe we are busier here—10 hours of school a day is too much—I'm getting kind tired of trying to rack my brain every day.*
>
> *The rest of the afternoon was a lot of fun. We played rich man's sports for about three hours, skeet shooting. At first I didn't do so good, but got better as I got more practice. Part of the time we shot at moving targets with 22s mounted so they could be used like the machine guns used in the air. That was fun also. Our fun ended at 5:00 when we had to take PT for an hour.*
>
> *From 6:45 until 11:45 this morning we studied machine guns, taking them apart and seeing what makes them tick and then putting them back together again. Don't know how much I'll do when I have to do it all alone.*

The following day, he added:

> *Yesterday while at the skeet range I operated the outfit that throws out the clay Pigeons for over an hour. It was a tough job for me- kept me busy all the time. At first I was a little cautious of the thing, because just before I started operating it one of the instructors was telling us what a dangerous thing it was. Told about guys getting their arm caught in it—even told of one guy who got his head caught in it. It wasn't as bad as I expected after working it for a while. I wouldn't mind this school so much if we got to do more shooting & did less going to school—maybe they know best though.*
>
> *For the first hour on the range today we were on the BB range. This may sound childish but it's good practice the*

way they set it up here. The guns are small machine guns with ring sights and operate automatically by pressing a button. They have planes running on tracks around a big room. The object is to follow the plane around and get as many hits as possible. It's lots of fun. The next hour we spent on the 22 range firing at moving targets. The guns are mounted like machine guns also. I'm not so hot but still I enjoy it.

Then the next two hours was the best sport of all—the ole rich man's sport, skeet shooting. We fired from a high tower. The clay pigeons come from three different houses at different times: one from the left of you, one from the right, and one directly under you. We use shotguns and do they ever more kick—especially for a guy like myself who doesn't know the first thing about 'em. Out of 25 shots I only hit 10, which is only fair. The best man is a Captain here who got 500 straight. In a way I'm glad we don't fire tomorrow, since I have a pretty sore shoulder.

On October 7, he shared a little more:

The day consisted of ten hours of classroom work—we worked on machine guns from 7 until noon. A washed-out pilot and I worked on one together—he knows even less than I do about them so we had to check each other pretty close to be sure and not lose any of the parts. Think I'm learning a little about them, but still have lots and lots to learn. We studied Consolidated Turrets, what the tail gunner on the B-24 sits in. I have a lot to learn about it too. The instructor gave us an oral quiz today—I managed to answer the questions, but didn't know exactly what I was talking about.

Oh yeah—I sure would like to listen to one or two of the World Series games. [St. Louis Cardinals vs. New York Yankees]. *If they play Sunday, maybe I will.*

Young men's departure to war put a strain on their families beyond the fear of war and its possible consequences, and Bud's situation was no different. In his letter of October 7, he also responded to comments mother had written:

> I'm glad mother is so happy with her work [at George's Department Store on Gay Street in Knoxville]. I suppose you're right in saying that it's good for her not to have to depend on me. I know it must make her feel much better to know she isn't totally dependent upon someone now. I hope she can keep on feeling well enough to work since she does enjoy it."

Three days later, in a letter to Thelma, he added;

> Sure was uneasy last nite when I read Evelyn's letter [both letters announced Bud's mother's hospitalization, but Evelyn's arrived first]. Yours didn't sound so bad though. So now I feel like mother is okay or will be in a few days. Would like to come home though, if possible. If I don't get to come now, it'll be a long time before I can get a furlough. We'll be here five weeks longer and then go straight to advanced. Will be there either twelve or eighteen weeks and then only get about a week traveling time to our assigned post. I think it would do me good to get home for a while as well as Mother.
>
> I got a letter just a few minutes ago written Friday (10/8/1943). You didn't mention any more about my coming home, so I suppose it's off. I'm glad Mother is better and sure hope she doesn't have to stay in the hospital long. I know how she worries about money and how much it's costing for her to stay there. I know she'll be better at home and would probably recover much faster not having to worry about how much it is costing to stay there.
>
> I want to call today—would have called last nite, but the phones were all so busy. I sent the telegram first to let you know I wanted to come home if it was at all possible. I hope you aren't going to too much trouble trying to arrange it. Maybe you'll decide it's best for me not to come.

If you do, it's all right—'cause I trust your judgment will be much better than mine.

I just heard that Grover missed the advanced ship-ment —It's too bad. I wouldn't be surprised if he isn't sent down here to Laredo in about ten days. If I happen to get a furlough, we'd probably be in the same class—but it looks like I might be getting set for a furlough, doesn't it. I won't be too disappointed if I don't get it though, 'cause I'll know you've done your best.

Expressing feelings without offending was difficult enough in person. In letters, with the pressures brought on by war and the time lag of mail service, it was virtually impossible. Bud showed this as he lamented.

I had a letter from Evelyn today. She was sorta upset about the letter I wrote mother. You know how they both were telling me their troubles. I was trying to console mother in my letter and mentioned something about try-ing to make the best of things as they were. Evelyn didn't understand what it was all about. Oh well, I guess I'll have to write her and explain that it wasn't about any-thing at home I was speaking of. I thought about what I had written later and was afraid Evelyn would get the letter first. Hope I didn't make things worse for them. Well my ole sweet baby, I've got to shine my shoes etc. for tomorrow's inspection.

Soon, Bud's hardship request for a leave to visit his hospitalized mother was granted. *Looks like I've finally received some of the Blevins good fortune,* he thought.

On October 11 at 10:30 a.m., Bud sent a money order for $55.00 to Thelma. On October 13, the Western Union office in Memphis called her at 7:15 p.m. with the message *"Will arrive Thursday morning at 6:40, Southern Station. STOP."*

Knoxville, Tennessee – October 13–27, 1943

The two weeks back home in Knoxville provided a welcome relief from the rigors of training but came with its own confining itinerary. However, family reunions came first. Bud's nephew saw to it that he was not without company, wanted (which it most often was) or unwanted (which it sometimes became).

The first sight of her son seemed to melt away Bud's mother's infirmity. "I can't tell you how much I've missed you," she said. "You look more like your Daddy than you did when you left nine months ago. It's been so long," she told him, her voice cracking as her boy held her close and her tears overflowed. Margie edged in for her own hug from her brother and hero, and he obliged.

After a few days of relaxing at their home on Chicago Avenue, he and Thelma drove the familiar route to the Power Board, where they made quite a stir in the outer reception area. Each employee-turned-serviceman who returned home from training was received warmly, but none created quite the stir that Ross Perrin, Jr., did. Staff from secretaries to managing directors all wanted to say hello. Managers Jimmy Hines and Howard Dycus got in line as did all the others to share handshakes, smiles, and good wishes.

After an hour or so, Bud and Thelma walked the three blocks north on Gay Street to Penney's, where the greeting party was smaller but equally enthusiastic. Thelma's co-workers, including Henrietta and their boss, Mr. Riggins, honored the young couple with their words and attention.

"We'd love to have you back, Thelma, but I know you're trying to get the Army to let Bud settle in one training location so you can go live with him," Mr. Riggins said.

"We hope it won't be too long for that," Bud added as he pulled Thelma close. "The next stop will probably be advanced bombardier training at either Midland or Big Spring, Texas. Then, I'll be close to real combat—if I can make the grade. The next training is a real weeding-out process, I've heard."

"You'll make it fine, I'm sure," Riggins said, patting Bud on the back.

On Sunday, October 17, the entire family attended services at

Broadway Baptist. Bud's Uncle Bill, his mother's brother, greeted him in his gregarious salesman-like manner. Bud's cousin Dick along with his wife, Mickey, was also there on leave. He had gone on active duty in an engineering branch of the Army in April of 1943.

"Looks like the answer to our questions back at the picnic two years ago came fast and clear, didn't they?" Bud said, as he and Dick shook hands and laughed.

"Sure did. I've kept up with your training moves. I know you're happy to be in the Air Corps—wish I could've done that, too. But this gives me a chance to get my engineering degree after the war is over, so I'm pretty lucky, too," Dick responded.

Bud and Thelma spent much of his leave at Evelyn and Leonard's new home at #9 Cherry Street. Much of this was spent with Bud's assertive young nephew sitting in his lap, vying for his attention and letting his displeasure be known when it wasn't forthcoming.

Leonard had undertaken significant renovations to their small home to provide mutual privacy for Evelyn's mother and sister as well as his own family. Bud and Leonard were more like brothers than brothers-in-law. Bud didn't consider himself a handyman, but there was no repair or fix-it-up job Leonard wouldn't tackle. They shared an interest in sports. Leonard played semi-pro baseball, and Bud had played in Knoxville's top amateur baseball league.

The two also thought alike. Conversations during Bud's leave always included Tennessee football and the war. But there wasn't much Vol football to discuss in 1943. The season had been called off. Now the discussion centered on whether or not the war would be over in time for the 1944 season.

October 27 came all too quickly. Bud didn't look forward either to the trip back to Laredo or to what he would face there. Still, in joining the military, he had already made his choice. So back to the Southern Railway depot and off to Texas he went.

Laredo, Texas – October 28–December 7, 1943

Bud wrote Thelma from the train on October 28:

> *Hello, Mama—I only have about three more hours of rid-*
> *ing to do before I get ready to get back in the saddle. I'm*

not very tired or hungry.—I was about this time yester-
day. Can't get used to sleeping on that fancy train. Spent
most of last in the smoker reading a couple of magazines
I bought in Chattanooga—almost missing the train there
too—had to catch it on the run. —My seat partner was
such a bad old lady. Didn't have much to say, which suit-
ed me just fine.

I have the same luck I had coming up in making train
connections. Stayed in San Antonio this morning just
long enough to get a good breakfast. About 45 minutes,
that's the longest I've had to eat at any place.

I can tell I'm getting close to Mexico now by merely
looking out the window and seeing how dry everything
looks. Most of the people on the train are Mexican. I've
read your little note at least ten times since Tuesday nite
and looked at your picture about ten times as much.

Over the next week, Bud almost regretted his trip home as he
found himself running hard to catch up with the class that seemed
to have raced ahead of him.

Dearest—I'm doing my best to get back in the swing of
things, but find it a little rough going after those twelve
wonderful days at home. Things have changed tremen-
dously since I left. They are teaching under a different
system, and I find myself racking my brain trying to
catch on to what's going on. Oh well, maybe I'll catch up
sooner or later I hope—I had a little trouble taking down
and putting that machine gun back together again with
a blindfold. Guess I would have trouble during that no
matter how much practice I got.

But—just as I thought might happen, Grover got
shipped here to Laredo. Seems like old times. This Army
stuff is easier to take with him around.

Training, like war itself, had an interesting way of leveling the
playing field. Young men came together regardless of social status,
economic state, religion, or profession. Bank officials and movie

actors often took their places with rank-and-file cadets. And Bud loved to tell aspiring actress Thelma when he rubbed elbows with someone in the acting profession. On November 2, he wrote,

> *Dearest—I only have a few minutes before lights out. I went over to the post theater tonight for a bit of enter-tainment—really had it too—one of the best all-round programs I've seen in a long time. To start things off—Al-bert talked to me for thirty minutes. He is a movie actor—played in "Wake Island" and several other well-known pictures. He spoke very well and furnished plenty of wit. He told us of a picture that was to be made here which we would be in. I doubt if we will be here then, however. They also showed several good short subjects—Pete Smith with all the highlights of 1942 football season—then a cartoon of dog life in the army. The picture was "Dr. Gillespie" with Lionel Barrymore taking the lead. It was very good. Grover and Bob went along with me.*

Grover's longtime interest grew to a lovesick state by the end of October and early November. Finally, he took the long-awaited step, as Bud reported to Thelma early in November.

> *Grover got the ring tonight [11/5/1943]. They had to send it to San Antonio to be cut down. He decided to have it sent from there to Henry [Henrietta], since it might take too long to send it to him and then to her, I think it's a very pretty little ring. I had a hard time again, wanted to buy one for you, but I didn't have $150.00 like Grover did. After buying the ring we ate supper at the Hamilton Hotel and then went to see Jack Benny in "The Meanest Man in the World." It was so good we sat through it al-most twice—we got out only a few minutes ago, stopped for a malted milk then walked straight to the post office.*

Like most of the cadets classified as bombardiers and navigators, Bud viewed gunnery school as necessary, if only to check the box that he had passed the required skill level. After all, navigators stayed busy charting the course, taking celestial shots in bad weather, and more. And bombardiers were charged with arming the bombs and making sure they hit the target. They had been told in passing of this new-fangled bomb sight that was supposed to make bombing more accurate, but it required a great deal of skill to operate. *At any rate, bombardiers and navigators have plenty of tasks in all those bombers the Army has, so how much time could be left to shoot a 50-caliber machine gun?* he wondered. He had seen a picture of the B-17G model that had guns out the side from the bombardier's perch and the chin turret mounted below that position, so maybe gunnery school wasn't just a box to check after all. *But I'm not being paid to speculate or analyze. They're paying me to pass the course, and pass I must. With only about a month left, I've come too far to screw up now.*

On November 4, he wrote, "*Did my best on the skeet range yesterday—broke 18 out of 25 birds the first time and 20 out of 25 the second. Got a new instructor that found all my faults, and bitched at me until I corrected them. I want to hit them all before this week is out.*"

A warm letter awaited him when he returned to his barracks November 18. Elated, he crawled up in his bunk to respond right away.

> *...pardon the pencil 'cause I've misplaced my pen—temporarily, I hope. I had one of the sweetest letters waiting on my bed for me this afternoon telling all about your Sunday morning activities. You sounded as though you enjoyed going to Sunday school over church. I'm glad you did. Also I'm happy that you enjoy taking little kids to church, 'cause I want you to take our boy to Sunday school real soon.*

As he was sweating out gunnery school, the saga on the home front continued. He knew well the sensitivity of both his mother and sister. He not only had great affection for his brother-in-law, but he had the utmost respect for the way he had taken on the daunting challenge of housing both his mother and handicapped sister. But as Leonard often said, "This is where we are and we'll just go on from here."

Bud added a few more words in his note to Thelma:

I plan to write Evelyn real soon and try to explain to her that I understand mother pretty well and don't have any hard feelings toward her or Leonard. I realize that it isn't the happiest sort of life living together as they do and imagine that both of them have complaints to make quite often. Mother takes things pretty seriously and so does Evelyn, but I believe mother lets things bother her. I'm sorry she had to read my letter though.

Four days later and impending graduation—or washback, whichever the case would be facing him, Bud wrote to Thelma while waiting for the weather to break.

I'm at the flying field now looking for my turn to go up and fire at the target. So far no one has gone up because of a fog which started closing in around 8:30 this morning. I was scheduled to fly at 1:30, but now it'll be 4:00 or five before I get to go—if I go up at all. Grover is not supposed to fly until tomorrow. We had hoped to be on the line the same day, but it didn't work out that way.

They finally caught up with Grover and put him on KP duty. He'll be on from noon today until about 8:30 tonight. Guess I'll get it tomorrow. I won't mind it though, 'cause you get to sleep about 4 or 5 hours during the day.

With only a few days left and a great deal to accomplish, Bud was on the range again, hoping get through the course. During a break, he wrote:

I'm waiting again to get an airplane ride. Had a mighty good one this morning in an AT-18, used to be called the Lockheed Hudson A-29 bomber. It's a fairly large plane, rides just like a train. I fired from a 200-round turret. I don't know my score yet, but I'm afraid it wasn't too good. We flew at 5,000 feet and my eyes gave me a little trouble, but not as much as they did in the pressure chamber. A lot of the boys are getting good hits, which puts the pressure on us fellows who aren't such good shots. We had to circle the field three times before we could land this morning, which put us over Mexico three times. I thought about stopping off to do a little shopping, but it was a little too far to drop.

I'm scheduled to go up on a camera mission in an hour or two, but it's been raining a little. This might knock me out of another trip today. A camera mission consists of taking a reel of film that operates from the trigger in the turret. An AT-6 dives down at your plane and you try and trash him all the way thru. Grover did it yesterday-—said it was lots of fun-—almost like being in combat.

On the fifth of December and feeling the pressure of the impending evaluation of all cadet's gunnery prowess, Bud wrote:

Once again on Saturday night I'm in my favorite spot to write my sweetheart. In the Post Office-—guess you are surprised that I'm still here. I may have another surprise if I have to stay here another two weeks. I'll try and tell you the whole story.

Well, it rained all day yesterday and today, so we didn't get to fly at all. Some of us fellows have maybe fired 600 rounds. In the end it seems that the minimum rounds to leave here is 1000 or 100 hits. So far I only have 72 out of the 600 which puts me in the same fix with about 50 or 75 other fellows who didn't get all their firing in. -—Out of a group of 38 navigators who were due to ship out today they held back 7 fellows in the same fix and told them they would have to take the last two weeks of the course over which means going back to Eagle Pass for a week. That's the only part of it I would hate.

If the weather clears tomorrow, I may get to fly and get enough hits in to leave. Right now it doesn't look as though it will clear at all. Grover, the lucky rascal, got in 800 rounds and has over 100 hits so he's okay. He got 69 of it of his last 200 rds. Which brought his average way up. We may be separated here if the weather doesn't break.

Did I tell you what happened on my last try when I thought I got so many hits? I really only got 27 hits. We all think that the fellows who marked the target got ours mixed up with someone else's. One man in the plane with me counted 30 of my tracers go thru the target which would mean 150 hits (every time a tracer goes thru, 5 more bullet go thru). I counted a lot of tracers for all the other fellows.

There is nothing we can do about it, but we still think we were gypped. I hate the thought of washing out and having to go back to Eagle Pass again. Sure hope I don't have to do it--hard on a fellow's nerves. I told Grover when I first heard about what might happen if I didn't get to fly tomorrow that I thought I'd just quit the cadets all together if I washed back. Later I changed my mind and decided I'd wait and let them be the judge.

Well, sweetheart, guess I'd better start closing now. Wish I could tell you something definite. In fact wish I knew something definite myself. This Army sure keeps us together. We may work it out, who knows?

The next day, Monday, brought some good and unexpected news as he related to Thelma:

Dearest--Well, I managed to pull through and get those wings even though I didn't fire but 600 rounds--only eleven men were washed back. Sure glad I wasn't one of them. We didn't have much of a graduation exercise, just a talk by one of our lieutenants, also a talk by a gunner who had been over in the Pacific for a year on a B-17. Then we marched by the Lt., picked up our wings, and came back to the squadron. We were told this morning

*that we would be here three or four more days, and ru-
mors of all kind started floating around. The best one was
that we would be given a 21-day delay in route, which
would mean being home for Christmas. This was hard to
believe, but of course everyone wanted to believe it. Grover and I got all excited about it and started planning
what we would do at home. This afternoon all that was
changed, and it was announced that we would ship out
tomorrow, probably to Advanced. We haven't been told
for sure, but we have a good hunch we will go to Midland, Texas for bombardier school.*

Bud would find that once again, his hunch was less than accurate. But he would soon make his home in yet one more Texas city,
the next stop on his journey toward war.

CHAPTER 10

A Seat in the Flying Fortress

Aircraft and Crew Assignment

Big Spring, Texas: Bombardier Training
December 9, 1943–April 8, 1944

BUD'S PREDICTION OF MIDLAND AS the location for advanced bombardier training proved incorrect. Big Spring, Texas, forty miles northeast of Midland, became his home for the winter of 1943 and the early spring of 1944. Grover accompanied Bud on the next phase of their training, but it took some mild shenanigans to make it happen. Bud explained the situation to Thelma in his letter before they left Laredo on December 7:

> *Dear Thelma, I'll write a little note now or when we either pass through San Antonio or stop—hope we stop. We left at noon today. Grover and I got together after a lotta trouble. At first they had us on different shipping orders. He was going to Midland. He and I went up to Personnel, and Grover put up a good speech about our wives being good friends and were coming down to be with us. Didn't know that about Grover having a wife, did you? Well it worked, and we are on our way.*

A sleepy town of four thousand in the early 1920s, Big Spring tripled in size over the next decade after the discovery of oil in the Permian Basin of west Texas. Its name came from a spring south of town that served as a major water source in the semi-arid area.

The Big Spring base hangar housed the training center operation for Bud's class of 1944–45. Its clear span was constructed with a unique wooden honeycomb roof system formed in an arc. Five buttresses on each side of the structure supported the system in a manner similar to Notre Dame Cathedral in Paris. Retractable doors on one side of the building and brick walls on the other three sides enclosed the hangar.

Inside, a rail system had been constructed on which moveable platforms on wheels with a simple chair seat served as reasonable facsimiles of bombardiers' operating positions in both a B-17 and a B-24. The zealously guarded Norden and Sperry bombsights were mounted in front of the chair on each of the twenty platforms. Maps below provided the students a target on which to sight as they determined the proper deployment procedure. This configuration served as the classroom for initial bombardier instruction. In addition, a Beechcraft AT-11 Kansan aircraft with two Pratt & Whitney radial engines served as the application laboratory for students to ply their trade in a more realistic environment.

The weather in that part of West Texas often included wide swings, and the '43-'44 period proved no exception. Bud related his first impressions to Thelma:

> . . . it's getting real cold here now. I'm thinking about putting on my long underwear again. Right now the wind is blowing pretty hard and it's raining just a little. Looks like it could turn into snow very easily. It hadn't rained in six months before we got here. Looks like we brought it from Laredo. It had not rained there in some time before we started, then it rained every other day—Two days later—there is a big blizzard carrying on now, it's the worst I've ever seen.

The Army was serious about the training regimen for airmen, as Bud related:

> This place is gonna be rough I'm thinking. We started off this morning like a house-a-fire. We've already had a lot of stuff thrown at us that ordinarily would take me weeks to learn. Since we are a week late getting started, they say it'll get even worse a time goes on. We'll have more & more night classes.

> ### THE BOMBARDIER'S OATH
>
> Mindful of the secret trust about to be placed in me by my
> Commander in Chief, the President of the United States, by
> whose direction I have been chosen for bombardier training...
> and mindful of the fact that I am to become guardian of one
> of my country's most priceless military assets, the American
> bombsight...I do here, in the presence of Almighty God,
> swear by the Bombardier's Code of Honor to keep inviolate
> the secrecy of any and all confidential information revealed
> to me, and further to uphold the honor and integrity of the
> Army Air Forces, if need be, with my life itself.

He later added, "... *we took the bombardier oath today and saw
the much-talked-of bombsight—that's about all I'll say about that.
In a few minutes we have to go have a picture taken for something
or other.*"

There was little to do in West Texas, and the weather during the
winter of '43-'44 further restricted the activities of the future bombardiers. Coupled with the intensity of study the Army required, almost all the airmen did was, study, train, write letters, watch movies, eat, and complain.

Christmas came and went. With the extreme cold and snow, New
Year's was bleak for the '44-'45 class, as Bud explained:

> *Last night was about the most miserable New Year's Eve
> I've ever spent. I was in a bad mood to start with because
> I didn't get a letter Thursday or Friday. Didn't get one
> Tuesday either, and there is no mail call today. There is
> a football game on now coming from the Sugar Bowl.*
> [Note: Georgia Tech beat Tulsa 20-17.] *This time last year
> my wife, sister-in-law, and I were listening to a game
> from the same bowl, remember?! Tennessee barely beat
> the great Glenn Dobbs and Tulsa 14-7. I also thought a
> lot about last New Year's Eve at Emma's and Dusty—re-
> member that awful fog we had to come home in?*

Over the course of his training, Bud had developed close friendships with two boys. Grover had been a friend and confidant since before they entered the service. Jay Pyles had also grown close to both Grover and Bud, as Bud wrote in a letter to Thelma: "*Got a letter from Jay Pyles, he is in pilot school. He's the best fellow I have met, except for Grover.*"

Their time in Big Spring served to add to Bud and Grover's cadre of cherished acquaintances. Lt. Bob Angevine was, as Bud put it, a "*genuinely nice, caring, and very smart guy. All the fellows like him, and he seems to like me and Grover too.*"

To let Thelma know how the other cadets felt about her "baby," Bud wrote in another letter:

> *Oh yeah. I've never told you about a boy in my barracks who has turned out to be a good friend of mine. I didn't know for quite a while that he was a preacher in civilian life. Always thought he was much nicer than the average of fellows, never gets mad enough to cuss like all the rest of us do. He's about the smartest guy in the squadron also. I think he's made the highest mark on every examine so far. Well, he seemed to take a liking to Grover and me—tries to eat with us every meal. Guess he would go to town with us but his wife lives here and I suppose he'd rather be with her. The other night he was telling us about our hearing a conversation between two boys in Grover's barracks. They were discussing Grover and the possibility of getting him a girlfriend for the weekend so he could go along with them. One of them spoke up with—"it couldn't do any good—he runs around with Perrin, and he's in love with his wife!" The preacher kinda likes us for that reason I suppose. Of course I do love my wife and I'm not at all interested in stepping out on her.*

Some lessons learned in training were expected. Others came with less warning but equal—or sometimes more—importance, as Bud explained:

> *Today the pilot had a little time so he took us up to 18,000*

feet. That's pretty high, you know. I was filling out my reports and thought all the time he was going down; therefore, had my oxygen mask off. Didn't take me long to realize I needed oxygen though and to get my mask on right away. That scared me, 'cause no oxygen will kill you "graveyard dead." It's even prettier from up there at 18,000 feet. I'll have to take you up that high with me sometime.

When evaluating his own skill level, Bud tended toward self-deprecation. But occasionally, he would deviate from his norm and reveal times when he performed well.

. . . got one shock today. A shock is the best you can get— it's the bullseye of the circle, only 15 ft. square so when you hit it from 13,000 ft. you're either pretty good or pretty lucky, which I was today. The instructor went along with all of us. Since the snow was still here, we hadn't been up for two days, [so] they figured we'd be a little rusty; however, mine didn't bother me. He stayed in the co-pilot's seat and left me all alone down in the nose. I made a few little mistakes, like almost forgetting to put on my headset, etc. The pilot could have told me to bail out, and I would have never have known it. There is a lot to remember while sitting in the nose—I guess they more or less expect us to forget something every now and then until we catch on a little better. Also had a little trouble picking up the targets at first. The snow and sun kinda blinded me, and the targets are white circles and looks just like the snow. I didn't line up a farmhouse like some of the boys have done though.

Don't know if I ever mentioned how many men have been eliminated from our class since we first started. I don't know exactly, but we started with 143 and now have somewhere in the neighborhood of 85 or 90—lost three more today or either they went before the board today. That usually means washing out. Look like we'll

have one of the smallest classes ever to graduate here.
Hope I'm one of the fellows to last that long—don't believe
I mentioned my grade on the test last week. Made 100—
my first one here—brought my average up to 89, which
isn't too bad considering that some of the tests were pret-
ty rough—we have another coming up tomorrow which
is supposed to be very tough, but I don't claim to know
too much about the subject.

The movie people must be in cahoots with the govern-
ment. Grover and I went to see one tonight—it was fair
but had the usual propaganda in it. It was "The Cross of
Lorraine." After it we decided to go eat at my favorite
place, the Hotel Settles. Maybe you can stay there when
you come." (Note: *The Cross of Lorraine* was one of the
many Hollywood World War II propaganda films showing
life in occupied Europe, with the purpose of explaining to
an American audience why US involvement in the European war was just as important as the war against the Japanese in the Pacific.)

Thelma and Bud had planned her trip to Big Spring for some
weeks, but things always seemed to crop up to thwart the plans. Finally, everything seemed to be in sync and arrangements were lining up: train tickets, reservations at the Settles Hotel, and a possible
boarding house to replace the more expensive hotel after a week or
so. Thelma was looking forward to escaping the snow and extreme
cold of Knoxville, but Bud told her she might be coming to more of
the same in Big Spring.

As she prepared for the trip, Thelma had a photo made of their
car, completely covered with snow except for a message she had
carved with her finger out of the white stuff: "THELMA LOVES
BUD." Next, she cut a heart out of card stock, ringed it with red
ribbon, and placed the photo inside. On the day after Valentine's
Day, Bud received this card, sent three days earlier. He then wrote.
"I knew you were a play actor, baby, but I didn't know you were
an artist too—can't wait to see you—All my love—your loving hus-
band and valentine.

Valentine from Thelma to Bud - February, 1944
Rosalind Perrin Davis Collection

After a long day and a half through Tennessee, Alabama, Mississippi, Arkansas, and East Texas, Thelma's train pulled into the station at Big Spring. The Settles Hotel rose fifteen stories high above the terminal and the buildings of the two blocks in between. Holding her coat across her arm and her suitcase in the other hand, she moved down the tight aisle past the washroom and on to the back of the coach. Stepping off with the help of the uniformed conductor, she paused to see which way to turn to reach the hotel. She moved to her right, turned left at the first corner, and walked the two blocks up a slight hill to the main entrance of the stunning building that was The Settles.

The Settles Hotel opened in 1930 to serve the trade brought on by the oil boom of the period. Its builders spared no expense in design and construction. A large central lobby rose three spectacular floors up from the terrazzo floor. Dark oak staircases on each side wound their way to the second floor. In the massive second-level ballroom, cut glass chandeliers adorned the ceilings and matching sconces lined the mirrored wall. (Note: the post-war years were not good for either Big Spring or The Settles, which closed in the early '80s. It stayed vacant until acquired in late 2006 by the Settles Hotel Development Corporation, restored to its original state, and reopened in the fall of 2012. On April 18, 2013, it was placed on the National Register of Historic Places.)

The reunion was wonderful for both Bud and Thelma. They knew it was likely they would be able to spend the next five or six months together before Bud had to ship out. The time would be hectic with his training taking priority, but at least they would be together. They took full advantage of the days Thelma stayed at The Settles, which included eating in the fine dining room and sleeping in a soft bed, neither of which had been a part of Bud's experience for some time. When they were able to borrow a car and the warmth of an early West Texas spring replaced the wrath of winter, they visited some of the historic sites in the area, even the Big Spring itself. But mostly they just enjoyed the luxury of being together.

Graduation Day finally came, and both Bud and Grover received their bombardier wings. Bud received orders to report to Lincoln, Nebraska not later than April 21, 1944. Grover was to report to Westover Field, Massachusetts not later than the April 28. Both had been assigned to B-24 Liberators. Neither was happy.

Knoxville, Tennessee – April 8–20, 1944

After two days on the train, Bud and Thelma arrived home to a welcoming family. Along the way, they decided to drive their '39 Ford to Nebraska. The week and a half at home was again a blur but an eventful and enjoyable one. Good food, family photographs, church at Broadway, conversations with Leonard, wrestling with J. Ross, a trip to Gatlinburg together, and then they were off to their new home. They left too early to see the article and photos in the newspaper about six Knoxvillians, including Bud, Grover, Arwyn Arnhart, T. G. Brown, Herman H. Coulter, and Robert F. Brooks, who had received bombardier wings. The trip west was not without difficulty, including a couple of flat tires and many long hours at slow speeds. But they arrived at last.

BELSKIS CREW – October 25,1944
Front Row: Walter R. Newman – *Top Turret Gunner,* Durward V. Suggs – *Waist Gunner,* Robert P. Rogers – *Tail Gunner,* Elvis McCoy – *Radioman-Gunner,* Lynn J. Laurel, Jr. – *Ball Turret Gunner, Back Row:* Leo P. Belskis – *Pilot,* Glenn C. Vaughn – *Co-Pilot,* James V. Collett – *Navigator,* Ross W. Perrin, Jr. – *Bombardier*
Perrin, Greene Family Collection

Thursday, April 20, 1944

The Knoxville Journal

Six Knoxvillians Become Bombardier-Navigators

R. F. Brooks   Arwyn Amhart   T.G. Brown, III   G. C. Blevins, Jr.   H. H. Coulter   R.W. Perrin, Jr.

Six Knoxvillians were graduated recently from the West Texas Bombardier Quadrangle after 18 weeks of training in a class of bombardier-navigators. They were:

Flight Officer Arwyn Arnhart, son of Mr. and Mrs.Arwyn W. Amhart, 1314 Lutrell Street. Amhart was a student at the University of Tennessee when he enlisted. He is a member of Sigma Nu fraternity.

Second Lt. Grover C. Blevins, Jr., son of Mr. and Mrs. Grover C. Blevins 210 Colonial Avenue.

Second Lt. Ross W. Perrin, Jr., son of Maude F. Perrin, 9 Cherry Street.

Second Lt. Robert F. Brooks, son of Mrs. M.D. Brooks, 1018 Tulip Street. Brooks attended the University of Tennessee.

Second Lt. Theodore C. Brown, son of Roy H. Brown, 2605 Kingston Pike. Brown attended the University of Tennessee and the University of North Carolina.

Second Lt. Herman H. Coulter, son of Mr. and Mrs. William H. Coulter, Route 3. Coulter also attended the University of Tennessee.

Article in *Knoxville Journal* about Bombardier Graduation from Big Spring, Texas-April 20,1944
Greene Family Collection

Lincoln, Nebraska – April 21–May 4, 1944

Bud was in a funk all the way to Nebraska over not getting a B-17 assignment. The group that left Lincoln earlier had been assigned to a B-24. But in true Army fashion, on April 30, Bud was placed in a B-17 crew. He was elated.

The crew was comprised of the following officers: pilot Leo Belskis from Illinois, co-pilot Glenn Vaughn from Virginia, and navigator James Collett from Maryland, with Bud as bombardier. The enlisted men and gunners included Elvis McCoy, radio operator and waist gunner; Durward Suggs, waist gunner; Robert Rogers, top turrett gunner; Lynn Laurett, ball turrett gunner; and Walter Newman, tail gunner. The crew had a short time to get acquainted but knew that in their next training base, Barksdale Field in Alexandria, Louisiana, they would have plenty of time to do just that.

On Thursday, May 4, Bud and Thelma hopped in their Ford coupe and set sail for Bayou country. The nine-hundred-mile trek was about the same distance they had driven from Knoxville to Lincoln just two short weeks earlier. The trip was similar in other ways: flat tires, slow speeds on crowded roads through Arkansas, bad coffee, and egg salad sandwiches. But they finally made it to Cajun country a day ahead of schedule, just in time for a much-needed rest.

Alexandria, Louisiana – May 6–July 10, 1944

Each successive training site upped the ante for the cadet airmen. Advanced crew training was the last and most critical stop before deployment overseas. Through the training regimen, Bud had survived numerous physical and intellectual concerns including his lack of a college education, his age, and even his eyesight, which had kept him from continuing on the pilot track. But for the last year and a half, he had proven equal to the challenge in each area. *And now I'm on a B-17 Flying Fortress crew—Wow!* he thought.

A week into crew training, the Belskis group had its first time up in the B-17. "What a twenty-eighth birthday gift!" Bud announced to Collett, whose navigator's seat was next to Bud's bombardier perch in the nose of the aircraft.

"Congrats, Grandpa," Jim, six years Bud's junior, responded with a grin.

"Hey guys, it's Perrin's birthday. Maybe we should put a rocking chair behind the Norden," Jim announced to Leo and Glenn as they swung through the front hatch and climbed toward the flight deck.

The crew was just getting acquainted, so Bud was pleased that the good-natured ribbing was already a part of their interaction. *Maybe it'll help us be more comfortable with each other and work better together—at least I hope so.*

Over the next two months, the routine was the same. First came practice bombing runs over designated targets. Longer-range trips designed to test the navigator's acumen at precision routing of the aircraft in a wide range of weather conditions also appeared frequently on the docket. Also important was large-group flying, designed to simulate the close formations the Air Corps increasingly employed to prevent enemy fighters from penetrating and wreaking havoc. Experiences in early 1943 had taught the 8th and 9th AF this important lesson.

Thelma's presence was a calming influence, Bud found. It also cut down on his letter-writing, a welcome change. "I feel like I'm continually repeating myself," he had lamented to Grover some months earlier. But now, some of those letters went to Grover and Henrietta. The two had written Bud and Thelma shortly after they arrived in Alexandria to say Grover was now taking Advanced Crew Training in Charleston, South Carolina. "Oh yes, we are getting married on May 18."

"That's today!" Bud shouted to Thelma as he read Grover's letter. "That rascal, he should've told me earlier."

A few days later, Evelyn wrote that it looked like Leonard might be drafted after all. It seemed the need for recruits was great and that others could be hired to work on the railroad, some of whom might have some medical reason for not entering the service. Leonard said, "I'm ready to trade places with Bud if they need me."

Bud sat down on the side of the bed, holding the letter in his lap. With a frown, he told Thelma, "I sure hope it doesn't come to that."

"I think we better let the family know about the new addition we're expecting, what do you think?" she responded.

On June 3, Thelma wrote to Bud's mother:

Dear "Granny"—Please tell Evelyn not to sell any more of J. Ross' baby things—and please tell her it is time to get that dress back that she's had lent out so long. Keep this "inside the family." There'll be plenty of time between now and January 1 to tell others. Bud's grinning—can't think what about tho, could you?—Love, Thelma

Thelma told her sister Edith in a more obtuse way. She sent her a catalog of maternity dresses and asked, "Which one do you think will look best on me?"

The newspapers on June 7 were filled with news of the previous day's invasion of France. Bud was able to get more information on D-Day from *Stars and Stripes,* available in the barracks. In a letter from Thelma to Evelyn on June 13 she wrote, *"What do you think about the invasion? The news sounded pretty encouraging. I'm glad all that is getting a good start before 'we' get too close to it."*

Two days after D-Day, Bud tore open a letter with the return address of Jay Pyles in Louisiana. "We got a letter from Jay and Dorothy!" he told Thelma. After weeks of no communication, Thelma had sent them a card asking the couple to write and let them know how they were doing.

"What did they say?" Thelma asked as Bud unfolded the letter.

"Hang on," Bud responded and began to read aloud:

Dear Bud and Thelma—Look where I am—just 100 miles from you. I'm a rat for not writing before this—no excuse, Sir. We got Thelma's card and immediately got to wondering when we could get together. Dorothy and I are going to get a weekend off and we'll come down there. Suit you? I'm going to try to get next weekend, June 17 and 18, off and we'll loop down there and see you.

My career since graduation has been in spending around 150 hours in a—guess what? Used to swear that I'd never pilot one of those things—that I'd fly any airplane but a B-26? Well, true to the Army custom, I was assigned to B-26's—the last thing I wanted. I was sent

Lt. James E. Collett-532nd Navigator,
in front of Barracks-Fall, 1944
Perrin, Greene Family Collection

Jim Collett, Durward Suggs, Leo Belskis and Elvis
McCoy-Fall, 1944
Rosalind Perrin Davis Collection

Alyce and Co-Pilot Lt. Glenn Vaughn-circa 1943
Vaughn Family Collection

Pilot Lt. Leo Belskis-Fall, 1944
Rosalind Perrin Davis Collection

Vernon and Norma Gatewood - April 4, 1944
Gatewood Family Collection

Julius W. "Jay" Pyles and wife Dorothy - Summer, 1944
Rosalind Perrin Davis Cllection

to Del Rio, Texas for 10 weeks. Right on the border. So Dorothy and I have been Texans for 10 weeks—now we're Louisianans.

I'm in the Replacement Depot here and it looks like a long time, too. We expect to get a furlough around the 24th of the month, about 15 days plus travel time. That sure won't be hard to take.

Bud, write me and let me know what you think of our coming down and getting together with you two over next weekend, will you? Give Thelma a big kiss for me and tell Thelma to give you one from Dorothy. Sincerely, Jay Pyles

"That's fantastic," Thelma said, her smile confirming the excitement in her voice. Bud slapped the letter across his left palm, grabbed Thelma and swung her around, and then put her down carefully as he remembered her condition. "Guess I better be more careful with you now that you are about to be Poppy's little Mommy."

"I'm not sick, just pregnant," Thelma said, adding, "Well, I guess a little sick," as she remembered the recent mornings spent hanging over the commode.

Next, a letter from Henrietta updated them on Grover's training in Charleston. *"Marriage is great—had dinner with the Gatewoods. Vernon and Norma are great folks as you know—wish we were all together."*

Bud responded to Grover, telling of him and the crew flying in a fifty-seven-ship formation on a long practice mission which took them over Montgomery and Atlanta. *"Pretty exciting—and nerve-racking, thinking of doing this in formations ten times that size in combat."* He also told about Jay and Dorothy Pyles coming down and how sorry he was to hear of their KHS schoolmate Milton Sutton's death in combat.

By this time, the crew members were getting to know each other quite well, and the chemistry was good. They were quite diverse with a down-to-earth stability. *"They're all really good fellows,"* Bud said in another letter home.

In the months ahead, the crew would spend even more hours

together getting to know not only the facts but also more of each other's idiosyncrasies. Consistent with the adage, "Boys will be boys," they took every opportunity to rag on their crewmates as they perceived weaknesses or embarrassing facts. This not only broke the tension of missions but also help spice up the monotony of the downtime between them.

2nd Lt. **Leo Belskis,** a twenty-five-year-old, five-foot-nine-inch Chicagoan of Lithuanian descent, was the much-respected pilot of the crew that bore his name. He always wore his crusher hat at a jaunty angle, befitting his immense confidence in his flying prowess, also held by his newly formed crew.

Leo's parents, Louis and Katherine, operated Marquette Gardens, a bar on 71st Street in the Windy City. In post-Depression Chicago, the financial pressures of two first-generation immigrants raising Leo; his three sisters, Estelle (Stella), Adele (Addie), and Katherine; and their brother, Charles, who now flew B-24s in the Pacific, were extreme. Often, the Belskis children were left to fend for themselves.

As a result, the siblings were close. The girls were especially captivated by big brother Leo's carefree nature and penchant for living on the edge. In his late teens, a car dealer hired him to deliver a vehicle to its new owner. But Leo didn't find the direct route to the buyer's residence in nearby Wisconsin either exciting or dramatic. Instead of opting for the mundane linear drive, he chose to take Katherine and her girlfriend Edith on a trek that took them through Colorado, which by his calculations, was only "slightly" out of the way.

Leo also had an eye for the ladies, and they for him. His magnetic charm and comedic persona constantly drew them his way. England would be new territory for this confident Midwesterner, and he would waste no time making sure the British beauties got to know him. He later wrote his sister Katherine of one special British girlfriend to whom he was becoming quite close.

Flying out of Scott Field in Madison, Wisconsin, Leo loved commanding the left seat and logged a great deal of air time prior to enlisting in the Air Corps early in 1941. When in the cockpit, he took the job of B-17 pilot seriously, becoming a man of intense focus and attention to detail. During their training time, it didn't take long for the crew to feel they were in extremely competent hands for the upcoming missions into enemy territory.

Second Lt. **Glenn C. Vaughn** was highly social and outgoing. But at twenty-two, the square-jawed, six-two athlete from near Danville, Virginia, may have felt too young for the old men of the crew, Belskis and Perrin. He was the fourth child of eight born to John, a salesman, and his homemaker wife, Agnes. Their home in Stokesland, Virginia, was always filled with music, and their living room piano a frequent gathering place for family songfests. In fact, the ten members of the "Vaughn Orchestra and Choir" often serenaded their neighbors with concerts of all styles.

The home place lay just outside the Danville city limits and immediately across the street from the Danville Country Club where the four boys—Curtis, John, Glenn, and Frank—spent much of their free time playing golf. Golf was Glenn's passion, and he was by far the best of the four brothers at the sport. They all caddied for the locals and the youngest brother, Frank, caddied for his older brother and hero, Glenn. The sisters—Clarice, Edith, Peggy, and Helen—didn't share their brothers' love of "pasture pool" as their father called it, revealing his disdain for what he considered a waste of time.

Glenn's prowess on the golf course permitted him to relieve some of the older club members of significant amounts of money when they summoned the courage to challenge this young upstart. He had a great mastery of most golf shots combined with, according to some, excessive confidence. This made him tough to beat. Since on most occasions he was playing with little or no money in his pocket, he felt more pressure than his more well-heeled opponents. This experience doubtless added to the coolness he exhibited when he held the stick of the B-17 in his capable hand.

Soon after signing on with the Air Corps, Glenn married a beautiful local girl, Alyce Turner, a devout Presbyterian whose family lived closer to town than the Vaughns. Now, a year later, their first child was two months from birth.

Like many of the Belskis crew, navigator and 2nd Lt. **James V. Collett** was slightly built at five foot nine and 135 pounds soaking wet. This twenty-two-year-old eccentric was born in West Virginia but lived in Maryland just outside of D.C. His eclectic approach to life kept all who knew him off guard and in stitches. His next words were always a mystery, and after he had spoken, the mystery often remained. He almost always wore a long coat that a 533rd pilot said looked like a horse blanket, furling and unfurling it as he walked as if it were the curtain for a stage production.

Jim was the oldest of four children born to parents Anna and Clarence, a World War I veteran. He had two younger sisters, Peggy Ruth, twenty, and Patricia, sixteen, and a much younger brother. Raymond, only six years old in mid-1944.

Jim, unlike all of the crew except Vaughn, had one year of college prior to enlisting in February of 1943. He had also worked as a skilled tradesman in the aircraft industry, which he claimed should have given him rank over the rest of the crew. No one, however, agreed with his viewpoint

Tech. Sgt. **Elvis A. McCoy**, the waist gunner and radio operator, was a dyed-in-the-wool country boy from Miami, Oklahoma. At the young age of twenty-one, he got some gentle needling from some who said that the real Miami was in Florida where it belonged and that Oklahoma hicks must be backwoods bumpkins. McCoy took the ribbing in stride and could, on most occasions, give as good as he got. His fellow southerners, Suggs, Rogers, and Perrin, often lent moral support—when they weren't among those doing the needling.

McCoy worked in the machine shop at Eagle-Picher Mining and Smelting prior to enlisting in April of 1942, only two years after his graduation from Miami High School. Like many mothers across the country, his mother, Lulu, was vehemently opposed to his enlistment.

Staff Sgt. **Durward V. Suggs**, known as "Woody" by most of the crew, was the other waist gunner. Texan Suggs, born in Dallas, was a well-liked, gregarious man of twenty-five years who wore a perpetual toothy grin, much to the delight of the British ladies. He had enlisted in May of 1941 at age twenty-two. He and McCoy developed an instant rapport, not only because as fellow waist gunners they often bounced off each other in the waist of the B-17, but also because they seemed to have so much in common.

Top gunner Tech Sgt. **Walter R. Newman** was also trim, standing five feet nine inches and weighing in at a lean 135 pounds. Affectionately known as "Hollywood," this straightforward twenty-five-year-old seemed a far cry from the moniker given by his crewmates. He was a student of his craft, determined to be the best gunner he could possibly be.

Staff Sgt. **Robert P. Rogers** was a man of few words. Being alone as tail gunner on the B-17 was fine with him; it gave him plenty of time to think. As he became more comfortable, his shyness ebbed away, and a slow-talking boy with a quick wit and a sharp tongue emerged. He was a young man with insight born of his agricultural upbringing in Palestine, Texas. His father, a chicken farmer, and mother, who had passed away a year or so earlier, had three sons, of whom Robert was the youngest. The eldest, Charles, served in the Army.

As the cramped conditions of his position as ball-turret gunner required, Staff Sgt. **Lynn Joseph Lauret, Jr.**, was the shortest of the crew and weighed "a buck and a quarter" in airman's terms. Lynn was the only son of Lynn, Sr., and Mary Alicia. At twenty-four years of age, this native of Alexandria, Louisiana also had three younger sisters: Dorothy, nineteen; Bettye Jane, seventeen; and Mary Alicia, fifteen.

In 1860, Jean Pierre Lauret, Lynn's grandfather, came to the States from France with his brother to escape military service. The two were separated upon landing and never saw each other again. One of Jean's twelve children was Lynn's father, Lynn, Sr.

Lynn would, at the drop of a hat, wax eloquent on his ancestral background. And in case no one else had the proverbial hat, he carried his own. He was quick to relate that his family descended from the owners of the wine estate Chateau des Lauret in Bordeaux, France. The associated vineyard of Puisseguin et Montagne, later to be owned by the Rothschild wine dynasty, provided three varieties of grapes for Rothschild wines: Merlot, Cabernet Franc, and Cabernet Sauvignon. This much-related story could only result in an appropriate nickname, "Baron Bayou." But no one knew that Lynn lived in fear that his mother's nickname for him, "Bootsie," would find its way into the hands of his crew, because the results of this revelation would be unmerciful.

When not in his office, submerged in the atmosphere a few feet below the belly of the B-17, Lynn was all fun. Upon entering his workplace he became laser-focused, with a warrior's intensity. All too soon, a warrior he would need to be.

A number of large-ship formations followed by intensive class-room work began the indoctrination of the crew to the vagaries of the European Theater that they had been informed would be their destination. *Finally, the puzzle parts have come together,* Bud thought.

The missing piece, their base location in England, would come soon enough.

CHAPTER 11

Jolly Ole England

Crossing the Pond and ETO Indoctrination

Various Stops en route to Great Britain:
August 14–31, 1944

AFTER EIGHTEEN MONTHS OF PHYSICAL, mental, educational, and tactical training in eight bases and four states connected by countless hours in jam-packed, smoke-filled trains and two car trips of almost a thousand miles each, Bud was anxious to get into the European battle. The entire Belskis crew felt ready. But the three years of the war made Air Force brass realize some logistical loose ends should be tied up before crews were ready for the big changes they would face in Europe.

First, the crews were given a week's leave to take care of personal matters and, if possible, have some family time before crossing the pond. Thelma had spent more than four months with Bud through some of the toughest part of training: Bombardier School at Big Spring, crew assignments and indoctrination in Lincoln, and battle simulations and bombing in Alexandria. Like Bud, she was looking forward to going home to Knoxville for a few days.

Both Bud and Thelma realized this extra leave would also mark the final time they would be together until his tour in Europe was concluded or the war ended. This realization made the seven-hundred-mile drive home bittersweet. Coupled with the intense heat and rough roads through the deep South along with the compromised comfort brought on by Thelma's pregnancy, the two-day trip was less than comfortable. On Tuesday afternoon, July 11, they rolled into Knoxville, where they were greeted at 1926 Chicago Avenue by some ecstatic Perrins, Greenes, and McGhees.

Knoxville, Tennessee – July 11–16, 1944

The next morning, the sudden clanging of the phone summoned Bud and Thelma from a deep sleep. After long months away from home, Bud struggled to remember the phone's location in the hallway just outside the bedroom. *Why don't they give up—and hang up?* his confused mind wondered. Stumbling into the hall, he answered on the tenth ring.

"Hello!" he barked.

"When are you coming?" came the insistent words on the other end of the line. "Momma's cooking bacon for you."

"OK," Bud's tone changed as he recognized the voice of his almost-four-year-old nephew. "We'll be there soon. Bye-bye."

"Hurry," came his namesake's orders.

"Looks like we have a full day that's starting early," Bud whispered to his still half-asleep wife. "Rise and shine."

They showered, dressed, and an hour later, completed the two-mile drive to his sister's home. Parking in the alleyway behind the house at #9 Cherry Street, they spied their self-appointed lookout sitting on the back steps.

"He's here!" J. Ross screamed as he stood and announced his uncle's long-awaited appearance. Running down the path, he jumped into Bud's outstretched arms and said, "I'm going to keep you here and never let you go away."

Evelyn met her brother at the top of the back steps. Bud said in low tones, "The little bugger is relentless."

"You don't know the half of it," she whispered back. "He was up at 6:30 this morning, driving me nuts to call you. We are sure thrilled to see you. You look great!"

"I haven't smelled bacon cooking in a long time," Bud announced with an ear-to-ear grin.

Family members had saved their ration stamps for weeks in anticipation of this homecoming. Meat, sugar, and flour as well as leather and rubber were tough to get during wartime. Ration stamps, doled out by the government, controlled the amount of these items citizens could buy—if they were available at all. Butter was also in short supply, often replaced by oleo, a margarine dyed yellow with a concentrated food coloring. On this special morning, Bud's sister Margie had ruptured the pellet containing the color concentrate for the oleo and stirred it in. Proud of her efforts, she took delight in the family's praise.

After the feast of bacon, eggs (not powdered this time), biscuits, and gravy, Bud pushed back from the table, extended his legs, and rubbed his tummy to confirm its full status. "Tell me about your neighbors," Bud asked as his nephew pushed his small body under the table, up his outstretched legs, and into his lap. Bud knew his sister and brother-in-law would waste no time making friends.

"I have a friend, Ol' Shooter Gay," J. Ross responded before his parents could say a word.

"OK, OK, I'll tell him," the little boy's father responded to what he recognized as a plea for help. "The Valentine family lives across Cherry Street. Their six-year old son, Gay, and J. Ross stare at each other across the street. I guess he calls him 'Shooter' because he has a holster and cap pistol."

"They're a nice family. And they also have two girls, Ann and Pat. Mr. Valentine is a prominent attorney, and Grace is very friendly," Evelyn added.

"How 'bout your next-door neighbors?" Bud asked.

"The LaRues on one side are kinda strange. He's quiet. Since Mother is diabetic, Mrs. LaRue is always trying to con her out of her sugar ration stamps," Evelyn said with a frown. "And she's big as a barn. Sugar's the last thing she needs."

"But the Davis family on the other side of us are great folks," Bud's sister continued. "Their oldest, Gene, is an Air Corp C-47 co-pilot. He graduated from Knox Hi in '41. I think they said he 'flies the Hump,' whatever that means," Evelyn said. "He was here on his way overseas, but we didn't meet him."

"He has a *tough* job, flying a heavy load in rough weather between Burma and China. I read about those missions in *Stars and Stripes* a few weeks ago," Bud responded in a voice that emphasized the difficulty of the task. "I sure don't envy him that duty."

"They have two girls, Lib, who graduated from Knox Hi last year, and Ann, a sophomore. J. Ross says he wants to marry her."

"Sounds like you really like it here."

"It's really convenient. The bus stops at the corner, and Leonard only has to walk three blocks to catch the Southern Railroad bus. We're three blocks from our new church, Fifth Avenue Baptist, and one block from Wray's Grocery Store. We're so happy here."

"Let's take some pictures," Thelma said. "I've got about seven shots left on this roll of film. I'd like to get them developed on Monday."

The family moved to the front yard, posed as Thelma instructed, and completed their task. "Make sure to roll the film back up so you won't expose it till you get the pictures developed." Bud said.

Thelma put her hands on her hips, dropped her chin to her chest, and shot Bud an evil look as she said, "I know what I'm doing, Lieutenant Perrin."

"Aye, aye, sir—I mean ma'am. I'm duly reprimanded," quipped her unrepentant husband. Then, turning to his sister, "We're going downtown to the Power Board. Can we take my Palsy Walsy with me? We'll bring him back after supper, if that's OK."

"Not just OK, that's great," Evelyn said, clearly thankful for the respite.

"We'll shine shoes and shave?" J. Ross asked.

"We'll see," Leonard said, trying to get Bud off the hook.

"Yes, sir," Bud replied. "I need help with my new shoes."

Bud and Thelma's homecoming was no secret. Thelma's friends from work, Mrs. Perrin's co-workers, and Knox Hi friends all awaited visits. And the Knoxville Electric Power Company was abuzz in anticipation. When one of the many employees they had lost to wartime service was coming through, word of the visit sped through the office.

Bud drove past Broadway Baptist and Knoxville High on the way to town, commenting as he passed each one. "You're a sentimental ole' bird," Thelma teased.

"Yep."

Bud turned right on Clinch, dropping into first gear to make sure he got up "Billy Goat Hill," as he called the steep incline. After finding a rare parking place at the hill's summit, they walked past the Tennessee Theater and one block south to Bud's company. Hugs and smiles greeted them at the front counter. As word of their

Evelyn Greene; Bud and his Mother Maude
at #9 Cherry St., Knoxville-July 16, 1944
Perrin, Greene Family Collection

J. Ross, Uncle Bud and Thelma Perrin
July, 1944
Perrin, Greene Family Collection

Above: Leonard, Evelyn and J. Ross Greene; Bud Perrin

Left: Leonard, J. Ross and Evelyn Greene; Thelma and
Bud Perrin-Big Ridge State Park-July, 1944
Perrin, Greene Family Collection

presence spread, the lobby filled with well-wishers. Bud's boss, Jimmy Hines, along with Emma Holder and Charlie Tombras, led the crowd. Someone pointed out the article from an April *Journal*, prominently displayed on a coffee table in the lobby, which told of Bud getting his bombardier's wings. Someone else gave him copies of each edition of the *Kilo-Water Account*, the company's monthly newsletter, from 1943 and 1944, "So you can catch up on what you've missed."

Bud soon took advantage of his ready-made audience. "We have an announcement to make," he said with a broad smile, pulling Thelma close. She gripped his arm as she looked into his eyes with pride and love. "My beautiful wife is expecting our first child sometime around the last of December, or maybe after the New Year. Since I'll probably be dropping some big exploding rocks on Germany before long, I expect you to watch out for her and our child."

Applause and cheers filled the room as the girls engulfed Thelma with hugs and congratulations. Bud received plenty of handshakes and slaps on the back along with more than a few jibes. "I didn't know you had it in you," someone said. Even Bud laughed at that one.

After supper at the S & W, they returned to Evelyn's with an exhausted three-year-old. Too tired to shine shoes, he was put to bed without his customary resistance. But Bud's mother and sister were wide awake and anxious to hear about his experiences in training and what he expected when he got to Europe. *They're like everyone else back home,* Bud thought. *They want to believe the war's going well. And they want to believe I'll only be overseas a short while— or maybe not have to go at all, God willing.*

They knew that D-Day had been quite a success for the Allies. Bud related what he had heard through the grapevine and military periodicals. "Our troops moved inland from Normandy beaches and recaptured many of the French towns around the coast. Fighting is still fierce in French towns nearer to Paris, but our Allied troops are on the march. Likewise, the Air Corps is pummeling the Reich." But then he added what no one wanted to hear. "We still haven't finished the job in Europe. Hitler's V-1 rockets keep terrifying London."

For the rest of the evening, Bud held not only their hearts, but their attention.

Mosquitoes vied for their attention as the family attempted to settle into backyard lawn chairs and deal with the sweltering mid-July temperatures. As the setting sun gave way to a full moon, the ever-present crickets hummed and lightning bugs swarmed in an apparent attempt to compete with the evening's flickering stars.

The questions started slowly but picked up intensity as the various fears and concerns, especially from Bud's mother and sister, surfaced. Thelma had lived through much of the training intensity, so she was more confident of her husband's ability to withstand what he would face. But she was not without fear of what combat might mean. Bud was about to encounter live ammo from people who hated the US and wanted to kill all Allied servicemen. That fact was not lost on anyone.

"Are you afraid?" "Have you ever been close to getting killed in training?" "What was the toughest part?" "Will you and Grover be together overseas?" "What's it like flying in a B-17?" "How long will you be gone?" "Do you have a good crew?" These questions and more made the conversational fire almost as challenging as what Bud expected to face overseas.

I want to answer honestly, he thought. *But it'll serve no purpose to tell them of my fears, especially those I know I'll have to face soon. I know from talking to the guys who've already been through it that the war in Europe's no walk in the park,* he told himself. *But I've got to downplay how I feel. I can handle the emotions better than they can. And I'll have plenty of time to reveal the details— most of them, anyway—in the months ahead.*

He did, however, want them to know of his confidence in his crew. "Our pilot, Leo Belskis, is a great handler of the airplane. So is co-pilot Glenn Vaughn. Our navigator, Jim Collett, is a funny guy, but committed to the job. The officers work well together and get along kinda like brothers. And the gunners in the back of the ship make us a formidable team." He paused before adding some words about the airplane itself. "And the B-17 is a beast. It truly is a Flying

Fortress, a real secure, powerful flying machine. We all feel safe in it." *As safe as you can be while being shot at from every direction,* he thought rather than said aloud.

Despite Bud's efforts, the mood of the evening had turned somber. Attempting to end the evening on a positive note, he proposed a day at the beach. "How 'bout a picnic at Big Ridge before I go back. Whaddya say?" he asked with a sharp handclap. "We can plan it for the day when Leonard's not working and could go with us—can't do it without him."

"I'll probably have a trip to Ashville, but I'm sure I'll be home on Friday," Leonard offered, accepting Bud's invitation.

"Friday it is," Bud responded as he stood up and took Thelma's hand.

"I'll have to work on Friday, but I'm not much of a swimmer anyway," Bud's mother added. "I'll be the cook."

The weather broke beautiful on Friday after a day of rain. "Somebody must have paid the preacher," Leonard said.

The cloudless day at Big Ridge was a tremendous success. The five of them—Leonard, Evelyn, J. Ross, Thelma, and Bud—canoed, swam, lay in the sun, and stuffed themselves with the delicious food prepared primarily by Mrs. Perrin. Thelma brought her Kodak camera, so the day was well-chronicled, her pregnancy barely visible in the photos.

As they sat by the fire, the sun hid behind the trees and the mosquitoes emerged. Conversation soon turned to the Labor Day picnic almost three years before. The questions raised on that day had been answered in much the way their subsequent investigation revealed.

In the summer of '44, isolationists were nowhere to be found. On US involvement in the war, the country had gone from ambivalent at best to fully committed and highly productive. Young men were ready to serve despite the risks. Some even lied about their age in their eagerness to enter the fray.

Bud's family knew only one day remained before he would leave again. In an eerily familiar scene, the picnickers cleaned up the area, strolled somberly to their cars, and drove off into the night.

The next afternoon, Thelma called Evelyn and asked her to bring Margie and Mrs. Perrin to their home on Chicago. "The weather's so pretty, and I have a full roll of twelve. We want to take some pictures of everyone with Bud."

An excited J. Ross had been chomping at the bit to "Go see my Bud," so he didn't have to be coaxed into the car.

Careful not to waste the film, the family worked hard to capture meaningful photos. Bud wore his uniform, so the pictures took on a regal look.

As Thelma watched for one more good shot, Bud bent down, and J. Ross saluted him. Thelma looked up and saw the moment framed before her. "Hold that salute!" she commanded, then snapped the photo and screamed with glee.

Alexandria, Louisiana – July 17–26, 1944

The multi-stop trek back to Alexandria gave Bud a chance to reflect on the previous Wednesday night's conversation with his family. The questions they asked and the emotions revealed showed him their deep concern for his safety. He had shared many details of the training activities, but wondered if censors would prevent such openness when he reached the war theater. *I'll learn soon enough,* he thought.

On July 18, he wrote Thelma: "I'm back at the field now—in the nice cool Officers' Club— passed by our old home on the way out here—and

J. Ross saluting Uncle Bud Perrin
at 1926 Chicago Ave. Knoxville - July 16, 1944
Perrin, Greene Family Collection

it didn't look very good to me 'cause you weren't there waiting for me. The trip as a whole wasn't too bad, although it had its bad moments—no air conditioning to Chattanooga—it was fixed for the trip to New Orleans—rode a 'cattle car' from N.O. to Alexandria—windows open and I got plenty dirty. I finally had a hot shower and feel much better."

The night Bud left, Thelma, reflecting her pain as Bud left for an unknown length of time, wrote:

> Today hasn't been too bad—we met Leonard after you left, and I asked him to "chauffeur" us. I enjoyed the ride and it gave me a chance to compose and steady myself—anyway, we passed by the park and J. Ross said so wistfully, "Daddy, last summer we came out here and rode the airplane"—it gave us all a good laugh. So Leonard promised they would come back this summer, too. I didn't stop at your family's—decided I had play-acted about all I could in one day, so I came home where I could cry in comfort!—not too much, just enough to let me know that my Poppy means more to me than anything in the world. Couldn't keep from wishing I was going back with you! Yep, even to hot Alexandria!

Over the next three days, before she had received any letters from Bud about his return trip, Thelma wrote:

> I took the snapshots to McLean's, and the proofs to Mr. Hines [Bud's boss at the Power Board]—they'll be ready in about two weeks—have a lot to tell you today—oh, nothing important—but if you were nearby I'd pin your ears back and coo into them for a couple of hours—at least. Mr. Kennedy offered his congratulations about our family to be—I then took your mother to lunch—I let her "take me"—she wanted to do it—she looked good and wasn't worrying about you at all, "big boy!"—she said that she has more money now than she ever had and didn't want anyone to worry about her. I know this makes you happy—one less thing to worry about while you are away.

*She was even bragging on Leonard because he kept Eve-
lyn from doing "lots of foolish things"—I've heard him say
many times, "Don't let your heart rule your head." He's a
smart man and a stable influence for all of us. We're in
good hands with him around.—so you can see, all is well
on the Perrin/Greene home front—your Mother called tonight, but before we could talk, J. Ross had to tell me he
had a card from you. He was so tickled.*

Bud hardly had time to get settled in Alexandria before he received orders to report to Kearney, Nebraska, the launching point
for his crew's departure for the war theater. That meant a return trip
to Knoxville, from which he would fly to Kearney. *"It only makes
Army sense,"* he wrote Thelma when she questioned why they had
sent him back to Alexandria in the first place. The return trip provided a couple of extra days at home. *Not a bad deal, and worth the
long train ride back,* he thought.

Bud's departure day, Wednesday, July 26, finally arrived. They
all knew this was the last time they would see him for months and
maybe even more than a year. This made the drive to McGhee Ty-
son Airport, a dozen miles south of Knoxville, bittersweet. J. Ross's
chatter about seeing the airplane kept the atmosphere lively. "A little of his jabbering goes a long way," his quieter father often said.

"I want to fly Unca Bud's plane," J. Ross insisted as he grabbed
his mother's hand, pulling her toward the DC-3 Delta twin-engine
plane parked inside the small fence just north of the terminal. Hearing the determined plea, the pilot motioned for Bud to bring him on
board for a tour. J. Ross ran to the steps rolled next to the plane
and pleaded, "Let's go." After a tour of the cockpit, Bud thanked the
pilot.

"Where are you off to, Lieutenant?" the pilot inquired.

"Kearney, Nebraska, then to England. Then a number of trips to
Berlin and its outskirts," Bud said with a nervous smile.

"Be safe, young man."

Stretching out his hand to grasp the pilot's in a long moment,
Bud responded, "Yes sir, I'll sure try my best."

The next thirty minutes passed all too quickly. First came a tearful and sisterly hug from Evelyn, then a long "Please come back soon" embrace from Thelma. Bud picked up his B-4 garment bag, shook Leonard's hand, saluted J. Ross, turned sharply toward the awaiting aircraft and took the steps two at a time as he entered the already-idling DC-3. Minutes later, the plane taxied to the end of the runway, revved its engines, traveled halfway down the newly constructed five-thousand-foot runway and parted the clouds into the wild blue yonder.

Kearney, Nebraska – July 28–August 1, 1944

Upon his arrival in Kearney, Bud reported to Thelma on his trip to the middle of the US:

I had a very good trip, got in Cincinnati about an hour after I left you. Caught a plane to Chicago 15 minutes later. We got there at 11:15 and I had to wait 3 hours for a plane to Omaha. I didn't get out of the airport—was afraid I'd get lost in such a big town. We were an hour and a half late getting to Omaha. I got to the station just in time to see my train leave. As I was checking my bags, I ran into Teddy Smith. He had missed the same train— next train was due to leave at 11:15—somehow Teddy and I managed to get on early and get a seat before the mad rush. It was lucky for us.

People were standing in every available spot. It was the most crowded train I've ever seen. I went to sleep as soon as the train pulled out and didn't wake up until five hours later when the conductor told me we were at Kearney. Belskis, Vaughn, Collett, and I are all in the same room—so far Vaughn hasn't come in—he is now officially AWOL.

I picked up a "Stars and Stripes" someone left on the plane. An article said that on July 20, some of Hitler's own people tried to kill him at one of his remote outposts. That's not the first time they tried. Too bad they failed or this mess might be over sooner rather than later. If we are able to fly out, we'll only be here about four or five days, if not, we'll stay about eight or nine. Chances are very good for us to get a plane—I sure love my little mama. Be sweet and take care of you all. All my love—Bud.

Saturday July 29, 1944—11:30 AM—Dearest, I've just come back from looking over a new beautiful B-17 airplane—assigned to us yesterday. We fly our ship for the first time tomorrow to calibrate the instruments. I'll tell you whether or not we like it after then. The fellows have a name for it, which I don't approve of. I'm not sure it's final, but they plan to call it "Pro-Kit"—corny, isn't it?

We had some more ground school this morning—wasn't too bad though. It was all repetition of what we've had the past years. I have another class at 1:00 PM.—I saw Teddy [Smith] in the barbershop getting a "GI"—he doesn't have much left now. Vaughn, Collett, and I went to see a movie—"Mrs. Skeffington"—I didn't like it any too well—never did care too much for Bette Davis. It's been pretty hot here all day but it's now nice and cool—one thing I like about this place is its cool nights—the first night here I almost froze.—You asked for some details this morning but I'm afraid I can't give you any. By the time you get this I may be on my way to—somewhere— All my Love—Bud

Bud was correct. The Belskis crew left Kearney on Wednesday, August 2, without a crew consensus on the name of *"Pro-Kit"* for their shiny new B-17.

Labrador and Iceland – August 4–10, 1944

The safest route from the U.S. to England was "over the top," through Newfoundland, Labrador, and Iceland before the last leg over the remainder of the Atlantic and into the UK. The route was not without peril. Even without attacks, numerous craft were lost attempting to ferry WWII aircraft to the theater. But this northern trip was still the route of choice.

The route took the crew to New York and on to Gander, Labrador.

B-17G 43-38780 VE-J, Markings as on aircraft flown by the Belskis crew on Mission #222 from Ridgewell.
USAAF - 381st

Land was almost always visible from the left side of the plane. After Leo told the crew they had passed over Newfoundland, Bud left the area behind the waist gunner locations, where a few of the guys had gathered to chat, moved through the narrow walkway in the bomb bay, dropped down under the flight deck, and took his bombardier's seat in the nose. *How beautiful,* he thought as he saw the vastness that lay ahead.

The 2,500 miles from Kearney seemed in the distant past as they took off from Gander three days later. Next stop: Reykjavik, Iceland. Even before they landed, the crew members discussed the stark beauty they expected to encounter there. "It may be beautiful, but it's not for me," Leo blurted as they exited the plane and walked toward the base. "Milwaukee's as far north as I want to go after this thing is over."

"I'm with you," Bud responded as he held the door to Flight Operations open and dropped his bag next to a locker.

The crew's seven-day sojourn through the two northern stopovers was similar and uneventful: young kids attacking the crew to beg for gum, extreme cold while on night duty guarding the plane on the hardstand, more than a couple of movies, twelve hours of sleep most days, more cold, and restlessness as they looked toward the future. Despite the specter of another six hours and a thousand miles to Ireland, they were all ready to move on. "Hey guys, let's get this plush chariot in the air," Leo said as they strode toward their imposing aircraft.

The B-17 was equipped for bombing missions, not luxury travel, and could be boarded from either of two doors. Using the first, a hatch under the front of the plane between the navigator's seat and the bomb bay, required some dexterity. One method of entering through that opening was to jump, grab the hatch frame, swing your legs up through the hatch, and pull your body through. Taller boys had the advantage of being able to reach the hatch without jumping, but their long legs impeded the final swing.

The other method of boarding was to climb up using a stepladder—if you could stand the crew's ribbing. Few wanted to face that. The officers and others who wanted to confirm their mettle used the front entrance, but heavier men could rarely enter the hatch without aid. However, the combination of physical training and poor food quality saw to it that few sported excess poundage.

The gunners typically used a more accessible door behind the right gunner position, easily entered by stepping up and over the frame. Seating was purely functional except for the pilot and co-pilot, who had the most comfortable seats in the ship. Drop-down wooden slatted benches lined both sides of the fuselage from behind the waist gunner's positions back to the rear entrance. "Bring your own cushions," was the customary word. Hard as they were, the benches became a gathering place for conversation during the ferrying of the B-17 across the pond.

The navigator, and radioman had seats of sorts at their battle stations behind a stationary desk. The bombardier had a backless, swivel seat directly behind the plexiglass nose of the plane.

The B-17 was thus a fortress without a moat, no-frills travel with questionable comfort built in. The crew's training had also taught them to "Take a leak before take-off" and "Make sure you can hit the pee bottle while in the air." Some found used ammo cans a better receptacle.

Great Britain – August 14–31, 1944

The journey over the North Atlantic lay on a route southeast from the crew's base in Iceland. As they got close to the coast of Ireland, Leo came on the mike to say, "We're almost here. Get your Limey accents ready, boys."

Glenn Vaughn quickly corrected his superior, "Irish brogue first, boys."

"Right," Leo confirmed.

Bud, who had been sitting on the bench with a few of the others, jumped up, stepped over McCoy's outstretched legs, and stumbled through the plane, lurching as it hit an air pocket, and toward his seat with its prime visibility in the nose of the aircraft.

"I wanna see this. I've never been to England," Lauret said, as Bud almost tripped over Newman's B-4 bag that had slid to the middle of the walkway.

"You've never even been to New England, much less England, you hick," quipped McCoy. They all chuckled, but Rogers and Newman laughed loudest.

"Two left-coasters, two tumbleweed Texans, and an Okie shouldn't make fun of a regal Louisiana boy with roots in France," Lauret came back, receiving a hoped-for laugh.

"Maybe we'll just drop your French butt out on your relatives' house when we pass over in a couple of weeks," McCoy drawled in his best Oklahoma accent, getting the last laugh.

The crew made a two-day stopover in Ireland before proceeding to England. On their approach to the first of a couple of airfield stops there, they found the beauty of the countryside almost breathtaking. The landscape formed an irregular patchwork, with foliage separating deep yellow fields of rapeseed and wheat-colored cornfields awaiting harvest. Tiny villages intertwined with narrow, meandering roads and larger towns here and there added an additional layer of interest.

On final approach, the crew noted another airfield, also dotted with B-17s, off to the west. "That aerodrome is mighty close to the one where we're landing," Bud said to Collett, preoccupied with the scene unfolding outside his window.

"There's a farmer working right next to the airfield," Bud said in amazement.

"We're landing at Bovingdon, where the 92nd BG is stationed," Leo told the crew over the intercom.

"What's that yellow stuff?" asked Collett.

"Rapeseed," Bud replied. "They use it to make the English version of oleo."

Leo greased the landing, to the applause of his crew. They appreciated both the smooth touchdown and their arrival in the European Theater at last.

Over the next two weeks the crew spent hours in the classroom and on training flights, familiarizing themselves with some of the terrain of East Anglia. It was relatively flat, not unlike Texas and Louisiana, but the perpetual cloud cover, more than occasional rain, and cool nights seemed like foreboding indications of the winter still to come.

The Belskis crew moved a couple of times during the indoctrination period, with each location providing specific instruction, medical attention, and equipment issue. First, they spent time learning how best to acclimate to the differences between the US and England.

A week into their training in England, Bud wrote to Thelma:

> *I've been a little busier today than usual. It's all been very interesting work however—much more so than I expected. I had a few beers with Teddy Smith last night—he hasn't heard from home yet either—he said he saw his brother the other day."* [Teddy's brother was in the 381st at Ridgewell.] *I wished I could feel free to write anything I wanted like I use to be able to do back in the States, but you never know. I haven't yet seen any rocket bombs there's been so much talk of. Don't care to either. I had my shoes stolen from my B-4 bag—sure hated that—gotta go—another indoctrination into the British way—it's really kinda interesting. We'll come back over here someday when all this is over—stay sweet and take care of Junior.—Bud*

Bud dropped off his letter and slid into his seat next to Leo just as the instructor began. "Remember, boys," he began, "We're in England, operating in their country, their cities and as you can see, in their backyards. Don't get too carried away with the thought that 'we're over here to save your ass,' regardless of how true you feel that is. Truthfully, we're here to help save the globe, including our homes. We don't want the Nazis marching down Main Street in our hometowns. If the Brits hadn't been able to hold off Goering and the Luftwaffe four years ago, this country would be speaking Kraut today. We don't want that! So treat these people with respect. They may seem docile, with their manners and all, but they have a toughness we can learn from." The instructor looked around the crowded room before he continued.

"In no way do I want to diminish the inconvenience this war has brought to the home front, but by comparison to the Brits, that's exactly what it is: an inconvenience. Sure, there's rationing in the States—sugar, butter, rubber, gasoline, leather, meat—but it only means they have to cut back slightly on some of these things while they still gripe about it. So your wife has to combine her trip to get her hair done with a trip to the bank. People here have to park their cars for the duration: no petrol, a flat on their bald tires, and no battery.

"Back home, they turn their noses up at cabbage and Brussels sprouts. These people fight to get 'em, but it does get tiresome. Our folks substitute oleo for butter. Big deal—these folks have neither. In the States we have a half-dozen things that are rationed—I mean cut back slightly. Over here, they have about the same number of things that *aren't* either rationed or non-existent. There's a big difference between inconvenience and austerity. Keep that in mind." Once again, the instructor paused to gaze at his students before continuing.

"If you get to London, you'll see the horrendous effects of living in the midst of bombing for over four years. V-1s and now V-2s sneak in from the sky unannounced almost every day. But these people get up and go to work, school, and church every day, too.

"And while our folks are eating pretty good back home, the Brits have a hard time getting many of the things you'll find on base. Chewing gum, chocolate, and cigarettes are like gold to these people—pretty good barter for a lot of things.

A snicker moved through the crowd. "Yeah, I know what you're thinking. Act your age. On second thought, act a lot older than that!"

the instructor added, recognizing his audience of virile boys, some just out of their teens with hormones raging. They laughed aloud as he too broke into a smile.

"Emotions among the Brits are mixed. They want us here because they know what's at stake, and they couldn't do this job without us. But on the other hand, they're proud people, a little chagrined that the neophyte nation that ran away from their way of life became so successful and strong that they have to call on us for help. And don't forget that this is a small country. England's about the same size as any one of southern states: Tennessee, Mississippi, Alabama, or Louisiana."

"I hope they're smarter here than in our South, don't you, Jim?" Leo whispered, just loud enough for Glenn and Bud to hear him. They didn't respond.

"This is a crowded space. You'll see it clearly when you fly your missions. England has about 125 fighter and bomber air bases in a space the size of Rhode Island. Stay awake. Keep those formations tight to keep the Jerries' fighters out." The instructor continued, "You've experienced some of the weather here, a little different from the extreme heat you did most of your flying in over the last six months. Well, you ain't seen nothing yet. A couple of months from now at 28,000 feet over the Continent and you'll see some real weather.

"I know you've studied the slick Me-109 and the blunt-nose Fw-190, and you know a little about the new Me-262. What do you think are the most formidable foes you'll face in combat?" No one answered. "The two Fs are your toughest opponents. Yeah, the Luftwaffe is a tough adversary. But your two biggest problems will come from frostbite and flak. Make no mistake about it—both will sneak up on you and kick your butt. And either one can kill you graveyard dead. You can easier combat frostbite than you can flak."

Flak, a contraction of the German word, *Fliegerabwehrkanonen*, meaning "Flyer defense," could be a devastating weapon, one hard to defend against. Fighters could be anticipated, seen, sometimes defended against and avoided, but not flak. It was insidious, indiscriminant, and showed up in waves. The puffs of smoke as 88 mm flak shots exploded were followed instantaneously by ragged white-hot metal shards flying in all directions. Resultant damage could include punctured aircraft, cut hydraulic lines, and holes ripped in the bodies of airmen. Further, as US and Allied forces from the West and the Russian Army from the East drove the *Wehrmacht* back toward Berlin, the concentric circles of flak emplacements became more concentrated around the targets they were protecting. So all mission crews knew they would face flak. Sometimes the Luftwaffe would be a no-show, but flak showed up consistently—and always in a bad mood.

"Now, let's make sure you blokes don't get yourselves in too much trouble by using the wrong words while you're here," the instructor said, trying unsuccessfully to put a proper British accent on the word *blokes*. "The US and England may very well be two countries separated by a common language. Let's not widen the chasm."

"First, don't punch someone if they address you as 'left-tenent;' that's just the way they pronounce *lieutenant*. And the 'h' is silent in the river Thames. It's '*Tims*,' not '*Thāmes*.'" He moved on to a topic he hoped would interest the roomful of young men staring back at him.

"Now, British sports are a little different, too. You baseball boys, don't try to understand cricket. You never will, and it ain't worth trying. Over here, cricket's a game, not a bug. If you do wander into a cricket match, just know that if you 'break the duck,' it means you score first.

"Also: shagging is not chasing down a fly ball, a hooker is a player in a rugby scrum, and a tart is not a pie but a 'working girl'." At this, the boys broke into laughter.

"All right, settle down. I realize you know by now that a pound is a quid or a bob. Their money is similar to ours, a pence is equivalent to our penny. And if they tell you to put two quid on the commode, don't panic. That means lay it on the desk or the cabinet.

"A jacket potato ain't got a shirt on, it's a baked spud, and you can get one at a pub along with fish and chips, which are French fries. Or you could order bangers and mash—sausage and mashed potatoes—with a biscuit, our cookies, for dessert."

"And oh yeah, your pecker is your nose, so keep it up and don't put it in somebody else's business." He had saved this gem till last, knowing it might cause him to lose control. It did.

"OK guys, settle down. As you head to the theater (the European Theater of Operations, or ETO), let me leave you with a final bit of advice: Remember what you promised and to whom you promised it when you left the States. Those people probably made promises to you, too, and you're expecting those to be kept, so keep yours. Don't trade a few minutes of pleasure for a lifetime of regret. I've got a boy of my own over here, and I told him to remember who and what you are."

The boys grew silent at the unexpected admonition. The verbal inoculation would take with many—but not all—of the young mustangs before him, and the sergeant knew it. *Sounds like what Dad would've told me,* Bud thought. *And, just like Dad's lectures, this guy's advice is worth the hearing.*

"Now, cinch up your jock strap, get this damn job done, and let's all go home," the older man growled. That last message was more what Bud expected from this gravelly voiced, battle-scarred veteran. But he heard both clearly.

That night, August 30, Bud wrote:

> *It's just six days till our second anniversary, and your poppy still hasn't been able to do a thing about it—all I can do is just wish I was there to give you a present in person. Fred Allen's program is being rebroadcast over our radio station here in the ETO. I'm listening to it out of one ear—hope you don't mind. He just did an imitation of a Southern boy, "Lt. Bob White you all." I had to stop and listen to him mimicking the way these British talk— he did a good job of it, too. I understand Bing Crosby is in the ETO. Maybe we'll get to see him—sure hope so. Boy, I'd give ten bucks for a nice big juicy hamburger with a big onion, tomatoes, and all the trimmings. If a fellow had a hot dog stand anywhere near here, he'd clean up. We saw a real good show tonight, Destination Tokyo. I believe I tried to take you to see it once and you wouldn't*

go. I enjoyed it a lot. Teddy Smith went along with us. He seems like one of our crew, everybody likes him.

Earlier tonight I packed all my clothes for another move which will take place very shortly—the next time I write I'll probably be some other place in England.

CHAPTER 12

Welcome to Ridgewell

381st Bomb Group (Heavy)

Ridgewell, England: September 1, 1944

THE BELSKIS CREW PULLED OUT from Bovington in mid-morning. After a bumpy three-hour ride in the back of a covered deuce and a half truck, they arrived at Ridgewell, Essex County, in the southeast corner of England. Ravenous after the uncomfortable trip, they headed straight for the mess hall.

Ridgewell was one of forty USAAF bomber bases in East Anglia during WWII. Designated as Station 167, it was the home of the 381st Bomb Group. The easternmost of the twelve heavy bomber bases, it joined the 91st at Bassingbourn and the 398th at Nuthampstead in the First Wing of the First Division of the 8th Air Force.

Some of the East Anglia airfields were newly constructed and others, like Ridgewell, were RAF aerodromes upgraded and made functional for B-17 and B-24 use. Ridgewell's 6,000-foot main runway was crossed by two other 4,200-foot runways. The resulting A-formation layout was ringed by a road, off of which came four sets of hardstands. At each, there was space for more than a dozen B-17s to park between missions. A main hangar was located near the center of the runways, and a second sat outside the runway area close to the village of Ashen.

East Anglia was chosen as the location for Eighth AF airfields used in the bombing of Western Europe for four basic reasons. First, this was the closest Allied land area from which Germany could be bombed, decreasing the amount of fuel and airtime required for each mission. Second, the land was relatively flat, requiring less time and construction expense. Third, numerous RAF airfields could be converted for use by the US Army Air Corps. And last was the large supply of available land that fit airfield requirements.

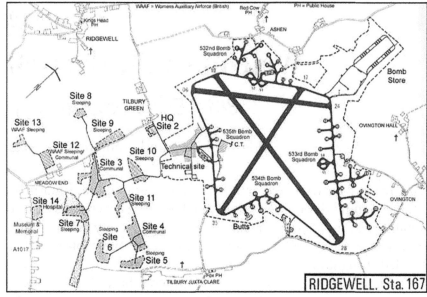

Map of Ridgewell - Station 167 during WWII
USAAF - 381st

Farming alongside Ridgewell Aerodrome during WWII
USAAF - 381st

There was, however, one slight problem with land acquisition. When the war began, most of the useable land was actively farmed. The British government didn't see this as a major impediment, informing select landowners that they planned to use their land for an airfield. At the war's conclusion, the land would be returned to the owner. Even when the facility was in active use, owners were allowed to farm the land outside the airfield area. Since landowners recognized the necessity of the US bombers in the battle for England's freedom, there was little if any resistance. And the airmen who came from farm families often helped the locals with crop information and machine repair.

Ridgewell began European operation in December of 1942, and the first mission was flown to Antwerp, Belgium, on June 22, 1943. Between that initial mission and September 1, 1944, 181 missions originated there.

After their first of many meals in the Ridgewell mess hall, the crew members retired to their barracks. Right away, they realized their home away from home was nothing like their stateside homes. However, since each of them had lived in as many as a dozen locations in the last two years, this move seemed to provide a sense of stability. The four officers were dropped off at their corrugated metal rectangular huts, and the five enlisted men at another.

Bud had hoped that the flight deck crew (Belskis, Vaughn, Collett and himself) would be billeted in the same hut the way most were, but that did not occur. *That's the Army for you*, he thought. Collett and Belskis were assigned to one hut, and Vaughn joined Bud in another, next to their crewmates in the cluster of 532nd Bomb Squad officers' quarters.

The crew had coalesced over the last few weeks. They did their work well, which was critical given the responsibilities they faced. But a personal unity was also growing day by day. In a letter to Thelma, on September 4, Bud wrote, "*I'm really crazy about our group, everyone here is [a] good fellow. They all seem to want to do something for each other. Everything is fine—rolling along smooth so far.*"

Barracks for airmen at Ridgewell were of two types. Nissen huts were functionally designed shells formed in a semi-circular shape from corrugated metal. Others were the more traditional rectangular shape. Both types were about twenty-four feet wide and approximately twice as long. Cots lined both sides of the structure and extended toward the center aisle. Each bunk had a footlocker at the end close to the aisle and a shelf on the wall above the bed. A wood-burning stove stood close to each end of the building. A few windows lined each side, cut from the metal sidewalls and projecting outward with a small ledge on the inside.

A washroom for shaving was off to one side of the building. Some huts had showers attached, but most did not. Neither the one occupied by Bud and Glenn nor the one to which Leo and Jim were

Thelma and J. Ross in photo folder Bud carried with him-Fall 1944

assigned had a shower. The closest one was thirty yards away.

Bud, who valued neatness, folded his clothes as best he could, arranged his footlocker, and placed photos on the shelf. One was of Thelma, the other was of his sister's son, J. Ross, whom he also claimed as his child, at least until his own came along.

Bud was anxious to check out the Officers' Club (OC). A chow-hound who would eat almost anything in sight, he had also become quite addicted to the game of bridge. He heard a rumor about a couple of similarly afflicted airmen who spent a lot of time engrossed in bridge games, and he was intent on tracking them down. One was the squad's lead bombardier, Harvey Tidwell.

"Hey Glenn, Let's take a jog to the OC before it gets too late. We might rustle up a bridge game."

"The last time you talked me into that, it cost me three bucks and two hours, and I have neither to spare. You're on your own," Vaughn responded. "Take your flashlight, it'll be dark soon."

"I probably ought to drop bread crumbs to lead me home," Bud said, laughing as he headed out.

After a ten-minute walk, Bud reached the Officers' Club, housed in a large Nissen hut. Bombs noting the group's various missions were painted on the panels that covered the semi-circular ceiling. A large rug bordered with two concentric squares woven into the pattern covered the concrete floor. Cushioned, straight-back armchairs lined the walls. Similar chairs ringed the tables in each corner. The atmosphere was homey—at least as homey as a corrugated metal building could be.

As Bud walked through the door, he scanned the room for any recognizable faces. He saw none.

Then came a familiar voice from his left, "Hey, Perrin." As he turned in the direction of the voice, he immediately recognized the wide smile and angular face.

"Lt. Angevine," Bud pushed away a chair and walked toward Lt. Robert H. Angevine, an instructor and friend from Big Spring. Bud stuck out his hand as he asked, "How in the world are you? How long have you been here?"

"Got here in mid-July," Bob replied. "How about you?

Just got here today—trying to get settled and ready to get started. What squad are you in? How many missions

Capt. Robert "Bob" Angevine-535th Navigator and "Mickey Man" on B-17 - 1944
Angevine Family Collection

have you flown?" Everyone kept close tabs on their mission count, which served as a ticket home. Everyone wanted to make sure that all-important ticket got punched.

"Let's go sit up there by the fire," Angevine said. They walked to the front of the large room. The fireplace rested on a brick hearth that extended outward about four feet. A brick arch framed the opening, and a two-foot deep brick mantle rested atop the entire width of the face of the fireplace.

Missions the 381st had flown were painted in black block letters on the wall above the hearth. The center of that wall boasted the insignia of the 381st BG, a shield with a red and blue bomb framed by the slogan, "Triumphant We Fly."

Flickering embers from the smoldering fire produced an occasional spark that flew to the front of the hearth. The heat seemed just right as these reunited friends removed their shoes and rested their feet on the hearth. "Just like home," Angevine said with a smile as he picked up the conversation.

"I'm in the 535th. Got five missions under my belt. They're slow since I've been flying lead navigator," Bob said with a slight grimace. "Wish they'd go faster. As the British winter progresses, the weather will worsen and missions may move even more slowly. Plus it'll be a lot colder aloft."

"Colder than forty below? How much colder can it get?" Bud asked.

"Probably fifty or sixty below in the winter," Angevine said.

"Where have your missions taken you?"

"Munich; Saarbrucken; Brest, France—but the first one was in July to Schweinfurt. That's a tough way to break in. You've heard of Schweinfurt, haven't you?"

"Yeah, they told us about it in ETO indoctrination. And I read something in *Yank* about the big losses on the raids in the fall of '43. Is it still a tough target?"

"You bet. The Germans are resilient. We hit 'em hard over and over, and they rebuilt each time. Ball bearings and Me-109s are the heart of the Luftwaffe, so I guess we'll keep on slugging 'em on the chin till they throw in the towel. You do know that Ridgewell lost

381st-Ridgewell Officers Club - December 1, 1944
USAAF - 381st

more planes in the August and October Schweinfurt/Regensberg raids than any other BG?"

"I didn't. Bet that was devastating to the morale around here," Bud lamented.

They continued sharing experiences, home situation, concerns, and even some fears. *I feel comfortable opening up to Angevine,* Bud thought. *Glad he ended up here.*

Soft-spoken and gentile, Angevine was the consummate gentleman, respected by every navigator and bombardier student he taught at Big Spring. A New Jersey native, he had a serious girlfriend waiting for him back in Texas.

After almost an hour of engaging conversation, "Wow, it's late," Bud said, standing up after a glance at his watch. "And who knows what they've got planned for us tomorrow?"

"Yeah, rumor has it there's no mission, but you never know."

The two walked out together. "I'd love to join you at church this Sunday, or soon," Bud said.

"Sounds good," Angevine replied. "I've been wanting to check out a couple of the churches in the village, or we can go to the base service and hear Colonel Brown. Which do you prefer?"

"Your call. Just let me know," Bud said with a smile.

Following the traditional handshake, both men disappeared into the crisp night. Bud followed the dim beam of his flashlight. *The breadcrumbs might have been a better idea*, he thought. All was quiet when he reached the hut, so he slipped into bed and fell asleep in minutes.

Later, on September 4, he mentioned this reunion in a letter to Thelma.

> *I know you've heard me mention Lt. Angevine, our flight instructor at Big Spring. I ran into him the first day here. He seemed glad to see someone from Big Spring—said he had been looking for some of us since he got here. He also mentioned that he had recommended me for an instructor there before he left. That was good to know.*

Ridgewell, England – September 2, 1944

As dawn broke, the creaking of the hinges on the hut's front door woke Bud from a deep sleep. Someone opened and then shut it before he could open his eyes. It was his first night there, so he did not yet know the normal sounds of his new home.

In the bunk next to his, Vaughn groaned his displeasure at the interruption. Since both had heard that no mission was scheduled for this Saturday, they simply turned over, pulled up their Army green blankets, and remained silent.

Bud was happy for the day off and time to acclimate to Ridgewell. This would be their base of operations until the conclusion of the war, or at least until they completed their required missions. Then home again. And home could not come soon enough. Earlier in the war, the airmen were required to fly twenty-five missions. The requirement was later raised to thirty and then quickly to thirty-five.

Home could be an earlier destination, however, if Hitler would finally surrender, which was highly unlikely, or the Nazis were bombed and beaten into submission, which was looking more like a possibility each day. Word was that Allied bombing was increasingly effective. It appeared that the Luftwaffe was running low on fuel as the 8th AF missions continued to blast German refineries and marshaling yards.

In his early-morning daze, Bud remembered being told upon their arrival the day before that Bing Crosby would be at the base for a show on Saturday afternoon. His mind drifted back to Christmas 1941. The attack on Pearl Harbor drastically changed the mood in the US and placed a somber tone on the holidays. But on Christmas day, the radio in the Perrin home was tuned to NBC's Kraft Music Hall when Crosby first sang "White Christmas." It created a warm, nostalgic mood for him and Thelma that evening. Later the next year, Crosby recorded the song that, unsurprisingly, became an immediate classic for Christmas seasons to follow.

As the cobwebs cleared from Bud's waking thoughts, he began to sing, "I'm dreaming of a white Christmas, just like the. . . ."

Vaughn interrupted Perrin's attempts at singing. "Hey, you're Bud, not Bing. . . can the crooning."

"I'm insulted. You've talked incessantly about your family's musical talents, so I thought you liked melodious music."

"I do, but that ain't it. And besides, Christmas is months away."

Chastised but undaunted, Bud finished the verse, ". . . and may all your Christmases be white."

The words and emotions of this Christmas classic caused Bud to reflect on the changes brought on by the events of the past four years:

Let's see: on September 1, 1940, Thelma was crowned Miss Knoxville. A year later during the Labor Day picnic at Big Ridge, the members of our newly-formed study group began pursuing the causes and effects of WWII. On Labor Day of the following year, Thelma and I were on our honeymoon. Early September of 1943 found me in Big Spring, Texas in the throes of bombardier training. And here I am today, waiting to fly my first live mission. It's mind-numbing to say the least.

Bud continued his musing as he remained in his bunk.

I'm excited about seeing combat action. But I'd be lying if I said I wasn't afraid. I feel a mixture of pride, resolve, anxiety, and insecurity, but these aren't things I talk about much. I know the other guys feel the same way, though. It just takes some intense homesickness or a night at a pub for them to admit it.

I wish I could tell Thelma the way I feel. Someday soon—the sooner the better, he thought. *No more censored letters. When this mess is over, I can tell her everything about what we did here. I miss my home and family, but I miss my wife and 'Junior' most of all. That January due date seems a long way off, but in other ways it seems like tomorrow.* He paused as he considered his mission requirements. *Hope I've got 'em done somewhere close to that time. But most of the boys say not to count on it.*

Once again, his mind returned to the pending arrival of his first-born. *Junior will want to know all that we did here and why,* Bud thought. He smiled as he envisioned adoring little eyes looking up at him as he related training, missions, and all. *It'll be like the way J. Ross looks at me. But Junior—Junior will be all mine. I can hardly wait.*

Leo Belskis bounded through the door with his ever-present grin and hat at its usual side-cocked angle. The James Cagney look befitted this fun-loving Midwesterner. In the six weeks since their crew was formed, he and Bud had developed quite a close relationship.

"Rise and shine, country boy," Leo chirped. "We gotta test the chow this place puts out."

Never one to miss a meal, Bud bounded up and dressed quickly. "Wonder if they'll have country ham, red-eye gravy, and hogshead biscuits?" Bud asked in his best country redneck accent while tying his shoes.

"You Tennessee boys sure have a weird culinary sense. Ever hear of bacon, eggs, and toast?"

"Just don't let him sing," Vaughn added as Bud and Leo scrambled through the door, laughing.

But there were no biscuits and gravy in the chow hall. Saturday was the Ridgewell mess hall's day for pancakes, and they were both plentiful and delicious. *The butter's real—probably local. And the syrup's thick, tasty, and not Karo!* Bud thought as he took his first bite.

On this weekend morning, the mood was almost festive. Maybe it was the fact that there was no mission for the day. Maybe it was the lack of rain, an English staple year-round. Or it could have been the knowledge that Crosby was coming to Ridgewell, no doubt accompanied by a couple of lovely young actresses or singers. Whatever the reason, the boys seemed to be in a good mood—at least as good a mood as they could be while four thousand miles from home and in the middle of a war.

Home meant a great deal to Bud. In fact, he was always on the lookout for boys from Tennessee, especially the Knoxville area. On this morning, he ran into a couple of them as he and Leo ate breakfast.

Bill Letson, a middle Tennessee native and fellow student at Southwestern in Memphis and later in bombardier training at Big Spring, recognized Bud and sat with him and Leo for a few minutes. Bill stood to Bud's left in the Big Spring class picture earlier in April of '44. He left quickly after remembering he had promised to meet a crewmate at the Officers' Club.

A few minutes later, Bud heard a voice from behind him that was unmistakably Southern, probably Tennessean, and possibly even Knoxvillian or somewhere close. He turned to see a tall, rail-thin young lieutenant walking by.

"What part of Tennessee are you from?" With that question, he took an educated geographical guess that surprised his new acquaintance. Many of the fellows looked younger than twenty-seven-year-old Bud, and this lieutenant could have passed for a high school student.

"Oakdale," said the startled airman. "C.D. Cash," he added as he extended his hand and broke into a wide grin. "How'd ya know?"

"Love the accent. Even more so since I've been away from God's country," Bud replied, indicating the reverence that most East Tennesseans held for their "neck of the woods." "I've heard a lot about Oakdale. My brother-in-law works for the Southern Railway and

Lt. Conan D. Cash - 1944
Peter Cash Collection

makes frequent trips to the coal mines there. If you've got a few minutes, sit down. Leo and I need to know what to expect here," Bud said. "We just arrived yesterday and haven't yet flown a mission. Oh yeah, this is my crew's pilot, Leo Belskis. He's a northerner, but still a pretty good guy. I'm trying to give him a southern linguistic education. Maybe you can help me."

"Where'd you read the word *linguistic*, country boy? Do you know what it means?" Leo chided.

"Be careful, buddy, I've got reinforcements now," Bud tilted his head toward Cash. "I see you're a bombardier. What crew?"

"I'm in the 532nd, the Seeley crew—Bill Seeley, but we call him Aloysius. We just got here too, on the twenty-fourth of August, a week after I turned twenty-one. We haven't flown a mission yet, either."

It didn't take long for the two to feel like long-lost buddies as they shared life stories in bursts of information. Cash said he graduated from Oakdale High School at seventeen, enrolled in the University of Tennessee, took two years of ROTC (required at all land-grant colleges like UT), enlisted in the Army Air Corps in November of 1942, and took basic training at Miami followed by more college at the University of Chattanooga.

After an hour or so of chitchat, Bud looked at his watch. "Uh-oh. The Crosby show's only an hour or so from starting. We'd better get a move on or we won't get a decent place to sit."

The trio stepped outside the mess hall into a light rain. The dark clouds forming to the west of the base made it clear that a downburst was imminent. Already wearing jackets, they ventured into the mist.

The show would take place at the base's main hangar, the largest facility at Ridgewell. Actor Edward G. Robinson had made a morale-boosting appearance in the same location earlier in the year. While there, he and his entourage christened a 532nd B-17G, adorned with the nose art "Happy Bottom." Eleven days after Robinson broke the champagne bottle over the craft's nose, its crew was forced to ditch in the English Channel on the way back from a mission over Germany.

Next, the friends made a quick fly-by of the Officers' Club to see if

Collett and Vaughn were there. They weren't. But they did commandeer a bumbershoot, as an umbrella is often called in the South.

The three then resumed their trek toward the hangar almost a half-mile away. Ridgewell, like most East Anglia bases, covered a broad area. One destination always seemed far away from the next.

Edward G. Robinson Christening B-17 *Happy Bottom*- July 5, 1944
USAAF - 381st

Church and pubs in the nearby towns were likewise distant, and the weather was, well, British. Pelting rain in East Anglia was commonplace. With winter approaching, daylight hours were getting shorter, and the snow was on its way. A bicycle was a necessity if one wanted to preserve shoe leather, energy, and time. As they continued to slog toward the hangar, they agreed they would each make the purchase of a bike a top priority.

As Bud, Leo, and C.D. topped the small rise in front of the theater that housed Chaplain Brown's office a few yards ahead, the hangar came into view. And so did the hundreds of other boys scurrying past the B-17 parked just outside the main doors. It seemed everyone had the idea of arriving early to capture a good vantage point from which to view the show. "Looks like we might be a little tardy for the party, boys," Leo said.

The excitement ginned up by the show should have been no surprise. Crosby was one of the top entertainers in the States. He was the star of a hit movie, *Going My Way*, then playing at the Odeon Theater in Leicester Square in London's West End. Earlier in the year, he had won the Academy Award for this starring role.

On the previous night, Crosby played to a sold-out crowd at the Stage Door Canteen, known as *the* place in London's entertainment center in the West End. The next day, *The London Daily Times*

Bing Crosby at Stage Door Canteen, London-September 1, 1944
London Times

reported the appearance in a lead article that estimated the crowd
at one thousand. Among those in attendance were Britain's Foreign
Secretary, Anthony Eden; and Air Vice-Marshall, Sir Arthur Ted-
der; as well as Crosby's supporting cast: Dorothy Dickson, Beatrice
Lillie, Fred Astaire, and Jack Buchanan.

In short, Bing Crosby was a hot ticket. He was playing a free show
for the boys at Ridgewell, and no one wanted to miss it. Since this
was also the anniversary of the opening of the Red Cross Club, the
festivities gained an extra boost.

As they entered the hangar through the open main door, C.D.
peeled off and joined a few boys from his own crew. Leo and Bud
scanned the already large and raucous crowd, looking in vain for a
place close to the stage.

The main hangar at Ridgewell reproduced those at other bases
all across East Anglia. Each consisted of an enclosed area about the
size of a football field, unencumbered by central columns. The hangar's height was about thirty-five feet at the walls and forty-five feet
at the midpoint. Its frame was comprised of a series of rigid arch
bents with a web frame, similar to bridge construction, across the
expanse of the building at the roofline. Purlins, horizontal beam-like

Bing Crosby on Stage at the Ridgewell Concert-September 2, 1944
USAAF - 381st

Airmen Audience at Bing Crosby Ridgewell Concert-September 2, 1944
USAAF - 381st

members that provided rigidity to the walls, connected the frame. Like most structures on the base, corrugated metal panels formed the hangar's exterior.

For the show, a small stage had been constructed by locating a number of flat-bed trailers next to each other at one end of the building, halfway between the two sidewalls. About fifteen rows of folding chairs filled in the areas in front of and on both sides of the stage. Dignitaries, some local residents, and 381st top brass occupied these seats, with the areas behind them jam-packed. Men were seated on the concrete floors and on any reasonable facsimile of a chair they could find. Hundreds had climbed the purlins ringing the building and were literally hanging from the rafters.

Two men climbed atop a workbench and scaled a column, taking one of the few vacant spots on a nearby purlin. Bud and Leo knifed their way into the vacated space fifty feet from the stage. Feeling lucky, they settled in to wait for Bing.

They didn't have long to wait. Just outside the open doors at the end of the hangar, a half-dozen cars pulled to a stop, and the boys craned their necks to see. Bing Crosby stepped from the first car, followed by Chaplain Brown and base commander Lt. Colonel Harry Leber. Someone in front of Bud said, loud enough to be heard over the din of the crowd, "There's Leber, where's the camera?" All those who had been at Ridgewell any amount of time knew Leber was a photo hound.

Crosby wore his trademark belted tan trench coat and the ever-present light gray felt hat set back on his head at a jaunty angle. Followed by the supporting cast of entertainers Darlene Garner, Jeannie Darrell, and comedian Joe DeRita, he made his way through the crowd. DeRita would, later in his career, have a short stint as Curly's replacement in *The Three Stooges*.

As Crosby stood in front of the group surrounding the stage, he removed his coat and hat, and handed them to his assistant. Those seated stood up to get a better view of the starlets and Crosby, in that order. Six hundred wounded servicemen from neighboring hospitals, guests of the 381st Group, were seated in the front.

Ever the dapper dresser, Crosby wore a perfectly tailored gray suit with a handkerchief in the left front pocket. He also had his left hand stuck characteristically in the pocket of his trousers.

After being introduced by Col. Leber and amid thunderous applause, whistles, and shouts, Crosby strode to the center of the stage, where two microphones magnified the sound. Helping all to hear in the vast facility, built for aircraft repair and protection rather than acoustics, was no easy task. One microphone was a traditional mic used in radio broadcasts, and the other resembled a fluted megaphone. In combination, they did their job, and the revved-up crowd roared its approval.

After introducing each person in his travelling cast and subjecting himself to jokes of which he was the butt, Bing fired off some barbs of his own. Then he began a concert that included most of the tunes that had fueled his ascent to the top of the US musical world.

Anticipating disapproval, he quipped, "I guess it's too soon to sing Christmas songs. . . " His voice trailed off in a chorus of boos, indicating the audience's hunger for music that would soothe their yearning for the sounds of home.

As he began the song that linked him with the Christmas season, the crowd's roar dropped to a hushed silence. "I'm dreaming of a white Christmas, just like the ones I used to know. . . . "

Bud didn't have to close his eyes to remember the first time he heard that song, but he did nonetheless. The vision of holding Thelma in his arms on that Christmas evening almost three years earlier was vivid. But the warmth of her body was missing. The vision blocked out the sea of men in front of him and also kept his welling tears from escaping. *Boo-hooing won't reflect the strength of a boy readying himself for his first bombing mission over Germany a few days from now,* he thought. *Or would it?*

When he opened his eyes, he saw the same "back home" look on other's faces as they, too, fought back tears. He brushed the moisture from his eyes and, encouraged by Crosby, began singing along. The sound in the hangar was surprisingly harmonious and certainly heartfelt.

"I'll be home for Christmas, You can count on me. Please have snow and mistletoe, and presents on the tree. . . " Another burgeoning Christmas classic after Crosby recorded it only a year earlier, this song evoked a hushed silence, followed by three-part harmony from the impromptu chorus of 2,000-plus Ridgewell voices.

The concert continued, as did the enthusiastic response after each song. In about two hours and against the crowd's clear disapproval, the show wound to a close, accompanied by a lengthy standing ovation.

Fighting a return to the realities of war, the crowd slowly dispersed into the cool autumn air of a British mid-afternoon. The rain had stopped, and as they strolled back to the mess hall, Bud turned to Leo and asked, "Wanna stow away on the next plane back to the States?" They both smiled, knowing the impossibility of the idea.

In his letter to Thelma on Sunday, September 4, Bud wrote,

> *I didn't have a chance to write Friday or Saturday—was busy getting settled, etc. Bing Crosby was here Saturday afternoon—that was one reason—I certainly enjoyed seeing him. Seems like a regular guy. He said it was sure good to be on the road without Bob Hope. One of his best I thought was—Gypsy Rose Lee was running for Congress and he would sure like to be there when she put the motion before the House. There were a couple of Hollywood gals with him but I can't remember their names—not very well-known.*

In the letter, Bud mentioned neither his longing to hold her in his arms nor his tears. *I don't have to. She'll know.*

A tea at the Aero Officers' Club followed the performance, but Bud and Leo took a pass. Later that evening at an enlisted men's dance in Great Yeldham, a stunning blonde private, Cynthia Burville, was chosen beauty queen by applause of the boisterous airmen. The following day she christened a Ridgewell B-17, *Smashing Time.* A photographer chronicled the event with pictures of the teenage beauty flanked by the Essex County Sheriff and none other than the camera-loving Colonel Leber

A few days later, Bud wrote Thelma, "*I wish Bing Crosby or some of the other celebrities would come around again soon. Bing sure did put on a good show for us here—wish you could have seen him with me."*

Angevine, Cash, and others had warned Bud that the missions might not come as fast as he would like. He hoped his experience would be different. But over the next few days, he would learn that he would experience the same delays they did. Letters and packages from home helped while away the time, but sometimes they simply made the longing more intense. On the base, mail call was the most coveted time of each day. Military restrictions prevented airmen from telling family back home anything about their military activities, location or thoughts. They were also not supposed to keep diaries of these activities. That made meaningful letter writing tough. "Can I say this, or can't I?" was a question they constantly faced.

Some skirted the rules. Others just plain didn't follow them. But Bud had a strong sense of responsibility and honest, so he kept most of his inner angst to himself. *How many times can I say, "I love and miss you" without seeming hackneyed?* he wondered.

Ridgewell, England – September 5, 1944

No mission was flown by 381st crews on that Tuesday. And the natives were restless. None of them were anxious to get shot at while shivering in the extreme cold, but no flights meant no missions marked off on their way to the milestone of thirty-five. And each airman knew his own count.

The Belskis crew weren't happy to have their count remain at zero, but they weren't idle on "no mission" days. They had ground school, flew practice runs, and dropped practice bombs. But none of these activities helped them mark off a number on their mission log.

The personal significance of this day kept Bud from focusing on the disappointment of waiting longer for their first mission. He used the day off to write a long letter to his bride.

> *Dearest,*
> *Well, this is my 2nd anniversary—yours too though*

isn't it—sure is wonderful remembering that only two years ago today I talked the sweetest gal in all the world into marrying a no good guy like me. I feel bad because I wasn't able to get a gift or something to let you know I was thinking of our anniversary. Hope you understand that it wasn't entirely my fault. What I'd like best of all is to be with you all day today. Maybe take a trip up to the [Smoky] mountains. We'll have plenty of those trips in not so many months from now don't you think?

Right at the moment you are fast asleep and don't realize that this is our day. It should be about 2:30 in the morning there so I hope you are asleep. Next year we'll have Junior to help in celebrating and that should be lots of fun.

I may go over to the club tonight and take a drink for you and me just to celebrate but I won't drink more than that. There isn't a Chinese café around here so I can't do as we did two years ago. Hope Junior is being a good boy today and not kicking around too much.

Vaughn may celebrate with me tonight—wish it was someone else, and you should know who.

We still get plenty of good food to eat. Much, much better than I ever expected to have over here. Matter of fact, it's 100% better than what we had at Alex.

Has Henrietta heard from Grover lately? How about sending me his APO I'll like to write him. If you have time go by the office and give them my APO so I can get that paper they put out every month ["The Kilo-water Account"*].*

Guess it's still hot at home—can't say that for here. Not too bad however. I'll have to go now baby be sweet and don't forget who loves you more than he did even two years ago today. Maybe I'll have a chance to write again later on today. —All my love, Bud.

Later that evening, he found time to share another declaration of love and longing:

"Once again on an anniversary I decided to write my sweet wife. I got five letters today, the first I've had since last Wed. I find it kinda hard to make out what you've told me though since the letters [I received] vary anywhere from July 31 to Aug 25th."

Ridgewell, England – September 6, 1944

This day also saw no mission activity at Ridgewell. Repeating the continual focus on coming home soon, Bud wrote to Thelma:

It's too bad we don't have a family already. I understand the fellows with families get to come home first after this thing winds up. Maybe I'll be in the second group though—.

Last night Leo, Vaughn, Jim and I celebrated our anniversary at a local pub drinking beer and throwing darts [an old English game]. *We didn't drink too much however and came in rather early. We brought a bunch of sandwiches along and toasted them on one of the fellow's toasters—didn't taste bad at all.*

Ridgewell, England – September 7, 1944

The early morning hours came and went without a knock at the door of barracks throughout Station 167. Once again, no mission would be flown on that day. Word spread quickly at the mess hall as the boys, sleepy-eyed and frustrated, shuffled in, grousing. The smell of grease mixed with cigarette smoke produced an unappetizing odor. But hunger overcame their compromised appetites, and the boys chowed down.

After breakfast, Glen decided to go into town. Bud declined an invitation to join him, choosing instead to ride his bike to the Officers' Club in search of a bridge game. Even at this early hour, he found one. Engrossed in the intense competition, he skipped lunch.

Leo came by the club looking for him. "I'm hungry, how 'bout you?" Leo asked, interrupting the bidding process for a new bridge hand.

"I'm starved—don't think I can wait for supper," Bud responded. "Let's go to The Fox Pub. How 'bout it?"

"I'm in."

Bud and Leo had each purchased a bike shortly after coming to Ridgewell. Hand- operated English brakes on bikes at the base befuddled all new airmen. Realizing their tendency to revert to the coaster brakes they were used to in the States, the two rode cautiously. Wrecks and injuries were commonplace on bases all across England until novice riders became accustomed to this different braking system.

While en route, they saw C.D. Cash riding toward them. "Where you going?" Bud asked.

"Been to town, just looking around," Cash said in his slow East Tennessee drawl. "Come on, we're going to The Fox. Go with us," Bud said. Cash turned without stopping and fell in behind them.

They arrived without incident and leaned their bikes into the neatly manicured ivy covering the side of the building. Bud grabbed the iron handle on the left of the oak front door, pushed hard, and entered the century-old structure. *This place reeks* of British history, Bud thought as he looked around. *I almost expect to see Charles Dickens at a corner table drawing on a long stem pipe and writing with a quill pen.*

Lunchtime had come and gone, and suppertime had not yet arrived, but the tavern was almost full of reveling airmen. It was teatime for Brits, but US airmen hadn't appropriated the custom. The three found a table in the rear and sat down. What are you drinking, Conan?" asked the bartender as he walked toward them.

"Bring us three cold ones," C.D. said with a sheepish grin.

"*Conan*—so that's what the *C* stands for," Bud said with a grin. "And how does he know you? He sure doesn't sound like he's from Oakdale."

I've been on base almost two weeks, so I've been here a couple of times," Conan replied. "Bill and I have had a couple of interesting conversations. He's a really nice guy. Been the publican here for about ten years, used to be a cop in London—a bobby, I think they call it."

"*Publican, bobby*—you've picked up the jargon pretty quickly," Leo said.

"English lingo with a country hick accent." They all laughed, Bud and C.D. more than the rest.

"Heard some accents this ol' Mississippi boy recognizes. Where you boys from?" drawled a shy young man who had approached their table.

"Two boys from God's country, Tennessee, and a lousy Yankee," Bud responded. "Get a load off your feet and sit with us. I'm Ross Perrin—call me Bud. This is C.D. Cash and my crew boss Leo Belskis. And you?"

"I can't believe it," the boy said. "I'm Teddy Smith's brother, Phil. He told me to look you up."

"You gotta be kidding," Bud said. "What a great guy he is! I was hoping he would be stationed with us. We've had many a brew together. What squad are you in?"

"I'm a gunner and radioman in the 533rd. Only got two missions to go, then back home for me. Man, am I ready! I'm gonna kiss me some Mississippi mud in a month or so."

Newman, Rogers, and Lauret sat at a table in the opposite corner. Once they spotted their crewmates, the gunners brought their drinks and joined the four. Bud introduced Cash and Smith. "Hey, one more Southern boy," Rogers said as the Texan stuck his hand out to greet them.

"Hey boss, when are we ever going to see combat?" Lauret asked Leo.

"Soon, I hope," came his reply. "Nobody's flown a mission since the one to Ludwigshafen on the third. There were two tries for missions to Berlin and then yesterday to Bremen, but both were scrubbed before takeoff."

"In ETO briefing they said that Ludwigshafen is a key target. The BASF chemical plant is there," Cash said. "And the Mannheim marshalling yard is right across the Rhine from the plant. The 8th has been there many times, I've heard."

"How did the mission on the third go, Leo?" Bud asked.

"The interrogation officer for that mission is in the barracks with Collett and me," Leo said. "He told me thirty-seven ships made a

Pff [bomb run led by an aircraft using the Pathfinder navigation system] run in a 9/10 undercast. Light flak and no enemy fighters at the target. However, one ship had to make a crash landing near Rheims. The 15th got 'em out—all except the navigator—don't know the scoop on him." The five boys hung on his every word.

I don't want to think about being in that situation myself. Hope it never happens, Bud thought.

The conversation drifted to lighter topics. Cash had done some scouting of surrounding areas and was able to fill the boys in on some local color. "There are a number of pubs here: the White Horse, Yeldham, Great Yeldham, Ashen—seems like there's one every hundred feet. I like The Fox, though—pretty simple, like my hometown. It's a basic fish and chips place. You can get a jacket potato—I mean baked potato," he said, correcting his use of British lingo. "There's a farmer that comes in here a lot, Bert Tanner. He brings fresh eggs to boys on the base sometimes. His wife washes and irons dress shirts for some of the fellows, too."

"Just like home back in Texas," Rogers said. *Speaking of home, how's your wife, Bud?*

"Letters have been kinda jumbled up since we left the States, with all our moving around and stops and everything. But she's doing great. Our first, 'Junior,' is due around Christmastime."

"So it's a boy. How do you know?' asked C.D.

"We've been asking that question for weeks," Rogers piped up. "We're betting girl."

Col. Joseph J. Nazzaro-
Ridgewell CO (1/5/43 to
1/9/45)

Col. Harry P. Leber, Jr.-
Ridgewell CO (1/9/44
to 2/6/45)

Lt. Col. Conway S. Hall,-
Ridgewell CO (2/6/45
to 6/45)

Commanding Officers at Ridgewell, England-Station 167
USAAF - 381st

"And Vaughn thinks his will be a girl, so we're betting boy for him," Leo chimed in.

"I'm plenty good with a girl," Bud said. "If she's a combination of my sister and my wife, I'd be a happy feller."

Changing the topic, Leo asked if anyone had met Captain Hall. "Conway Hall?" asked Cash. "I saw him a couple of times at the OC."

"Whadja think of him?" Leo responded.

"He seemed a little cocky to me." C.D. said.

"Supposed to be a crack pilot," the crew chief said. "From what I've heard, he has a right to be a little cocky. I heard he was ticked off that he didn't get Leber's job. He relishes the tough missions, someone said. Did you hear the story of Hall rescuing the crew that had the stuck landing gear?" The men looked at each other, shaking their heads *no*.

"I heard this from a couple of guys, so it seems to be spot-on. On April 8, the *Carolina Queen* (B-17 42-97214) was returning from a mission to Oldenburg, Germany. They radioed the tower saying that they couldn't get the landing gear down. Hall was in the tower and told 'em to jettison the ball turret and they might be able to bring her in for a safe belly landing. The pilot said they didn't have the special wrench needed to free the turret. Hall—recognizing their plight—told 'em to circle the field. He was coming up.

"He jumped in an A-10, and took her up. They hovered over the *Queen*, but couldn't make the transfer. The rope was too short. Hall confirmed that their fuel supply was adequate and told them to 'keep it in the air.' He landed, put the wrench on a longer rope and inside a bag of sand so the rope wouldn't sway, and took off again, this time in a Fort. He was then able to drop the rope through the hatch. The crew dislodged the ball turret, and dropped it into the English Channel. Pilot Lt. Leslie Bond then greased a turretless belly landing."

"That took a real set," Bud said. "I'd fly with him any day."

"You got that right," Leo agreed. The rest nodded their heads.

A few more beers, a more than ample supply of fish and chips, and numerous stories about why each of their hometowns was the best, and before the boys knew it, the time approached 9:00. Not knowing if a mission might be called for the next day, they decided they'd better get back to base.

Having forgotten their flashlights, Bud and Leo would have had trouble finding their way, but C.D.'s flashlight allowed him to lead them back to the hut. Before retiring, Bud scribbled a few lines to Thelma. *I'd love to tell the Hall story, but it's against rules*, he lamented to himself. *And I wouldn't tell her about the casualties on the missions even if I could.* Instead he kept his note short and sweet, with few meaningful details.

> *Leo and I rode our bicycles down to a pub about a five minute ride from here last night and had a couple of beers. Oh I didn't tell you about my bike. Bought it for 4 British pounds—they call it quid—which is 16 bucks in our money of course. It's second-hand. Saves lots of shoe leather and lots of walking—you know everything is so far apart over here.*
>
> *Did I tell you that we now have sheets and pillow cases? I couldn't sleep on them the first night—guess I was getting used to sleeping on blankets alone.*
>
> *Hey, I met Phil Smith, Teddy's brother tonight at The Fox—seemed like a great guy, just like Teddy. Too bad they couldn't be based together.*
>
> *And did Emma go back with Dusty the last time or have I got your letter mixed up? I enjoyed mother's letter a lot, she didn't sound a bit worried and that's what I like—good news is always the best news, isn't it, baby?*

Ridgewell, England – September 8, 1944

On this date, a mission was finally flown out of the Ridgeway base. The target was Ludwigshafen. The 532nd had a number of crews assigned to this effort, including the Seeley crew, with Cash flying bombardier in his first taste of combat. The Belskis crew, however, was still waiting.

Thirty-seven crews, led by Lt. Col. Charles Halsey, encountered a solid undercast over the target and bombed with a Pff. Flak was moderate but intense with most of it below the formation. The crews saw no enemy aircraft.

Bud spent the late afternoon and evening playing bridge at the Officers' Club. Before retiring, he wrote to Thelma.

I know I must have gained 5 or 6 lbs.—since we've been here—I eat more than I ever did and you can imagine how much that must be.

I'm getting legs like a football player from riding my bike. They were a little sore at first, but I'm getting used to it. Think I'll bring it home for Junior. Don't believe he'd like it though since it doesn't have brakes like American bikes. I almost ran over a hundred fellows before I learned how to put on the brakes. I rode over to the club with Leo and Glenn last night and forgot to take my flashlight. Had a hard time finding my way home but finally made it.

Ridgewell, England – September 9, 1944

This was another day when the 381st went to battle over Germany without help from the Belskis crew. The Group diary recorded the following:

After a mission to Gaggenau was cancelled, a force of 49 aircraft, commanded by Lt. Col John Fitzgerald, Jr. with 1st Lt. Harris Sluyter as his pilot headed to Ludwigshafen. A 3/10 to 4/10 undercast, which had built up during the trip to Northern Europe, cleared when the Fortresses reached Belgium. Scouts reported that weather socked in again and it was 10/10 over the target. Ludwigshafen was, therefore, passed up, and the formation went, instead, across the Rhine River to Mannheim, which was the Pff target for the day. It looked for a while, as if the bombing would be visual, but the clouds stacked up, after a visual run had been begun and the instrument men took over to complete the job. Results were unobserved. Four Me-109's were reported in the vicinity of the target but they made no attempt to attack. The flak, however, was fairly accurate, although it was rated as only "moderate," and 16 381st ships sustained battle damage. There were no losses. (381st Bomb Group Diary, 381st Archives).

The weather at the base was raw. It seemed as cold in the barracks as it did outside. Despite his frustration at not yet racking up missions, Bud wrote home on September 9:

> *I'm sitting here in bed under three wool blankets—have on my long handles and my outing pajamas on over them, and I'm still not hot—only comfortable. Wonder how the weather is back in Knoxville town.*
>
> *I haven't written anyone at the Power Board since my APO changed—how about giving somebody down there a buzz, I'd like to get their paper and hear from some of them—Is Emma still working or has she joined Dusty again?*

Ridgewell, England – September 10, 1944

On this day the 381st flew to Gaggenau. The mission on the ninth was scheduled to attack this target, but weather caused it to be diverted. Once again, today's mission took place without the Belskis boys. After church, Bud wrote to Thelma:

> *Guess about this time you are either still sleeping or just getting up to those good hot biscuits. This morning I had real good hot cakes for breakfast, then came back and slept until time to go to church.*
>
> *Couldn't get Vaughn out of bed so I went alone. The service was very good and so was the singing—lots of English civilians attended the service. After church I had a chicken dinner with hot biscuits and lots of vegetables then topped it off with ice cream for dessert. I stay hungry around here most of the time. Can't understand it either since I eat so much every meal.*
>
> *Think I'll go to London on my first pass, which should be before long. Understand it's pretty quiet over there*

now. Want to come along? Sure wish you could. Did you ever hear Lilly Anne Carroll sing "I Walk Alone?" They play it about a dozen times a day over the AFN [Air Force Network]. *She's about as popular with GIs over here as Frank Sinatra is with the women at home.*

Bob Crosby's program is on now. He's pretty good but not as good as Bing. Guess Tennessee has started playing football now. How about sending me the clippings of their games I'd like to see one of their big games this year. That is if they have any. [Actually, the first Tennessee football game of 1944 would not be played until September 30.]

Baby hope you understand why I don't talk about activities here other than personal ones. It's all for security. When I come home I'll tell you all about everything you are probably wondering about. There are many things I'd like to write about, but think its best that I don't.

May go to a show in the club tonight, don't know what's playing but it doesn't matter much. Think I'll take a nap now so I'll close now. Hope you are getting mail regular now.—All my love, Bud.

Bud also wrote his mother in one of what had become his infrequent letters to anyone except Thelma:

I wonder if Leonard, Evelyn, and J. Ross took the annual trip to Big Ridge on Labor Day. I sure miss those days. I remember the one three years ago so vividly. We really began to focus on the war we are now in. I guess our conclusions were right. Tell Evelyn we'll go together and take Junior next year.

Frustrated and homesick, but also "plumb tuckered out" at the end of a long day, Bud had no trouble getting to sleep.

CHAPTER 13

Finally Going to Battle

Mission #1

Merseburg, Germany: September 11, 1944

THE CLICK OF THE DOOR handle followed by the squeak of an un-oiled hinge pierced the quiet of the cold hut. It could mean only one thing: a mission to Germany at last.

As the beam from his flashlight cut through the darkness scanning the cots that lined the walls, the CQ (officer in charge of quarters) barked, "Perrin, Vaughn, you're flying today. Chow at 0400. Briefing at 0500." He called other names too, but Bud only heard his and Glenn's.

"Where to?" Bud asked, the nervous reaction of a novice airman about to fly his first mission. He should have known better.

"You'll learn soon enough, lieutenant." His job complete, the CQ turned and exited. The whole interaction took less than thirty seconds, but its impact was both palpable and lasting.

No time to dawdle, Bud thought as he squinted, seeing that his watch read 3:30 a.m. He took a minute to think about Thelma, Junior, and home. Then a quick prayer. "Lord, protect us as we fly," he whispered. He threw the blanket back, swung his legs to the left, and put his feet on the cold, dank floor.

The waning fire in the coke stove gasped its last breath as heat vacated the drafty hut. The adrenaline surging through each crew member kept the lack of heat from their thoughts.

There was little talk, just nervous groans and the rustling of six men stumbling to awaken from fitful sleep while dressing for the day. Another crew in their hut joined Bud and Glenn in readying for the day's mission. Although this was not their first, they shared the fear that gripped the stomachs of the two Belskis crewmen. They tried to keep it from showing, but it was there.

Bud dressed quickly. First, wool uniform pants on top of the long johns in which he had slept. Then socks: a cotton pair for now, with wool ones added later. Then shoes. A cotton undershirt and a wool sweatshirt followed, then his uniform shirt. He winced as he splashed tepid water over his face. *I sure don't need it to wake up*, he thought. *Knowing what we're facing today took care of that. Sure would like to have a hot shower, though.* He chose not to shave.

It was now 3:52, and they had a five-minute walk up the hill to the mess hall. "Ready, Glenn?" Bud whispered, trying not to awaken those men in the hut who weren't flying that day.

"To eat or to fly?" Glenn shot back.

"Both."

"You bet. Let's go get 'em."

They put on their fleece-lined bomber jackets and strode to the door, merging with other 532nd crewmen who were funneling into the path leading to the mess hall. Belskis and Collett had exited their adjacent quarters at the same time. They joined Bud and Glenn, and the four made their way through the chill and dark of this very significant September day.

Each day's final mission decisions were made at headquarters of the U S Eighth Air Force, located in the town of High Wycombe, in Buckinghamshire County thirty miles northwest of the center of London. This nerve center for the 8th, code-named "Pinetree," was located in the facilities and grounds formerly occupied by an elite girls school, Wycombe Abbey. This exclusive school was founded by Miss Frances Dove, the daughter of a Lincolnshire clergyman, on Victoria's Day, September 26, 1896 and was its first headmistress. She died in 1942, shortly before her ninety-fifth birthday. (Lorna Flint, *Wycombe Abbey School 1896-1986 Partial History* (United Kingdom: Wycombe Abbey School, Private Printing, 1989.)

After the outbreak of the war in Europe, the British government, fearing an escalation of the conflict, sought an existing location for conversion into a hub for possible bombing activities into the continent. In the spring of 1942, the British Air Ministry requisitioned Wycombe for this purpose. The school's staff and two hundred

Left: Wycombe Abbey School-
"Pinetree"-circa 1943
Bursar John Luke

Below: Wycombe Abbey - Pinetree
in WWII, 9-27-2013
Photo by J. Ross Greene

Left: Mission Planning
Room, "Pinetree"-circa
1943
Bursar John Luke

female students were given just over two weeks to vacate the campus. Engineers immediately began converting existing facilities and grounds for command use and construction of the requisite infrastructure to serve the needs of the Eighth Bomber Command of the US Army Air Corps. Girls were relocated in numerous private schools all across Great Britain in hopes that when the war ended, they would return to Wycombe Abbey. As it turned out, only a handful did, because most had graduated by the time the war in Europe was over. However, the first class after the war was larger than the number of girls who left in the spring of 1942.

Behind the gate in the brick wall entrance to the school grounds stood a stately three-story, ivy-covered stone structure that served both teaching and administration functions. In front of it, mossy stone walkways led to concrete and stone fountains. Dense greenery, century-old trees, and manicured hedges stood at attention, guarding the pristine beauty of the imposing structure and the Abbey campus.

Behind the main buildings and up a road that wound its way a half a mile through a pine thicket, stood Dawes Hill. There, engineers constructed an underground bunker to house the critical military planning operations.

Inside the bunker, the command center walls were covered with maps of Europe. State-of-the-art communication tools rested neatly on small tables that encircled the large oak table at the center of the room. On the center table lay manuals, photos, and files with details of bombing targets in Western Europe. Each showed the ragged effects of intense and frequent use. Ashtrays filled with snuffed-out cigarette butts, gray ashes, half-full and coffee-stained cups, opened packs of cigarettes, and other items identified the bunker as a well-used and busy facility. This building housed the nerve center of the 8th Air Force's activities and remained on constant alert and as secretive as possible.

Planning for each day's bombing mission began the day before, even before the present day's run had been completed and returning airmen had landed. The results of the current mission factored into the decisions for the upcoming day's assault but did not define it. Bombing success and losses incurred did, however, determine the availability of crews and aircraft.

Weather was also a critical factor, and Britain's weather was especially hard to predict—more so as autumn staggered into winter. Weather projections would often change even as aircraft were forming up (getting into battle formation) over the bases throughout England. After takeoff, each plane circled over the base until all were airborne. Then they would move into their assigned positions in the bomber formation, and all would proceed en masse to the mission target in Germany. The fickle weather would occasionally curtail the day's activities but did not thwart the necessity for a constant focus on the ever-changing conditions. In fact, this never-ending process of iteration had produced the increasingly accurate forecasts so important to mission success.

The aim of the Eighth was to destroy the war-making machinery and capability of the Third Reich. So oil refineries, aircraft manufacturing facilities, ball bearing plants, and munitions factories were among the targets most attacked by all Army Air Corps units. Bridges and marshalling yards, accumulation points for the distribution of these elements of war, were likewise frequent objects of bombing missions.

As each of these elements important to the decision—timing, targets, size of effort and battle order—came together, the final plan for the following day's mission began to take shape. A couple of hours before midnight at Pinetree, information about the probable mission for the next day began to be disseminated by a noisy but effective Teletype machine to the First and Second Air Divisions of the Eighth. The First Division at Brampton Grange, Huntingdon, would then transmit the preliminary alert to its three bomb wings.

Wing officers, in conjunction with operational personnel, would then begin to calculate the more tactical elements of the upcoming mission. These key bombing tactics included bomb loads, routes of flight, fighter support availability and assignments, assembly points, group lead, and formation elements.

The bomb groups in each wing were alerted next. Three bomb groups comprised the 1st Wing of the 1st Division of the 8th AF: the 381st Bomb Group (Heavy) at Ridgewell, the 91st Bomb Group at

Bassingbourn, and the 398th at Nuthampstead. Each group would take the information from the wing commander and begin to make specific preparations for their mission responsibilities. Twenty-four Forts from the 381st had been assigned to bomb the Daimler-Benz Diesel Lorry Works at Gaggenau, Germany, on the tenth.

Intelligence reports indicated that the plant at Gaggenau had been turning out V-1 and V-2 "vengeance" flying bombs. Ridgewell was in a direct line between London and the European launch pads for these terrifying weapons, which were thus more than a nuisance to the boys at Station 167. Occasionally, one would fall short of its intended target and land at Ridgewell, Great Yeldham, or other nearby hamlets. That put taking out the place where these sinister weapons were made high on the Eighth Air Force's list.

Weather on the tenth was good over the Gaggenau target. Visual evaluation deemed bombing results excellent, and there were no enemy aircraft observed. However, one ship was lost to what the report termed "meager inaccurate flak." Try telling any crew ever hit by it that the flak was meager. Flak was both random and insidious, no respecter of airmen or aircraft.

While crews from the Gaggenau mission were finishing interrogation and downing a well-deserved meal, alerts went out to lead group officers selected to participate in the upcoming mission. Successive reports indicated that conditions the next day could be affected by inclement weather. The decision makers at Pinetree would continue monitoring the weather and evaluating enemy flak emplacements and movement. Later, bomb loads would be defined and assembled. The mission was still a go.

A coded Teletype message had communicated the target for the day to the wing intelligence officer (IO), who then referred to the top-secret codebook that identified it by name. That officer then extracted the folders containing photos and intelligence data on the site from the locked file drawer. On each mission, cameras located in "Tail-End Charlie," the last aircraft in the formation, took photographs of the target location. Not only did this chronicle the mission's effectiveness, but it also provided additional intelligence for future missions.

The 1st Wing's target for September 11 had been identified as the dreaded Merseburg, Germany.

Hitler relied heavily on synthetic petroleum products to keep his war machinery running. The chemical firm IG Farben Leuna works, located just south of Merseburg, was one of the two dozen principal production facilities for this fuel. In addition, IG made all of Germany's synthetic rubber and lubricating oil, most of its nickel and magnesium, virtually all of its poison (such as Zyklon-B used in the gas chambers at concentration camps), and most of the gasoline and explosives used by the vengeance rockets. Because of the high production capacity of the plant and the critical nature of its products, Nazi protection of the facility was intense. Berlin, or the "Big B" as it was commonly called, was a formidable target and heavily fortified, as were Cologne, Munich, Ludwigshafen, and others. But no target was better protected by flak emplacements or better guarded by Me-109s and Fw-190s than Merseburg. So when the 8th received their assignment to this city, they knew they were in for a tough day.

Next, the squads scheduled for the following day's run were identified. Their lead officers: pilot, navigator and bombardier, along with other operational staff, would work well into the night defining all the times so critical to an efficiently run mission. Any inaccuracy, miscalculation, or oversight could be disastrous, costing lives and equipment. The 8th had learned that lesson in spades on the first mission to Schweinfurt-Regensburg on August 17, 1943, when weather conditions, miscalculations, and poor tactical decisions contributed to the loss of sixty B-17s and six hundred men. This devastating loss, coupled with a similar one to the same target two months later, crippled the Eighth's daylight bombing efforts for five months. *Schweinfurt* and *Regensburg* were two words that took up permanent residence in the minds of mission planners from that day forward.

By 0300 all planning was complete, and the process of alerting the boys designated for the mission began. A last cup of coffee bolstered the planners as they realized their job was done for another day. But the chosen ones were about to embark on a mission that would put their lives in significant danger. The more spiritual

among the planners prayed their calculations had been right and
the weather would cooperate. They also prayed the airmen would
do their jobs well and return unharmed. On bases throughout England, few servicemen checked the "non-religious" box on a personnel form. War had a way of intensifying and galvanizing a boy's
religious views.

A tense and somber atmosphere hung over the mess hall. The
crowd at lunch and supper meals was more evenly dispersed. Boys
ate at different times within the hour and a half allotted for each
meal. But on mission days, everyone descended on the hall at the
same time. Since there was no place to put their hats at the crowded tables, the boys wore them as they ate. Maybe their mothers
wouldn't know or care about manners, as long as their sons were
safe.

Most conversations took place among crew members, who usually sat together. Coffee was plentiful and tasty. Eggs were fresh, as
they usually were on mission days. Some boys couldn't eat because
of nerves. Others took candy bars to devour on the return trip. For
the most part, the appetites would be much better coming home.
But there would be nothing to eat until the peanut butter and jelly sandwich and shot of rotgut whiskey provided at post-mission
interrogation. Unlike most men on their first mission, the Belskis
crew all ate well.

At 0420 airmen began to leave the mess hall for the mission briefing room. Trucks idled outside. The five-minute ride over a bumpy
road went quickly but added to the nausea that overtook a few of
the airmen. Some got sick before every mission. Others overcame it
after a few turns. But no one took missions in stride. Everyone knew
what was at stake.

As the trucks eased to a stop, the increasingly nervous airmen
crowded toward the entrance to the briefing room. After checking
off his name on the master crew load list, each man grabbed a spot
near the stage at the front. A few stood. Most sat.

Acrid smoke hung over the crowded briefing room. Bud knew
his smoking went against all the physical conditioning he had done

over the years. *I'll quit when I get home*, he thought. No one else in his family had taken up the habit except Leonard, whose Wesleyan Methodist mother didn't know he smoked.

Bud's mother didn't know of his tobacco use either. Neither woman would approve. Despite Bud's new habit, either the smoke that morning or his thoughts about the day's events made him queasy.

His thoughts were interrupted by a gruff command from an officer entering the door to Bud's right: "Ten-hut." It was 0430 on the nose. Punctuality was essential in the Air Force; lives depended on it. The 381st officers scrambled to their feet, standing at attention as the group commander made his way forward. Just as in the

381st Mission Briefing Quarters-September 12, 1943
USAAF - 381st

training film they had watched, a black cotton sheet covered the three-legged easel at center stage. "Take your seats, gentlemen," the officer barked.

In contrast, the group commander then used a firm, positive tone to give the troops a pep talk about the job that lay ahead and commendations for their work up to this day. "After takeoff, those jitters will go away," he said, continuing his encouragement.

I don't believe him, Bud thought, *but I'd best keep that to myself.*

His introduction completed and aware of his audience's eagerness to know today's target, the command officer (CO) turned the briefing over to the IO, who stepped up, pointer in hand. He immediately pulled the black cover away from the easel as he said, "The target for today is Merseburg."

Bud was relieved. He had expected Berlin instead. Instead of sighs of relief or cheers, though, moans came from men all across the room. *Those are boys who've flown missions before,* Bud observed. *That can't be good news.*

"OK boys, control your happiness," the IO said with a tinge of sarcasm. "Merseburg's a tough target, no doubt, but our intelligence information and fighter aircraft protection have improved with each visit there. And today, we're going in with a real powerful load."

The room fell silent. The officer then used his pointer to follow the red ribbon that snaked its way along the map from Ridgewell up the east coast of England, across the English Channel, down across France to the target at Merseburg, and then back to England.

The flak officer then took over the briefing. "Merseburg is a critical refinery of the Reich. There should be fighter resistance well before the IP (initial point, the designated point at which the bomb run commenced), both Me-109 and Fw-190. We haven't seen any Me-262s on recent missions. Flak will be heavy, increasing as you get closer to the target. You'll have plenty of escorts during the entire mission, from the coast to the target and back. (Note: without escort from P-38, P-47 and in particular P-51 aircraft, USAAF B-17 and B-24 heavies were vulnerable to the power of Luftwaffe fighters. With escorts, they were better able to get through and stay on course throughout a bomb run from IP to RP [rally point, or location where the aircraft were to re-group for the return leg of the mission] and back to base.) Stay on the target all the way through to the RP. Then hightail it on back."

He then moved to some photographic maps of the target area displayed via an overhead projector with key topographic elements of the terrain identified. "Bombing with visual identification may be difficult, as it looks like you'll encounter a moderately-dense undercast at the target. We have a Pff ship leading the group, so the weather won't control the bombing."

He defined escape routes into Holland and Belgium and also reminded them of a 381st airman from the first Schweinfurt raid who had been protected by the French underground and ultimately returned to Ridgewell. Some thought this information was reassuring; others, terrifying. But no one dismissed it out of hand.

"Don't forget your escape and evasion pack," the Ops officer reminded them. "You'll probably never need them, but don't get

Escape and Evasion Photos of Lt. Ross W. Perrin, Jr.-September, 1944
Perrin Family Collection

caught without them. No personal items—check those with the quartermaster. Dog tags only. No personal photos, only the European ones in your evasion kit. (Note: airmen carried photos made to look European, so evasion documents could be made if they found their way to the Underground.) Name, rank, and serial number is all you give if captured. Stay safe, gentlemen, and bust their chops."

The group navigator then called each pilot's name, identifying his respective position in the formation. The Belskis crew would be flying in the outside of the high element. He then went over the times. "Stations: 0700, Start Engines: 0715, Taxi: 0730, First Take Off: 0745, Last Take Off: 0855." Bud wrote the times on his palm but, along with Leo, Glenn, and Jim, he would receive a formation sheet that would list them all. The navigator called for a time hack, a time coordination process intended to further ensure precision: "Five, four, three, two, one, hack." Each man noted the hack time on his watch.

The CO then returned to the stage with some final reminders. "We went to Merseburg two times late in July with reported direct hits on the big refineries. Flak was moderate on the twenty-eighth but more intense the next day. On the twenty-eighth the Nazis used fire pots to obscure the target. We bombed effectively with Pathfinders. They've rebuilt some, so we're going back. Expect opposition, and probably significant undercast. It's a tough target, but you're a tough group of boys. Keep the formations tight. Stay on the target. No evasive movement during the run. We'd like this to be the last time we have to go to Merseburg, so do a great job" (Note: 381st Bomb Group War Diaries, data for missions on July 28 and 29, 1944).

The group briefing adjourned, and each officer moved to an informal briefing with other officers of his discipline. Bud and his fellow bombardiers studied maps, noting key landmarks connected with the target, the Luna refinery. *I can do this,* he told himself. *I'm ready.*

The time was now 6:15, forty-five minutes to station time. Bud lined up to pick up his flight gear. He had left his personal effects in the barracks. *That was probably a mistake,* he thought. *I've heard about theft in some huts, as hard as it is to believe.* Next, his musings turned somber. *And if I don't make it back, vultures will descend on anything left in the barracks. My rings, the watch Dad gave me, my billfold and money will be more likely to get to Thelma if I check 'em. Next time. Too late now.*

He donned the flight gear. First came the flight suit with insulated wires that would be plugged into the aircraft's electrical system. This lifeline would provide the heat to help him survive in the fifty-below-zero temperatures they would experience at 30,000 feet. Another pair of protective pants covered his wool uniform trousers. Heated shoe covers inserted into rubber flight boots would provide heat to his lower body. A yellow Mae West life preserver in case they had to ditch in water and leather flight helmet completed his critical protection from the extreme conditions he would experience for the next seven hours.

Lastly, Bud checked out the secret Norden bombsight, the aiming device used by bombardiers to sight in on the target for minimum error and maximum effectiveness and treated like gold. He had to check it out with a signature, carry it to the aircraft in a black protective container, and return it to the locked and guarded Norden repository after the flight. In the event of a crash landing and imminent capture, he was to destroy it with his forty-five caliber hand gun.

The entire Belskis crew, four officers and five enlisted men, met in front of the combat locker for the truck ride across the field to the 532nd's group of hardstands where the assigned B-17 was parked. The boys were quiet, each lost in his thoughts as they prepared for their maiden voyage under real enemy fire. They had practiced much of what they would do, but that was practice. Today would be for keeps.

The truck stopped by the drab green but elegant bird that would be both their protection and their weapon for that day. It was 0700. Each man relieved himself on the ground around the hardstand, not an easy task with all the bulky clothing and electrical wires. It was, however, a lot easier than using a relief tube would be at 30,000 feet, buffeted by winds, unable to escape the piercing cold on their exposed parts, and balancing a walk-around oxygen bottle.

At the eastern end of the main runway, the light of morning was peeking just above the horizon. A slight breeze blew from the west, and a fine mist hung ominously over the airfield. The corn in the field next to the runway wafted in the breeze, unconcerned at the danger the men were about to face. The ground crew was busy attending to their final checklists. The auxiliary power unit hummed as it provided initial service to the Fort.

Bud, the first officer to enter the aircraft, placed the Norden and his flight bag inside the lower hatch just below and behind his bombardier's position. Grabbing the cold steel rail of the opening, he easily swung his 156-pound body up through the hatch.

Bud put the bombsight in position, locked it into place, and began his checklist for takeoff. He carefully checked the positions of toggle switches on the instrument board to his left. The bomb bay tank safety switches were properly in the off position as were the others on the board. His interphone worked. He confirmed the equipment list: bombardier kit, target folder and weather data, oxygen and mask, parachute, life vest, and spare fuses. He then confirmed pre-flighting of the Norden, including calibrating the internal disc

Norden Bombsite,
Liberty Belle
January, 2010
*Photo by J. Ross
Greene*

Bombardier Instrument Panel
Liberty Belle-January, 2010
Photo by J. Ross Greene

View from B-17 bombardier seat, *Liberty Belle*-January, 2010
Photo by J. Ross Greene

using the Jaeger tachometer. Lastly he confirmed the airworthiness of the guns, turrets, gun sights, and camera intervalometer.

He plugged into the interphone. Even before flipping the switch to the communication system, he could hear Belskis and Vaughn walking through their critical checklist: "Gear switch?"

"Neutral."

"Turbos?"

"Off."

"Throttles?"

"Closed."

"Autopilot?""Off."

"Generators?"

"Off" and so on.

With checklist complete, at precisely 0715 the number two engine strained, choked, turned over, caught, and started. Its initial rattling disguised the power of the Fortress. The same engine then coughed, sputtered and belched dark gray smoke. After almost a minute, it smoothed out, and the powerful hum that resulted brought confident smiles to the ground crew who took loving care of their baby. Each engine progressed methodically through the same ritual until all four motors strained like stallions, eager to get on with the day's work.

All four squadrons of the 381st BG: the 532nd, 533rd, 534th, and 535th, had crews assigned to the total of thirty-seven that would attack the refinery. With additional spare crews, including a Mickey ship (a B-17 outfitted with a Pathfinder navigation system, an early radar device that assisted bombing missions in the often-cloudy skies of Europe) assigned to the mission, a total of forty-one B-17s would rise over Ridgewell airspace that Monday morning. Capt. Douglas L. Winter, an experienced and respected pilot, commanded the lead ship.

Leo looked at the thin sheet of onionskin he and the other officers were issued at pre-flight in the crew room. This important document identified each aircraft in the formation. Appropriately nicknamed a "flimsie," it also listed all times pertinent to takeoff and gave a diagram of the three elements of the group's formation: lead, low and high. Each aircraft was further designated on the flimsie by the pilot's name and the identification number on the tail of each aircraft. To prevent this critical data from falling into enemy hands, they were instructed at briefing that the flimsie could be chewed and swallowed. It did resemble a thin sheet of phyllo pastry, but no one admitted checking to see if it possessed a similar taste.

At the appropriate time, each pilot turned his ship from the hardstand to the perimeter path connecting his parking position to the runway. Guided by the flimsie, Leo followed suit. Each Flying Fortress moved along in a halting single file, lunging forward and then stopping abruptly as the pilots tried to maintain continuity of the lumbering bomber parade.

The stench of fuel and belching smoke from the tightly-bunched aircraft hung low over the field. The open mic allowed all to hear Elvis McCoy cough and clear his throat, irritated by the heated fumes wafting through the waist window. "Sorry, boys," McCoy said.

"It's getting to me, too," Collett chimed in. Despite the semi-tight seals on windows and other openings, the flight deck crew sat in the wake of the exhaust from the aircraft ahead of them. Further back, the gunners had even less protection due to the open waist windows. Their eyes and throats also suffered from the effects of the fumes. "OK, boys, hold down the chatter, we're about to launch this eggbeater. We'll get some clean air in a few minutes," instructed Leo.

Urging the craft forward, he turned it ninety degrees to the right and guided it to an abrupt stop at the end of the main runway. Out of the exhaust stream, the air cleared somewhat.

Aircraft were scheduled to take off at one-minute intervals. As the plane in front of them gained speed down the swell of the main runway, Leo and Glenn moved the throttles forward, revving engine power to its full level. With the brakes also fully applied, the Fort seemed to groan as it strained to be loosed from its restraint. Finally, the plane ahead lifted off and disappeared into the mist. Leo then released the brakes, allowing the Fortress to lurch forward. It gained speed over the next 3,500 feet, reached takeoff speed of 115 miles per hour, rotated, and lifted off to begin their nine-hour journey. "We're on our way, boys," Leo said across the interphone. "Strap it on."

The takeoff, one of the most terrifying portions of a mission, had been successful. Next to the bomb run, the flight segment that followed takeoff was probably the most dangerous. In excess of one thousand bombers, B-17s and B-24 Liberators would form up (align the aircraft into the assigned formation for the trip to the target) over southeast England on each mission day. Coupled with the unpredictable and often soupy weather over the continent, the crowded sky was hazardous at best. Add topped-off fuel tanks and each aircraft's full rack of 500-pound bombs to the mix, and the airspace over England was a boiling cauldron of risk.

Looking through the plastic canopy that gave him what was probably the best view of the entire crew, Bud could see that they were still "in the soup." Visibility was nil as they continued their climb to the elevation where they would form up. On large missions it would take well over an hour to allow each bomb squad, group, and wing in the First Division to maneuver into the assigned slot for the three-hour, 600-mile trip to central Germany. When the Second and Third Air Divisions were also involved, as they were on that day, the process could take two hours.

After what seemed an eternity but was only about fifteen minutes, the Belskis crew's B-17 broke through the cloud cover. As they looked around, they found a semblance of order among the aircraft as each moved above the cloud formation. Some of the planes were olive drab like theirs. Others were unpainted, glistening like silver in the early-morning sun.

In early 1944, combat aircraft were left unpainted. For the B-17, the resulting weight reduction was close to a hundred pounds. Multiplied by the thousands of planes produced, the change yielded a significant savings in fuel costs.

Belskis then came over the interphone, "Radio check." Each man checked in, confirming that his communication link to other crewmates was working. "Let's go to oxygen," the pilot instructed. "We've got another hour before we head for the continent. Let's preserve our energy. We'll need it."

Following his orders, the men donned the masks that kept them connected to the oxygen supply. Since the B-17 was unpressurized, this umbilical attachment was essential. Without it, anoxia could occur in minutes, resulting in a blackout and quick death. As their altitude increased, the necessity for a constant connection became greater. The cruising altitude for the trip to Germany would be 28,000 feet, close to the maximum recommended for the B-17.

When a crew member had to move from his station for any reason, it was essential that he attach himself to a walk-around oxygen bottle. Found at numerous locations throughout the airplane, these metal containers provided the crew with essential mobility. The excitement of the flight made it easy to forget this necessary step. Each boy looked out for the others, constantly reminding anyone who left his station to "hook up to air." Anoxia and frostbite had proved to be almost as great a risk to crew safety as flak and the Luftwaffe. Anoxia was controllable by attention to protocol. Frostbite, however, was more sinister. Temperatures at altitude often dipped to sixty below zero Fahrenheit. Failure of the electrical system could render heated suits and gloves inoperable. Even when the system worked perfectly, cold often overcame the level of heat it produced. And keeping all parts of the body protected from the biting cold at all times was nearly impossible. A few seconds of exposure to this extreme cold could result in severe and sometimes permanent impairment of extremities.

The thirty-seven 381st B-17s had successfully formed around the guiding flare ship. The other 1st Wing groups had done likewise, as had the aircraft from the 2nd and 3rd Wings. United, they all then turned toward northern Europe for the next phase of the mission.

As they crossed the English coast, the weather was a clear 2/10 (twenty percent cloud cover under the formation), providing a good view of the gigantic bomber stream boring holes in the sky and taking the fight to Hitler. As they moved further across the channel, the undercast cloud cover they had been told to expect became a reality at 3/10.

"Think we oughtta check guns, Leo?" Vaughn inquired of his boss.

"Good idea," Leo responded and opened his mic. "Check your guns, boys."

The two turret gunners, Newman in the ball turret and Lauret in the top one, quickly entered the cramped environment that would hold them captive until they got back to the Channel later in the day. Rogers had already crawled the twenty-five feet back through the narrowing fuselage and into the tail gunner position. McCoy and Suggs stood at the ready behind the 50mm guns on either side of the waist. Unlike Lauret and Rogers, the waist gunners could stand as they operated their weapons. The five enlisted gunners quickly fired off bursts of ammo, making sure no blockage existed. Bud fired the chin turret on either side of the nose and Collett likewise checked his guns. All were operational.

They each reported the good news to the cockpit, and none too soon. As they crossed the French border, three Me-109s darted beneath the bomber stream. As quickly as they came into view, they disappeared again. "Let's be alert, boys, no chatter," Leo warned. The Messerschmitt Bf Me-109 was easy to distinguish from the Focke Wulf Fw-190. Both were fast, but the Messerschmitt had a sleeker profile as a result of its in-line engine. In contrast to the 109s, the 190 had a blunt nose resulting from its radial engine, much like the American P-47.

Walkway through Bomb Bay -
Liberty Belle B-17G-January, 2010
Photo by J. Ross Greene

Time to arm the ordinance, Bud thought. He grabbed the walk-around bottle in one hand as he turned and exited toward the bomb bay immediately behind and below his position. Next, he gingerly navigated the six-inch wide metal walkway leading to the bomb rack. Each bombardier was well aware that the bomb doors below the walkway would open if he made a misstep and dropped onto them. Three 500-pound bombs hung in the rack on his left and two in the one on his right. One by one, he removed the fuse pin from each bomb, releasing a small propeller in its tip. When the bomb was dropped, this propeller caused the ordnance to fall true and straight without tumbling and falling off target. His task accomplished, Bud turned and retraced his steps back to his seat in the nose of the plane.

Following the enemy sighting, the trip became quiet. *I guess this is the calm before the storm,* Bud thought. *I wonder what Thelma's doing right now? It's a little after midnight in Knoxville. That little night owl's probably banging out a letter to me on the used Royal machine, the one with the "errant 8."* For some odd reason, when Thelma tried to type an apostrophe, the machine inserted an 8 instead, so words like *I'm* usually came out as "*I8m.*" Bud smiled as he pictured Thelma in her pajamas and housecoat sitting cross-legged at the dining room table. But Leo's voice crackled over the interphone, jolting him back to reality.

"Communication check." The OKs came back one by one.

"I gotta take a leak." Rogers interjected with a slight laugh.

"Use the tube, Tex," Vaughn shot back.

Collett was engrossed in the maps on the table in front of him, making sure that the plane was on course. The lead navigator and the Mickey man in the Pathfinder ship at the front of the 381st bomber formation directed the course of the group. Each bomb group (BG) and wing, as well as each division, had a lead ship. But as the craft neared the IP, the navigator and bombardier in each aircraft were charged with finding the visible landmarks that would identify their position relative to it. If the mission was operating by instruments, intricate calculations would replace visual sighting.

Upon reaching the IP, the lead ship would fire a flare, alerting the combat element that he was about to turn. After the flare, the lead pilot would proceed for twenty seconds, then make his turn. Ships in his element would follow. Successive groups would proceed for fifteen more seconds before turning to the bomb run. Through this maneuver, the tight three-element formation would be broken and each element would follow the other in a single-line formation. At that point, the most critical and dangerous segment of the mission began.

Flak began to appear. First it was light, small puffs of smoke that looked like pregnant cherry bombs, no larger than 50mm. Then the explosions were much more plentiful, intense, and larger. *Probably 88mm,* Bud thought. *And the ones that seem like exploding fifty-gallon oil drums must be the dreaded 105s. They warned us that the Nazis had concentrated flak guns in concentric circles around key targets,* he recalled. *If oil supplies aren't key targets, I don't know what are. The explosions are getting worse, and we're not even on the bomb run.*

Leo noticed a group of 190s off to the right. "Fighters at two o'clock," came his warning over the interphone. But the intruders zoomed away, chased by a group of P-51s.

Flak is terrifying, Bud thought. *The fighters are finite and visible. But flak is indiscriminate. You don't know where it will explode and what it will do. This is some welcome to combat.* In mid-thought, multiple pieces of flak metal struck the fuselage right under where he was sitting. "Crap!" he said aloud.

From his wooden desk to the left and behind Perrin's bombardier position in the nose, navigator Jim Collett leaned to the right and caught Bud's eye through the bomb bay. He pulled his mask slightly away from his face so Bud could read his lips and hopefully hear above the drone of the engines and bursts of flak. "We're not far from the IP," Collett said in a loud voice. Bud pointed upward to the flight deck, indicating that he should alert Leo and Glenn. Collett complied.

In minutes, the lead ship confirmed the IP. In concert with the entire bomber stream, Belskis and Vaughn had spent the last quarter hour dropping the altitude to 20,000 feet. Following the element in front of him, Leo banked right, intercepting the IP. "We're on the bomb run now, boys. This is what we came for," Collett told the crew.

The next fifteen minutes were stark terror. Bud and the rest of the Belskis crew had heard countless stories about B-17s taking incredible beatings in combat and returning to base with the crew distraught but alive. But at this moment, they found themselves discounting what they had heard. Buffeted by the slipstream created by the planes ahead and the bursts of air from exploding flak, the B-17G strained and creaked. *Will this mighty ship come apart?* Bud wondered.

About that time a loud pinging sound announced the entrance of a metal flak shard. It came through at Bud's left, just below the toggle switches that would activate the bomb drop, careened across behind his swivel seat, and came to rest beneath the instrument panel on his right. *It looks like the kind of metal bolt that gave me a punctured tire on Magnolia Avenue in Knoxville late one evening,* Bud thought. *But that was frustrating. This is surreal.*

Bud toggled open the bomb bay doors and twisted the right knob on the Norden, adjusting the crosshairs to find the midpoint of the target area. The adjustments for wind, drift, elevation, and air speed had already been programmed into the bombsight. He flipped the toggle switch with his right hand and announced, "Bombs away."

500# Bomb in Bay of B-17 *Liberty Belle*, January 2010
Photo by J. Ross Greene

The plane lurched upward, losing a ton of its total weight via the five descending bombs.

We did it! thought Bud. *Now for the rest of the job.* Fighter opposition was sparse on the run, but it could show up at any moment. Gunners had to be ready.

As the bomb run concluded, Leo was already searching for the RP. Following the stream of bombers, he dropped the craft the assigned thousand feet below the bomb run altitude. Upon reaching the RP, he maneuvered the thirty-ton behemoth into the normal pattern for the return home. Flak was still moderately heavy, but the group reported no Luftwaffe sightings for an hour. As they approached the Belgian border, they sighted a squadron of FW-190s off to the east, but the German fighters didn't approach the bomber stream.

As they crossed over the channel, the famed white cliffs of Dover came into view off to the right. *What a beautiful sight,* Bud thought. *Even more so than* [British singer] *Vera Lynn's mellow rendition of that song I love.*

By now, chatter on the interphone among the Belskis crewmates was lively—and a little bawdy. *One mission down, thirty-four to go,* Bud thought. *If the rest are like this one, we'll all be gray-headed by Christmas.*

The landing was uneventful. After rolling to their assigned

hardstand, Leo turned the ship around to position it well for the next mission, but he didn't need to. The ground crew had work to do to prepare it for any upcoming flights. In addition to normal service, the flak holes in the aluminum skin needed repair.

Not only was each mission designed to destroy Hitler's ability to wage war, but it also served as a reconnaissance effort for future attacks on the Reich. That made post-flight interrogation an important follow-up to the day's work. But first, the ravenous airmen had to be fed—at least a snack to tide them over until they could get to the mess hall. A peanut butter and jelly sandwich served with some low-grade whiskey was the bill of fare at these Ridgewell sessions. Not milk, not Coca-Cola, not water, but whiskey. The choice seemed consistent with the many other aspects of military life that didn't make sense.

Bud downed his sandwich in short order, but the shot of whiskey was another matter. He was a beer man. Beer-drinking was only an occasional activity before he joined the service, although his taste had increased in the last couple of years—but not for hard liquor. One sip of the whiskey confirmed his disdain. "Got any water?" he asked.

The interrogation officers first wanted to know if anything unusual had happened on the mission. Since this was their first foray into the belly of the beast, everything was unusual to the Belskis crew. But for the questioners, that answer wouldn't suffice.

"See any aircraft shot down?" "What enemy aircraft were present?" "Where were you?" "When?" "What was your altitude at the time?" "How did your craft perform?" "What problems did you have?" Each crew member answered the questions pertinent to him. Sometimes two or more gave input on the same question.

The interviewing officers took meticulous notes, which would become a valuable part of the repository of intelligence that aided the planning of future missions and could save crew's lives. Everyone took the debriefing sessions seriously.

Bud told of the Me-109 sighting prior to the IP and the large group before they reached the Belgian coast on the return. All agreed that the flak on the run was heavy. "The lead Pff crew called it moderate and inaccurate," one of the IOs revealed.

"Inaccurate I can buy," Bud said. "But if that was moderate, I hate to know what heavy looks like."

Vaughn nodded his head in agreement. In unison, Belskis and Collet said, "Right."

With interrogation complete, the men scurried off to the mess hall, where conversation about the mission continued with other crews. All 381st crews returned to Ridgewell without injuries. Unknown to them, on this day, eleven aircraft from the Bloody 100th Bomb Group (Heavy) at Thorpe Abbotts were lost on the Merseburg mission. Eight of the ships and seventy-six of the men came from one bomb squadron, the 305th, stationed seventy miles from Ridgewell, a devastating tally.

Bud fell into bed at 8:00 p.m., spent and relieved. Compared to the sixty-below temperature at 28,000 feet, the current sixty-but-drafty degrees in the barracks seemed toasty. He slept hard and well.

(Note: 8th AAF Mission 623 was flown on Monday September 11, 1944: 1,131 bombers and 440 fighters were dispatched to hit both synthetic oil plants and refineries in Germany. On the total mission an estimated 525 Luftwaffe fighters were encountered; 111 of 351 B-17s were dispatched to hit oil refineries at Merseburg; 13 B-17s were lost, 2 damaged beyond repair and 106 damaged; 2 airmen were KIA, 21 WIA and 120 MIA. Fighter escort was provided by 247 P-47s and P-51s; they claimed kills of 13 aircraft in the air and 4 on the ground; 3 P-51s were lost, 2 damaged beyond repair and 2 P-47s and 4 P-51s damaged; 3 pilots were MIA. Source: WWII 8th AAF Combat Chronology-www.8thafhs.org.)

CHAPTER 14

Hurry Up and Wait

Slowly Counting Missions

Ridgewell, England: September 12–24, 1944

THE FOLLOWING MORNING, RAUCOUS LAUGHTER from the other end of the barracks jarred Bud awake. Checking his watch, he realized he had no time to waste. He had a scheduled navigator training session at 0930. Addled from the deep sleep that followed the long-awaited first mission, he rolled over, pulled the blanket over his head, and closed his eyes. Nothing, however, could protect him from the abrasive cackle spewing from the other end of the room. From beneath the nominal protection of his blanket, he whispered to Glenn, "Who is that idiot?"

"Some friend of the other crew," Vaughn grunted as he glared at the source of the unwelcome sound, wiping shaving cream from his face as he sat down on his bunk.

Mumbling his displeasure, Bud struggled from the warmth of the bed to the chill of the barracks. *Better write Thelma while I've got a few minutes,* he thought. Grabbing his pen and paper, he slid halfway back under the covers to begin his note. The unwanted clamor from the other end of the room continued as Bud wrote:

> *Good Morning Sweetheart,—Your ole poppy was too tired to write last night, sorta had a long and rough day—went to bed at eight and slept until almost eight this morning.*
>
> *I had a letter from mother waiting for me last night, but none from you. Hers was written Aug. 10th—must have been delayed somewhere. Just heard one of the fellows who was going home singing, "No more fighters, no more flak. Ho ho ho. I'm going back."—thought that was*

*pretty good. Anyway, he was happy and quite boister-
ous. I'll have to make this short since I have something
on my schedule in a few minutes. Just wanted to get a
note in the mail to you. I also need to escape the boisterous activities of some visitors who are interrupting our
otherwise quiet morning. Be a sweet gal and take care
of Junior. Hope you ain't having any trouble with him.
I'll write again tonight but right now I've got to run—so
long. All my love, Bud*

With little time to spare, Bud splashed cold water onto his face,
threw on his clothes, and rushed into the still-foggy morning of East
Anglia. The ground school meeting would take place fifteen minutes
away. Thanks to his trusty bike, he made it in twelve.

On days when crews stood down or no missions were flown from
Ridgewell, the boys kept busy with ground schools and updates. Updates usually included changes in enemy protocol, locations of flak
emplacements, Luftwaffe air assault changes, and sometimes new
Nazi aircraft. Air Force Intelligence had information on a jet-pro-
pelled fighter, the Me-262 Swallow, introduced by the Luftwaffe
late in the summer. Reports of its speed were quite impressive and
led to increased concern among fliers. The fighter was said to be
fifty percent faster than the P-51 and British Spitfire. If it rivaled the
P-51, it certainly commanded the airmen's attention.

But today, Bud was taking additional navigator training. Nearing
reclassification to this new position meant he had spent a number of
hours studying, attending classes, and flying local training missions
to practice the skills needed to guide bomber crews safely to the
heart of the Reich and back. This class was one of the final requirements between him and the coveted assignment. Certification as a
navigator would also mean he could fly as both a bombardier and
a navigator. But on flights as a navigator, he might have to fly as a
crew replacement (substitute in crews other than his regular assignment). It could also mean that missions would not be as frequent.
It's not in my hands, Bud thought. *Let's just see what happens.*

The class design kept the discussion and interrogation rapid and
intense. Quick but well-analyzed decisions were essential when

flying a 1,200-mile round-trip mission to Germany under the severe conditions of extreme cold, 10/10 cloud cover, tight formations, and fire from both flak and darting Luftwaffe fighters. The
intensity of pre-flight training had helped Bud increase focus in the
classroom and sharpen application in the practical environment.
He not only kept up with the intense pace, he thrived on it. The
training also gave him renewed enthusiasm for whatever vocation
he would pursue at war's end.

The class concluded shortly before noon, and Bud hurried to
his bike leaning against the building, slung his leg over the seat,
and rode off toward the officers' mess. The front wheel wobbled
as he navigated the ruts, rocks, and mud puddles that, along with
the bike's hand brakes, served as constant challenges to the biker's
skill. Ten adventurous minutes later, he arrived at the mess hall,
parked his ride among a hundred others placed in ragged fashion
either against the building or on the ground, and joined the other
eager officers as they streamed inside.

The officers' mess consisted of two long Nissen huts parallel to
each other and connected in the middle of each to form a T-shaped
structure. Red brick walls covered with rough-cast concrete stucco
enclosed the end of each building. Adjacent to the adjoined buildings at their connecting point was a smaller Nissan hut, similarly
constructed, where all the food was prepared. A concrete walkway
roughened by stone aggregate popping out on the surface connected the kitchen to the mess hall. There, the staff served the hordes of
hungry airmen from two parallel central serving lines.

Bud got his food and headed toward a vacant table at the end of
one leg of the hall. Almost immediately, he noticed the 532nd bombardier leader, Harvey Tidwell. Someone had pointed out Harvey at
the OC a few days earlier, and Bud saw him again at the Merseburg
briefing the day before, but the two had never met. Today, he took
the opportunity to become better acquainted. Not only did his bombardier position make him someone to know, but "Harv," as he was
known, was by all accounts a card fanatic and much-sought-after
bridge partner.

"Captain Tidwell, I'm Ross Perrin of your 532nd, may I join you?"
Bud asked.

Bombardier-Lt. Harvey Tidwell,
532nd BS Lead Bombardier-1944
Tidwell Family Collection

"Call me Harv, and absolutely, Lieutenant," Tidwell shot back with friendly acceptance. "Have a seat."

"Where are you from, Captain?"

"Originally, West Tennessee."

Bud smiled and chuckled, "I'm from the other end of the Volunteer state, Knoxville."

"A hillbilly and a river-rat flatlander. Think England can survive the combination?"

"It's a tossup," Bud said. "I hear you're quite a bridge player."

"Fly, eat, sleep, write home, stay warm, and play cards. What else can you do in jolly ole England? After I finish this grub I'm off to the OC to see if I can make a buck or two—or should I say a quid or two. Wanna come?"

Amid the din of airmen's chatter and the ever-present cigarette smoke, Bud and Tidwell talked of the upcoming World Series, the presidential election a couple of months hence, and the war. After the last sip of what was by then tepid coffee, the two headed outside and off to the OC.

"Hey Tidwell, looks like you've found another sucker?" a laughing airman two tables away hollered as they strode by.

Tidwell smiled and mumbled to Bud, "Some of my *friends*." Not one to let anyone get the best of him, the captain shot back, "I have plenty of money that I won from you two last week before I have to risk any of my own."

The antagonist shook his head as the boys at his table roared with laughter. Bud and Harv smiled at each other and made a beeline to the door. Tidwell's confidence and engaging persona captivated Bud as much as his reputation had before they met. A strong friendship had clearly begun.

Over the next four hours, the two played what seemed like hundreds of hands of gin rummy, smoked far more cigarettes than they should have, and won the tremendous sum of three dollars and change between them. It wasn't the best use of an afternoon, but they both enjoyed it. They decided to call it a day, pushed their chairs from the table, and stood, stretching to relieve their cramped limbs. As they did so, Bud pulled out his billfold to show his new friend Thelma's picture.

"Wow," exclaimed Tidwell. "Those East Tennessee gals sure are pretty, and yours is at the top of the list."

"She was Miss Knoxville in 1940 and competed in the Miss America contest in Atlantic City. I met her after that. and we married in 1942. We're expecting our first little one the last of this year."

"Well then, who's this little guy?" Tidwell asked, pointing to the picture of Bud's nephew next to the one of Thelma.

"That's my sister's boy, named after me," said the proud uncle. "I've told a lot of the boys that he's my son, though. Maybe we'll have one like him or maybe a prissy little girl—it doesn't matter to us."

Tidwell took another look at Thelma's picture, gave a muffled wolf whistle, and handed the billfold back. As they left the OC, he said with a laugh, "I believe this will be the first of many miss-spent days of cards with you, Perrin." His prediction would prove prophetic.

Later that evening Bud, excited to tell Thelma about meeting Tidwell, added to the letter begun twelve hours earlier. By then, the chill of the afternoon had become outright cold.

"I'm sitting here under three wool blankets—have on my long handles and my pajamas over them and I'm just barely comfortable. I'm wondering how the weather is back in K-town," Bud scribbled, trying to balance the book he was using as a desk while keeping the blankets from sliding off onto the floor.

Just then, the boy whose abrasive laugh began Bud's day earlier that morning flung the door open and entered, announcing, "Did you guys miss me?" No one dared state the obvious answer. The uninvited and unwanted visitor strode to the other end of the room, taking up the same seat he occupied earlier. Loud and lewd talk, obviously bolstered by a significant amount of booze, flowed in an almost continuous stream over the next fifteen minutes. "Who's that guy again?" Bud asked Glenn who, like Bud, was writing a letter to his pregnant wife, Alyce.

"I think his name is Tony Fabiani," Vaughn said. "He's been in and out of here all day. I think he has only a couple of missions left. and he's living it up before going home."

"Hey Tony, pipe it down a little bit," Bud hollered. That was a mistake. Fabiani bounded up and strode toward him.

"The name's Antonio, hotshot. What's your problem?"

Both Bud and Glenn stood up quickly. Their 6'0" and 6'2" frames slowed the 5'6" Antonio's advance and muted his belligerence.

"No problem, just interested in a little peace and quiet so we can listen to the radio," Bud responded.

"Oh, we got a hillbilly here." Antonio mocked, recognizing the southern drawl.

"Make that two of us," Vaughn declared.

His antagonist noticed the brown New Testament next to Bud's bunk and decided it might be his way out of a pending physical altercation. He blustered, "Surely you don't believe the fairy tales in that book."

"Every word of it," Bud replied.

"What's your name? You a preacher?"

"Ross. Ross Perrin, and no, I'm not a preacher, just a Christian."

"Yeah, I've heard that Jesus stuff since I was a kid—from nuns who slapped my head and played the bongo drums on my knuckles with a damned ruler. I don't want no more of that malarkey," he said with a smirk. "Keep it to yourself," he added as he turned and walked away.

"That guy could deprive you of your solitude without providing you with company," Bud said to Glenn.

With a little less wind in his sails, Tony quieted down a bit and left a few minutes later. "Good riddance," Glenn said.

Bud returned to his letter.

> . . . *Oh yes, I got a letter from Dorothy Pyles, giving me Jay's address. He's supposed to go to the Pacific on the 23rd, eleven days from now. So sorry to hear about Jimmy Allen.* [James G. Allen, a twenty-year-old from Knoxville, was killed in action on August 15, less than a month earlier.] *I guess you sent flowers—horrible! The Fred Allen show is being broadcast on Armed Forces Radio.*

*Chattanooga Choo Choo is playing right now—wouldn't
mind being on that Choo Choo heading West. I probably
won't write for a couple of days. I'm heading to London
on a 48-hour pass—pretty good huh? One mission and I
get a two-day pass. At this rate I won't be home 'till next
Christmas. I don't want to think about that. I'll close for
now. Remember who loves you. Your Poppy*

Off to London – September 15, 1944

London was about thirty-five miles from Ridgewell as the crow
flies. But the Ridgewell airmen couldn't catch a ride on a crow.
Reaching the downtown area required a short hop in a truck, three
train rides, and a taxi. The trip usually took about three hours, but
any trip to London was worth the hassle.

Bud, Leo, and Collett were all making their initial visits to the
city by the Thames. Forced to stand on the crowded final leg from
Halsted, they exited quickly as the train slowed to a stop. The crowd
in the Liverpool station was uncharacteristically light for a Friday
morning and the wait for a taxi quite short. This made for a good
start to what the boys hoped would be a fun-packed weekend.

A taxi pulled up to the curb, and Bud opened the door. "Hop in,
Yanks, where to?" the driver asked.

"The center of the action," Collett blurted out as they each
dropped their B-4 Air Corps issue clothes bag on the floor of the
taxi.

I guess you mean Piccadilly, right, mate?"

"Sounds good to us," Bud responded as he leaned forward for a
better look out of the front window as the cabbie left the station.
They peered ahead as he navigated the midday traffic. First a right
on Bishopsgate, then as they approached Cannon Street, a bridge
with two large tower structures appeared in the distance to their
left.

"There's London Bridge," Collett exclaimed, "I've seen the picture many times."

"Sorry, mate, that's Tower Bridge. It's a common error made by
many first-timers to the city—it is your first time, isn't it?"

"Rookie mistake," Bud affirmed. "Well, where's London Bridge?

It didn't really fall down, did it?" His attempt at humor landed with a thud.

"Straight away—it's the bridge right in front of us," the driver responded as he turned West on Cannon Street.

It's a pretty plain bridge, nothing fancy. I wonder why people make such a fuss over it. Bud thought, choosing not to offend their impromptu tour guide by sharing his opinion.

As they followed the path of the River Thames past Trafalgar Square and on to Piccadilly Circus, the three airmen turned tourist, continued to gawk at London's sights. But they refrained from confirming their novice status either by asking questions or again asserting their lack of knowledge through false identification of London's attractions.

"We're here, mates. That'll be two quid forty," the driver announced as he screeched to a stop at the intersection of Regent and Piccadilly Streets. "Hope you guys are well-protected. Watch out for the Commandos, they're pretty aggressive," he added with a chuckle.

"I got it," Jim said as he pulled the fare from his pocket. "Thanks for the advice. You're about the thousandth person to school us on that fact."

In their indoctrination to the European Theater of Operation (ETO), all crews received warnings about the young— and old—ladies of the evening who patrolled London streets. The city's West End theater district at Leicester Square and Piccadilly was the center of operation for many of the Piccadilly Commandos, the moniker assigned them by the British press and adopted by Yanks and locals alike.

A familiar (and well-earned) British adage about American servicemen identified them as: "Overpaid, oversexed, and over here." Service men had money, candy, and "smokes." On occasion, each could be used as trade currency, and foolishly chosen companionship was one of many options.

They stood on the corner and gazed across the circular street (intersected by five others) known as Piccadilly Circus. The sidewalks bustled with a mass of people, eyes pointing straight ahead or down at the sidewalk, all in a hurry. Times were tough across the whole of Europe, but London had taken an extra measure of abuse at the hands of both the Luftwaffe and Hitler's Vengeance rockets. Neither pedestrians nor cars were in a mood to dawdle. Black cars and taxis intermingled with double-decker red buses, all honking as

Picadilly Circus, London- circa 1940
Public Domain

they hurried to reach their destinations.

Bud scanned the many large lighted signs adorning the ornate buildings. "Schweppes Tonic Water. . . Wrigley's—for vim and vigor. . . Gordon's Gin," he read aloud.

"Hey Perrin, 'Guinness Time—Guinness is good for you,'" Collett exclaimed as he read the ad for the liquor that was a staple for British imbibers. The slogan adorned the popular black sign featuring a prominent clock next to the Schweppes logo. "Sounds right to this old boy."

"What's 'Bovril'?" Bud asked as he looked at the large capital letters above the Schweppes sign. "It's gotta be good to have an advertisement that big."

"Or horrible," Jim shot back. "Have you ever tasted that stuff? It tastes like over salted. . . " He stopped mid-sentence, unable to describe the disdain he held for the popular British meat extract used as a condiment. Most servicemen considered Bovril foul-tasting and odiferous, an unappetizing delicacy that required time to get used to. And most of them didn't want to give time to such a task.

The three neophyte tourists spent a few more minutes gawking. "I wonder what that is," said Bud, pointing to a large monument, its top adorned with an angel, in the center of Piccadilly. Apparently, Collett was not the only one to hear him.

"Need a guide, boys?" inquired a shapely young woman.

"Yes, ma'am," Bud replied respectfully.

"You can drop the ma'am, flyboy. I'm younger than you," she said coyly, cocking her head to one side and smiling. "That's the Shaftsbury Memorial Fountain topped by the statue called the *Angel of Christian Charity*. It's been there for over fifty years. Anything else I can help you with?" she asked in her best come-hither voice.

"That's about it, thanks much—*ma'am*," Bud said, using the pause to emphasize that his answer to the implied but well-understood question was, "Nope, I'm not buying what you're selling."

She smiled, gave a little four-finger wave, and strutted down Piccadilly toward Leicester Square. Bud and Jim looked at each other and laughed. "London may be in the same country as Ridgewell, but it's in a different world," Bud said.

"Right, let's get to the Officers' Club, drop the luggage, and get some fish and chips," Collett barked as he glanced right, remembering the different traffic flow direction in England.

"Think I'll stay here a while," said Leo. "Let's meet up later tonight for some dinner and a few brews. How 'bout the corner pub behind Leicester Square at 1900, I mean seven. OK?"

"I may go back early," Bud said. "You boys meet and if I don't go back to Ridgewell, I'll join you."

Looking right just before crossing the street instead of left, as was the imperative in the States, was tough for visitors to the UK to learn. Mental muscle memory had been programmed the opposite way for more than two decades. But failure to remember that traffic flowed on the left side of the road could be lethal. Reminding each other to look right, Jim and Bud walked the two blocks to the OC, checked in, washed up, and were off again to take in more of the city.

Trafalgar Square was the first of many stops that Friday afternoon.

From the steps of the National Gallery they could see the stately St. Martin's in the Field Church, with its towering spire, to their left. As they scanned clockwise, the panorama improved. Below were the fountains of Trafalgar and Lord Nelson's Column rising up tall and silent amidst the hubbub below. The four massive male lion statues that surrounded the fountains seemed to protect Big Ben, the classic clock atop Parliament clearly visible in the distance. After a half hour immersed in the historic beauty of the setting, they walked down Trafalgar, through Admiralty Arch, and turned down the long straight Mall Road toward Buckingham Palace.

"Reckon King George is expecting us?" Bud asked with a laugh. "Let's go pick him up, then run by Ten Downing, get Churchill, and head to his favorite pub for an evening of elbow-bending. Sound like fun?"

"Dream on. I think George and Winston have their hands full, as do we," Jim said as they wasted no time making their way to Buckingham Palace.

"There's nothing like this in the US," Bud asserted, gazing at the massive structure.

"Probably not, but how would you know? You'd never been out of the South until you joined the Army. And you've still never been west of Texas or north of Kentucky. This is your first exposure to class and history," Collett teased with a sarcastic smile.

"Hey, world traveler, I remember you whining the other night about having no money and not being able to go anywhere as a kid. And here you are, ragging on me."

They both knew the good-natured ribbing was just that. So they took the path through Green Park and headed to Hyde Park. "*Hyde Park is pretty, but I've seen lots better at home. It would have been prettier if you had been with me, though*," Bud would later write to Thelma. "*I know you never give it a thought, but your old Poppy is still just as true as could be to Mommy and always will be. Just wanted to mention that after some of the things I've seen here in London*," he would say, reflecting on the questionable conduct he witnessed there.

The two days passed quickly. Shopping at the PX for white socks and another wool shirt, a brew or two at a couple of pubs, and visiting other sites on the tourist list kept them all busy. Bud decided he would go back to Ridgewell a little early. He hadn't heard from Thelma in some time and was concerned. "I hope I have letters waiting when I get back," he told Jim and Leo.

His return trip to Ridgewell was faster than Friday's journey to London. He got a seat on both trains and was able to catch a welcome catnap on the segment out of London. *Back to the war,* he thought.

Ridgewell, England – September 18, 1944

No letters awaited Bud when he returned, which left him wishing he had stayed in London. But two from Thelma the following day lifted his spirits for a short time. *"Grover has been shot down and is listed as MIA,"* she wrote. *"He was on his 5th mission on August 23rd. Henrietta is quite upset as could be expected, but hopeful because witnesses reported seeing parachutes open after the plane was hit."*

The news stunned Bud. Holding the letter, he dropped his hands to his side. *I wonder how he's handling it—or if he's even alive,* he thought. *He's such a sensitive guy, and so devoted to Henrietta. He must be terrified.*

A few days earlier in the OC, Bud had heard about one member of a 381st crew who was shot down in the Schweinfurt mission in August of 1943. He came walking into Ridgewell a few months later after being found and aided by the French underground. A Knoxville boy in the same crew, Corky Moulton, was also being held as a POW.

All these thoughts swirled in Bud's head as he contemplated their fate—and his potential one. He tried to erase the thoughts but couldn't. In that day's letter to Thelma, he tried to mute the anguish he felt over Grover. But unlike his usual writing, his letter was a disjointed staccato of disconnected facts:

> *I was so very sorry to hear about Grover. I sure hope and pray everything does work out okay. I'm just before being converted into a Navigator, so I won't be flying for a few days I suppose—got a haircut today—line was*

*long—J. Pyles is a pilot on a B-26 instead of B-25—saw
"Three Men in White" at base theater tonight—now listening to Eddie Cantor and Joan Davis on the radio—went
to see Jim and Leo, they stayed in London an extra day.*

He ended his letter with insight into how much he was thinking of the plight of other boys in different theaters or in captivity.

*More and more, I realize how much better a deal we fel-
lows in the air have than those poor fellows fighting on the
front lines. We at least have a good place to sleep after a
hard day's work. They sure deserve lots more credit than
they get. It's time for me to go to sleep now sweetheart. So
I'll say goodnight. I love you more and more—Bud.*

Mission #2; Hamm, Germany – September 19, 1944

Finally, mission number two is actually here, Bud thought, as the CQ broke the silence of the early morning in the barracks. "Perrin, Vaughn, you're flying today. Chow at 0700, briefing at 0745, first takeoff at 0930. Look alive, gentlemen." He turned and exited as quickly as he entered.

"The phantom strikes again," Bud whispered to Vaughn as they each wiped the sleep from their eyes and stepped onto the cold floor to meet the long and even colder day.

"The target for the day is Hamm," the crew learned from the IO at briefing. The resulting groan was typical and consistent. "Flack should be heavy. We expect light to zero fighter resistance, but don't be caught off guard. The weather will probably be soupy. Initial reports show a 5/10 undercast at the target. Don't forget your escape packs, and be alert."

Bud was still new enough not to be cavalier as the various officers gave their portion of the briefings. He had been well-schooled in ground training, had completed one mission, and always paid strict attention to detail, so the thirty-minute briefing kept him at rapt attention.

After being dismissed, Bud met with the other 381st bombardiers. He saw Cash in the corner and sat down beside him. "Where are you positioned today?" Bud inquired, referring to the placement of Cash's aircraft in the bomber formation.

"I'm flying with Seeley in the low element, how 'bout you?" C.D. replied as he studied the flimsie that denoted the aircraft, tail number, and pilot of each of the 381st crews.

"I'm with my normal Belskis crew. We're in the lead element," Bud responded. "Looks like your take off's thirty-six minutes behind us. We'll warm up the air for you."

Cash managed a wry grin that reflected the morning's tension.

The objective for the Hamm mission was the marshalling yard that had increasingly become a key distribution point for the Reich. The mission on September 19 was only the second time the 381st had bombed Hamm, but the 8th AF had peppered the marshalling yards there on numerous other occasions. On the first Hamm mission by the 381st almost five months earlier (April 22), the flak was meager and there was no Luftwaffe resistance. The participating crews landed back in Ridgewell as late at 2200 on the earlier mission. With their late takeoff on this mission, it looked like they might repeat the tardy return.

Under the command of Lt. Col. David E. Kunkel, Jr., thirty-seven aircraft bombed Hamm that day.

There was a 10/10 undercast to five degrees east of the target. The weather cleared, so the group began a visual run on the target. Closer to the IP the weather socked in and bombing was done by Pff. Results were unobserved. There was moderate but very accurate flak and ten of the aircraft, including the Liberty Belle in which the Belskis crew flew, experienced damage—major for five of them. The Luftwaffe wisely chose not to show up as a large contingent of P-51s and P-47s were protecting the mission (381st Bomb Group Diary, April 22, 1944).

The increasing dearth of Luftwaffe resistance was no coincidence. The introduction of the P-51 in early 1944 and the growing number of Mustangs protecting Fortresses and Liberators caused the Reich leaders to protect both their rapidly dwindling fighter force and the increasingly low supply of petrol. However, with declining fighter force came an increasing quantity and intensity of flak. So the risk of missions was not reduced, just changed.

381st Bombardiers & Navigators (Ross Perrin on back row extreme right)-October, 1944
Robert Lane Album-Dr. Mike Thomas

After settling in after the Hamm mission, Bud scribbled a quick note to Thelma.

Last night I told you I'd be taking it easy for a few days, but it turned out that I had a pretty rough day. I'm really tired and am already in bed. Now all I have to do is stay awake long enough to tell you I love you more today than I did yesterday. By the way, I found the letter I wrote last night in my jacket pocket. It's a little wrinkled up 'cause it's been lots of places today.

A second mission to Hamm was cancelled the following day. The weather in East Anglia normally didn't get blustery until mid-October, but not in 1944. It was raw that year from almost the first of September and would continue so for the remainder of the year.

On September 21, the 381st BG sent three squads to Mainz, one of which was the Belskis crew, minus Ross W. Perrin, Jr. Still awaiting his advancement to navigator, he was left behind. He took the opportunity to "... *beat our Squadron Bombardier, Tidwell, about five or six games of gin rummy...guess I'm pretty good, eh?*" as he wrote to Thelma with pride. On a more important note, he added, "*Teddy Smith's brother* [Phillip], *left for home the other day, the lucky rascal. He's done his share though, so I don't suppose I should envy him much.*"

On the mission to Kassel on September 22, the Belskis crew flew, again without Bud. If his qualification as an ETO navigator had come a day earlier, he might have been able to fly and thereby carve the proverbial notch in the Norden bombsight. But his new status didn't become effective until Saturday, September 23.

That Saturday was also eventful for another reason. Late in the evening, Bud was sprawled out on his bed, humming as he wrote to Thelma, "*Some hillbilly music is on now. Makes an East Tennessee fellow a little homesick, even though I wouldn't listen to it at home.*" At that moment, an ear-splitting explosion rattled the windows in the barrack and caused all to dive for cover on the floor. The boys immediately recognized it as a V-2 rocket that had landed somewhere close. Two of them scurried outside and, aided by the glow from the exploding rocket, saw the smoke rising above the trees a few hundred yards away (Robert Armstrong, *Friendly and Enemy Skies* [Hutchinson, Kansas: Robert Armstrong, 2003]). Bud continued to write. "*We had a little excitement a few minutes ago—fun in a way, but pretty close.*"

His gross understatement of the incident didn't escape Bud. But he was hamstrung by the rules requiring minimal discussion of base and mission information. *I'll tell my kids about this night someday,* he vowed.

The Vengance-2 or V-2 rocket was quite different from its predecessor, the V-1, or "Doodle Bug," as many named it, or "Buzz Bomb" as it was known by others. Had the bomb that descended near Ridgeway that night been the latter, the cessation of its trademark buzzing sound when under full power would have acted as a warning of the impending crash. But there was no such warning by an incoming V-2. Also, the second-generation rocket was many times more devastating, with almost twice the range and an ability to fly at a height of fifty miles and ten times as fast as its predecessor.

V-1 rockets were often detected in flight and shot down. Occasionally, British fighters that could tip the bomb with the wing of the aircraft and knock the weapon off its course chased them down. But there was no effective defense against the V-2. Werner von Braun, its chief architect, would immigrate to the US after the war and become the designer of the early rockets used by the space program at NASA.

Humble, honorable Bob Angevine remained a positive influence on Bud and a growing friend. Bud shared his enthusiasm about their relationship in a letter the following Sunday:

> *I had two meals with Lt. Angevine yesterday. We're getting to be pretty good buddies. This morning I went back to bed after breakfast, but got back up in time to go to church with him. The service was short, but very good. All the songs they sang weren't very familiar—not like home. I did the best I could.*

With that, Bud closed, *"All my love—your Pappy."*

CHAPTER 15

Four Tough Days

Mixing Boredom and Terror

Ridgewell, England: September 25 –28, 1944

BUD'S FIRST FOUR B-17 COMBAT missions confirmed his long-held desire to be assigned to the Flying Fortress. Even with its lack of comfort, tight quarters, and extreme cold, especially at high altitudes, its crews trusted its airworthiness. Few who knew the Boeing-designed B-17 firsthand challenged its ability to both pack and take a punch. It had proven it could be shot up to resemble Swiss cheese, lose an engine or two, have control surfaces blown away, and still chug its way back across the English Channel to land safely on British soil.

Its sister bomber, the B-24 Liberator, was faster, carried a heavier bomb load, and had a greater range but was also more difficult to fly and had poor performance characteristics in the tight bomber formations used over Europe. Even more devastating in its comparisons to the Fortress was its inability to withstand significant battle damage and remain airworthy. Many called the B-24 a "Flying Coffin," an obvious reflection on its comparative weakness to the sturdier Fortress.

Unlike the supremely offensive weapon the B-17 ultimately became, its birth was quite inauspicious. In a USAAC-initiated competition with Douglas and Martin, Boeing produced the superior aircraft, a much-advanced blending of its XB-15 Bomber and 247 air cargo craft. At its inaugural flight on July 28, 1935, a local *Seattle Times* reporter christened it "The Flying Fortress." The name stuck.

However, due to a crew oversight in its preflight check, the B-17 crashed on its second test flight in October of 1935. This caused Boeing to be scratched from the competition in favor of the Douglas entry. However, the perceived value of the Boeing design was not lost on the USAAC engineers. After modifications and further tests, the Army placed an initial order for a dozen B-17s for extensive testing. Before Pearl Harbor, fewer than two hundred were in use. But, by the end of the war in 1945, more than twelve thousand Fortresses were built by Boeing, Douglas, and Vega. The crash that almost left Boeing bankrupt ultimately led its engineers and combat crews to redesign, upgrade, and advance the craft to the formidable weapon it became by war's end.

Frankfurt, Germany
Ridgewell Mission #192 – September 25, 1944

After a few days of raw weather in East Anglia as well as over the prime target areas on the Continent, a slight respite came on September 25. With this break, the Pinetree staff scheduled a mission to Frankfurt, and Ridgewell crews were included. Following breakfast, briefing, and dressing for the long day to the Frankfurt marshalling yards, the Belskis crew boarded the truck for the mile-long trip to the hardstand.

Weather that September had been predictably raw, even more so than the same harsh period in 1943. Heavy bomber use of the H2X Pathfinder navigation system (Pff) was the major difference that allowed the 8th to fly more missions that September than in September of 1943. This system, developed at the Massachusetts Institute of Technology, marked the first deployment of air-to-ground radar in an aircraft. "Neither enemy fighters nor enemy aircraft caused a single mission to be cancelled or aborted," was the claim touted by the 8th AF.

But the same could not be said about the mercurial European weather. Poor weather at or near the operating base or the target caused the cessation of numerous missions. However, the Pff significantly altered the number of missions lost to inclement weather. Early on, this system was housed beneath the bombardier's location. Later it was located mid-ship, replacing the ball turret.

Aircraft outfitted with a Pff led most missions flown in the fall and winter of 1944. Ridgewell had three Pff aircraft and six to ten "Mickey Men," the name affectionately given to Pathfinder-trained navigators. The moniker became commonplace among fliers because the system looked somewhat "Mickey Mouse." However, it was anything but. Rather, the Pff permitted as many as fifty percent more missions to be flown than before its advent, with enhanced bombing accuracy.

The Belskis crew's ten-minute trip to the hardstand began in relative quiet, broken only by tail gunner Rogers's infrequent comments. "This is our fifth mission—thirty more to go before going home—I hope," he said. The halting end of his statement was almost a question.

"Long way to go," responded Lauret.

"Yep."

After that interchange, each boy seemed lost in his own thoughts. Revealing his inner trepidation, Rogers added, "I overheard another tail gunner, Ivory something—I think Wilson—yeah, Wilson, telling someone that when he first got here, he asked a veteran to give him some tips about how to be the best gunner possible. He said the guy told him to forget that crap, he probably wouldn't last that long."

"All right guys, none of that stuff. We're going to make this trip and thirty more. Let's hang together," Leo commanded, taking charge of both crew and conversation.

No one else spoke as the truck splashed through puddles in the rutted road leading to the hardstand where bomb-laden aircraft 42-97442 awaited their arrival. The ship was devoid of the nose art that adorned many bombers in the 8th AF. The boys scurried out of the back of the truck, each carrying the tools his assignment required. It was 0700, three hours since wake-up and thirty minutes until scheduled takeoff.

Heeding their crew chief's directive, the Belskis crew quietly entered the assigned aircraft and began the pre-flight sequence for each position. Bud and Collett studied the route of flight and weather predictions provided at briefing. "Can't decide whether I like the bombardier or navigator position better," Bud said as he turned away from the maps to complete positioning the Norden and calibrating it for the mission. "I love the rush of the bomb run, but I also like the dead-reckoning calculation process. There's a lot of pressure, but I like it. It keeps you focused and your mind off the flak."

"Well, I've never done your job, but I understand the excitement of tracking the route from the IP and then the drop," Collett responded.

"Communication check," came Belskis's voice over the intercom. The five gunners checked in, followed by Jim, Bud, and Glenn. The engine startup sequence was smooth, as were the takeoff and Wing form up over Ridgewell. Boring holes in the sky, the bomber stream droned from the British coast across the Channel and turned eastward toward Frankfurt.

As they came into the heart of the Reich and got closer to the IP, the crew encountered increasing amounts of flak. McCoy, who manned the radio and also fired the 50mm gun from the right waist position, dropped chaff, small shreds of metal foil designed to confuse German radar. This tactic worked well on days of heavy undercast, as on this mission.

The Luftwaffe had decided to stay at home on this blustery September day. As the war progressed, the German fighters had smaller amounts of essential fuel, so their opposition waned somewhat. However, Allied ground and air forces drove the Germans back toward Berlin, and the flak rings around the Reich became more concentrated and intense. In this way, confusion and diversionary tactics such as radar-jamming chaff were welcomed defenses for the flight crews.

The uncharacteristically long bomb run from the IP to "bombs away" was a terrifying twenty-two minutes. The following day, the *Stars and Stripes* reported that 1200 Fortress and Liberator bombers assaulted the Reich. A fighter presence of 750 Mustangs, Thunderbolts, and Lightings increased the crew's confidence.

They salvoed (released all at once) their bomb load, proceeded to the RP, turned for home, and after a long but uneventful journey landed safely at Ridgewell at 1400. "Five down, thirty to go," Leo announced as he slid through the front hatch onto the hardstand. Later, the airmen learned that one Fort was brought down by flak, but the entire crew bailed out and were taken prisoner.

Expecting another mission the following day, Bud was anxious to "hit the hay" early, as he told Thelma in a note before retiring. *"Your ole poppy didn't have too rough a day today—and then again it wasn't too easy. I'm a little tired tonight. Oh yes—Lt. Angevine was awarded a Distinguished Flying Cross today for his work on a mission a few weeks ago. I'll write again tomorrow. Remember who loves you—Your devoted husband—Bud."*

Osnabrück, Germany
Ridgewell Mission #193 – September 26, 1944

The prediction of a mission on September 26 was accurate. Vaughn and Perrin were awakened at 0700, somewhat later than normal for missions. At briefing, Bud learned that he would be flying navigator with another crew, and Vaughn would be in his normal position with the Belskis crew. Bud sat with C.D. Cash at briefing. C.D.'s Seeley crew would also be in the twelve crews flying from the 532nd.

Their target, they learned, was the marshalling yards in the Lower Saxony town of Osnabruck, with Lt. Colonel George G. Shackley in the command ship of the thirty-seven from the 381st. The run used visual bombing for only the second time in the month of September, with some Pff assistance, and flak was reported as meager.

"I'll take a bunch of milk runs like that one," Bud said to the flight deck crew as they strode off to interrogation. Since they arrived home early, they were able to have their gas masks, an important protection at altitude, inspected along with those of other fliers on the base.

Following dinner, Bud refused requests for bridge at the Officers' Club, opting instead for a quiet evening and some letter-writing. *I haven't written the family enough lately,* he thought. *I can't believe I've slacked off the way I have.* He had been derelict in his scribe duties and felt ashamed at his lack of communication.

However, if Bud had a fetish, it was love of and care for his shoes. His three pairs of footwear were suffering from a pronounced dearth of attention, so he decided to give at least one pair some TLC before writing Thelma. He had cleaned and applied the first of three coats of polish to his best pair when through the door came an unexpected, unwanted guest. Tony Fabiani, the abrasive antagonist whom

Bud had hoped since their first meeting would show up either not at all or at least infrequently, made his unwelcomed appearance. And Bud's attempt to make him think he didn't see him failed.

"Hey Parrot, long time no see," came the acerbic greeting.

Not long enough, Bud thought but didn't say. *I wonder if he mispronounced my name by accident or on purpose,* he fumed. *Either way, it doesn't matter.* Bud chose to ignore both the mispronunciation and the greeting. Once again, his attempts failed.

"Hey Shine Boy, what'll it take to get a shoe shine? About three pence?" Fabiani said with a bawdy laugh.

"Thirty quid wouldn't be enough," Bud responded uncharacteristically. As soon as the words left his mouth, he knew he'd made a mistake. He remembered his brother-in-law Leonard's truism a bit too late: "When you wrestle a pig, you both get dirty, but the pig likes it."

Bud was now in a tussle with a pig, and the potential outcome was foreboding. Thoughts of decking Fabiani crossed Bud's mind, but so did the possibility of being pulled from flight status and spending a day or so in confinement. He collected his emotions and kept brushing away at his shoes.

Luckily, Tony's friend in the opposite corner of the barracks beckoned him. He walked away with one parting shot. "When you finish, read some of those foot washing stories in that Bible of yours," Fabiani cackled. Bud steamed but said nothing.

All done, he thought as he finished shining one pair. *The others'll have to wait.* He wrote Thelma without mentioning the conflict.

Cologne, Germany
Ridgewell Mission #194 – September 27, 1944

A wake-up came early the next morning, but not as early as the V-1 buzz bombs that streaked across the base at 0400. Many of the boys scrambled and retreated to the nearby bomb shelters in anticipation of more assaults by the destructive devices Hitler had devised to harass and kill both US troops and London residents. Ridgewell lay in a direct line between most of the V-1 and V-2 European launch points and the city of London, so the bombs often showed up unannounced to do their damage. On this morning, many of those who chose to evacuate their beds in favor of the bomb shelter were able to witness an RAF night fighter shoot down the sputtering missile.

Bud was still half-awake from the commotion when, only thirty minutes later, the officer entered his still-dark barracks and called his name. "Perrin, you're flying, 0630 briefing, rise and shine." Since Vaughn's name wasn't called, Bud knew he was flying navigator with another crew and the Belskis crew would stand down.

Cologne was the target that day. Under command of Capt. Douglas L. Winter, thirty-seven 381st aircraft participated in what turned out to be another milk run.

At interrogation, they learned of one significant problem suffered by another crew. "Hey guys, we had a ball turret gunner pass out from anoxia today. We couldn't revive him in the air, so the ship aborted to Brussels. He's going to be OK, but be careful up there," the captain said.

"Sounds like you guys had it pretty easy today," Vaughn said as Bud entered the barracks and plopped down on his adjacent cot.

"It would've been easier if I'd gotten the sleep I lost from the V-1

Cologne Cathedral, Cologne, Germany-May, 1945
Bill Palmer WWII Photo Album

scare this morning," Bud responded. "You must've had a long night last night; you slept right through it."

"Wasn't feeling too good—had a bad cold—think I'll go to the infirmary," Glenn answered.

"We went to Cologne today," Bud said. "The city sits right up next to the train station and marshalling yards we bombed. The place looks like a pile of rubble except for this beautiful cathedral with a very tall elegant spire atop it. The whole church looks like it's almost untouched, just like St. Paul's in London," he paused to emphasize his next statement. "God is either protecting his house or we are all great bombardiers trying not to hit it. Personally, I don't think we're that good—good, but not that good."

Disappointed to go without a "sugar report" from Thelma, Bud began scribbling a note to her before trying to fight the cold, dank conditions of the barracks by hibernating as best he could under three thin blankets and a bomber jacket:

> *I'm a little tired tonight as usual, so this will be a short note. Only had one V-mail letter waiting for me this afternoon from Evelyn. It was written Sept 17th to my new APO which is pretty good service.*
>
> *I played a little bridge with three other fellows who were a little better than me. Of course, I didn't get the cards either, so I didn't do so hot.*
>
> *Being a navigator isn't so bad. Keeps a fellow busy and makes the time pass by much faster.*
>
> *Evelyn said J. Ross backed out at the dentist. He's just a big talker, I'm beginning to believe. Don't blame him though. I was worse than that the first time I went to have my teeth worked on—and I was a lot older than he is. I'm kinda tired—had to work three days in a row—not too rough a day today, but was awakened by a commotion early this morning and couldn't get back to sleep. I sure hope to hear from you tomorrow. Wish you were here beside me—every night. All my love—Bud."*

The barracks was quiet by 2200 hours, as all its occupants except

Vaughn had flown that day and were exhausted. The sleep monster attacked them all, and the snoring commenced.

Magdeburg, Germany
Ridgewell Mission #195 – September 28, 1944

The snoring was rudely interrupted at 0400 by the all-too-familiar creaking of the door hinges and the raspy voice of the CQ officer. "Perrin, Vaughn, you're flying today."

The snoring stopped. The morning calm, present until the officer exited, was broken by the gravelly but grateful voice of a boy not summoned for the day's mission. "Thank you, Lord." He fell back to his flimsy pillow as Bud swung his legs from the warmth of his cot and onto the cold floor.

Pilot-Lt. Robert "Bob" Armstrong- Fall 1944
Bob Armstrong WWII Album

At briefing, Bud learned that the Belskis crew was flying the mission to Magdeburg that day, but another bombardier would fill his position. Bud would be flying navigator, replacing Lt. White with the Reed crew. Harley L. Reed was an accomplished pilot, as was his co-pilot, Bob Armstrong. The flight deck duo, with the well-earned respect of superior officers and crew members alike, would be flying element lead, now their normal position. Bud relished the responsibility that accompanied lead duty. He hated to fly with an unfamiliar group but loved the challenge presented by flying with this esteemed crew.

In the ten-minute truck ride to the hardstand, an uneasy quiet reigned. An occasional groan was heard from those jostled when the driver failed to avoid some of the many potholes on the road ringing the airfield. The freeze-thaw cycles of the harsh British winters, the intense traffic of heavy trucks, and the compromised concrete mixture used in construction had, over the previous two years, caused the potholes to grow in both number and size.

Armstrong introduced himself to Bud and, in turn, introduced him to the remainder of the crew. Smiles constrained by the anxiety that accompanied each mission crept onto the welcoming faces. "White sick?" asked Reed.

"Yes, sir," Armstrong responded. "Mauldin, too," referring to bombardier "Slim" Mauldin, who was replaced by a togglier (an enlisted man trained to occasionally substitute for the bombardier and toggle the bomb drop from his aircraft when so instructed by the lead bombardier) for the Magdeburg mission.

The truck finally came to a halt in front of the B-17 that would be their workplace for what would become their almost twelve-hour mission. *Little Guy* was emblazoned in bold black block letters underneath the two windows aft of the flight deck on each side of the aircraft. Each of the two t's in the word *Little* was painted to resemble a bomb hanging from the cross bar at the top of the T. The designation 2K-6994, signifying the Douglas-built aircraft VE 42-106994, was lettered across the tail. *VE* was the designation for a 532nd Bomb Squad aircraft and was located beneath a large black *L* inside a triangle. This "Triangle L" identified the 381st Bomb Group.

The expected mist of the early hour on this late September morning made visibility of the thirty-six other Fortresses scheduled for the Magdeburg mission difficult. "Looks like a tough start for the day," Bud commented to Armstrong as the two dropped off their bags and exited the truck.

"Yep, we got our work cut out for us," Bob replied.

"That's why we get the big bucks." They both smiled, understanding the fallacy of the assertion.

The departure of bombers from East Anglia was dangerous to say the least. Thirty-seven ships taking off one after the other at one-minute intervals caused every crew member to wince and "pucker up," as the saying went. Put that together with thirty-plus ships taking off at the same time from twenty other airfields in the geographically tight confines of the bomber fields, and it was no wonder that accidents often occurred.

The flare shot from the base of the tower burst in red hazy smoke above the main runway, indicating that the first aircraft could take off. Forty-five minutes later, the thirty-seven Fortresses from the

381st were forming in concentric circles at 10,000 feet. They then proceeded to the beginning of the bomber stream in the area of Felixstowe, England, northeast of London. On a heading almost due east, the stream crossed the North Sea and entered enemy territory as they hit landfall over Belgium.

Anti-aircraft fire met them as soon as they entered enemy range and continued all the way to the target. Bud's responsibility for the mission was to make sure they maintained course and heading to the IP, where the control of the ship was turned over to the Norden bombsight that guided the craft on its twenty-minute bomb run. With a socked-in 10/10 undercast, bombing was directed by the Pff ship leading the 381st.

The crew encountered heavy flak throughout the run. "Bombs away," came the announcement by the togglier, indicating he had deployed the ten 500-pound demolition bombs and two 100-pound

LITTLE GUY CREW: AC #42-106994 - October 25, 1944
Top: Jensen, Pendleton, Kuhfuss, Hansen, Brauder.
Bottom: Reed, Armstrong, White, Mauldin (Combs missing).
(Note: Ross Perrin replaced White on this crew for the mission to Magdeburg on 9/28/44-10/25/44)
USAAF - 381st

incendiaries. Flak continued past the target and on to the RP. Later, co-pilot Bob Armstrong reported in his diary that it seemed "the Luftwaffe had resigned en masse" for the mission. (Armstrong, *Friendly and Enemy Skies*, 99).

"Did you see the big orange flak burst?" Bud asked as *Little Guy* banked, joining the formation and turning toward home.

"Sure did," came a voice from the flight deck. "Might have been one of the new flak rounds designed to resemble an aircraft that's blown up. Or. . . " the voice trailed off, with no need to complete the sentence. Most flak bursts emitted either white or black bursts of smoke. The orange ones were fewer in number, but larger, bringing with them a heightened sense of terror.

The fear of a sudden and unannounced explosion hung over every crew. The presence of the Luftwaffe heightened the anxiety of boys on a mission, and their absence permitted a more relaxed state. But only after exiting flak range over the English Channel or the North Sea did any calm replace fear in the minds of the crew.

They arrived at Station 167 and after receiving clearance from the tower, landed at 1540, thirteen hours after wake-up and more than eleven hours since takeoff. "Do we get time and a half for overtime today?" the tail gunner asked as the crew strode toward the truck.

"In your dreams," came the reply from the rear of the group.

"Great job today, boys," said Lt. Reed as they struggled into the back of the truck.

"You too, boss," Bud replied, giving him a weary smile.

Darkness was fast approaching as the crew entered the interrogation building munching on the traditional peanut butter and jelly sandwiches. "This mission was from *can* to *can't*," Bud said through a grin. No one responded. Southernisms lacked humor after a full day's journey over hostile Nazi-land.

After four straight days of getting up early, ten hours of being shot at while buffeted about in subzero temperatures, and going to bed late, a day off on September 29 seemed to Bud like the return of a long-lost friend. He awoke to a drafty barracks that seemed to invite the fog and mist of the last Saturday in September to take up residence inside. And it obliged. The single wood-burning stove was woefully inadequate to drive out the pervasive cold of the British winter, even if there was enough fuel to feed it, which there wasn't. When legitimate means of obtaining fuel didn't work, airmen resorted to petty thievery. They scavenged for cardboard, ammo boxes, fence posts--almost anything that would stand still and burn. In his letter to Thelma, Bud wrote,

> *I just built a fire. Yeah. I ain't kidding. I really did build a fire in our stove and put a big piece of the tree some of us fellows cut down the other day. Ain't that awful—cutting down one of the King's trees. Maybe he won't miss it though and it does furnish us with quite a bit of heat.*

A leisurely lunch at the mess hall with Leo, Glenn, and Cash served as a welcomed respite from the rushed, dry, and tasteless meals at 25,000 feet. The other three stayed to drink coffee, but the magnetic draw of bridge at the Officers' Club was more than Bud could resist. Four hours and three quid later, he braved the cold and returned through the light mist to his Ridgewell home.

When he entered the barracks, he realized Armed Forces Radio was broadcasting the season-opening Tennessee football game. In the continuation of the letter started hours earlier, he wrote:

> *I'd like to be wherever that football game between Tennessee and Kentucky is being played along about now. If it's Knoxville, it would be wonderful, but if it's Lexington, we could have a second honeymoon. I'll listen and hear how the game comes out, but I'd like for you to send me the clippings from the paper."* (Note: Tennessee won its season opener against Kentucky in Knoxville 26-13. They played the Wildcats again in Lexington two months later on November 25, 1944. Tennessee also won that one, 21-7. The Tennessee stadium capacity was 31,390 that year after an increase from 19,000 in 1938).
>
> *After a very slow start I got in seven missions in the first month. At this rate I could be home before Junior is born—if you can hold off 'till late January. No pressure, just have a healthy one—boy or girl. I'll be home as soon as I can—I love you more than I can really express.—Bud*

CHAPTER 16

Slogging Through the British Winter

When It Snows, It Pours

Ridgewell, England: October 1944

OCTOBER BEGAN WITH A BANG, or rather a buzz. On the snowy evening of the first, two doodlebug V-1 bombs passed low and close over headquarters with RAF fighters on their tails. Leon Wagner, control tower operator on duty, excitedly furnished a blow-by-blow description of the encounter over the Tannoy, the generic trademark name airmen had come to use in referring to the base's public address system. Bud chose not to mention it in his letter to Thelma the next day. *She has enough to worry about as it is*, he thought.

East Anglia weather in September of 1944 had been uncharacteristically cold and snowy. October brought more of the same. In fact, uneven weather characterized the entire southeastern portion of England. The elevations of First Wing bomber and fighter bases were just different enough to cause significant difficulty with early-morning takeoffs and forming up of aircraft. Cloud cover obstructed ground visibility over some bases at elevations only a few meters lower than others only a few miles away, where the extra elevation blocked the cloud cover and visibility was clear.

Even though Allied advances indicated that Jerrie was on the run, it became more and more evident that the word *kapitulation* must have been expunged from the Reich's dictionary. US brass found their opponents' continued efforts to prosecute the war were both frustrating and unbelievable. Whether their persistence was due to strength of will, the lunacy of Hitler and his minions, a hope for some magical breakthrough, or the knowledge that their crimes were so horrendous that resulting post-war prosecution would be both inevitable and harsh, the Reich fought on (*First Combat Wing–8th Air Force War Diary,* October 1944).

Bud was certified as an ETO navigator in late September, a critical time in the operations of the 8th AF. A summary from First Wing operations in late September chronicled the increasing importance of this key crew position.

> There is a vast difference between Pathfinder [Pff or Mickey ship] attacks and visual attacks. Pathfinder equipment is a scientific miracle, but there was no denying that it is in its early infancy. For one thing, only a few types of targets are vulnerable to it.
>
> More than ever before, however, the navigator has become a key man in the crew. . . . pilots guard our ships against the dangers of the air. Gunners and fighter escorts protect against enemy air attack. But the navigator is the sole defense against flak. Faulty navigation can lead the ships off the briefed course and over non-essential flak. When it comes to the attack and withdrawal there is no getting around the flak guarding the target, but every attack is planned on the basis of a carefully considered estimate of the flak situation involving a computation of the exact number of rounds that could be fired on each possible axis of attack and withdrawal. Studies prepared by our own Hal Hanes show conclusively that losses and battle damages through flak vary inversely to the accuracy with which the briefed course by the navigators is flown. And, of course, you have to be there at the practice time laid down in order to get the benefit of the chaff dropped by the screening force.
>
> Hence, it became a source of genuine concern when it became apparent that there was a tendency for our navigators to relax and rely too much on the Mickey Operators. H2X, or Mickey, was a perfect navigation medium above the overcast when it was working, but it had a fatal tendency to become inoperative, especially on long missions. The dead-reckoning navigators couldn't afford to relax a

moment. Fix-crawling was all right as long as the Mickey was working, but a navigator who lost contact with it while the Mickey was working was certain to be lost the minute it went out. In one case a Group went astray when the Mickey operator suffered from anoxia and started giving crazy directions to the Pilot. Briefed to come out over the Zuider Zee, another Group wandered off on its own and came out via Hamburg before the Mickey operator was able to re-establish his position and navigation could start anew. It was apparent that we would have to maintain eternal vigilance in this matter. Constant indoctrination would be required to insure that Mickey was used as an aid to navigation, not as a substitute for it. Soon, we were told, we would have Gee coverage all the way to Berlin. Then it will now be a case of preventing Gee "fix-crawling" from becoming another substitute.

Ridgewell Main Runway-Snow and Minimum Visibility- October, 1944
Bill Palmer WWII Photo Album

Kassel, Germany
Ridgewell Mission #196 – October 2, 1944

On October 2, the 381st put up thirty-seven Forts on the mission to bomb the Henschel und Sohn (Henschel & Son) factory in Kassel. This highly advanced heavy machinery operation was the result of a merger of Carl Henschel's company, founded in 1810, with one founded in 1837 by his son, Carl Anton Henschel. By the end of the nineteenth century, the combined company had become the largest manufacturer of locomotives in all of Germany. In 1935, Henschel und Sohn began manufacturing Panzer I tanks for the Reich and shortly thereafter initiated a large-scale production of the Panzer III tank. As the sole supplier of Tiger I and Tiger II tanks, the factory in Kassel became a mission-critical target in disrupting the Reich's ability to wage war on the ground.

There was one snafu at takeoff on this run. *The Railroader*, BG-17 #42-97357, a plane of the 533rd BS, collided with another craft during taxi, and one plane tore off the other's tail section. Luckily the tail gunner was not at his combat post when the accident occurred. The extensive damage was repaired in record time, and the aircraft returned to service the following day. Just three days later, it was again damaged in a takeoff accident. The pilot, Lt. Ed Stevens, was unable to get the plane airborne, and it crashed at the end of the runway in a ditch. Upon entering the ditch, the aircraft "nosed over," damaging the chin turret and supporting members. When it landed on the tail, the wheel and axle were torn from their mounting, and the compressive load on the fuselage, now greater than that for which the ship was designed, broke its back.

Mizpah - B-17G, AC #42-31575, 7/4/44, With Ground Crew
USAAF - 381st

Flying in B17-G, 2P 42-31575, *Mizpah,* the Belskis crew incurred intense flak in the Ruhr Valley on the return to base and, along with thirteen other of the 381st Forts, suffered significant to major battle damage. The First CBW had also informed the 381st that indications were that the persistent cloud blankets of recent weeks had allowed the Jerries' (WWII slang for the German army) fighter picture to improve. Under these conditions, they were able to repair some production facilities and move others underground. This intelligence was passed on to the crews at briefing, but resistance on the Kassel mission came from the increasingly concentrated flak batteries (*First Combat Wing–8th Air Force War Diary,* October, 1944).

The crews agreed that "buying the farm" was a distinct possibility. But the strength of the Fortress, the skill of Leo and Glenn, and God's blessing allowed them to return to England. The white cliffs of Dover to the south of their return flight path were a welcome sight. In his understated depiction of his "day at the office," Bud wrote to Thelma, *"I'm a little tired tonight so I'll have to make this short." I'll make sure tell her about this someday soon,* he thought as he fell asleep.

East Anglia was cloudy, blustery, and cold on Tuesday the third, so Glenn and Bud spent the day shuttling between the mess hall and the Officers' Club. No mission call came on the early morning of the fourth, and it seemed a carbon copy of the day before except for one change: Wednesday's cold now combined with spitting snow from dawn till late morning with no end in sight. Crews were very happy that no bomber takeoff into the low-visibility soup was scheduled.

The boys sequestered in the barracks took turns stoking the ever-dwindling fire. Scraps of wood, lumps of coal scrounged from big-hearted townspeople, and the theft of limbs from King George's trees, as the boys laughingly called the sticks they scavenged, provided minimal fuel to drive the cold from the drafty huts.

Carrying some much-needed firewood, Leo and Jim arrived just after noon. "Beware of northerners bearing gifts," Bud said, laughing as he grabbed the dry wood and placed a portion into the smoldering fire. Glenn pulled up a chair, and the four sat close as the flames increased over the next few minutes. The blaze wouldn't last long, but whatever heat it provided was welcome.

By late afternoon, the fire was again gasping to stay alive, the stash of fuel was exhausted, and the boys were restless. Trekking through the mush to the OC was an option, but not a good one. Regardless of the weather, a trip to the nearby pub, The Fox, was deemed a great idea. "Let's evacuate this icebox," Bud said standing up and dropping the blanket in which he was wrapped onto his bed. The four Belskis crew officers grabbed hats and coats and, almost in unison, bounded through the door. Turning their heads to ward off the icy snow that pelted their faces, they scurried toward the pub.

Above: The Fox Pub, Ridgewell - Fall, 1944
Bob Armstrong WWII Album

Right: The Fox Pub Building-Now a Private
Residence, October, 2013
Photo by J. Ross Greene

The Fox Public House was a cozy respite on a small road just outside the base fence. Resourceful airmen had cut a hole in the fence to allow easy access. Since base brass had repaired the hole, a makeshift ladder was now kept hidden by a tree next to the fence. This helped airmen, especially those of the 532nd who were billeted nearby, to easily escape the base for a few hours of food, brew, and often-raucous conversation.

The Fox's much-loved publican, Bill, greeted the boys as they scurried out of the pelting snow and into the warm pub. In turn, they laid their crusher hats on the table and hung their coats on the rack at the front wall. "Welcome, chaps. Two days of relaxation—how'd you rate that?" Bill asked with a wide grin.

"Did you have to arrest anybody today?" Collett asked, referring to Bill's former job as a London bobby.

Never one to let a patron get the best of him, Bill responded, "Not yet, but the night is young, and with you on the loose, I'll probably be called back into service." The crew broke into laughter, none louder than Bill's.

"You're ahead of the crowd today, so I've got a prized table in the corner just for you chaps," their host said, pointing to one next to the fireplace.

"This'll be the first time I've been warm all day," Leo said.

"The heat will cost two-bob-fifty (two pounds and fifty pence) extra," Bill joked.

"No problem," Bud said, rubbing his hands in front of the blazing fireplace.

"Let's start with four pints," Leo called out. Bill's wife soon brought four dark ales and placed them on the wooden plank table in front of each airman. The suds billowed down each handled mug like a small wave crashing on a sandy beach, coming to rest in a frothy pool on the table. The crackling fire emitted a warm orange-yellow glow that cast shadows on the walls. Everything about the intimate setting was perfect except for its location, more than four thousand miles from the hometowns of the Belskis flight deck crew.

"This may be a long night," Leo noted after taking a long swig of the brew in front of him.

"Not too long," Glenn responded. "There's a rumor we'll fly tomorrow, come hell or high water."

"Or snow?" Bud asked.

"Yes, or snow," Glenn agreed.

Warm ambiance, good friends, and cold British ale had a way of evoking a wide range of emotions and conversational topics. Over the next two hours, the discussions among the quartet ranged from the perils of war to the longing for home, touching on a myriad of personal matters in the process.

Monday's accident of *The Railroader* on the taxiway evoked a discussion of some stories that made the rounds with each replacement group that came to Ridgewell. Almost always when airmen discussed 381st tragedies, they included the June 23, 1943 incident when the 533rd B-17F, *The Caroline,* was incinerated by an explosion of sixteen three-hundred-pound bombs. And that Monday was no exception.

"I heard twenty-three of our boys and one local were lost that day," Leo said. "I saw a picture taken after the explosion, and there was nothing left bigger than a bolt."

"I think that was the first week missions were flown out of Ridgewell," Bud added. A somber quiet ensued, the boys lost in their individual evaluations of the extreme dangers of aircraft being readied for a day's work. Other than witnessing such an incident firsthand, nothing could sober them more than the story of that horrendous 1943 explosion.

The topic turned to their good fortune in their assignment to a B-17 instead of the B-24. The Fortress had proven to be just that, a Fortress, with the ability to take multiple punches, get up off the mat, and return to battle.

The ill-fated mission of the *Tinker Toy*, a 533rd B-17F, was another incredible story invariably discussed as a tribute to the Fort. Its gruesome tragedy took place a year earlier. "The *Tinker Toy*'s mission to Bremen in October of 1943 was a bloody one, I heard," Glenn said.

"You mean December, don't you?" Jim asked.

"No, the December crash with the Me-109 occurred two months after the one where the crew got it back to Ridgewell," Bud said. "My wife heard about that one from a newscast in the States and asked me

Tinker Toy - B-17G, AC #42-5846, after Mishap on 10/8/43, Lt. Sellers on left
USAAF - 381st

about it. I tried to slough it off, not wanting to worry her, but it sure worried me."

"Yeah, the pilot was killed but the co-pilot, Sellers I think his name was, limped her back. I saw a picture of the plane. The entire canopy was destroyed. I don't see how they withstood the cold coming in through the open cockpit," Glenn put in.

"All got back but one: the pilot, who was decapitated," Leo added, emphasizing the vulnerability of his position.

(Note: The 381st War diary of the 535th BS depicted the incident this way:

> Thirteen officers, including the squadron commander, Major Ingenhutt, Capt. Jukes, squadron operations officer and 11 enlisted men of this squadron are missing in action after the group's 36th mission, an attack on Bremen. Lt. Tom Sellers, co-pilot to Lt. William J. Minerich, has been recommended for the Distinguished Service Cross for his courage and skill over the target. Lt. Minerich was killed instantly when a 20mm shell exploded in his face. A second shell wounded Sellers in his left arm. His navigator and bombardier were both wounded. His engineer was unable to stand on his turret platform because of the slick layer of blood covering it. Sellers flew the ship home alone, holding perfect formation and successfully performing evasive action. Two months later, on December 20, Tinker Toy was lost when it collided with a Bf Mc-109 on another mission to Bremen.)

The intensity of the devastating Tinker Toy story put a pall on the mood of the flight deck crew. "Enough of this morbid stuff. Let's think about something else," Bud implored. "The World Series starts today. Who's going to win it: the Cards or the Browns?

"Hey Perrin, I'm surprised you don't want to talk Tennessee football," Leo needled.

The boys decided to put in a quid apiece and choose an inning in which the most runs would be scored in the first Series game. To make the wager work correctly, each of the four drew small pieces of paper out of a hat on which they had written numbers zero through nine. Each of the crew drew two innings, Bill drew one, and an airman at an adjacent table drew the tenth. "Hey, I got zero," Leo wailed. "What gives?"

"Looks like you'll be hoping for extra innings so your 'tenth inning' will be in play. Good luck," Bud explained with a laugh.

Since the game was broadcast over Armed Forces Radio, the group listened to most of it as they continued their conversation, interrupted only by the focus of each boy as his innings came up during the game. Leo eventually won the ten pounds and used it to pay the chit accumulated to that point in the evening. "You're a great guy—for a Yankee Yank," Glenn teased.

Just as the game ended, with Denny Galehouse having twirled a 2-1 victory for the St. Louis Cardinals over the St. Louis Browns, the front door swung open and two unwelcomed guests entered. The first was a blast of cold air. The second and even less pleasant was Tony Fabiani. "Look what the cat drug in," Glenn mumbled.

"Oh no. He's as welcome as a fart in church," added Bud.

"Who's he?" Leo asked. Since Leo and Jim didn't live with their two fellow officers, they hadn't been exposed to the ill-tempered, irascible airman.

"He's a pain in the butt, that's what he is," Glenn said, his voice low and firm in his effort to escape Fabiani's notice. Perrin, Belskis, Collett, and Vaughn had exhausted their discussion of aircraft accidents and were expecting to fly the following day, so they snuck out the door unseen.

Cologne, Germany
Ridgewell Mission #197 – October 5, 1944

An early morning wake-up and mission to Cologne had always made for a rough day, and the one flown to Cologne on the fifth by the complete Belskis crew in *Our Boarding House* would prove no exception. The Rhine River bisected the city of Cologne. The industrial area and marshalling yards near the center of town, nestled up against beautiful Cologne Cathedral (*Kolner Dom*), were key to the manufacture and distribution of material to the Reich's offensive.

(Note: On May 31, 1942, the city was attacked by 1042 RAF bombers, the first attack by more than one thousand aircraft on one mission of the war. Before the end of the war, Cologne would endure 262 air raids by Allied aircraft, resulting in the loss of more than twenty thousand civilians. Even after such numerous attacks, the Cologne Cathedral still stood on VE Day.)

The next day, Bud scribbled a note to Thelma.

Our Boarding House - B-17G, AC #42-38103 VP - 9/6/1944
USAAF - 381st

Baby I was too tired to do any letter writing last night. I'll try to make up for it tonight.

I hit the jackpot on getting letters yesterday. Got five big fat letters from you—sure was nice to see them laying on my bed after coming back from a rough day. I enjoyed the clipping or rather the sports sections you sent. In fact I wasn't the only one who had the pleasure—a lot of the other fellow Tennessee football fans enjoyed it, especially our Squadron Bombardier who was born in Tennessee, Harv Tidwell—I mentioned him before.

Today I got another letter, but it was written September 16th. The ones yesterday were from the 23rd, 24th, and 25th. I don't care how old they are when they come just as long as they keep coming and contain all that sweet stuff.

Looks like mama is getting pretty chubby now. 123 lbs. really isn't very heavy, though, considering that's for you and junior together.

I played bridge with Tidwell this afternoon. We won a pound apiece from the other fellows—they always like to make the game interesting and play for small stakes. It isn't very often that you can win that much for no more than we were playing for.

I just finished writing mother for the first time in quite a while. You said she didn't say much about my not writing her much, but I know I should write more often—also Evelyn. I won't promise but I will try to do better. Baby, it's time for me to let the sack now so I'll close this up. Hope those letters keep coming as regular as they have been the last three days. Be a sweet mama. I love you as ever—Bud

Politz/Zwickau, Germany
Ridgewell Mission #199 – October 7, 1944

The Douglas-built B-17G *Century Note* was awaiting the Belskis crew as at 0650 on Saturday morning as they rolled up to the hardstand on which the beast was parked. The assigned mission targets for the day were the depot at Zwickau and the high-volume Hydrierwerke Politz synthetic petroleum hydrogenation plant on the Oder River. With Germany's increasing need for and decreasing supply of fuel and lubricants, the remaining refineries, undamaged or destroyed by Allied bombing, were well-fortified with flak emplacements and heavily guarded by the Luftwaffe. Consequently, every mission to bomb a German-controlled refinery was a tough day for bomb groups.

Century Note - B-17G, AC #42-107100-532nd BS
USAAF - 381st

Heavy flak was present on that day's bomb run as were Messerschmitt-109s and Focke Wulf 190s. However, the large contingent of P-51 Mustangs and a few P-47 Thunderbolts did their usual great job of preventing enemy fighters from scuttling the mission's effectiveness. Flak pinged away at the entire thirty-seven aircraft formation on the bomb run and did some damage to all aircraft. But through the hail of anti-aircraft fire, they were all able to deploy their ordnances.

As the 381st hit the rally point and turned from the scary but successful raid toward the safety of England, the crew members chattered about their confidence in their resilient Fort. This confidence was directly proportional to the effective protection of their airplane by their "little friends," principally the P-51 Mustangs, and they knew it. Without them, missions to the heart of the Reich were devastating-ly dangerous and often lethal.

The Flying Fortress was, as its name touted, one tough, battle-test-ed war bird. With all its proven toughness it was, however, still pro-foundly vulnerable to the Luftwaffe until the P-51 entered the fray in early 1944.

But one fact was known only to a limited number of military lead-ers and certainly none of the Belskis crew. If not for a combination of significant bomber losses in 1942 and '43 and the resulting inter-vention of a few courageous and experienced airmen in the turf bat-tle among hard-headed Air Force brass, the Mustang may well have never entered the European Theater as a USAF airship.

Only slightly over a decade after the Wright Brothers' first flight of twelve seconds and 120 feet on December 17, 1903, air combat was introduced in WWI. When the battle ended with the armistice in the fall of 1918, fighter aircraft had become an integral part of the combat arsenal of competing nations. And the decorated flying aces piloting these machines had become icons.

In the ensuing twenty years, aircraft technology developed expo-nentially. The widely-held theory among military leaders was that bomber aircraft, capable of carrying payloads greater than those of fighters, would be the workhorse of future wars should they erupt. With the breakout of WWII in the fall of 1939, fighters and bombers would initially vie for preeminence and ultimately work in unison to bring the conflict to a welcome conclusion.

In the summer of 1940, Britain used two primary fighters, the Supermarine Spitfire and the Hawker Hurricane, in a successful at-tempt to protect its homeland from the destructive onslaught of the German Luftwaffe. Even before Hitler's abrupt about-face in June of 1941 when he refocused his wrath on his former ally, Russia, Chur-chill felt that the Allied success would only result from devastating bombing attacks on the Nazi homeland. While still defending Britain, the RAF began what proved to be a rather unsuccessful attempt to destroy both German production and civilian morale through strate-gic nighttime bombing.

Army Air Corps Chief of Staff Hap Arnold and his lieutenants felt that where Britain had failed, the US could prevail. They believed their bombers, sufficiently equipped with fifty-caliber machine guns and an ability to fly high and fast, could do the job unaided by additional fighter protection.

Arnold had taken flying lessons from the Wright brothers and his Chief of Staff, General Carl "Tooey" Spaatz, had been a combat pilot in World War I. A highly competitive and proud man, Arnold was anxious to prove the superiority of the US forces so as to obtain independence and status equal to that of the Army and Navy. But the battle task they faced was daunting, and success proved elusive.

A number of factors worked against the US flying effort. First, it was almost a year after the initial mobilization of a small force in England before there were enough trained airmen and functional aircraft to mount a significant effort. Second, training of pilots and other airmen was done primarily in the flat, arid land of the West. Training conditions varied significantly from the rain, fog, intense cold, and unpredictable conditions of England and continental Europe. The airmen found frostbite and anoxia due to high-altitude flying and somewhat unreliable oxygen systems as formidable foes as the German war machine.

But the most devastating impediment faced by the US air effort was the lack of protection afforded the long-range heavy bombers as the strategic bombing plan called for missions deeper and deeper into Germany territory. The P-47 Thunderbolt and P-38 Lightning could protect the bombers only so far into the continent. Without bases or refueling outposts in Europe, the fighters had to turn around at a point short of the mission's target. That left the then-unprotected bombers as sitting ducks for the Luftwaffe fighters. They knew well the limited range of their US counterparts and took full and consistent advantage of that weakness. The perceived invincibility of the independent US bomber proved a mere pipe dream.

On August 17, 1943, the Eighth conducted a massive raid on two well-fortified German production targets, the ball bearing plant at Schweinfurt and the Messerschmitt plant at Regensburg. Significant damage was done to both, but at just as significant a cost to the Eighth. The P-47 fighter escorts had to turn back just before reaching the German border, leaving the bombers alone for the final and most dangerous segment of the mission. A WWII writer for *Stars and Stripes*, Tex McCrary, characterized a mission like Schweinfurt as: "You're driving one of 24 fifty-ton trucks down Broadway, fender to fender at 275 miles per hour, while the whole NY police force is blazing away at you with Tommy guns" (Olson, *Citizens of London*, 256). Sixty bombers and six hundred men were lost in the Schweinfurt raid, inaccurately touted as a strategic success although both plants were back in full operation in short order. A follow-up raid to the same targets two months later on October 14 was equally devastating to both US aircraft crews and base morale.

Amid the consternation of the compromised bombing effort in Europe and the political and public relations efforts among US air brass, two seemingly unconnected things were occurring. First, his superiors assigned WWI-tested and air-savvy pilot Tommy Hitchcock to an assistant military attaché position in London. At age seventeen, unwilling to wait until the US entered WWI, he had pulled strings and was permitted to fly in France's Lafayette Escadrille. After shooting down two German aircraft, he too was shot down and imprisoned in a POW camp. He later escaped and made his way to Switzerland, spending the time between wars creating a national reputation as a polo player and investment banker.

When WWII broke out, the forty-one-year-old Hitchcock tried unsuccessfully to gain permission to fly for the USAAC. The desk job at the US Embassy in London was the closest he could get to the cockpit, but it didn't deter his zeal to have a meaningful impact on the war.

Concurrent with Hitchcock's move across the pond came intransigent internal resistance by Arnold, Spaatz, and Eaker to considering numerous proven British flying techniques and equipment. But this narrow perspective did not restrict Hitchcock. On the contrary, he had a great respect for the British experience and design prowess. At Duxford, the RAF airfield outside Cambridge, he observed test flights of a new fighter that was faster and more maneuverable than the Spitfire.

P-51 Mustang WWII Vintage
Public Domain

In October of 1942, Hitchcock wrote a memo to Washington suggesting its marriage with the British-made Rolls-Royce Merlin 61 engine. After the substitution, knowledgeable observers thought the sleek Mustang would prove to be the best fighter in the European Theater.

The Air Force top brass were stubborn, unimpressed, or both. They considered the plane a British product because of its made-in-England Merlin. The best American airplane of the war was actually designed by a German, Edgar Schmued, who had once worked for Willie Messerschmidt and built for the British by North American Aviation (Donald Miller, *Masters of the Air: America's Bomber Boys Who Fought the Air War Against Nazi Germany* [New York: Simon & Schuster, 2007], 252). At worst, the Mustang was a half-breed. At best, it was the premier hope the 8th AF had to protect its bombers on the long trip to the heart of the Reich and back.

In his early years at St. Paul's School in New Hampshire, Hitchcock was a student of Professor John Gilbert Winant. They had remained friends and had both served as pilots in WWI. Winant's career had taken him from college professor to the first director of the Social Security Administration under Roosevelt and ultimately to the critical position of US Ambassador to the Court of St. James, with an office in Grosvenor Square, close to that of his friend and confidant. After more than a year of fighting the politics of war, Hitchcock and Winant, who had also taken up the case for the Mustang, finally got the fighter to the Theater in early 1944.

The magnificent machine proved an instant success. With added drop fuel tanks, the Mustang was able to provide cover for the bombers all the way to Berlin and back. After the war, Arnold admitted that this aircraft was instrumental in the Allies' victory. Historian Donald Miller is quoted as saying that the failure to employ the Mustang earlier was "one of the most egregious errors in the history of American airpower" (Donald Miller, *Masters of the Air: America's Bomber Boys Who Fought the Air War Against Nazi Germany* [New York: Simon & Schuster, 2007], 253). Tommy Hitchcock used his business skills, dogged competitive style, and firsthand knowledge of the needs of the Air Force to keep the error from being a supremely lethal one.

The sight of the English Channel came none too quickly for Bud and the crew. "Home safe again," Leo announced proudly.

"Afghan VE 2D-7100 *Century Note*, requesting permission to land," Glenn Vaughn called to the tower at Ridgewell.

"Permission granted, put her down. Welcome home, boys," came the reply.

At debriefing, Bud learned that the buzz bomb that rocked the camp the night before had smashed down in the nearby small hamlet of Little Yeldham, only a mile and a half from the base. No known fatalities had occurred. He chose to only tell Thelma that, *"There was a lot of excitement at the base on Saturday evening."* He likewise understated the risk and difficulty of the mission on the seventh, only saying he was too tired to write after a tough day.

London, England – October 9–11, 1944

Few things outside of an Air Force mandate to fly would get an airman out of bed early on a cold October day. But a two-day pass to London was one of them. By noon, after a truck ride, whistle stops in Great Yeldham and Mark's Tey—a final leg into Paddington, and a fifteen-minute taxi ride—Leo, Jim, and Bud again found themselves at Piccadilly Circus in the center of London. With each trip, they found the bustling British city more familiar and interesting.

Train at Marks Tey to London
Bob Armstrong WWII Album

Bud had chosen the time away over treatment for an aching wisdom tooth. No sooner had he exited the taxi that he realized his decision had been a poor one. Aspirin muted but didn't kill the pain. With Jim's help, he was able to find an Army clinic where, after an hour wait, he saw a dentist at last. An X-ray showed no reason for the trouble, but Bud convinced the man to pull the tooth anyway. The almost-immediate relief from the nagging and sometimes-intense pain confirmed his decision.

After a few drinks at a Leicester Square watering hole, the boys got a room in a private home that another Knoxville boy had recommended. Upon his return to base, Bud later wrote to Thelma, ". .

. it was a very nice home with the most expensive-looking fixtures and furniture I've ever seen. It was a little weather-beaten or maybe something else, like bomb damage, could have caused the outside to look a little shabby. The lady who owned it said General Arnold always stayed there, so I said what's good enough for 'Hap' is good enough for me."

The next morning, feeling much better, Bud rose early and rousted Jim out of a deep sleep, leaving Leo to rest. "Come on, navigator, plot a course to the blacksmith. I need to be reshod," Bud said as he shook a groggy Jim until he finally rolled out. By noon, Bud had accomplished his prime goal, the purchase of another pair of fine high-top British shoes. *"I sold my buckle ones to our radio man, McCoy, 'cause they didn't fit me, and he liked them. My new ones are OK for dress and work—you'll love them,"* he wrote to Thelma. After more purchases of pajamas, wool socks, long drawers, and some fish and chips, the two met up with Leo and reversed the two-hour trip back to Ridgewell.

When he reached his barracks, Bud

> *. . . found just what I had hoped for and thought about all the way home—this big letter and another containing a lot of sports news, all from my sweet mama. One of the letters was quite a large volume in itself and contained lots of news which I'm always eager to know. I know you couldn't possibly make all the letters that long and newsy but they sure are nice to get sweetheart. Was very sorry to hear of Gatewood* [Thelma had informed him that Vernon Gatewood, a friend from Big Spring, had been shot down on September 10, 1944 and was a POW in the same camp as Grover Blevins.] *and I do hope that things work out all right for him and Grover. There is every reason to have hope.*

Cologne, Germany
Ridgewell Mission #197 – October 14, 1944

On Saturday night, Bud settled in his uncomfortable but familiar bed and began a letter to his love. *"Dear Baby—Your ole poppy hasn't changed as far as keeping up with his belongings. I've been looking for my fountain pen for over 30 minutes so I could write you—finally found it in my shirt pocket where it usually is. Sorta expected some mail today when I got in—but none at all. Maybe it'll come tomorrow."* Then Bud gave Thelma his standard understated analysis of the mission he had flown earlier in the day: *"—had another rough day today—so I'm a little tired tonight."*

On that "rough day," flak, the ultimate weapon used against Allied aircraft, wreaked havoc on a ship of the 381st. The Belskis crew was flying in *Mizpah* in the high squadron. The *Pella Tulip* , piloted by 1st Lt. Charles W. Reseigh, was flying at the tail end of the low squadron, taking off near the squadron's end at 0956.

After a three-hour flight and two minutes before bombs away over Cologne, the Tulip was hit by a flak burst that lit up the front area of the aircraft. The *Tulip* was visible to *Mizpah*'s tail gunner Robert Rogers low to his left and three rows behind. When the flak struck the *Tulip*, Rogers hollered into the mic, "Oh no—holy crap—that ain't good."

"What ain't good?" Leo asked.

"One of our boys is hit, and it looks bad," Newman shot back. "It's either *Little Guy* or *Tulip*, can't tell which. They dropped out of formation and down to their right—they're struggling."

"Keep your mind on our business," Leo commanded the crew. "We're now on target. Perrin has the controls," he added, knowing the edict from Eighth brass that after the controls are handed over to the bombardier and the Norden, they must stay on mission all the way through the bomb run and past the target to the rally point.

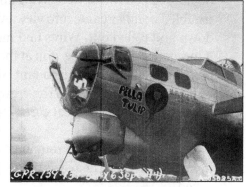

Pella Tulip - B17G, AC #42-102703, 532nd VE-9/6/44
USAAF - 381st

Bud added. "Stand by—steady." All was quiet in the *Mizpah* except for the continuous pinging of flak striking various parts of the B-17. Each caused an instant flinch and surge of fear throughout the crew, who wondered if the metal had entered the craft and damaged a critical control element. The plane surged slightly forward, and at the same instant, Bud announced, "Bombs away."

The Norden held the *Mizpah* steady, completing the run, then Leo took control, pulled the bomber up to the right, and proceeded to the rally point for the trip home. "Any more info, Rogers?" he asked.

"Can't see; too much flak smoke."

At that instant shards of metal tore through the cabin between Rogers and the left waist of the ship. "Let's get the heck out of here," Suggs hollered.

Two turns, and the formation was intact for the return to England except for the *Tulip*, which was nowhere in sight. "We're on our way, boys," Leo said. "Eyes open, stay alert, can the chatter. We've got a long way home."

The ride back was unusually quiet. The crew knew something awful had occurred; they just didn't know how awful. They worried about the crew of the other ship—whichever one it was. *It could have been us—and may well be someday*, Bud thought.

At last, they landed safely in Ridgewell. Word of the problem on the bomb run quickly found its way through the crowd watching the returning planes land. Few of the thirty-six other crews saw the strike on the *Tulip*, as most were flying ahead of it. After almost an hour, the troubled bomber came into view. After a wobbly approach, it touched down and rolled out. Wires and metal shards hanging from its nose, it lurched to a struggling stop at the end of the runway amid thunderous applause from the remnant who had remained along the flight line, hoping and praying. The crew was extracted from the plane and rushed to receive medical care. The *Tulip's* bombardier canopy was completely destroyed.

The Belskis crew had remained near the tower. "That's absolutely incredible. How in heaven's name did that ship make it back?" Lauret asked.

"It must have been eighty below with the wind factor," Newman said, shaking his head in disbelief.

Over the next hour in the interrogation session, the unpleasant facts of the situation became clear. A hushed respect prevailed throughout the normally loud briefing process.

The flak strike on the *Tulip* shattered its nose and cockpit, knocking the bomber out of formation. Flak bursts hit Reseigh in the face and both arms, breaking one of his legs and rendering him unconscious. The co-pilot, 1st Lt. David R. Rautio, was also knocked out by the blast, but regained consciousness, pulled the ship out of its dive, and salvoed the bomb load.

T/Sgt. John M. Nushy, the engineer and top turret gunner, put out a fire in the cockpit and helped remove the pilot to the radio room, where the bombardier administered first aid. Nushy then climbed into the pilot's seat where he acted as co-pilot for Rautio and intermittently massaged the twenty-one-year-old's face and neck to minimize danger from frostbite. For the next four hours, Rautio fought with the damaged but stubborn Fortress. Despite the streaming cold of the open cockpit, he nursed the damaged Fort back to England with only the two left side engines working.

Nushy suffered mainly from conjunctivitis caused by the flying plexiglass from the plane's shattered nose. Navigator and First Officer Maryan J. Winicki narrowly escaped serious injury when, at Rautio's order, he stooped down to pick up a flak helmet. At the same time, Nushy bent over to check a flaw in his oxygen equipment. At that moment, a flak burst slammed right past the spot where their heads had been only moments before.

For the next week, Bud did not fly. Sunday, October 15 was a day to give prayers of thanks for the safety of the crew over the previous six weeks since coming to Ridgewell and especially on the Cologne mission. He attended the base church service and shared a hymnal with Lt. Bob Angevine during the exuberant singing.

After church, he and Angevine ate at the mess hall and then went to the Officers' Club for a few hours of camaraderie and conversation. "Hey, Bob," Bud called to Angevine as he looked over the previous day's London edition of *Stars and Stripes*. "Ike was fifty-four yesterday." He read more before adding; "It says here that Bing Crosby returned after his eight weeks tour of US camp shows in Britain and France and told newspaper correspondents, 'The only serious question I was asked a hundred times by American soldiers was if the people back home think the war is over? They are concerned about the reports of the complacent attitude throughout America and do not want to hear about post-war plans at the moment—and — the closer you get to the front, the higher the morale.'"

"Do you think that's true? I wonder if he interviewed anyone at Ridgewell while he was here," Bud wondered aloud. "If the folks back home are complacent, it's either because top brass won't let us tell them what we really face, or they just can't imagine what it's like here."

With time off from missions for the next few days, Bud wrote a few important notes to keep family informed of his well-being and continued thoughts about them.

> *I met Bob Angevine going in to church on Sunday so we sat together and sang together. For once they sang a few songs I know. And I was able to carry a tune. Chaplain Brown's talk was rather interesting and broad minded— matter of fact it didn't sound like a sermon at all. He told how much he like movies, baseball, and all sort of amusement. Said he told Bing Crosby when he was here that he thought he and his type did more for the boys in service than the chaplains. Edward G. Robinson was here not so long ago and he told the chaplain that he was going to induct him into his gang.*

Ridgewell Chaplain James Goode Brown
USAAF - 381st

On the seventeenth, Bud wrote again:

> *We had a crew photo taken in front of a B-17 yesterday—We didn't fly but had to dress as if we were and stand in front of a plane while the photographer snapped away. A number of crews had to do the same. We used the same plane as a background—Chug-A-Lug IV. All the crews commented that they had never flown the plane. So don't think it was one of ours (the 532nd BS).*
>
> *...today is Evelyn's birthday—30*

years old—I've thought of it several times but never when I could do anything about getting her something or even getting a card in time to get it there by her birthday. Explain to her that I didn't forget, only failed to do a thing about it. Hope she enjoys her 30th. Boy, that's getting up there, isn't it?

I'm glad you and Junior are getting plenty of fresh air, and I'm sure he will be a naughty, husky brat, especially if he takes after his mama. By the way, what if he is a beautiful little girl? You've only mentioned Junior lately. I'll be happy either way. There's always another chance.

By the way, I'm still with the crew. When I navigate, I fly with another crew, but so far only three or four times.

On Tuesday, October 24, the Belskis crew traveled fifty miles away to the aerodrome base at Bassingbourn, west of Ridgewell and south of Cambridge. Bud thought Thelma would like to know, since the famous crew of *The Memphis Belle* from that base had been on a tour through the States to promote sales of savings bonds to support the War effort.

I took a little trip today over to another field for some special training. It was the home of the Memphis Belle *and also where Clark Gable was located during his stay here in the ETO. They had lots of pictures, both of Gable and the Memphis Belle crew. It's a rather nice base, much nicer than ours, but this place* [Ridgewell] *is beginning to seem more like home so I was glad to come back after spending the day away.*

I will write J. Ross and tell him to be a big boy about having his tonsils out. [Thelma had informed him that his nephew was scheduled to have them removed due to repeated infections.] *He is a little young for it, isn't he? Was glad to hear that mother's check was for sixty bucks this time.*

I found a pretty cute little dog in my bed this morning. He belongs to the Colonel [Leber] *who is away for a few*

Memphis Belle Crew - after 25th Mission -1943
Harold Loch , Cecil Scott , Robert Hanson, James Verinis, Robert Morgan,
Charles Leighton, John Quinlan, Casmir Nastal, Vincent Evans, Clarence Winchell
USAAF

days and left him with one of the fellows in our barracks to
keep. Two fellows brought him back from France about a
month ago. He was too young to understand French when
he first got here so they didn't have the trouble of teaching
him English. I think he's about the cutest little dog I've ever
seen. I gave him a piece of my peanut brittle because he
begged so hard for it. He liked it as much as I did—stay
sweet, Love, Bud

On October 26, the full Belskis crew flew the *Liberty Bell* to Munster, Wehrmecht headquarters for a significant portion of the Reich's ground operations in Western Germany and Belgium. Munster was socked in, so Bielefeld was chosen as the day's target of opportunity. Bombing was carried out by Pff through a 10/10 undercast, with unobserved results. On the previous day, other First Wing bases engaged in a mission to Munster, but the 381st bombed Hamburg with good success and no losses.

The next day, a mission to Mannheim was scrubbed after briefing. Some boys had a hard time getting to sleep after missions were scrubbed. But the 0430 wake up call for the cancelled Mannheim mission and the hard day on the Munster mission the day before left Bud so sleep-deprived that he crawled back into bed and slept until noon. His report to Thelma read, *"I didn't write last night, sweetheart, as I was a little too tired to do anything other than hit the sack after a pretty rough day. Today was almost the same—but not quite. Got up kinda early, so I imagine I'll be turning in early also."*

Once again, he did.

Münster, Germany
Ridgeway Mission #207 – October 28, 1944

Bud awoke at 0600 and realized that all the other barracks residents remained in bed. That could only mean that there would be no mission that day or there would be a mission but no crew from the 532nd or 535th, the other squad with crew billeted with them, would be involved. *But that doesn't seem likely, so I guess we have no mission today,* he thought as he rolled over to return to sleep.

Bud was wrong. At 0800, the familiar squeak of the door knob and the quick steps of the CQ dispelled his hopes. "Perrin, Vaughn, you lucky boys are flying today. Chow at 0830."

"Well, looks like they're keeping us flying together," Glenn whispered to Bud. At briefing, they both learned that this assumption was also inaccurate. Bud was informed that he would be flying as bombardier in the squadron's lead ship, *Sunkist Special,* a Pathfinder piloted by Lt. Edwin A. Bryce Jr. and Lt. William Seeley. The 381st formation would be led by Major Taylor, also in a Mickey ship with Maj. Demaglski flying co-pilot.

It'll be odd, flying in a formation with the rest of my crew family in the Mizpah, Bud thought. *We've flown together in that ship twice before this month. But I won't take time to dwell on it now.*

This would be his first mission flying squadron lead as a bombardier. He had flown squadron and division lead as a navigator with Reed and Armstrong to Magdeburg back in September, but not as a bombardier, and not with this crew.

Bud had seen but never met either Lt. Bryce or Seeley. At the conclusion of briefing, he sought both out and made the introduction himself. "Lt. Ross Perrin," Bud said, extending his hand and smiling. Bryce

Sunkist Special - B-17G, Pff AC #42-97625,
with Ground Crew - 7/27/44
USAAF - 381st

turned to Seeley and said, "Bill, this is Lt. Perrin—Ross Perrin, he'll be dropping the ordnance for us today."

"Sir, I'm a good friend of your crew's bombardier, C.D. Cash—great guy," Bud responded politely.

"You're right, lieutenant —you go by Bud, I think. Or at least that's what Lt. Cash calls you. He speaks highly of you."

Bud smiled as they divided up for the sub-briefing for each of their flight positions. After that, the ride to the hardstand was its normal one, bumpy and cold, with the canvas truck sides that protected the boys from the early-morning chill flapping along the way. Some of the crew took this as an opportunity to stretch out the kinks, readying for a long day's ride to Munster and back. Others chose to take a leak off the side of the hardstand, and one boy performed his ritual of throwing up before entering the ship. *I don't know if he does that for good luck or to get rid of tension*, Bud mused. *Guess it doesn't matter much either way.*

"The flimsie says our load is five 500-pounders. Looks like all is in order," Bud said as he looked down the throat of the bomb bay after swinging himself up through the entrance hatch aft of the bombardier station.

Take off beginning at 1010 was orderly. The *Sunkist Special* lifted off at 1051, right on schedule. Assembly over the base was just as orderly, and the bomber formation was on its way for the two-and-a-half-hour trip to the IP. Also on the mission with the 381st were the 351st—Polebrook, 398th — Nuthampstead, 401st — Deenethorpe and the 457th — Glatton.

All checkpoints over England were made good, and the formation left the English coast on course and on time. With his Norden bombsight checked out and locked in, Bud had a little time to let his mind wander. *Bombing's supposed to be by Pff with a heavy undercast approaching 10/10*, he thought. *But the weather seems to be clearing the further we go into Europe.* The clear visibility made more vivid the beauty of this late-morning Channel crossing and trip over the beautiful countryside of Belgium and northwestern Germany.

All I keep remembering are those trips to the Smokeys with Thelma, Bud thought. *But that makes me count missions and project when I might complete my 35 and be able to head home. Münster's my thirteenth, so I'm about forty percent done.* He did a few more mental calculations. *At this rate, I'll probably finish in late February unless, of course, Germany throws in the towel earlier. Fat chance.*

"OK boys, we're thirty minutes from the IP. Let's get ready." came the voice of Lt. Bryce over the intercom. "Gunners, check your guns."

In rapid succession, each of the fifty calibers in all six of the B-17 gun locations clicked off a few rounds, making sure none had jammed. "Oxygen check," instructed Bryce. Each crew member reported back. "Make sure to take a walk-around bottle if you move. We don't want any anoxia." Quiet prevailed throughout the *Sunkist Special* for the next ten minutes.

Boyce again came over the intercom to announce, "We're approaching the IP—ten out." Almost immediately, he added, "Lead Squadron's Mickey is out of commission; we're taking over. Perrin, it's all yours."

Boyce maneuvered the ship into the lead position of the Lead Squadron as Taylor dropped back to the lead of the Low Squadron. *Squadron lead and now Division Lead.* The thoughts raced through Bud's mind. But all he said was, "Let's put these rocks down the smokestack."

He made minor adjustments as navigator Ed Dvorak read out coordinates and wind speed. The formation continued from the IP along the bomb run. At 21,900 feet and at a time of 1424, Bud called out, "Bombs away." The five five-hundred pound bombs were released and fell true. The bomb run time was three minutes—three long and terrifying minutes as intense and accurate flak pelted the ships, each holding its course steady throughout the run.

The ships then made two turns toward the RP, and the formation turned for home. Boyce's lead ship greased a landing at 1656, rolled out, and returned to its parking spot at the 532nd hardstands. After their return, the crews learned that one ship was damaged so badly it had to land in Belgium. A half-dozen airmen suffered flak-penetrating wounds, and one was hospitalized due to failure of equipment. This was not just another day at the office, but the work was completed with efficiency by the 381st and its sister BGs.

"My first Squadron lead turned out to be a Division lead—not a bad job, Remember, I ain't no hero. So keep it in the family," Bud reported to Thelma in his letter that evening. He was unusually chatty that evening, due in part to the euphoria of his position on the mission.

Lt. Teddy A. Smith - 303rd
BG, 359th BS - 1944
303rd BG website

A letter from Thelma had confirmed that Grover was a POW. *". . . that was good news about Grover. I know Mrs. Blevins and Henrietta were happy to learn about it. I felt all along that it would turn out okay."*

In the letter Bud also received the bad news that Gene Davis, son of Evelyn and Leonard's neighbor, was killed on August 7, when his C-47 crashed west of Warazup, Burma. He was not yet 23. His wife Evelyn would later give birth to a daughter, Eugenia, on November 3, 1944.

On Sunday afternoon, October 29, he added to his letter of the previous day:

> *I planned to go to church this morning, but woke up rather late and was so sleepy anyway. I wasn't quite sure what day it was. That makes two Sundays straight I've missed now. I saw in* Stars and Stripes *where Tennessee won Saturday* (Note: Tennessee 26-Clemson 7.)
>
> *I got a letter from Teddy Smith's brother, Phil, which I hate to answer. He was inquiring about Teddy and I can't give him any good news, I'm sorry to say. However I will answer his letter real soon—I love you baby, your husband.*

(Note: Unknown to Bud was the fact that Teddy had bailed out of his damaged plane on the Magdeburg mission on September 28 and was murdered by Germans after reaching the ground [Source: www.303rdbg.com/missionreports/248.pdf]. The mission to Magdeburg was the one on which Bud flew with Bob Armstrong.)

There was much more work to be done.

CHAPTER 17

A Clash of Culture and Worldview

Differences and Distinctions

Ridgewell, England:
October 30–November 13, 1944

AFTER THE TWO TRIPS TO Münster, the 381st put up ships for missions to Gelsenkirchen on October 30 and Harburg on November 4. But each time, someone else took Bud's spot in the crew. He found it frustrating to hear Vaughn rousted from sleep each morning and his own name not called. *I need the missions,* he thought. *I guess I'm being held back for lead crew work. Just let me fly!*

A mission to Frankfurt took place on the fifth, but none of the Belskis crew participated. Glenn slept late, and after breakfast and the church service at the base chapel, Bud curled up in his bed and read some magazines he had borrowed the day before. Belskis and Collett showed up mid-afternoon and convinced their two partners to trade the cold, dank confines of the barrack for a warm fire, interesting conversation, the possibility of darts, and more than a few tankards of British ale.

It was late in the afternoon when the four reached The Fox, usually a busy time for the pub, but on that Sunday, only a couple of boys were there, so their favorite table in the corner by the fireplace was open. "Saved it just for you chaps," Bill said as he pulled the chair back for Leo.

"Four cold ones," Collett said.

"I want some fish and mash," Bud put in, asking for mashed potatoes with the haddock served at The Fox.

"Make it two fish and mash," added Leo.

"Three," Glenn said.

"I'll pass on the sea burgers," Collett added with a grimace. "Bring me some bangers (British sausage) and mash."

The warmth of The Fox, the friendliness of its owner, and some pretty good food almost made the boys forget about home for a few hours. Almost.

"Hey, Perrin—sure was strange flying to Münster a couple of days ago knowing you were in another ship right ahead of us," Leo said.

"Byron Weir flew with us and toggled off of your bomb drop," Collett explained. "As soon as he heard the transmission, Leo told us Maj. Taylor's Pff went south on him and your ship took the division lead."

"From all reports, the bombing was quite a success. Great job," Leo added.

He didn't want to show it, but Bud was quite proud of his performance and the recognition of his peers.

They had just finished their dinner and a couple of extra brews when out of the corner of his eye, Bud saw Tony Fabiani again enter The Fox. "Look what the cat drug in." Bud said, dropping his head in hopes he had gone unnoticed.

As usual, his ploy was unsuccessful. In his normal abrasive manner, Tony pushed his way through and sat at the table next to the Belskis boys. *I hope he doesn't insert himself into our conversation again,* Bud thought. *Maybe if I don't look at him, he'll leave us alone.*

He didn't.

"Hey Perry," Tony said in an obvious attempt to get a rise out of Bud by again mispronouncing his name. Bud didn't take the bait, so Tony made another cast. "You guys talking baseball, football, war, or religion?" The quartet looked at each other but no one responded.

"I've been thinking about something. Tell me. How does war fit into religion? If you believe in God, how do you justify war?" Fabiani asked in a voice dripping with sarcasm.

"Self-protection is evident throughout the Bible," Vaughn replied. *I'm glad Glenn's helping me,* Bud thought. *I sure don't want to take on this discussion solo.*

"Okay, how 'bout this: You say you're a Christian, right?"

"Yes," Bud responded.

Glenn nodded in agreement, but Collett didn't move.

Leo said, "Does Catholic count? If so, count me in."

"All right. So why do you think you're right and other religions are wrong?" Fabiani pressed.

All four were quiet. After a few seconds that seemed like an hour, Bud broke the deafening silence. "Before we answer that question, let me ask you one. By what source or standard do you determine right from wrong, or what's true from what isn't?" Bud's verbal volley achieved the unbelievable and rendered Tony silent—at least for a moment or two.

"Truth is different for everyone," their antagonist said haltingly. Feeling that he had put Bud, Glenn, and Leo on the defensive, his voice became more strident as he volleyed back to the group. "It's what each person determines it to be for himself. Are we talking about your truth or my truth?"

"Truth, by definition, is one thing. So how can you say it's different for everyone?" Bud asked, with an accompanying nod from Leo.

"We all have the right to our own beliefs, so it has to be different for everyone," Tony responded.

"So you are saying that truth is relative and not absolute, correct?" Bud questioned.

"Absolutely," Tony shot back. By then, their audience had grown to more than a dozen. No one else had the will to expose his lack of conviction by either answering or asking a question, so the talk remained a two-airman conversation.

Bud then followed with a query that stunned the group. "So would you say it's absolutely true that truth is relative?"

Tony sat mute, elbows resting on the table, chin in his hands. Realizing he'd been snookered, he removed his elbows from the table, leaned back, and folded his arms to his chest.

"You're just playing with words now. What if I believe there's no God?" he shot back in one more attempt to take the offensive.

"We all have a right to believe what we want," Bud replied.

"But you said what you believe is true, Perrin," said another boy at the second table, putting his toe in the waters of debate.

"No, I said you can believe what you want, but belief doesn't make something true. You can believe goats can fly, but that doesn't mean you'll see them soaring over our airfield," Bud countered.

"In Texas, they can fly," came an alcohol-laced voice from another table. Laughter erupted. Even the two principal debaters joined the chorus that seemed to take the edge from the tense discussion.

"If I believe accepting Christ is the way to heaven and you don't believe that, then we both can't be right because we believe opposite things," Bud explained. "Doesn't that make sense?"

"I don't believe in God or heaven. This right here is as good as it gets," Tony replied.

"I sure hope not," came the reply from the Texan who had said that Texas goats could fly.

After the laughter died down, Bud added; "You certainly have that right, but I believe in both God and heaven."

"How many gods do you believe there are, one or many?" a pilot from the 535th asked.

"I believe there is one God. And you believe that God doesn't exist, right?" Bud responded to the question but addressed Tony with his own.

His opponent nodded as he again leaned forward, resting his elbows on the table, wet from beer that had flowed over the rim of mugs jostled by the crowd surrounding the debate forum.

"Well, we both can be wrong—there could be many gods, but we can't both be right. If one is right, the other has to be wrong, because one contradicts the other," Bud asserted.

"This is getting too heavy," Tony said, slamming his fist to the table. "You believe what you want and I'll believe what I want," he added as he stood up and waved both palms. This gesture affirmed his rejection of further discussion and signaled the end of the debate.

It's over for now, Bud thought. *But somehow, I don't think it's over.* For the next hour, he and the crew finished their meal without mentioning the evening's intense discussion. But his frustration was obvious.

As the boys ventured from his pub into the cold, dark evening, Bill shouted his traditional goodbye from behind the bar. "Tally-ho, Yanks!"

The snow had stopped, but the biting cold persisted. The boys walked toward the makeshift back entrance to the base and climbed over the fence. "I'll be along in a few minutes," Bud said. "I need to think about a couple of things."

"Don't let that horse's butt bug you, Perrin," Collett said. "He's not worth it."

I know better, Bud thought, *but I don't want to let on to them. Wonder if I've won the battle but lost the war, as Dr. Wallace used to say?*

William Wallace (Back Row Center) Sunday School - RWPJr - Row 3, #3
Greene Family Collection

Dr. Wallace was his former Sunday school teacher in the Juniors class back at Broadway Baptist Church, who had often given his students advice on debates over faith matters. *Maybe God will give me an opportunity for a one-on-one talk about Christianity with Tony outside the spotlight of a pub setting*, Bud thought. *I sure hope so.* Their debate and its abrupt conclusion had softened his feelings toward his erstwhile antagonist. *I can't believe I feel this way, but it's gotta be a good thing.*

As his crewmates walked toward the barracks, Bud took the opposite route that led to the hardstand where the 532nd Forts were parked. After a few minutes, he stood at the edge of the parking area, his eyes scanning the profile of the massive bomber in front of him. *It seems a lot more ominous in the dark*, he thought. His eyes came to rest on the craft's name, *Mizpah*, emblazoned on the nose just behind the bombardier canopy, just below a small painted cross.

Before his time in England, Bud knew nothing of the name *Mizpah* or its Hebrew origins. Angevine had told him the meaning from Genesis 31:49, "The Lord watch between me and thee when we are absent one from another." Its import haunted him only two days before when he flew it on the on the mission to Kassel. As he stood shivering beneath it on that cold night, the name's wartime significance again moved his heart.

A hundred feet away, *Century Note* loomed out of the night. *Liberty Bell* and *Our Boarding House* stood nearby as silent guards for the Ridgewell aerodrome and the airmen who lived and worked there. *Hell's Angel* was also visible in the distance. Bud chuckled to himself as he pondered the name's perverse message.

The strength these mighty ships carried was obvious to anyone who caught a glimpse of them or heard the rumbling sound they made either at engine startup or in full flight. The B-17's nickname accurately defined its ability not only to endure damage to which lesser craft would succumb but to continue the fight as well.

The evening's debate about his Christian beliefs continued to haunt Bud. As he looked up at the ship in front of him, he began to hum and then to sing the familiar hymn: "A mighty fortress is our God, a bulwark never failing, our helper He amid the flood, of mortal ills prevailing."

How I wish Dr. Wallace's free-flowing words would come back to me when my beliefs are challenged as they were tonight, Bud thought. *He always said we should be able to defend our faith—"Christian apologetics," he called it. And when I get home, I'll prepare myself to do just that, but in a way that beckons, not blasts.*

Warm tears flowed down his cheeks in the quiet of that frigid night as he sang more of the hymn. "Did we in our own strength confide, our striving would be losing, were not the right man on our side, the man of God's own choosing. Let goods and kindred go, this mortal life also; the body they may kill; God's truth abideth still; his kingdom is forever."

Is there a greater mission here than the ones to Kassel, Cologne, Merseburg, or Münster? he thought. *Sure, the overall mission of preserving peace and stopping Schicklegruber is the big one.* The name at which Miss Neubert had so often scoffed returned to his mind as he thought of those days of study in 1941. *But is there another mission?* he wondered. *Do I have one that's the same as the one that so captivated Dr. Wallace? That one may well be the biggest mission of all.*

His vision blurred, he stared down at the mushy ice in which he stood. The mixture of oil, aircraft fuel, dirt, and engine grime painted a lustrous but indefinable miniature landscape on the hardstand. He brushed his sleeve across his eyes, attempting to wipe away the tears as he tried to focus on the concrete canvas at his feet. Then, glancing up at the underbelly of the *Mizpah*, the dual meaning of Fortress came into sharp focus. The stillness and meditation of the brief few minutes on the hardstand brought comfort as he turned and began the ten-minute walk back to his barracks. He slipped into the quietness of his hut, crawled into bed, and slept soundly.

(Note: Mr. Wallace was Dr. William Wallace who in 1929, as a twenty-one-year-old medical student, taught a group of teenage boys in a Sunday school class at Broadway Baptist Church in Knoxville, Tennessee. In 1925, he had committed his life to being a medical missionary, a commitment he fulfilled when he became a missionary doctor and surgeon at a hospital in Wuchouw, China. Withstanding numerous wartime difficulties, he remained at his post, ministering both the gospel of Christ and his medical abilities to the people there. On December 20, 1950, he was imprisoned where he continued to share his faith in Christ with both inmates and guards. He was murdered by his Communist captors two months later, at age forty-two. Jesse C. Fletcher, *Bill Wallace of China*, [Nashville: Broadman Press, 1963].)

Bud wrote to Thelma a couple of days later, without relating the encounter at The Fox.

I'm enclosing the picture of our crew taken a few weeks ago. You know the four of us standing in the back. In the front are Newman, Suggs, Rogers, McCoy, and Lauret—I think it's a good crew and wish I was still flying with them, but since they've put me in the lead I doubt if I'll fly with them very often. Notice the ink spots—I had to censor the picture before I could send it home.

Our barracks acquired a couple of pets and they are something I never did like—cats. However, they have helped the mice situation. I think they are twins both are black with white spots one of them has a black moustache looks like it has been painted on. We call him Hitler.

Oh yeah—I almost forgot the play. "Blithe Spirit" is playing on our base tonight with the New York cast. Last night Leo and I had a few drinks at the club with Peggy Word, a lady about forty years old, who plays the part of the 2nd wife in the play. I told her all about my play-acting wife and that I was going to be a papa. She was interesting to talk to. Said she would love to go on a mission with us, but we couldn't arrange it.

I'm hoping to go to London this weekend. All my love— your loving poppy to be.

(Note: *Blithe Spirit*, considered the most successful of all the twenty-nine plays Noel Coward wrote during his illustrious career, premiered in London's Piccadilly Theater on July 2, 1941 where it enjoyed a run of 1997 performances. It also had an eighty-seven week, 657-performance Broadway run. Ever-popular, it enjoyed a fifty-three major city transcontinental tour, including Ridgewell and other bases in England. Peggy Word also played Ruth, the second wife, in the Broadway cast. Wikipedia Contributors, "Blithe Spirit," *Wikipedia, The Free Encyclopedia*, http://en.wikipedia. org/wiki/Blithe_Spirit_%28play%29.)

Cambridge

Cambridge and London were by far the two most common destinations for Ridgewell airmen on two- or three-day passes. Cambridge was closer, about forty miles and one hour away. But London, even though almost seventy miles, three train rides, an underground jaunt, and fifteen minutes by taxi away, had other attractive elements. Far more diverse and bustling, it was therefore more appealing to

Ridgewell boys looking for a hot shower, comfortable beds, and some R & R.

On Thursday, November 9, Bud and Leo decided that rather than going directly to London, they should take in some of Cambridge's academic culture and architecture. The base provided regular transportation to Cambridge, so they boarded the transport truck and an hour later piled out in front of King's College Chapel.

"Incredible," Bud said as the two walked alongside the architectural marvel and sat on the bank of the River Cam. They relaxed, watching some young boys decked out in bow ties and flat-brimmed straw hats navigate the almost-stagnant stream. They used long poles to push and guide their flat-bottomed, square-nosed boats along. "So this is punting?" Bud asked, a tinge of humor in his voice. "It's done differently on The Hill [referring to the kickers for the Tennessee football team]."

"Can't refrain from talking football, can you?" Leo said with feigned disgust.

They walked back through the quadrangle alongside the Chapel to Trinity Street, turned right, and caught sight of Jim Collett a few paces in front of them. "Jim," Leo hollered.

Collett, who had come to Cambridge the night before, turned and asked, "Where are you blokes going?"

"We're heading to The Eagle for some grub," Bud replied.

"Me, too. Let's go."

The trio walked to Bene't Street, turned left and immediately saw the sign for The Eagle Pub, a popular watering hole where RAF and USAAF airmen were known to bend an elbow.

The Eagle was replete with old-world charm. Entering the pub, the boys walked past the ornate oaken bar on the left, lined two-deep with a raucous crowd of tippling airmen and engaging young ladies. The small room that separated the front bar from their back-room destination was adorned with photos of British and American patrons, and Bud stopped to see if he recognized any. Generals Hap Arnold and Jimmy Doolittle stood out, but no one else.

The Eagle was also well-known for a most unusual tradition. Since the beginning of WWII, visiting airmen would emblazon their names on the ceiling of the backroom bar with the soot from a burning

Eagle Pub Ceiling-Cambridge,
England-2013
Photo by J. Ross Greene

candle or cigarette lighter. One patron with a well-developed artistic flair had drawn the outline of a curvaceous woman there as well. Bud wanted to join the tradition but had never followed through. "Wanna do it?" Leo asked, pointing upward.

"Maybe later."

As usual, the back-room bar was two-deep with revelers. Consistent with British protocol, they ordered beers at the stand to the left of the bar and nursed them until a couple of seats came available at a table near the back wall. The couple seated at the four-top table motioned for the boys to join them.

Jim, having taken full notice of an attractive lady who appeared to be alone at the bar, had already begun his attempts to attract her attention. Instead of joining his friends, he continued his pursuit.

"Dr. Colin and Maude Barnsley," the man said extending his hand first to Bud, then to Leo.

"Ross Perrin and Leo Belskis," said Bud. "Hey, my mother's name is Maude. Love that name!" he beamed.

"Where are you chaps from?"

"I'm from Tennessee—Knoxville."

"I'm a Yankee from Chicago," responded Leo.

"You mean a Yank," Maude said.

"No, a Yankee. In the States, we refer to people from up north as Yankees. The term *Yank* goes for all US servicemen. So I'm a 'Yankee Yank.' I guess you'd say," Leo explained.

"I see," said Dr. Barnsley, shaking his head.

"Can we buy you a drink?" Bud asked.

"Thanks. You're a kind chap, offering to take care of a couple of Limeys. We really should be buying for you after all you do to make living in England safer by the day."

"We'll let you get the next one, OK?" Leo said.

"Is this your first time here?" Maude asked.

"No, we've been to Cambridge a number of times. We usually

Below: The Eagle Pub
Cambridge, England-1944
Photo by J. Ross Greene

Above: The Eagle Pub
Cambridge, England
Fall 2013
Photo by Lynne H. Greene

come to The Eagle each time. We really love the upbeat atmosphere, so different from the small pubs around the base," Bud responded. "What about you all?"

"We're regulars. We've been coming here since we moved from London almost five years ago, right before the Blitz. We love to meet new people, and The Eagle is the best place in the city for that. We're people-watchers—"

Maude interrupted her husband mid-sentence to correct him: "No, we're people-assessors," she said with a smile. "We both love to investigate different cultures under different conditions."

"I guess you meet mostly British and Americans here, and maybe a few Canadians, right?" Leo asked.

"We met a couple of Polish aviators a couple of weeks ago. But the Americans from different states are so different it seems like they don't come from the same country," Dr. Barnsley said. "And American aviators' attitudes have changed markedly over the last couple of years."

"Tell us about you and your families," Colin urged. It seemed that the people assessment had begun, but the boys didn't care. Comfortable that the Barnsleys seemed honest and harmless, Bud and Leo offered a brief rundown of those they'd left behind.

"A new baby in a few months. I'm sure you're excited," Maude said to Bud.

"Beyond excited," he answered with a broad smile. "Now, tell us about your family."

"I'm a professor of economics here. Maude is taking a year's sabbatical from teaching English Composition. We have a twenty-six-year-old daughter, Elizabeth, a graduate of the London School of Economics. She was a home guard spotter on the eastern coast until after the Blitz and Battle of London. Now, she works as a typist at a place called Bletchley Park, south of London.

The professor continued. "Our son, Colin, is a fourth-term philosophy student at Cambridge College, trying to make sense out of the world, and has no idea what he wants to do. He recently met a young woman who is trying to help him balance the socialistic philosophy so prevalent on the college campus with the practical realities of today's world."

"You mentioned the changing attitudes of our airmen in recent years. What do you mean?" Bud asked.

"I would say there's a more hopeful, positive attitude in today's airmen, including you two. Two years ago, the aviators who came in here held an attitude I would call fatalistic hedonism. The US was losing so many planes that they seemed to fear they might not make it through, so they might as well live it up. From what we read, air superiority has now shifted to the Allied side, and the Nazis are on the run. Is that true?"

"Well, we see fewer Luftwaffe on our missions than a few months ago, and a lot less than crews did in '43. So from that standpoint, things may seem marginally safer or at least less risky," Leo said. "However, flak is equally, if not more, intense. The enemy concentrates anti-aircraft locations to protect critical targets: rail yards, oil production equipment, aircraft, and the like. It just takes one blast from a flak gun to bring down a bomber, and we know it. So we never feel safe."

"Not even in bed," Bud added. "Two doodlebug V-1s landed close by our hut a few days ago. We're sure not playing a game of pinochle. Before enlisting and after FDR was reelected in 1940, I tried to get a better handle on how and why the war started and if the US would have to get involved," he shared. "Pearl Harbor answered that question. Looking back, it seems that Lend-Lease virtually ensured our eventual involvement. But the average citizen like me couldn't see it, even though Edward R. Murrow continued to tell us so. By the way, how did you Brits feel about us when Churchill became PM in 1940 and before Roosevelt's reelection six months later?"

"Good question. I believe the answer is clear but not short." Dr. Barnsley responded. "First, we were unsure whether Roosevelt and other US politicians recognized our plight: we couldn't remain free without your help. At best, we could hold Germany, Italy, and Russia at bay until the States came to our aid. And if you waited too long to join in, we might not have been able to win even with your partnership. Churchill intimated as much in veiled comments during his public statements." He paused as if to emphasize his point. "Then when Hitler turned on Russia and the shelling of England slowed, we became more hopeful. Pearl Harbor and your immediate entrance into the war effort let us know we had a chance. Even with his prickliness, Churchill was able to keep people's spirits up. His famous words, 'Keep calm and carry on,' kept us going.

"As an economist, I've also dug into the supply and demand balance of many segments of the war. One of the most important things your country did for us was to help us with food supplies. Having our shipping channels cut off could have starved us—and nearly did. Few realize that the US's ability to more effectively produce high-quality dried milk and eggs—fit for human, not animal consumption—helped us as much as the rickety old tankers you provided under Lend-Lease. You have continued to ship four times as much food in dried protein value in twenty-five percent of the weight as before."

"We can't stand the dried milk and eggs they serve us at the base," Leo said. "We only get fresh eggs on the days we fly a mission, and that's not a good trade."

"Dried food isn't as good as fresh, to be sure, but it has helped keep our island alive." Dr. Barnsley said. "There are a number of war-related differences between the US and the UK. For us, it's 'over here' and not 'over there.' Second, your pre-war productive capacity has been refocused and increased, while much of ours has been damaged or destroyed."

He took a long drink before continuing. "Rationing—both the necessity and the intensity—in your country has been a mere inconvenience, a significant one I'll agree, but still only an inconvenience. For us it has been pervasive and deep, and in many areas, a threat to our very existence. Contrary to the pre-war view held by many US isolationists, there was really no way you could stay out of the war. If you hadn't come here, the war would have sought you out. And I guess it did—at Pearl Harbor."

Both Leo and Bud nodded as they listened to the professor's insightful analysis. *I bet his students love him*, Bud thought.

The conversation covered many more topics of comparison between their two countries: baseball and cricket, football as played by each nation, the B-17 and the Lancaster, the P-51 and the Spitfire, FDR and Winston. After an hour and a half, three beers, and some fish and chips, the boys realized they were too late to get the train to London. They'd have to find a room in Cambridge and continue their trip the next day.

Officers Red Cross
Cambridge, England-1941
Bob Armstrong WWII Album

After exchanging contact information with the Barnsleys, Leo, Bud, and Jim (who had enjoyed a fine dinner with someone who turned out to be a very nice young lady) exited The Eagle, made their way to the Red Cross Officers' Club, rented a room with three "very wide bunk beds," and slept late on Friday morning. After realizing they were again too late to catch the train that would get them to London in time to get to the PX before it closed, Jim and Bud decided to stay in Cambridge and go to London on Saturday. Leo went on ahead.

Friday was filled with sightseeing and then a movie, *White Cliffs of Dover*, with Irene Dunne and Roddy McDowell. "If only these folks knew what it was like to see those cliffs when we get back from a mission, they'd really appreciate it," Bud told Jim. "I think Vera Lynn's rendition of 'White Cliffs of Dover' is one of my favorite songs next to 'White Christmas.' In fact, I love all her songs—and her voice—and she's pretty easy on the eyes, too."

"Hey, you're a married man. No roving eyes, bomber boy," Jim chided.

London

A two-hour train ride with multiple stops the next morning put Jim and Bud in the heart of the city. They caught a cab and went straight to the PX, only to discover it was closed because of Armistice Day. Not to be thwarted in his desire for some new clothes, Bud ordered a bomber jacket from a local shop. *"It'll be ready in about ten days,"* he later wrote to Thelma.

After dinner they met up with Leo; saw the movie *Going My Way,* the story of a parish priest in New York with Bing Crosby and Rise Stevens; and headed for a pub at Covent Garden. Bud later complained in a letter to Thelma that the show *". . . cost 6 shillings, which is $7.20, to sit in the balcony. That's a little too much money."* He also wrote that the play was *". . . too long, about three hours."* It was actually just over two hours long, but Bud's patience was wearing as thin as the elbows of the jacket he was about to replace.

Covent Garden, a three-story marketplace a couple of blocks behind The Strand and a mile from Leicester Square, contained numerous shops and pubs. One in particular, The Punch and Judy, an eighteenth-century public establishment on the lower level at one end of the building, attracted a diverse clientele that included a large number of airmen. The lively conversation and bustling staff made the atmosphere jovial, fun, and a favorite of both Bud and Leo.

It was unusually easy to get a table on that Saturday night. A flirtatious waitress quickly served three beers, with suds pouring down all sides of the cold mugs. "Want some food, loves?" the waitress asked in a bawdy tone.

"We're good for now," Leo said. "Maybe later."

"This may be our last trip to London till after Thanksgiving or maybe even Christmas," Bud told his friends. "We can't miss that last train, though. We need to get a cab in the next hour or so."

A thin, well-dressed, elderly gentleman sitting alone at the next table leaned over and asked, "Where are you chaps stationed?"

"Ridgewell," Jim and Leo said in unison.

"Essex County," Bud added.

"Yes. I know it well. I was born in Halstead," the man said. "Allister T. Crumbley," he added, extending his right hand as he twirled the end of his mustache with his left. "I'm a solicitor—office inside the city of London, at least it was this morning. Nowadays, we live day to day. You never know what each night—or day— will bring."

The three introduced themselves and asked Mr. Crumbley to join them. "Lovely," he said, moving across to the vacant chair.

"I saw the Ridgewell aerodrome when RAF Bomber Command flew Short Stirlings out of it early on, before it was turned over to you chaps. I guess they've done a lot of construction since the end of '42. It must look quite different now. I guess you chaps have taken the population of Ridgewell from seventy-five to what, three thousand?"

"'Bout right," Jim said.

"Hope to take it back to seventy-five soon, if we can get this thing over with," Leo added.

"I guess The White Horse and The King's Head are still operating," Allister said.

"And a few more," Bud added. "We like The Fox, a smaller one at the edge of the base. How long you been in London, sir?"

"Since the mid-thirties, 1936 to be exact. I've lived through some tough days here in the city. My house got bombed in June of '40. Winnie came calling the next day, top hat bouncing and swinging his walking stick. Quite a chap, that Winnie. I then moved in with my brother and his wife."

Changing his topic to the US brass in London, Crumbley ventured into a comparison of US leaders assigned to the long-standing position of Ambassador to the Court of Saint James. "The current US ambassador sure is better than Joe Kennedy, the Hitler-loving chap Roosevelt placed here before. After Kennedy, we Brits were expecting another self-serving big shot. Your country's new choice was quite a surprise."

The airmen nodded their heads in affirmation, although they had no idea who the current ambassador was.

"This chap, John Winant, sure is different. He's always at the sight of a bombing, just like he's one of us. He's become quite close to Winnie and Clemmie, I hear—maybe even closer to their daughter, Sarah," Allister added with a wry chuckle and another twirl of his mustache.

"I think I've seen his picture in the London paper, but I don't know anything about him. Sounds like he's well-liked and an effective representative of our country," Bud said. *I don't really know much about Winant, but I want to hear more about what Crumbley thinks. Who knows, I might learn something,* he told himself.

"We had a coal strike back in mid-'42, and Winant was asked to speak to the striking miners about why they should focus on the important role they could play in winning the war," Crumbley continued. "By cracky, they listened, and went back to work—made our own politicians look pretty bad, he did. But I bet ol' Winnie was glad to have him on our side."

The boys took in this unexpected education with more nods. *Better to keep quiet and not expose my limited understanding of the British economic picture by saying too much,* Bud thought.

"And we also really like that radio guy, Eddie Murrow," their British instructor added.

"He's quite a favorite in the States, too," Leo offered, smiling at the refined Brit's characterization of Murrow as "Eddie." "Before Pearl Harbor, he kept the home front up on what was happening in England and especially in London. It seemed like he had actually become British and was begging America to come to the aid of his country."

"Yeah, my wife and sister say they never miss his daily broadcast," Bud added.

In early November of 1941, Murrow had returned from Britain for a scheduled three-month series of stateside lectures, his first visit home since 1937. Conflicted about taking the trip at a time when he was most needed in England, he feared his adopted country would not survive without US intervention. He was also fearful that the widespread apathy then permeating American thinking might prevent the US from entering the fray. He felt increasingly "convinced that the hour is much later than most people at home appreciate"

(Olson, *Citizens of London*, 50). His reluctance tempered by a steely resolve, Murrow crossed the Pond to reinforce the message he had long trumpeted.

He was welcomed at the airport in New York with an overwhelming enthusiasm that shocked both him and his wife, Janet. According to one report, prior to this time, Murrow had no idea the impact that his daily broadcast, *London Calling,* had on his loyal American listeners. He was the voice of reality about the war. But much like others who returned from prolonged stays in the UK, Murrow was appalled at Americans' complacency about conditions in Europe.

On Tuesday, December 2, a banquet was held in Murrow's honor at the Waldorf-Astoria. Speaker after speaker lauded him for helping quiet the voices of isolationists and giving credence to the interventionists. Roosevelt capped the deluge of appreciation in a telegram read at the dinner that said, ". . . you who gather tonight to honor Ed Murrow repay but a tiny fraction of the debt owed him by millions of Americans." (A.M. Serber, *Murrow: His Life And Times* [New York: Fordham University Press, 1998], 204.)

Moved by Murrow's contribution to bringing the hearts and minds of Americans into concert with his conviction that America must lock arms with Britain, the president invited the Murrows to dine with him and Eleanor at the White House on Sunday, December 7.

Unaware of what was to occur on that ominous day, Gil Winant had accepted a typical invitation to spend December 7 with the Churchills at their weekend retreat, Chequers. He was thus with Churchill at the moment he heard, over a cheap American-made radio, that Japan had attacked the US at Pearl Harbor. Back in DC, the Murrows joined the Roosevelts on the night of the attack. America's inevitable involvement had come to pass, with British and American leaders both together and apart.

Crumbley, the quintessential English gentleman, entertained the three airmen for the next hour with anecdotal British history. He described both the stoic resolve of his fellow British citizens and the unrelenting combination of rowdiness and heroism of the American ex-pats as he held court.

Bud and Leo responded with their profound respect of the Brits, garnered as they observed Londoners going about their daily lives amid the chaos and need the war had foisted upon them. "They never seem to succumb to despair, even as they step over bombing rubble from the night before," Bud commented.

"And the people around our base are always trying to help us, bringing eggs, bread, and the like," Leo added.

"Yeah, a guy in the town, Bert Tanner, is always giving us bread. And man, is it good!" Bud said with relish.

"You know that here in the Isles, bread is stretched with potato flour because of the shortage of hard wheat, don't you?" Crumbley asked. The negative answer remained unspoken.

Realizing their time must draw to a close, the friends reluctantly bid Allister goodbye, paid the chit, and hustled out to catch a cab for the ride to Paddington Station where they would begin the three-train ride to Essex County. After returning to Ridgewell, Bud wrote to Thelma:

> I spent the best pass I've had so far. . . . the first thing I had to do when I got back to the base was to get some fuel for our fire—sure was good to not have to stoke the fire while in Cambridge and London—our wood supply is running rather low. We have some coke, but it doesn't put out the heat wood does, especially in our type of a stove. The other day we brought a bunch of boxes back from the bomb dump for our stove—we discovered one box wasn't empty yet. Lucky we always cut the boxes up before we put them in the stove—slept well in both Cambridge and London— and it was surprisingly quiet for London. Didn't hear a single bomb alert all night—Sunday morning we started to church but got lost several times and ended up seeing Buckingham Palace and a few of the old cathedrals. Then caught the train for home—by the way Vaughn heard yesterday that he's the poppy of a baby boy—no cigar yet though—cause they are rationed—the baby was born November 5th.

No call came the following morning, November 13, and Bud learned that the last Ridgewell mission flown was to Cologne on

Friday, November 10. Talk at the Officers' Club later in the morning was all about that mission. Just after the bomb run, three 110-pound bombs that had jammed in an aircraft above fell clear and struck the 535th aircraft, *Hell's Angel*, flying below. Two of the bombs fell all the way through and tore off the plexiglass nose of the ship. The third entered the nose compartment between the astrodome and the windshield, striking and killing the bombardier, 1st Lt. Leroy Drummond. The bomb remained jammed in the floor of the nose compartment for about forty-five minutes before it could be dislodged and dropped out the forward escape hatch. The pilot, 1st Lt. Floyd Metts, nursed the Fortress back to Ridgewell. Metts and the rest of the crew were uninjured and hospitalized overnight for rest. Top turret gunner Sgt. Albert Atz remained unaware of Drummond's death until *Hell's Angel* had landed, although he knew the ship had been hit.

The nerve-racking event rattled the base as airmen recognized anew the real flight risk they all faced. *I can't imagine what they must have felt,* Bud thought as he considered the horrors of the accident.

The base would not participate in another mission until November 16.

Hell's Angel - B-17G, AC #42-97265, with Battle Damage -11/10/44
USAAF - 381st

CHAPTER 18

A Radio Message to the Folks Back Home

Thanksgiving 1944

Ridgewell and London, England:
November 14–16, 1944 and November 23, 1944

WITH EACH PASSING MONTH IN the fall of 1944, the German Wehrmacht was being worn down. Fuel supplies were declining, reducing the strength of Goering's Luftwaffe. Territory captured earlier was being challenged and taken back by Allied forces. But even with their hard-earned success, the US military and the government both recognized the economic necessity of continuing the sale of war bonds.

As Thanksgiving and Christmas approached, FDR, fresh from his fourth-term presidential victory, combined the promotion of the bonds with the opportunity to raise the nation's spirits by airing interviews with servicemen stationed in Europe and other theaters of battle. Two Knoxville servicemen were among those chosen to represent the 8th AAC. Bud Perrin was one of them.

Their correspondence reflected the shared excitement of Bud in England and his family in Knoxville. On Tuesday night, November 14, Bud wrote to Thelma from London:

> *Dearest—Your ole Poppy is back in London tonight but not on a pass this time I'm travelling on orders. And can you imagine what I'm gonna do? I'm supposed to talk over the radio directly to WROL, Knoxville, Tenn. I thought they were kidding me when they told me at first that I was to go to London and broadcast to Knoxville, but I guess they weren't. Here I am, orders and all. Hope you listen in— don't know what time it will be but sometime Thursday.*

[Thursday, Nov 23, Thanksgiving Day.] *We work on script tomorrow, I am told.*

I got lots of mail today before I left and didn't have time to read it. So for the past hour and half I've been sitting here in the Red Cross Club (where I'm staying) reading about six letters, five from you and one from mother (11-14) and also a lot of clippings [Tennessee football articles] *you sent.*

The first thing I did when I got here was visit the snack bar. You know your ole poppy is a chowhound and can't resist anything to eat. May go in and eat again after a while.

I was sure glad to know that you had finally heard from me. Can't imagine what the holdup could have been, but everyone was having the same trouble it seems. You must have really gotten a good buy in that pen [playpen] *for Junior. I agree that he would probably tear a wooden one down pretty quick.*

Baby, I'll try to find something for him—I may have some time here this time. Don't know how busy Col. Ben Lyon plans to keep me these two days yet. But I can't see how it should be an all day job.

You tell J. Ross I thought about him Oct. 30 and was hoping that he'd be a brave boy about his operation [the planned removal of his tonsils]. *I'm certainly glad he's getting along so well.*

You asked about the Knoxville boy in the next barracks—thought I mentioned him before, but he's a bombardier also, C.D. Cash. He's only about 21 so I don't imagine you know him. I didn't before we met here.

I'm here in the lounge. It's full of flying officers so the conversation has been for the past two hours about ground officers and their dislike for them—can't seem to get along with them for some reason or the other—Pretty easy to understand why though.

The clipping you sent about the Sgt. flying his plane back after losing his pilot and co-pilot sounds like a true story to me, baby. He was an engineer, and they do know an awful lot about the plane. In fact they know a lot more than the pilots about some things.

They are supposed to get stick time as often as possible and be able to take over in case of an emergency. Of course what he said about the bombardier not knowing anything about the plane was probably a little fake—or that could have been true also.

It's now after eleven so I'd better close, get a snack and hit the sack—will write you again tomorrow—I love you lots and sure appreciate all those letters I got today.

Be sweet. Hope I dream of you and Junior tonight.

All my love, Bud

On November 17, Bud again wrote to Thelma, this time from Ridgewell:

Dearest,

Baby, I feel like I've neglected you again because I didn't write yesterday or the day before. So I'll start off by telling you all about the past couple of days.

I wrote you Tuesday night while at the Red Cross Officers' Club in London. Then Wed. morning early I had to go to Col. Ben Lyons' office. After waiting around for a good while, I was interviewed by a BBC girl which took about an hour—then this fellow, Jimmy Warwick from Knoxville, (you'll hear him on the air) took me over to his billet to eat with him. I was near the PX so stopped by there and bought me some more wool socks and a trench coat. My trench coat hasn't been keeping me too warm. That took all afternoon since there's always a big line in that place.

Jimmy Warwick wanted me to meet him and go to a show that night - so we met about 6:30 at a hotel lobby— while waiting for him I ran into T.G. Brown , so we talked for a good while. He said he was also a lead bombardier and his missions were coming slow. R.F. Brooks is with

T.G. Brown, Grover Blevins and Ross Perrin-1944
Perrin Family Collection

him and is getting along great. He was on his way back to his base so we, Jimmy and I, left him there.

We couldn't decide on a show so found a pub and drank beer instead. We talked over our beers for about three hours. Was good to talk to someone from home, especially someone who knew so many people that I know. He knew Leonard real well, he says, and used to play ball with lots of fellows that I also played with. I was staying across the street from this pub at the Red Cross. So about eleven o' clock I left him and went to bed. —Slept real well that night, much better than the night before. Wasn't quite so much noise

I got up rather late yesterday—about 10 am—ate breakfast and decided I'd try and shop for something for Junior, but I know you can guess the answer—I didn't find a thing I could send. They have a lot of big fluffy toys that aren't rationed but I couldn't see buying one of them somehow. I haven't given up though. I'll go into Cambridge soon and try my luck there.

Baby I'll know when you hear that record[ing] we made yesterday that you can tell I was reading every word of it. I heard the thing after it was finished and that's the way it sounded to me—but after all you are the play actor of the family.

Some of the things they had in the script for me I didn't say, but they try and make everything sound dramatic, so I had to cooperate. You can probably tell we didn't have a rehearsal either and I stumbled over a few words.

Back to yesterday, I went by for Jimmy about three.

We had a grilled cheese sandwich and a Coca-Cola at his snack bar—was good. Met another fellow from Knoxville who works in his office, a Lt. Col. Burns. I didn't know him at home. Must have been a big shot through or has a lot of pull.

We finished our record-making about eight last night. There were only three of us there. I understand there were some WACs [members of the Women's Army Corps] *on the program also, but their part of it was made about two weeks ago. They told me their names, but they didn't sound familiar.*

We [Tech Sgt. Shrouse and I] *caught a train for the base about 8:45 and came on home. It was a little late when I got back; everyone was in bed so I couldn't write then.*

Had two letters waiting for me which I didn't get to read until this morning. They were written Nov. 2nd and 3rd and had lots of clippings in them and were very sweet letters, baby—one of them told me about me about my baby being a little fat. I expected that, since Junior's getting bigger every day. Hope you do have a chance to take some pictures soon. I'll like to see my Momma just one time when she wasn't the most glamorous gal in all the world. Wouldn't be surprise of you aren't still just as glamorous though even if you are a little chubby.

I had a dream about Evelyn and J. Ross last night. Dreamed he had a new car and was driving Evelyn over to your house. Could see him turning the car into your drive way just as plain. He looked a little small, but yet seemed to be so big. I thought he looked at me out of the corner of his eye as if to say, "Ain't I the big one?"

I have the script that we used so I'll send it to you for our scrapbook.

Better close now, sweetheart—may go over to the club with Leo and the boys for a little while. Be sweet and I love you lots and lots. Good night—Your Husband

On Tuesday night, November 21, Thelma wrote to Bud from Knoxville:

> *Dearest—Your baby is singing tonight—"what a differ-*
> *ence a day makes." —for today was really a red-letter*
> *day for me. To begin with, I heard that your grandmother*
> *Perrin had received a letter from you dated October 30th,*
> *as I mentioned in the letter I mailed today—then my letter*
> *came, for the same date, with the wonderful news that at*
> *last Pappy had received some packages—(and can once*
> *again keep his hair greased).*
> *. . . and that isn't all. I know that yesterday at 12:15*
> *my sweet ole pappy was in a British Broadcasting Station*
> *sending a message across the ocean to WROL in Knox-*
> *ville! You can't IMAGINE how wonderful having such re-*
> *cent news of you is after all the delays we've had in mail.*
> *Here's how I know so much. Mr. Graybeal,* [an executive
> at the Knoxville Chrysler dealer, Kerr Motor Company—
> where Evelyn worked] *who gets his Sentinel early in the*
> *afternoon, phoned your mother (or Evelyn) to tell them*
> *about the article stating that you and several other Knox-*
> *ville boys and two WACs were to be in a special Thanks-*
> *giving broadcast from London.*
> *It was too late when your mother phoned me (about*
> *five-thirty) to see if I had seen the article to contact anyone*
> *at the Sentinel for more information, but I thought about*
> *John Reese at WROL and so called him right then. That*
> *proved the correct thing, for the program is all WROL's*
> *doings. He was writing me a card when I called to tell me*
> *of the program but didn't know my telephone number, or*
> *how to look it up. So instead, he gave me all the dope.*
> *In case you don't know all the details, here they are.*
> *They asked the British Broadcasting Company to line up*
> *all the Knoxville boys in London or about, for this pro-*
> *gram they'd like to use Thanksgiving. But since the wave*
> *lengths would be slightly crowded on Thanksgiving, the*
> *program was sent to WROL yesterday on shortwave.*

However, they were unable to pick it up very clearly here but New York says they got a fairly clear recording, and are shipping the record, or transcription, immediately. If nothing happens, it will arrive in time for the scheduled [broadcast] time but in case it shouldn't, John assured me that we would have a chance to hear it regardless.

He says, from what he could gather from the recording they made, you had quite a bit to say. Also another boy mentioned just meeting you and learning that your sister had married a friend of his! So we are all very anxious to hear the program. Naturally, John is going to try and get records enough to make recordings of each boy's part, for a member of his family. (It will be nice to have my Pappy's voice on record, so I can play it when I get lonesome for him!) John said his mother was a very good friend of Mrs. Perrin and had told him to be sure and let her know about the broadcast! I thought that was sweet of her. Of course, he is contacting all the boys' families. He was so pleased that they located you. Of course, they didn't have any idea of who the BBC would be able to line up for the show. You'll have to supply us with that part of the information how they located you, etc. We will be anxious to know "every little thing" of course.

. . . I'm worn out with excitement and so much going on, baby. Think I'll stop and hear Bob Hope, and continue in the morning. I love you and wanted you to remember that 'til I get back to writing you!

Well sweetheart, I must close now. Will write you again later today or tonight. Be sweet, and don't forget who thinks you are the best hubby in all the world.

Bye for now—All my Love, and Junior's too—Your Wife

The Lever Brothers-sponsored *Bob Hope Show* had, for almost a decade, been the premier family radio show in virtually all US markets. Enjoyed by a vast cross section of the listening public, its hour-long weekly broadcast drew families like a magnet. In early 1944, Lever Brothers expanded beyond its traditional soap product line when it bought the Pepsodent Company, and Hope became the spokesman for their new toothpaste product. The catchy advertising phrase "You'll wonder where the yellow went, when you brush your teeth with Pepsodent" catapulted them to the top sales position.

On the show that night, Hope and regular guest Jerry Colonna entertained the nationwide audience with their pithy barbs and comedic one-liners. During WWII, the show was broadcast on the Armed Forces Network (AFN) to troops stationed all across the globe. For many servicemen, some of whom were wartime guests on the show, this became a warm connection to home. But a preoccupied Bud somehow missed the delayed broadcast.

From Ridgewell, on Thursday morning, Thanksgiving Day, Bud wrote to Thelma:

> *It's a beautiful Thanksgiving Day, about the same as most of the days in England this time of year.*
>
> *I'm up a little earlier than usual this morning considering that I got up of my own accord. I had a sneaking feeling that we'd have fresh eggs for breakfast this morning, and that suspicion was right. Were the first ones I'd had in almost a month.*
>
> *I didn't write last night—had planned to write you and several others, but Leo and Glenn decided that we should go in to a local pub and drink a few beers to celebrate our seven-day leave which starts tomorrow. And we leave today. Think I told you we are going to a rest home where we are allowed to wear civilian clothes—play golf—baseball—have breakfast in bed and just relax and take it easy.*
>
> *I had three letters from you yesterday, the first in almost a week. Two were old ones and one was new written Nov. 5th.*
>
> *So my baby weighs 130, now that ain't bad at all. Let's see now, you used to weigh 112. That means junior will weigh about 18 lbs. doesn't it?*
>
> *I noticed in some of the clippings you sent—an article when you had written August 1, Sept. 2, Oct. 3, Nov. 4, Dec. 5, Jan. 6, Feb. 7—that could be correct, but—right at*

present things are going very slow. I started out pretty good but after getting in the lead, I don't fly as often.

I was tickled at you writing about our relatives. I know you never used to talk about people. I guess you've been associating with the Perrin family enough to where they've got you doing it too.

I've been wondering if they notified you and mother so you know to tune in to WROL today. Hope you ain't disappointed in your poppy's acting. I wanted to say something about you and Junior, but they wouldn't give me a choice.

I have a lot of packing to do and you know what a good packer I am. If I do it the way it should be done it'll take me all day, but I suppose I'll do as I usually do and throw everything in a bag about ten minutes before time to leave.

Be a sweet baby, I'll be writing you every night but won't be able to get my mail for a week. I don't like that.

All my love, Bud

When Bud wrote on Thanksgiving morning at 9:30, it was a little more than three hours past midnight in Tennessee. The broadcast made days earlier had not yet aired in Knoxville. The transcript of the broadcast that follows was aired a little over sixteen hours later at 8:00 p.m. EST.

Transcript of the Thanksgiving Interview Aired On WROL in Knoxville, Tennessee on November 23, 1944:

EFFECTS:

Interviewer, Mr. Alban: This is BBC London calling WROL Knoxville.

EFFECTS: FADE UP MUSIC—FADE DOWN AFTER

Alban: (Over fade) Hello WROL—hello Knoxville, and greetings for Thanksgiving from all American servicemen and women this side of the Atlantic. For many of us—as for many of you at home —Thanksgiving this year will be a day of work, but even so, there's going to be time

for the turkey and cranberry sauce and all the
trimmings. Men and women from Knoxville are
in the BBC studio today, and we'll be introducing a sergeant in the London Headquarters
of Air Transport Command, a bombardier, and a
top turret gunner—both of the 8th Air Force,
and two members of the fair sex, in the Women's
Army Corps. Well, to start the program rolling,
I'm going to introduce you to the 8th Air Force
bombardier—he's a lieutenant, and his name is
. . .

Perrin: Ross Perrin.

Alban: From Knoxville?

Perrin: All the way from Knoxville. . .

Alban: Was it a long journey?

Perrin: Well, I think I know what you mean. Yes, it
was a long journey. The first stop was Miami,
Florida, where I took my basic training.

Alban: When did you join the Army, Ross?

Perrin: I enlisted in October 1942—I was a cadet,
and then I was called to service in January
1943.

Alban: Okay, errr, what was the next stop after Miami?

Perrin: Memphis, back in good old Tennessee. I had
my college training there.

Alban: Did you get your commission there, too?

Perrin: No, I went to Big Spring, Texas, for that.

Alban: Were you assigned to an outfit then?

Perrin: Well, I'd been assigned to the job of bombardier before then, but

when I received my commission, I became part of a
B-17 Group.

Alban: In other words, you were a bombardier on a

Flying Fortress?

Perrin: That's right, and after more training in Louisiana, I came to Britain last August.

Alban: And how many missions have you done since then?

Perrin: 13.

Alban: Then you have the Air Medal—and, let me see—the Oak Leaf Cluster—is that right?

Perrin: Quite right.

Alban: Have you had any close calls?

Perrin: Not really—all my missions have been to Germany, and none of them easy, there isn't such a thing as an easy mission. I think maybe the first mission I went on was the toughest.

Alban: What was that?

Perrin: We picked a day on which the Luftwaffe appeared—and it so happened it was the first time it had appeared for ages.

Alban: Did you get any down?

Perrin: No, we didn't, but altogether 186 of their aircraft were shot down that day.

Alban: Well, that's not to be sniffed at. Where also have you been?

Perrin: Cologne—there was plenty of flak there, too.

Alban: But there isn't anymore?

Perrin: I don't think there's anything there anymore.

Alban: I don't suppose you know what kind of day Thanksgiving Day is going to be for you?

Perrin: No, I guess not. But one thing I know is that we'll be having a turkey and a service at the base.

Alban: Where will the service be held?

Perrin: In our church at the base—I expect there'll be some English people there, too.

Alban: But they don't have a Thanksgiving Day.

Perrin: No, but there are a lot of English people who come to our chapel for our services, and we often go to theirs. We went to their Harvest Festival Services, which is almost the equivalent of our Thanksgiving.

Alban: They decorate the church, don't they?

Perrin: Yes, the service is held at the end of the harvesting season, and the people decorate the church with the flowers, fruit, wheat, and corn they've reaped. They make large, decorative loaves of bread too, especially for the occasion.

Alban: Do you know any of these English people?

Perrin: Oh yes, I do. There's one man we all know. He came to our base after every mission to check and see that we're all back safely. He brings us fresh eggs too—he's a farmer, and sometimes has some to spare.

Alban: I was beginning to wonder. . . You know, Ross, I'd be interested to know what a bombardier feels thankful for at Thanksgiving?

Perrin: I'm thankful for my life mostly. But I'm thankful to have a strong ship to fly, and that the folks at home are working along with us, and backing us all the way. We couldn't have the faith we have if we weren't sure about that.

Alban: Well, thank you Ross, now I know. I hope you'll have a restful day this year, and no missions just for once.

Perrin: Thank you, Lieutenant—I hope so too. Goodbye everyone at home, and a happy Thanksgiving.

Alban: Goodbye, Lieutenant Ross Perrin. And now here's someone in the Air Transport Command—his name is Technical Sargent James Warwick—I strongly suspect he's called Jimmy—am I right, James?

Warwick: Yes, I'm called Jimmy.

Alban: I think all that sounds more complicated than it really is—I'll call you Jimmy anyway, and that settles everything. Do you come from Knoxville too?

Warwick: Yes, I was born there. As a matter of fact, the Lieutenant and I have just discovered that one of my friends married his sister.

Alban: Is that right, Ross?

Perrin: Sure—we were talking before we came into the studio, and it's really a fact.

Alban: Well, to coin a phrase—it's a small world—and it's getting smaller every day.

Warwick:Well, time seems to go by quicker than it used to—it seems ages since I enlisted in February, 1942.

Alban: Did you enlist in the Army?

Warwick: No, I joined the Air Force.

Alban: Where were you sent?

Warwick: To Kessler Field, Mississippi, and then to Palm Beach, Florida. . . believe it or not, but I stayed at Palm Beach for twelve months.

Alban: I believe you—but I think you were a lucky man. What outfit were you assigned to?

Warwick: The Ferrying Division—later, that Division developed into the Air Transport Command.

Alban: And what was your job?

Warwick: I was doing personnel work, and I still do
the same job here in London.

Alban: When did you come overseas?

Warwick: In May 1943.

Alban: Well, you're an old-timer then.

Warwick: Yes, I know my way around—even in the
blackout.

Alban: Well, you'd need to in the blackout. Who's
listening to this program at home, Jimmy?

Warwick: My wife, Cassie, and my daughter, Bunny.
My daughter's fourteen months old, and I hav-
en't even seen her yet.

Alban: Then you weren't home for Thanksgiving last
year?

Warwick: No—I'm hoping I'll be back for the family
dinner next year, though. I'd sure like to see
little Bunny.

Alban: I'll bet you would. I suppose you'll be
working this Thanksgiving Day?

Warwick: Yes, that's right. I'd give a lot to be
going to Shields Watkins Field to see a football game. Guess that'll have to wait though.

Alban: Guess it will, Jimmy. Anyway, thanks for
coming along today—I know you ATE people are
busy these days getting your new air base in
order. . . .

(Script prepared at BBC studio in conjunction with USAAF, used
in BBC interview sent to WROL in Knoxville, November 23, 1944.)
From November 23-25 of 1944, Thelma wrote a long letter to Bud:

*23rd: It has been a nice Thanksgiving in many ways—get-
ting to hear my pappy's voice, and having so much mail
yesterday. But if I don't watch, I'll be getting ahead of myself and won't make much sense to you. Let's see, I wrote
last before we went into town yesterday—at that time I*

didn't know that the mailman was going to bring me five letters. Some pretty recent ones for a change! But that's what was waiting for me when I got home—and, baby, they really contained some news! I hurried over to your mother and read them all to them. . . . and we have been so elated and excited over them—I had one letter Tuesday, written October 30th, which mentioned two packages, These were for Oct 27, 29, and 31st and November 2nd and 3rd—the ones that came yesterday, I mean. (I see now that I'm NOT making sense tonight, sweetheart, but you can blame it on excitement!) Think I'd better reread the letters as I write maybe that will help me get in all I want to say. . . .

24th: Your mother and I had a busy time answering the telephone last night after that program—think she told me later that Grace [Evelyn's sister-in-law, Grace Hill], Mrs. Evans, and Virginia Russell had called her up to that time. And Mrs. Bell, Mr. Riggins, and Virginia had called me. Also Martha Carlise, or McDonald, phoned beforehand to be sure of the time. Wednesday, when I was in town, a number of people told me they had heard about the program and would be listening.

Mr. Riggins said he believed Mrs. Riggins was as thrilled as I was—and that the kids were excited to death over hearing "Thelma's husband"! Everyone talked about how clear it was, and how much it sounded like you—that is, everybody but your mother and me. Maybe we were too excited, but I'm going to arrange to hear it again at WROL.

25th: Guess what! We just heard a rebroadcast of my sweetheart's little Thanksgiving speech. And this time it seemed much plainer to both your mother and me. She happened to be walking in the kitchen and heard the announcer say that they had had so many requests for the special program carried last Thursday night that it would be repeated at this time—she ran in and called me, and we both got to hear it again, much to our delight.

Maybe we weren't so excited this time, but I understood you much better, and it sounded like my pappy. And it sounded like you to Mrs. Perrin, too. I talked to her afterwards—it did her a lot of good, she said—pepped her up! I started to write you immediately afterwards, but stopped when she called me, and again when Trula Clift called to say she had heard it. At first Trula didn't know it was you—said to tell you she enjoyed hearing you! I thought it was nice of her to phone me—guess your mother will be getting lots of calls again tonight, too! —

I love you, darling—will write you again later.

Bye for now, baby—your wife

About your program, baby. Think I have already told you that we thought it sounded good. Wouldn't be surprised if I couldn't turn my pappy into a pretty good play-actor! Only he'd have to play all love scenes with me, for I wouldn't have him even play-acting and making love to another gal. As for them writing in things you didn't say, I understand how that is, for I have done some scriptwriting myself, as well as reading scripts other people wrote. But you sounded quite natural, and if you did stumble, that makes a program of that kind sound more natural. But I didn't notice any. I did get a kick out of one place in the script which called for you to call "Quite right"—that sound a little more like an Englishman than my pappy! Don't think I've ever heard you use THAT expression.

I'll have to call John Reese, and tell him about your account of the program, for he was thinking you were in the studio the day they received the program by shortwave.

Being chosen by the USAAF for the honor of talking to all the folks back in Knoxville elevated Bud's spirits, if only momentarily. *I'd trade this experience for thirty-five missions done and a ticket home any day,* he thought. *It sure ain't as good as talking to 'em in person. But it'll have to do for now.*

CHAPTER 19

A Welcomed Rest

There's No Flak in this Flak House

Roke Manor, Romsey, England:
November 23–December 1, 1944

IN THE NUMEROUS LETTERS THEY sent back home, most airmen painted a benign picture of their everyday lives. Military brass demanded this ruse to prevent sensitive information from falling into Axis hands and thereby compromising both the safety of Allied troops and their ability to prosecute the war. Further, the limited reports given out helped protect those on the home front from the reality of the fears and horrors men faced in battle.

In an earlier letter (September 12, 1944), Bud explained this policy to Thelma: *"In case my letters aren't clear at times, it's because we have to follow a procedure as to what we can write about which is almost nothing at all. Like I can't say when I flew last, etc."*

This portrayal of calm was in no way accurate. The atmosphere in Allied aircraft on missions over the Third Reich was bathed in angst on good days, brimming with stark terror on others. As their mission count mounted, the airmen's need of a break increased.

Late in 1944, a report by the Office of the Surgeon in the Headquarters of the Eighth Air Force chronicled the initial perceived need for and subsequent implementation of rest homes to help provide this time of emotional, physical, and spiritual regeneration. The study stated:

> From beginning of operations by the Eighth Air Force it was apparent that fatigue and staleness in flyers would necessitate special measures. Flyer weariness had been known to flight surgeons for a long time. Under ordinary conditions of flying in peace time it responded to short

periods of rest, but under combat conditions there is a great amount of stress added to the tension ordinarily connected with flying. Consequently, combat crew members experience fatigue in a relatively few months of operational flying. Ideally periods of leave spent at their own homes would be best. As it would be highly improbable to disrupt operational tours by sending airmen home, the next best substitute evolved. Rest homes came into being.

Rest homes should provide an atmosphere of ease and freedom. . . . Moreover, it has been attempted to actually maintain a homelike environment throughout all the rest homes. The facilities of the homes provide an exceptionally good cuisine, comfortable beds with good springs and mattresses, a minimum of military routine, bathing accommodations, excellent recreational and athletic equipment, and medical care when required. Special emphasis has been placed on the opportunities offered for recreation. Athletic equipment and grounds have been provided for golf, baseball, basketball, football, tennis, badminton, archery, skeet shooting, bicycling, boating, horseback riding and other sports. Dances and motion pictures are offered several times weekly. Besides these there are opportunities and facilities for furthering hobbies such as photography. Each home has a small, well-equipped dispensary where medical care is administered. The policy of removing guests from military environment is carried to the extent of providing sport clothes for them to wear during their stays at the homes.

The staffs at the respective institutions comprise an administrative commanding officer, an adjutant, plus several enlisted helpers, and two female Red Cross representatives, who act as hostesses and supervise the recreation and feeding of the guests. A medical officer rotated each week from the groups and squadrons of the Eighth Air Force is in attendance for emergency medical care and is

in an advisory capacity at each home. Civilian chamber-
maids, cleaners, and ground keepers are provided by the
American Red Cross. (Eighth Air Force, Office of the Surgeon, "The Use of Rest Homes in the Eighth Air Force for
the Two Year Period November 1942 to November 1944,"
December 11, 1944, 1.)

In July 1942, before the first 8th AF plane flew in combat, the
official arrangements for rest homes began. By late November,
combat crewmen could be sent, albeit unofficially, to a rest center.
By January 1943, the first official rest home was activated at Stanbridge Earle, Hampshire, The same report described it as "an estate
of historic interest which has recently been thoroughly modernized
and refurbished, has central heating, is surrounded by beautiful
grounds and gardens, and is being equipped for recreation and
athletics, including excellent fishing in season" ("The Use of Rest
Homes," 2). This home originally provided accommodations for
just twenty-five officers.

The aforementioned study either failed to recognize or chose to
ignore one critical fact concerning rest homes: they had come to be
known by a colloquial but accurate name, "flak houses." After all,
they were designed to relieve the stress of the most insidious weapons Nazi forces used against airmen. In fact, a boy whose nerves
were frayed (or worse) from the rigors of combat was often referred
to as "flak happy."

These rest home stays were intended to relax airmen so they
could go back into combat refreshed and ready. But the times away
also posed a risk. An airman could realize that this flak house life
reminded him of home and decide not to return to duty. But the
homes did serve their purpose. Most men who stayed there re-
charged their batteries and returned to the flight line with calmer
nerves and a measure of renewed zeal

Bud and the Belskis crew had happily received orders to take
a seven-day sojourn to a rest home away from the sound of starting and revving B-17 engines, the specter of a V-2 rocket landing
in their bunk, and lethal shrapnel from exploding 88-mm ammo
launched from powerful ground guns over targets in Germany, or

flak. "Somewhere in south central England" was all the information they had about Roke Manor. It didn't matter. Their stay meant relief from the day-to-day tension, at least for a short while.

On November 20, 1944, Bud wrote to Thelma from Ridgewell:

> *Sometime this week we go to the Rest Home for a week. I'm looking forward to that—means 7 days of living like a civilian, playing golf and all that sort of thing.*
>
> *I've thought of you and Junior so much lately—guess I'm getting a little anxious, but no more than you are I suppose—I wrote my cable address in a letter the other day so you can let me know as soon as Junior arrives.*
>
> *Heard our song on the Hit Parade last night sung by Frankie. It's still my favorite 'cause it lets you know just how I feel about you, sweetheart. Speaking about Sinatra, he's on the radio right now singing "Come Out."*
>
> *Better get ready for chow right now—may have to do a little practice flying this afternoon. Don't forget that pappy loves momma and Junior an awful lot.*
>
> *All my love—Bud*
>
> *November 23: Seven days leave which starts tomorrow—and we leave today. Think I told you we are going to a rest home—where we are allowed to wear civilian clothes, play—golf, baseball, have breakfast in bed, and just relax and take it easy.*

A motor car was awaiting them as they exited from the train in Romsey.

"I phoned ahead and arranged for this chariot—pretty good service, boys, right?" Leo said in his best British accent, which, because it sounded a lot like the south side of Chicago, left a lot to be desired.

"Is Roke stocked up with Guinness?" Collett inquired of the driver as the crew climbed aboard the makeshift taxi for the short drive to their vacation spot.

"It's quite stocked up with a large quantity of proper liquid refreshments, sir," the driver replied with typical British precision.

"You are not the first Yanks we have hosted. We are quite prepared, as you will see. I might add that we are eternally grateful for the support of your country in protecting the Commonwealth."

As a fleeting thought about the Revolutionary War came to his mind, Bud mused to himself, *You lost the fight to control us, so it's no surprise you're glad to see us come back. But I bet you didn't think it would be to save your butt.* He almost shared his joke, but thought better and held his tongue. *We've got plenty of time for humor*, he thought. "Hey, we like this place already. What's your name?" he asked.

"Reginald, sir, Reginald Shipsworth. But I would be most pleased if you would call me Reggie."

"How 'bout 'Ship'? We want you to remember us well when we leave next week. So is it OK if we call you 'Ship'?" Bud asked.

"I'd be honored, sir," Reginald replied. "And your names, please?"

"Jim, Leo, Glenn, and. . . " Bud thought for a second. "Ross." *It sounds more British than Bud*, he told himself.

The crew chattered like a gaggle of geese as they drove the two bumpy miles to the manor. Collett said that even though it was close to the sea, the landscape didn't look like his beloved eastern Maryland.

Bud told the crew, "It reminds me of Kentucky or good ol' East Tennessee."

"You mean in Tennessee, sheep have the right of way?" Leo shot back as Ship slowed and came to a stop, allowing a dozen sheep to amble across the road in front of them.

Even Bud had to join his fellow crewmates' belly laughs at another of their chief's putdowns of his beloved home state.

As the laughter died down, Ship turned left between two ornate wrought-iron gates flanked by two precisely manicured pine trees, deep green and ten feet tall. The circular pebble stone drive framed an exquisite manor home that seemed to epitomize the stateliness of British tradition.

The two-story structure was topped by a smaller third level adorned with five dormers jutting from the tile roof. Eight brick chimneys rose from the roofline. *Wow. It's got eight, maybe sixteen fireplaces, if each serves two floors. Stunning. There's nothing*

Roke Manor "Flak House"-Romsey, England-1944
Ted Homdrom Collection

like this in Knoxville. But there's no way I'll say that aloud. For one thing, I'd never serve up such a fat pitch to Belskis, Bud thought, remembering how Leo had skewered him with the sheep comment.

The admiring boys entered the double front door, taking in as many of the home's architectural details as they could. None of them had seen anything like this. Little did they know that this building was constructed more than two hundred years before the signing of the Declaration of Independence.

In the days ahead, the intricacies of this stately mansion, the peacefulness of its pastoral surroundings, and the quantity and quality of the food (it didn't seem proper to call it grub) would both calm and energize them. The treatment by the manor staff and the Red Cross team would also prove stellar. *And every bedroom has a soft bed and a connecting bathroom with hot water,* thought Bud. *A fellow could get used to this pretty quickly.*

Roke Manor was added to the Allies' list of rest homes on April 10, 1944. It was the seventh facility in what would be, by October 1944, a total of fourteen homes so designated by the 8th AF.

Roke was situated approximately 150 miles from Ridgewell. Nestled in south central England, twenty miles northwest of Portsmouth, it was located two and a half miles from the center of Romsey, nine miles from Winchester Cathedral, and close to the original 8th AF rest home, Stanbridge Earle.

The home's storied history dated back to the sixteenth century. After many transfers of ownership, the manor house was sold to the Birmingham-based brewery firm of Ansell in 1935. The company owned the facility until the end of the war in Europe.

Bud wrote as best he could about what he was experiencing in his next letter to Thelma:

25th: We are now settled down to a week's vacation at the rest home known as Roke Manor—a nice quiet English estate located in Southern England away from airplanes, etc.

25th, cont.: Didn't write yesterday—we were on the train most of the day —left early yesterday morning stopped off in London and picked up my Battle Jacket—Leo got one also just like mine—you should see the bright red silk lining. Think I'll wear it wrong side out. Jim and Leo wanted to go to the PX so I went along with them and bought another wool undershirt—makes about seven I have now.

We got here just in time for tea last night—then about an hour later they served us a drink of scotch—then thirty minutes later some of the best food I've had in ages.

There is a small village nearby and last night the mayor was giving his annual formal ball. We were forced to go even though no one was very enthused about it. It turned out more or less as I expected. High-class, if you know what I mean. You know I never cared too much for things like that. Leo and I spent the night in the bar until the cars were there to bring us back to our home for a week. This morning a butler woke us up and gave us some sort of fruit juice—don't remember what kind it was—guess I wasn't too wide-awake, but do remember that it tasted pretty good.

A few minutes later I went down to breakfast and got my fresh egg. That's one meal I won't miss here. Vaughn and another fellow talked me into a golf game, so they got us a staff car and put us in civilian clothes, then drove us down to a golf course about ten miles from here. I was surprised at my game—much better than I expected after the years laying off the game.

We played another rest home near by a game of softball this afternoon for some sort of trophy which we won. Guess I'll be a little sore tomorrow. No PT for some time.

I'm gonna miss those letters from you, baby—won't get

any for a week now and didn't get any yesterday so that means almost ten days without sugar reports. I'll be glad to get back for that reason.

This place is more like being home. If you were only here—everything would be perfect, I'm not very good at describing a house, but it's beautiful I think.

Just had a bath in a great big tub, big enough to lie down and soak in and I did just that for about thirty minutes.

It's almost time for our drink—wish you could join me.

I'll write again tomorrow, sweetheart, don't forget that your old poppy loves you more all the time.

Your husband

26th: It's a little late and I should be going to bed since this is the rest home and we are supposed to get plenty of sleep. But bet you can't guess what I've been doing all day—I found some more bridge players and we've been doing quite a bit of playing today. Also played all night last night until two this morning. Just can't get away from the game even at the rest home.

That fellow woke me up again this morning with a glass of tomato juice about nine o'clock, then I got up and ate eggs, bacon, toast, jelly, and coffee—my favorite breakfast.

I read most of the morning then when it came time to freeze the ice cream I helped out and what a job that was. It's a big three-gallon freezer and sure gets hard to turn toward the end.

We had a very good lunch. Fried chicken, mashed potatoes, string beans, and salad, then the good desert. The ice cream was for supper, which we cooked ourselves—it was lots of fun. Cooked hamburgers, cheeseburgers and St. Paul's—some fellow's own creation which consists of cheese, onions, and hamburger meat all rolled together before it's cooked. It wasn't bad—we also had potato salad and baked beans.

That's about all I can think of at the present. May get up early and go

horseback riding in the morning. I sure do love my little momma so goodnight and sweet dreams.

All my love—Your husband

28th: I just finished eating my fresh eggs for the morning. All I need to make things feel like home now is the morning paper—and you.

I wrote Mother yesterday morning and had planned to write you yesterday afternoon as last night but we had another ball game yesterday afternoon with another rest home—this one didn't turn out so good for us. We lost in extra innings and therefore had to leave our trophy with them.

Right after supper last night four of us started playing bridge and played until midnight. My partner was the Red Cross lady here, and we didn't do bad at all with the two other fellow.

It's a bad day today so I imagine we will all have to be content to stay indoors and take it easy—I had planned to play golf this morning, but it wouldn't be very healthy this morning.

This part of England is really beautiful. The grass and trees are still pretty and green. They must stay that way the year around it reminds me a lot of some parts of Kentucky.

While at this other rest home yesterday, I saw some of the funniest looking little dogs I've ever seen. They had legs shorter than Dimout's [Thelma's dog] but had real fat bodies, but not as long. Someone told one the type dog they were, but I've forgotten—some sort of Wales dog though.

I don't know what we will do this afternoon, but if the weather remains the same I guess it'll be another bridge game. Well sweetheart, I'd like to have four or five sweet letters from my baby this morning.

I'll go now—don't forget how much poppy loves you— Your husband

Winchester Cathedral
Winchester, Hampshire, England.
Public Domain

29th: There isn't much too write about this morning. Yesterday was a day with very little activities. Played quite a bit of bridge, in fact most of the day and most of the night.

We (about 12 fellows) may take a trip into Winchester today for a sightseeing tour. Understand these are quite a few historical things to see there.

Sure wish I had a letter from you so I could have something to answer. I'll cut this about now and write again after we come back from Winchester.

30th: Well, only one day more at this beautiful rest home. Sure hate to leave this place.

Yesterday afternoon, about twelve of us escorted by the Red Cross lady went to Winchester for a tour of the city. They have this real old cathedral there—was built or rather they started building it in 1064 and I understand it took sixty years to complete it. It's a huge thing—supposed to be the largest church in Europe. Some of the statues carved out of pure marble look almost human. It was really beautiful. I thought of you all the time we were going through it. Wish you could have gone along. I bought a postcard of part of the inside of the church. I'll send it to you.

It was well worth the trip just seeing the church. We spent most of our time there but did manage to get around to visiting the place where they have King Arthur's round table. We saw the table, but don't believe it was the original.

We had a movie in the living room last night—was Wallace Beery and Margie Maine in "Rationing." I had seen it before. Believe we saw it together. I enjoyed it the second time however—always did like Wallace Beery.

This afternoon we played another softball game and won—had a lot of fun.

I may not have chance to write tomorrow, may be on the train all day. But I probably will though. I'll be glad to get back and see if I have some mail—letters and packages—especially letters.

So long for now, baby.

2nd: I have lots I would like to write about tonight, but it's so late I won't be able to write very much. As I told you Thursday night, I would probably be on the train yesterday. That's the way it turned out. We left the rest home at noon yesterday and expected to be back here last night, but after changing trains at least nine or ten times we made it as far as Cambridge last night and stayed at the Red Cross there. We got up this morning but didn't catch the train until noon, got here this afternoon.

I may go to church in the morning, then come back and start in on my letter-writing. So now I'll say goodnight to my sweet little mama and hit the sack.

I love you an awful lot—Your husband

V-1 Buzz Bomb Rocket that landed at Ridgewell-December 1,1944
Bob Armstrong WWII Album

Crater caused by the V-1 Rocket - December 1, 1944
Bob Armstrong WWII Album

Bud chose not to mention the V-1 Buzz Bomb that terrorized the base the day before he got back from Cambridge. As he viewed the bomb in its crater adjacent to the main runway, he thought, *This will be quite a story to tell Junior and Thelma.*

Roke did its job, he thought later as he tumbled into the lumpy but familiar cot to which he thought he had become accustomed until he experienced the plush bed at Roke Manor. *This country boy has returned to reality.* Almost instantly, fatigue overtook the feel of the uncomfortable mattress, and sleep came just as fast.

CHAPTER 20

Duty Calls

Ridgewell Mission #222

Mannheim-Ludwigshafen, Germany:
December 11, 1944

A Bombardier's Prayer

Apprehension, fear, and longing; duty calls to drive away.
Never knowing what lies yonder, nothing calms but yes, to pray.

Yanks are teeming in formation, chasing Jerry 'cross the Rhine
Pray Godspeed for each to come back, landing safely in due time.

Once the fields of oat and barley, wafted gently all the day.
Now the drone of mighty Fortress, takes the place of new-mown hay.

You the Fortress all-sustaining, bring us home with freedom sure.
Whilst in England keep us ever, in your heart both safe and pure.

On the run, no turning back now. Courage comes, the heart beats fast.
Let me always act with honor, my faith proven now to last.

Run complete, we turn for home now, safe to fight another day.
Thank you, Lord, who doth sustain me, for your light that guides my way.

If you will I'm at the ready, strong by your sustaining grace.
With each test I see more clearly boundless love upon your face.

But if you choose to take me home now, final rest at last I'll see.
In your hands I place my future, in your arms my victory.

By J. Ross Greene, October 17, 2009

MUFFLED CONVERSATIONS AMONG TIRED AIRMEN created a soft din in the officers' mess. It was 0430, and except for being able to mark off another mission in their slow trek to thirty-five, the boys flying on that Monday morning saw no reason to be awake. Wakeup, or more accurately, get-up, was at 0400. Full wake-up was just occurring for most of the boys who made up the thirty-seven crews that would fly on that clear but bitterly cold, damp day. Real eggs, a treat reserved for mission days, were the morning's fare.

Bud's thoughts of his frustration the night before were rolling around in his mind as he went through the food line. *I'm not sure I should have mailed last night's letter to Thelma this morning. I was discouraged and my writing showed it. Hope it doesn't worry her. Too late now, it's posted,* Bud thought as he took a seat across the long table from Vaughn. *I'll write a cheery one when I get back tonight.*

"Looks like Tennessee's heading to the Rose Bowl," C. D. Cash said as he plopped his tray down across from Bud and Vaughn and eased into the seat between Leo and Jim Collett.

"Yep. Hope they do better than they did five years ago," Bud replied, referring to Tennessee's 14–0 spanking by Southern Cal on January 1, 1940. That appearance, Tennessee's first in the "Granddaddy of all Bowls," followed an undefeated season in which the Vols scored 222 points and held their opponents scoreless in every game. Supporters of the men in orange had smarted over that loss for half a decade and were hungry for revenge.

"You got that right," Cash agreed. "I think they might have won that game if Cafego hadn't been hurt." George Cafego, Tennessee's gritty tailback, sported a crooked smile and a slashing running style in his march to All-American status in 1939.

"Walt Slater isn't quite as good, but he's no slouch, either," Bud added his perspective on Cafego's replacement.

"Is UT football all you hillbillies can talk about?" Leo said, his ever-present smile belying the sarcasm in his voice.

"Don't talk with your mouth full," Vaughn barked. No one else seemed willing to enter the mock fray, so attention turned to eating and the mission ahead.

"Early get-up. Must be a long one today," Vaughn offered. "Hope it's not to Hitler's house." Numerous flak emplacements and an active Luftwaffe in and around the dreaded Berlin always made those missions tough and long.

"We might be flyin' further south along the Rhine. It was Stuttgart two days ago, and the scrubbed one yesterday was scheduled for Mainz," Cash said.

"We'll know soon enough," Collett added.

Cash joined the Belskis crew in the short truck ride to the briefing room. The flapping canvas sides did little to ward off the cold, and the ground was wet from the overnight melting snow. *Must be about 32.01 degrees. It seems like it's below freezing, but that's water, not ice, on the ground,* Bud thought. He swung his leg over the back of the truck bed, stepped on the makeshift bumper, and dropped to the ground. The crew checked their names off the master crew load list and took seats together in the back of the almost-full briefing room. Cash saw the other officers in his crew and joined them just in front of the curtain that kept secret the target and map for the day's mission.

"Ten-hut," came the command from a briefing officer as he entered the room from behind the assembled men. The conversations ended, some in mid-sentence. Metal folding chairs clanked and screeched as the boys rose to stand at attention. It was 0500 sharp. Each man checked his watch to make sure it showed the correct time. There would be a time-hack at the end of briefing, but they knew they could almost always set their watches by the start time. Punctuality was critical to safety. And safety was supremely critical to life in the menacing skies over Europe

"At ease, gentlemen. Take your seats." The briefing officer gave the standard rah-rah talk, which the boys had heard many times before. But even the most battle-hardened among them devoured every small bit of encouragement.

We all know we're playing for keeps, Bud thought, noting the somber looks on the faces surrounding him.

"Gentlemen, pay close attention." The briefing officer's directive was redundant, since all eyes and ears were trained on him. "The formation sheets you were given must be corrected. Our mission times have been accelerated in an attempt to take advantage of as much good weather as possible. The skies will be crowded today. Stations will be at 0600, Start Engines at 0610, Taxi at 0620, first takeoff at 0630, leave the field at 0753, last takeoff at 0757. And the

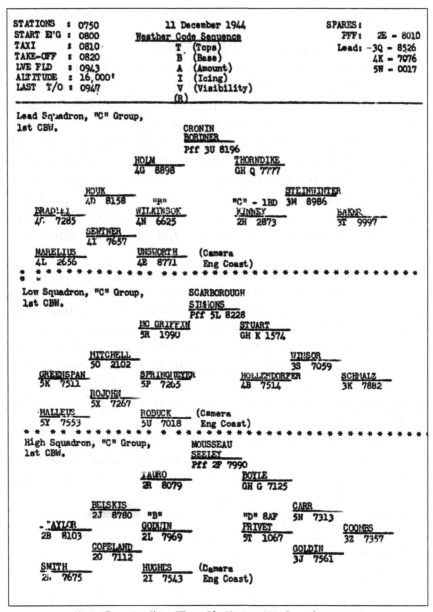

```
STATIONS   :  0750              11 December 1944              SPARES:
START E'G  :  0800           Weather Code Sequence            PFF:  2E - 8010
TAXI       :  0810               T  (Tops)                    Lead: -3Q - 8526
TAKE-OFF   :  0820               B  (Base)                          4K - 7076
LVE FLD    :  0943               A  (Amount)                        5W - 0017
ALTITUDE   :  16,000'            I  (Icing)
LAST T/O   :  0947               V  (Visibility)
                                (R)
```

Lead Squadron, "C" Group,
1st CBW.

```
                                    CRONIN
                                    BORDNER
                                    Pff 3U 8196
                        HOLM                THORNDIKE
                        4G  8898            GH Q 7777
                 HOUK                           STEINWINTER
                 4D 8158      "B"               3M  8986
        BRADLEY           WILKINSON    "C" - 1BD   KINNEY           BAKER
        4C  7285          4N  6625               2H  2873          3T  9997
                 SENTNER
                 4I 7657
        MARELIUS          UNSWORTH    (Camera
        4L  2656          4E  8771    Eng Coast)
```

* *

Low Squadron, "C" Group,
1st CBW.

```
                                    SCARBOROUGH
                                    SIMMONS
                                    Pff 5L 8228
                        MC GRIFFIN          STUART
                        5R  1990            GH K 1574
                 MITCHELL                        WINSOR
                 50  2102                         3S  7059
        GREENSPAN         SPRINGMEYER   HOLLENDORFER      SCHMALZ
        5K  7511          5P  7265      4B  7514          3K  7882
                 ROJOHN
                 5X  7267
        MALLEUS           RODUCK     (Camera
        5Y  7553          5U  7018   Eng Coast)
```

* *

High Squadron, "C" Group,
1st CBW.

```
                                    MOUSSEAU
                                    SEELEY
                                    Pff 2F 7990
                        TAURO               BOYLE
                        2R  8079            GH G 7125
                 BELSKIS                         CARR
                 2J  8780     "B"            "D" 8AF  5N  7313
        TAYLOR            GODWIN        PRIVET           COOMBS
        2B  8103          2L  7969      5T  1067         3Z  7357
                 COPELAND                        GOLDIN
                 2O  7112                         3J  7561
        SMITH            HUGHES     (Camera
        2N  7675         2I  7543   Eng Coast)
```

Mission Formation Sheet-"Flimsie" for Mission #222 - December 11, 1944
381st BG Collection-Everette Worrell

altitude will be 16,700 till further notice." The airmen scribbled the changes on their flimsies.

"As you can see, men, the weather is cold and wet. It will be clear at takeoff, at least at low levels. As I said, you're scheduled to form over the base at 16,700 feet, a slight change from what's shown on the formation sheet. Clouds are reaching higher, so it's possible that that will be increased at station time of 0600. Weather over the target will probably not be clear. On virtually all of our missions there, we've had to bomb by Pff with 10/10 cloud cover. But our Mickey Men have been putting us right on the target, so we'll kick their butts, regardless of whether we're bombing in soup or not.

"This will be our third mission of the month. We had some off days and a couple of late scrubs. We've been to Soest and Stuttgart with good results. And this one will be an effective one, too. We've got 'em on the run. Let's stay after 'em!" (Note: Unbeknownst to the Eighth AF or the broader Allied forces, Hitler had lined up his lethal tank forces along the Belgian border for a supreme offensive that would come to be known as the Battle of the Bulge. That battle began five days after the December 11 mission and continued in the abusive European winter until January 25. History would deem it one of the most bloody and critical battles of WWII.)

As the briefing officer took his seat, the IO stepped in front of the draped easel. As he drew the curtain open, men strained to get a clear view of the location where his four-foot pointer came to rest. "Gentlemen, today's target is Mannheim-Ludwigshafen."

This had become a more critical bombing target for the Eighth in 1944. The 381st had been there a couple of months earlier, on October 19. Three other scheduled missions to bomb that area along the Rhine were scrubbed. The previous month, the group had flown three missions in a row there, immediately preceding the Belskis crew's first mission on September 11 to bomb the I.G. Farben Chemical plant in Merseburg.

Ludwigshafen was the location of the BASF chemical plant that in 1925 had been merged into IG Farben. In conjunction with the Merseburg plant, the Ludwigshafen location was a main producer of the synthetic fuels and lubricants critical to the Reich's continued war efforts.

Additionally, the Mannheim rail yard, directly across the Rhine River from Ludwigshafen, was the hub of an arterial system that carried war materiel to German troops. Toward the end of 1944, much of the BASF plant was decimated, but still in production with a much-reduced output. But the marshalling yards in Mannheim, although put out of commission numerous times by RAF and USAAF bombing, were always repaired and back in operation in what seemed like no time.

Mannheim Ludwigshafen Bridge before bombing missions by Allies, circa late 1930s
Photo by J. Ross Greene

Despite repeated attempts to destroy it, the massive steel truss bridge that connected these important German war components still stood. That made these targets the increasing locus of and quarry for continuous and intense Allied bombing efforts. It also rendered them heavily guarded by German flak emplacements and occasionally by the Luftwaffe, when they could rustle up enough fuel and seasoned pilots for the task.

Bud had been to Cologne four times but never to Mannheim. He first heard about the key target from Bob Angevine, who flew a Mickey ship there on two of the early September missions. Bob had told him he had seen few Me-109s or Fw-190s, but flak was usually intense and accurate. *It's gonna be a busy day,* Bud told himself with a sigh.

The briefing concluded, the forty-one bombardiers met, thirty-seven scheduled for the mission and four spares in case of difficulty with one or more of the ships at takeoff. They finished dressing for the anticipated sixty-below temperatures, gathered their assigned Norden bombsights, and joined their respective crews for the bumpy ride to the hardstand.

"Hey boss, where are we positioned today?" Collett asked.

"We're in the number four position of the low element; the Seeley crew is leading our element," replied Leo, glancing at the flimsie showing the position of each ship in the formation.

"What ship are we in?" asked Lynn Lauret. "I hope it's *Liberty Bell*. The seat in the ball of that one is the most comfortable of all the uncomfortable turrets in our ships." No one joined his accompanying chuckle.

"This road ought to be named Washboard Avenue," Bud mumbled as the truck bounded along on its brief journey to the hardstand. The nine men being jostled by the rutted access road were about to spend ten hours fighting low visibility, extreme cold, uncomfortable seats, and compromised breathing conditions while fending off cannon fire and flak from an enemy intent on their destruction.

As they exited the truck for the fourth time that morning, Bud stopped to take in the eerie, yet poignant sight from below the wing of their assigned Fortress. Day was slowly crowding out night as the sun peeked its head cautiously above the eastern horizon. Ground crewmen splashed through water puddles glistening with hues of combined reds, blues, and yellows created by the mixture of oil and petrol.

The airmen methodically entered their unnamed B-17 offices for the day's work as ground personnel made their last-minute adjustments. Those on the ground knew well the risk to which these young men would be exposed, and many offered short but heartfelt words of encouragement: "Go get 'em," "Kick ass," "Give 'em hell," "Be safe," and "Godspeed," were often heard and much appreciated.

Bud was usually one of the first in the plane for each mission. On that day he tarried, continuing to gaze over the field until everyone else was aboard. He then swung himself up through the front hatch, walked past Collett, seated at the navigator's desk on the left, and took his place on the swivel seat behind the Norden. "Let's get on with it," he said with confidence. It was 0555, five minutes ahead of the station time the flight deck crew had scribbled on the formation sheet and twenty-five minutes until the beginning of taxi.

The crew-members all checked their oxygen systems and mics. On this and every mission, constant communication was as critical as access to oxygen.

The Curtiss-Wright radial engines of the sleek new B-17 fired in order. It was 0610, right on time. First, Engine #2 turned over, belching smoke as if it were flooded and then smoothing out to an idle. Engine #3 followed, then #1 and finally #4, each rattling, chugging and smoothing out until in unison they bellowed the familiar hum. "She's ready," Leo told Vaughn as he gently increased the idle speed of all four engines.

The formidable Forts began their slow, plodding taxi to the eastern end of the main runway. Bud had a box seat to the beasts' methodical nose-to-tail march to the takeoff point. As the ships ahead of them took off, heading west into the prevailing wind, he got a good look at each aircraft. The 534th ships led the procession, then the 535th low squadron planes. *Hell's Angel,* piloted by Lt. Springmeyer, was sporting a new front canopy after the disastrous accident of November 5 that took the pilot's life and destroyed the bombardier's perch.

Immediately ahead of them, *Carnival Queen* began its journey to attack the Reich as Leo stopped short of the main runway. With clearance from the tower, he then turned the B-17 into takeoff position and increased power to the engines. Like a young colt anxious to break free from its bridle and bit, the Fort strained its disapproval of the momentary confinement as Jim and Leo maintained full pressure on the brakes. From the tower came the word, "2J-8780, cleared for takeoff. Godspeed, Lieutenant." The brakes were released, and the now-unshackled Flying Fortress lurched forward and began its roll down the runway.

Number fifteen, twenty to go, Bud thought about his missions as the ships taking off behind them came into view on his left. "*Our Boarding House—flew that one to Cologne in early October. And I flew the Liberty Bell to Hamm and Münster,*" he thought as they passed the last plane in the procession.

At 0803, four minutes after the designated time, the thirty-seventh plane lifted off and fell in line with the 381st formation at 20,000 feet. This was higher than the briefing altitude of 16,700 feet, a change made due to contrails and cloud cover. The planes then made their way northeast toward the Belgian coast on their way to attack enemy installations with thirty tons of potentially devastating ordnance.

McCoy, Suggs, Lauret, Newman, and Rogers sat on the bench seats that lined each side of the fuselage, behind the waist gunner positions and forward of the rear hatch entrance to the aircraft. The noise from the engines combined with the wind whistling past the gun openings used by the waist gunners made conversation difficult but not impossible. But as they left the English coast, making their way across the Dover Cliffs and over the English Channel, instructions came to reconnect to oxygen and mics as they would soon be approaching enemy territory.

Bud and Collett, along with Leo and Glenn, had been in their battle positions from takeoff. As they approached land over Western Europe, Leo called for a time hack, oxygen check, and roll call to make sure all were in place and ready for the mission. All airmen checked in, and Leo had another command. "OK boys, check the guns." Bursts of fire from the 50-mm guns at each position added their rat-a-tat-tat to the mixture of deafening sounds, only partially drowned out by the headset connected to the intercommunication system.

"Make sure your oxygen lines and masks are clear, boys," Leo said.

"All clear," came responses from six voices with diverse geographical accents.

"Let me hear from you. Okie," Leo chided Elvis McCoy, whose distinctive Oklahoma drawl was missing from the responses.

"Sorry, boss. I'm OK," Elvis shot back.

With an hour or so to go until they approached the IP, Bud used the idle time to let his mind travel the long distance back home. *In just three weeks, I'll be a father. . . can't wait.* He smiled at the thought. Other thoughts came and went over the next half an hour, some fleeting and some longer-lived. *Hope Mother is OK and not too worried—sure am glad Leonard's there to watch over Thelma, Mother Evelyn, and my Palsy Walsy,* he mused. *I sure loved William Wallace's Sunday school class. He taught me so much, but I think Thelma and I will join Dr. Barbour's church in the spring when I get home.* His mind skipped through the past two years, in which his life had taken such a circuitous route. *I can't wait to just relax at home. I hope Grover and Gate are OK and not being mistreated. Wonder what Miss Neubert thinks about what's goin' on in the world today. I hope my letter last night wasn't too much of a downer—don't want Thelma and everyone to worry—I'll write a more upbeat one tonight or tomorrow, depending on how tired I am tonight.*

"We're getting close, boys, time to strap on your jocks," Leo's voice announced over the intercom. Jolted from his reverie, Bud grabbed a walk-around oxygen bottle, strapped it to his waist, and plugged in his breathing hose. He then began the treacherous walk back over the narrow catwalk between the two bomb racks directly over the bomb bay. He removed the pins that restricted the small guiding propellers in the nose of each bomb and put them in his pocket. This would keep the bombs running true and free from tumbling on their flight to the target. He then returned to his position in the nose of the plane and made a second check of the Norden bombsight. All was in order.

True to the briefing information, weather cleared up over the Channel and remained so over Belgium. But as the bomber stream approached Germany, weather conditions deteriorated. Chatter on the frequency heard by flight deck crews of the 381st ships indicated some equipment problems with other of their ships. The Pff ship of the lead squadron lost its #1 engine and fell into the slot, yielding the squadron's position to the 535th. *Egg Haid,* piloted by Lt. Greenspan of the 535th, also lost its #1 engine.

The high squadron and the Belskis crew were holding their position at 24,000 feet about thirty minutes from the IP. No enemy aircraft had been sighted up to that point, but flak had begun to rattle both the aircraft and the crew. "Sounds like bolts rattling in a tin can," Bud said to Collett as he slid his mask to the side so Jim could hear him and also read his lips above the rattles. At about that time, their craft took a pretty good direct hit from an 88mm flak gun on the ground. "They have us zeroed in," Bud said over the intercom, heard only by the flight deck crew.

"Yeah, we've been here before. We'll be OK," Glenn said, referring to the many times their ships have been pelted and punctured

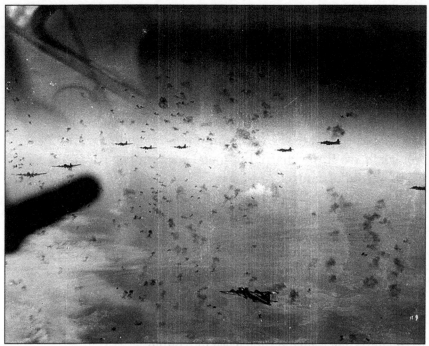

Flak in 381st Bomber Stream over Germany - 1944
USAAF - 381st

but remained relatively unscathed. Each time, they were able to remain aloft, returning safe but rattled to Ridgewell.

In letters to Thelma after those missions Bud only wrote, *"We
had a rough day." Someday, I'll define rough,* Bud thought. But
then came another thought. *I'll be so happy to get home I'll probably never talk about this stuff.*

At that moment, an orange, almost-blinding flak burst flashed in
front of their plane, interrupting his musings. "Holy crap, a 105,"
Bud whispered as he recognized the results of an exploding flak
ordnance from the dreaded 105-mm gun the Germans used to protect key targets. "This ain't good."

"We're coming up to the IP," Jim confirmed to Leo.

"Roger," Leo replied.

Bud readied the Norden for its takeover of the guidance system
on the bomb run. They had dropped their altitude to approach
ten thousand feet for a more accurate bomb run. The soup had

thickened as guidance was transferred to the Norden. Buffeted by the clouds and the wind from the crab angle (the amount of correction an aircraft must be turned into the wind in order to maintain the desired course) taken to maintain the proper heading on the bomb run, the Fortress rattled and shook. Flak ricocheted off its aluminum skin, and some entered the ship, making a pinging sound as shards of metal hit the Fort's skeletal frame. The crew had one shared thought: *Just don't hit the wires that operate the control surfaces.* If the sharp, hot metal sheared key wires, their ship would go out of control—and fast.

"Bombs away," Bud announced as the first of six bombs rolled out its perch and through the bomb bay.

Suddenly a deafening, bone-rattling explosion sounded as a flak ordnance burst open, hitting the wing behind and just to his left. A massive red-and-yellow fireball engulfed the #2 engine, creating immediate chaos throughout unnamed ship #2J-38780. The four men on the flight deck crew heard, saw, and felt the searing heat of the strike. As the five gunners felt the ship jolt and lurch downward to the left, they realized they were in trouble.

Glenn Vaughn's calm voice came across the still-intact intercom, "Bail out, bail out." *Why Vaughn and not Leo?* Bud thought, realizing the order should have come from Leo. *Unless—.*

Suddenly Suggs and McCoy were out their waist windows and hurtling toward earth from about 9,000 feet. The blazing #2 engine broke loose from the wing as the plane began to roll. Glenn fought to maintain control as the remaining crew members scrambled through the chaos, united in their attempt to exit what now seemed a doomed aircraft.

Ablaze, spinning, and without its #2 engine, the once proud B-17 plummeted toward Earth like a falling rock. The now-uncontrollable craft leveled briefly, crashed to the ground, and careened through an open field, coming to rest upside down in a mangled heap. Only a smoldering fire interrupted the pervasive silence at the crash site.

In Mannheim-Neckarau, Germany, the time was just past noon.

CHAPTER 21

Missing Aircraft at Station 167

One Ship to Go

Ridgewell, England: December 11, 1944

As word spread that aircraft were returning from Mission #222 to Mannheim-Ludwigshafen, a crowd began to gather at Ridgewell's airfield. Top brass, including Colonel Harry Leber, stood behind the pipe railing atop the two-story control tower. They looked eastward en masse toward the end of the main runway, straining to hear the unmistakable drone of the Fortresses' Curtiss-Wright engines and to catch a glimpse of the first returning ship as the early dark of the short winter day crept across the base.

The icy snow swirled about the men, pelting their faces and setting their cheeks aflame. The windsock adjacent to the concrete pad identifying Ridgewell as Station 167 remained full, giving an occasional wild flap in the gusting wind before returning to its prevailing west-to-east pattern. These swirling conditions took away the officers' breath and bit their extremities as they stomped their feet in an attempt to increase blood flow and ward off the cold.

Well aware of the 8th AF's commitment to attack the heavily fortified area on the Rhine, the waiting officers remained undaunted and anxious for the return of their bomber boys. The pervasive inclement winter that gripped all of Western Europe and Britain further compromised the crews' safety and added to the anxiety of those gathered in the spitting snow.

Other airmen huddled in small groups along the flight line, rubbing their hands together in a vain attempt to resist the biting cold of this December day. It was difficult to tell the difference between the smoke breathed out by those with cigarettes and the frosty exhale from those without them.

"I went to Ludwigshafen back in early September," one

357

bombardier said. "We had some pretty good weather that day, not like today, but flak was heavy. The Luftwaffe doesn't always show up like they used to, but flak guns are always there in spades. They really protect that big-ass bridge across the Rhine next to the railway yards." (Note: Ridgewell had previously participated in eleven missions to the Mannheim-Ludwigshafen area since January of 1944. On four of these missions, crews and aircraft were lost. None of the three previous Mannheim missions in September of 1944 experienced losses from the 381st. [381st Bomb Group War Diaries of the 532nd, 533rd, 534th, and 535th Bomb Squads, September, 1944.])

Ground crews stationed themselves near the hardstands assigned to each aircraft. They chatted nervously, awaiting the return of their "babies," hoping and praying that each one would land safely with little or no damage from the day's combat. Often they had to nurse their adopted Forts off of life support and back to health through the night in Ridgewell's B-17 hospital after the damage of a tough mission. Before sending the planes back into the fray, they wanted to make them airworthy and safe by every means possible. No member of any flight crew took more pride in their aircraft than did the ground crews and technical specialists. The tech specialists, electricians, mechanics, sheet metal workers, and aeronautics technicians usually stationed themselves near the control tower. Breathing life back into these gigantic birds was both an art and a science. Day after day, night after night, or both, these craftsmen plied their well-honed skills.

Often, area farmers would be seen waiting for the return of the boys who had become almost like family to residents of Ridgewell and surrounding villages. Many of the airmen attended local churches. Young ladies would often come to dances and parties held on the base, and US boys would return the favor with relish and attend functions in the nearby towns. Invariably, romance emerged, and marriage of GIs to local girls was not uncommon. But on the cold, snowy day of December 11, no local residents were seen around the base. If there were non-military spectators awaiting the return of the B-17 crews, they watched through the windows in the warmth of their cottages.

"AFGHAN, this is VP-8196 requesting permission to land," came the call to the tower from the Pathfinder lead ship piloted by William R. Cronin and Charles W. Bordner.

"Eighty-one-ninety-six clear to land. Bring her in," came the reply from the tower. The aircraft was not yet visible, and the chatter among the tower denizens blocked out the sound of the approaching B-17 engines.

Ridgewell Tower- Awaiting ships returning from a mission - 1944
USAAF - 381st

"Here they come, boys," Colonel Leber shouted to the airmen below, "Let's count 'em in." All eyes searched the eastern dusk for the first sighting of the returning ships.

"There's number one," came a shout. And the countdown began.

One by one, Fortresses came into view on final approach and landed to the west, rolling out quickly to clear the runway for the remainder of aircraft. *Smashing Time, Patsy Anne, The Fox, Stage Door Canteen, Egg Haid, Hell's Angel*—one by one, the nose-art names on the planes were called out as they landed. *Our Boarding*

House, Sleepy Time Gal, Liberty Bell, Old Iron Gut, Flak Magnet.
Occasional cheers erupted as each ship's crew members were welcomed home by friends, barracks mates, and bridge partners.

The countdown of returning aircraft continued: "33 . . . 34. . . 35.
. . 36. . . ," then stopped abruptly. Was there a straggler among the thirty-seven crews that launched on this cold morning? Or did one land in Allied territory because of engine trouble or worse? Word began to spread that a ship had been hit over the target.

As they exited the aircraft, crews were quickly hustled off to debriefing in a building near the tower. The Air Force wanted to capture information about conditions they experienced with regard to their aircraft, the enemy, and the weather. They also wanted critical information on aircraft hit by flak or enemy fighter fire. Eyewitness perspectives often differed when men under the intense stress of oxygen deprivation and high-altitude combat tried to recall and relate what they saw—or thought they saw—in the fleeting seconds when a mishap occurred. Stark terror, pressure of the job at hand, confusion, and changing weather conditions compromised not only visibility and eyesight but memory as well. For all these reasons, airmen were not supposed to discuss events of the day until interrogation began.

On that day's mission, the Seeley crew flew the Pathfinder ship in the high squadron of the formation. From his position as tail gunner, Staff Sgt. Wallace McCallair was in the best position to observe a heart-stopping event that occurred over the target a few hours earlier. He knew he was not supposed to talk, but he could no longer hold in the horror he had just witnessed. He chose to tell C.D. Cash, his crew's bombardier, what he saw.

"What ship was it?" Cash asked, his voice cracking as he questioned his crewmate.

McCallair's voice trembled as he replied, "I hate to say, but I think it was the Belskis crew. Your friend's their bombardier, isn't he?"

"Bud, yes, Ross Perrin. I saw him at breakfast and briefing."

Stunned and silenced, Cash stepped into the briefing room and took his seat with the Seeley crew, his normally calm demeanor shaken. Like McCallair, he struggled to come to grips with what he knew must be true.

Metal folding chairs encircled the three-by-six foot tables jammed into the crowded interrogation room. Naked light bulbs dangled from the ceiling, casting a concentrated light on the maps and papers strewn about. Acrid smoke hung heavy and merged with the stench of stale cigarette butts in the ashtrays throughout the room. Discussions of the day's mission focused on the intensity of flak, the absence of the Luftwaffe, the 10/10 soup at the target, and the presumed loss of an aircraft on the Mannheim side of the Rhine River. The confirmation came quickly: one plane and its crew had not returned. McCallair was determined to be the last one to have seen aircraft VE 2J-38780 piloted by 1st Lt. Leo Belskis. The investigation of the tragedy began with him.

First Lt. Alpheus S. Hodge was the IO assigned to interrogate the crews and complete the Missing Air Crew Report # 11341, or MACR, as it was commonly called. Hodge, a soft-spoken, sensitive South Carolinian, was thirty-five years old and a devout Christian. He had attended both Furman University and the University of South Carolina and aspired to teach in college after the war. His obvious empathy helped him coax information from young airmen disturbed by the carnage they sometimes saw in the skies over continental Europe.

From McCallair's last sighting of the downed aircraft, it was determined that its approximate position was at coordinates 49 degrees 29' N.–08 degrees 28' E., at 21,800 feet and heading 300 degrees north, and 500-600 yards out of position. The damaged aircraft was not seen to have a US fighter escort nearby.

Normally, one bomb squad at each base stood down during each mission, protecting the viability of the bomb group in the unlikely but possible wipeout of multiple aircraft. The extensive losses on the two Schweinfurt missions in 1943 taught a lesson well-remembered. The mission to Mannheim, however, called for "maximum effort," so all four 381st bomb squads participated. The war diary prepared each day by the four squads had a similar view of the enemy opposition on that day. It said they experienced "moderate, continuous, and accurate [flak] fire with no enemy A/C (aircraft) sighted" (381st Bomb Group War Diaries of the 532nd, 533rd, 534th, and

535th Bomb Squads, Ridgwell Mission #222 to Mannheim-Ludwigshafen, December 11, 1944).

First Lt. and 532nd BS Pilot Gottfried H. Klinksink ("Klink") was assigned as the preparing officer of MACR #11341 for Mission #222, so he and Hodge worked in tandem to gather the pertinent data. They derived their information from the responses to specific, calculating questions designed by the Air Force to result in an accurate, clear, and succinct report. Some crews provided cryptic information via staccato responses. Others went to the opposite extreme. Klink and Hodge's job was to whittle down the conversations to pertinent facts.

Boys who came forward as witnesses to various aspects of the mishap included two pilots, Charles F. Houk, 1st Lt. in the 534th BS and commander of aircraft 4D, 43-38158, named *Smashing Time*; and 1st Lt. Alton E. Copeland of the 532nd flying A/C 2O, 42-107112, *Sleepy Time Gal*; plus two gunners from the crew of 1st Lt. Edward Carr's aircraft VE-5N, 42-87313, *The Columbus Miss,* Staff Sgt. Robert J. Whitaker and S. Sgt. Leland D. Graham.

The witnesses agreed that "Flak struck [the] aircraft in the #2 engine (to the pilot's immediate left). It erupted in fire and fell off. Fire extended back to the waist of the craft. The left wing exploded and the A/C went into a deep spin, then fell over on its back."

But beyond that analysis, the perception of facts differed somewhat between the four. "Four men bailed out of [the] waist at 21,000 feet. Two more were seen to come out later when explosion occurred. Chutes were not seen to open," was the account settled on by the investigators. However, Hodge also reported another's view that "Four parachutes were seen to open." In a section of the report entitled "Other Remarks," it was stated that, "Two objects were seen to come out, possibly from nose, one object was on fire. Objects were not identified" (Missing Air Crew Report # 11341, Page 5, Response 7).

It seems clear that, in the interrogation room, some facts were in dispute. What was not in dispute, however, was that a horrific tragedy had occurred over Mannheim at about noon on December 11, 1944. There was no way the aircraft could have survived; it was coming apart as it fell from the sky. It was possible, but not probable, that one or all of the crew members could have survived. The report that preparing officer Klinksink signed that day was nominally accurate but woefully incomplete.

In the days ahead, some data would be made clearer and some data further obscured. It would take decades to add more clarity, but some of the facts of that day would remain known only to God.

Loss of aircraft and the boys who flew them had become a common occurrence during WWII. But it was never accepted without intense emotion. Most men on airbases kept their cadre of friends to a minimum: crew members, barracks mates, boys from home, and few others. Building close friendships with those who one day might not return was more than most wanted to face.

The more than 360 airmen of the 381st who returned from the mission that December afternoon could not walk away feeling it was "just another day at the office." But they had to shove their emotions aside or stuff them down. Odds were high that the next day would find them boring holes in the sky again on their way to destroy some German factory, rail yard, or city. As best they could, they did what they must to leave the day's sadness behind and move forward into the everyday work they now realized was both a mission and a legacy.

Sleepy Time Gal - B-17G.
AC# 42-107112 VE-O, 532nd BS
USAAF - 381st

The Columbus Miss - B-17G
AC# 42-97313 MS-N, 535th BS
USAAF - 381st

MacGregor Crew: Back Row: Schomberg, J. Kre, A. Stepanich, J. MacGregor, C. Hodges
Front Row: J. Marinace, L. Roedding, L. Alexander, A. Kazen, (Absent- J. Smith)

Missions Flown by Ross W. Perrin, Jr.

Date	Mission #		Mission Target	Aircraft	Position Flown
	RWP	Ridgewell	(all Targets in Germany)		
9/11/1944	1	186	Merseburg	Unknown (2)	Bombardier
9/19/1944	2	189	Hamm	Liberty Bell	Bombardier
9/21/1944	3	190	Mainz	No Nose Art (3)	Bombardier
9/25/1944	4	192	Frankfurt	No Nose Art (3)	Bomb/Navig. ? (1)
9/26/1944	5	193	Osnabruck	Unknown (2)	Bomb/Navig. ? (1)
9/27/1944	6	194	Cologne	Unknown (2)	Navigator
9/28/1944	7	195	Magdeburg	Little Guy	Navigator-Division Lead
10/2/1944	8	196	Kassell	Mizpah	Bombardier
10/5/1944	9	197	Cologne	Our Boarding House	Bombardier
10/7/1944	10	199	Politz-Zwickau	Century Note	Bombardier
10/14/1944	11	201	Cologne	Mizpah	Bombardier
10/26/1944	12	206	Munster	Liberty Bell	Bombardier
10/28/1944	13	207	Munster	Sunkist Special	Bombardier-Division Lead
12/9/1944	14	221	Stuttgart	Unknown (2)	Bomb/Navig. ? (1)
12/11/1944	15	222	Mannheim-Ludwigshafen	No Nose Art (3)	Bombardier

1   Position unknown
2   Records incomplete-Nose Art unknown
3   Plane had no Nose Art

Missions flown by Ross W. Perrin, Jr. during WWII.

CHAPTER 22

A Search for Truth

Waiting, Hoping and Praying

Knoxville and other cities in the United States: Winter and Spring 1945

ON THE FOLLOWING DAY, DECEMBER 12, the headline of the *Stars and Stripes* read: "Mightiest Bomber Fleet Hits Reich." The accompanying article told the story:

> The mightiest heavy bomber fleet ever hurled against the Nazis by the Eighth Air Force—more than 1,600 Liberators and Flying Fortresses—thundered over the Reich yesterday, blasting rail-yards in the Frankfurt area with nearly 6,000 tons of explosives. Flak was meager. Escorted by 800 fighters and flying in columns 300 miles long, the armada of heavies pounded the rail network behind the Rhine at Frankfurt, Hanau and Giessen, unloading its bombs through heavy low-flying clouds which prevented observation of results of the raid. (*Stars and Stripes,* Vol. I, No. 138, Dec. 12, 1944, Paris edition.)

The *New York Times* headline on the same day trumpeted: "Eighth Air Force Rips German Rail Center." The accompanying article said that "...weather was so thick and bad that bombing results were unobserved....Luftwaffe let them bomb without hindrance. German aircraft fire was meager." But it also added a crucial phrase: "[only] 12 bombers and 2 fighters were lost out of a procession that extended 300 miles over land and sea."

The *Stars and Stripes* was a daily WWII publication read almost entirely by military personnel. Because of this, finding it in Knoxville; or Miami, Oklahoma; Frankston, Texas; or even in the suburbs of the larger cities of Baltimore or Chicago or any of the other hometowns of the Belskis crew was virtually impossible. The *New York Times* could have been purchased at the newsstand on Gay Street or read at the Lawson McGhee Library in Knoxville. But the article's relative obscurity, despite its presence on the front page of both publications, would have hidden the information from anyone without access to the details of exactly which aircraft and crews flew the mission that day.

Furthermore, even if all the families of any of the thirty-seven crews from Ridgewell had read the articles and realized that only twelve bombers were lost—a mere seven-tenths of one percent of all that flew the mission—they would have dismissed the thought that any of their boys was one of the twelve. And both articles stressed the important fact that flak was "meager" that day.

Back in the States, life went on as usual in the lives of the families of the Belksis crew. "As usual," that is, if anything was "usual" with their boys fighting in the protracted war thousands of miles away.

On the same day the article appeared, J. Ross chattered and tugged insistently at his mother's dress as she attempted to write a letter to her brother. Evelyn wrote:

> *Thelma and I were talking on the phone the other day and she told me to ask Leonard if he was ready to take your place about January 1st. He said yes, he was ready, and for her to have plenty of cigarettes ready for him.* [This referred to the potential change in status of men like Leonard who had previously been exempt from the draft.]
>
> *I'm getting real anxious for the little Perrin baby to arrive. I told Thelma I would probably worry her to death coming to see it. J. Ross talks about it a lot. I'm afraid he will be a little jealous of it. He has been the King Bee so long. Thelma said she didn't want Leonard to say that her baby was ugly. I said that would be paying you back. You must remember saying that J. Ross was ugly . . . he really was the ugliest little thing.*
>
> *J. Ross asked me the other day if you would be home*

for Christmas, and I said no. He said, "Boy, when he does
come I'm going to lock the doors so he will have to stay
here with me." Hope you come home soon—your sister
who loves you loads—Evelyn

Mid-December brought many happenings that required preparation. Christmas was less than two weeks away, and Thelma's baby
was due a week later. Both required trips to town for what the wom-
en of the family termed "essential purchases." On the same morning that Evelyn wrote her letter, Thelma had made the trek to downtown Knoxville, returning just ahead of the snow that threatened to
lock down the city for a few days.

Following a bowl of piping hot soup that warmed her from the
inside out, Thelma arranged her makeshift office in the drafty dining room. Huddled beneath a heavy flowered blanket, feet tucked in
front of her, she hammered away on the Royal typewriter perched
on the dining room table. Snow had already blanketed the small
yard in front of 1926 Chicago Avenue, but the falling flakes were
coming thicker and faster. This spelled trouble for merchants across
the city, who needed good weather to keep shoppers active. Beneath
her feet, her dachshund, Dimout, whined his disapproval at her lack
of attention as she concentrated on reminding Bud how much she
loved and missed her Poppy.

Her letter included a lament: "...the Ford's battery is dead again*
so I had to take the bus to town. You wouldn't believe the crowds.
Sometimes the sidewalk was so crowded that Evelyn and I had to
step off the curb and walk in the street. Don't be mad at me—I was
careful."

Mail service in both directions between England and Knoxville
was erratic. Often letters would come after one written two weeks
later had already been received. Thelma, Evelyn, and Bud's mother—especially Bud's mother—worried when there was too much of a
time lag between letters. All were ecstatic when one arrived because
it marked one more day that they knew he was alive—at least on the
date of the letter.

Bud's letter of Saturday, December 2, written just after returning from Roke Manor, was awaiting when Thelma returned from

shopping over two weeks later on the eighteenth. And the next day, two more, written November 27 and 28, showed up in the morning mail.

Thelma smiled and read the letter of the second aloud for her brother, Garland, and her mother to hear: "... *we left the rest home at noon yesterday and expected to be back here last night, but after changing trains at least nine or ten times we made it as far as Cambridge last night and stayed at the Red Cross there. We got up this morning but didn't catch the train until noon and got here this afternoon.*"

At this point, Garland interrupted Thelma's reading. "I would love to see Cambridge. The architecture there is stunning."

"Let her finish," Mrs. McGhee chided as Dimout barked his own brand of displeasure. Thelma continued her letter:

> *I had lots of mail—about seven letters and six packages, I have lots to answer in those letters and lots to talk about what's in the packages. I'll do that tomorrow in a long letter. I had ones from Mother and Evelyn besides the ones from you. I may go to church in the morning then come back and start in on my letter-writing. So now I'll say goodnight to my sweet little mama and hit the sack. I love you an awful lot—Your husband*

With only four days left until Christmas and possibly only a few more before the arrival of their first child, Thelma, excited about her visit to the doctor, hurriedly scribbled a letter to Bud.

> *Our baby has two arms, two legs, a head and a beautiful spine on the X-ray photo I had taken today! And he's in the normal position he should be, "head first" which is the main information the doctor wants from the X-ray. The technician also took a side view, but Junior, the wiggly-worm, moved, and spoiled the picture! It wasn't me that moved—I was holding my breath to be perfectly still. He just can't seem to be still a minute. I (or we) weigh 134 lbs. now. That's about right—112 lbs. (my normal weight) +22 = 134! Don't believe I'll gain much more between*

*now and January 1st—gained only two pounds since De-
cember 1st. I was thinking the scales showed 137 but I
was wrong—it was 132.*

Two weeks after the event over Mannheim-Ludwigshafen, Christmas Day arrived, as did a smattering of snow atop the remnants of the large snowfall that also occurred two weeks earlier. An encouraging but long and hectic day at Evelyn and Leonard's uplifted Thelma's spirits but also tired her out. The mother-to-be arrived just past noon and didn't get back home until after nine. After a hot bath in water that nearly overflowed the claw- foot tub, she put on her new robe, a Christmas gift from Evelyn, cleared a spot on the dining room table, and began another epistle to her Poppy. Because everyone else was asleep, and for fear that she would awaken Dimout, she chose to write instead of type the letter.

> *Why should it be harder for me to write you tonight than
> usual? I've begun three times already—the other two tries
> are in the wastebasket! Guess it is because I have so much
> to say to you, for you have seemed close today in spite of
> that ocean between us. I spent most of the day with your
> family, had a good Christmas dinner, was "showered"
> with pretty gifts, and enjoyed myself—in SPITE of the
> realization that an important part of the "picture" was
> missing. Honestly, I shouldn't have said that, for you DID
> seem to be there. I won't go much further with this sort of
> talk, sweetheart, for I'd hate to get sissy [cry] after being
> able to stay dry-eyed THIS long, and that's what would
> happen.*
>
> *I hardly know where to begin—or how far I'll get to-
> night—but there has to be a start, so here goes.*

Thelma shared with Bud the details of her Christmas, pausing sometimes to smile and often to cry, thinking about her dreams for next year's Christmas. Margie, Bud's sister, and J. Ross had both received an abundance of presents, small in size but great in quantity. The chaos of gifts and greetings kept the family from focusing on Bud's absence. Thelma's letter continued:

After J. Ross and Margie opened their gifts, we had our dinner—baked chicken, dressing, potatoes, frozen asparagus tips, green beans, carrots, and Evelyn's fabulous hot biscuits, with pineapple and fruitcake for dessert. I ate PLENTY, in spite of Junior! Guess I sorta crowded HIM this time, but it was really good. You know both Evelyn and your mother are good cooks. J. Ross didn't eat much, tho—he was too excited.

About the fruitcake, before I forget it—YOU were more or less responsible for that! When Evelyn told Leonard about your seeing T. G. Brown in London, Leonard kidded that he bet that was worth a fruitcake—and sure enough, when he went by Kerns and told Mr. Brown [Lt. T. G. Brown's father, founder and owner of Kerns, Knoxville's largest bakery, where Leonard once worked as a baker], *about your seeing his son, he ended up coming home with a big cake! So we thank you! Uncle Sam furnished the dessert pineapple, too—Leonard brought it from one of his "trips" —you know we poor civilians can't find pineapple very often!*

All thru the dinner I kept wondering if you were having a good Christmas meal. I was afraid to bring up the subject but your mother did—she said she bet you did have, if you were at the base, and not "at work." I'm glad to tell you that we all stayed quite cheerful, and nobody looked near tears at any time. Of course, J. Ross kept us amused.

The normal post-Christmas letdown started the next morning. Thelma decided to enhance her sharing of the holiday with her husband with another note.

I DIDN'T listen to the Christmas music this year—it is what always gives me that Christmas feeling, but also makes me sissy—so I just keep the radios off! The first Christmas we are together, baby, we are going to SIT

BY THE RADIO and make up for all the pretty music I'm missing!

I still wish I could have sent you a Christmas present, baby—something you could have had for Christmas day. But I'll keep that on the "I-owe-you list" and make it up when you come home. And that reminds me—J. Ross took out one of his Christmas dollars, folded it up, and insisted on Evelyn sending it to you! Said he was afraid you might need it—and so far, he has refused to take it back!

On the last day of the year, the mailman brought the letter Bud wrote on the night of December 10 before the Mannheim-Ludwigshafen mission the following morning. After reading it, Thelma felt a need to cheer him up as he seemed to be dragging.

Dear Poppy, (almost anyway!) —There aren't many more minutes in this ole year 1944. It hasn't been such a bad year, considering—has it? I was lucky enough to spend several months of it with my Poppy, and we got a start on our family and so far we both have been lucky in lots of ways sweetheart—I could name them, but you know what they are. Of course, I'd like for my sweetheart to be here with me to ring out the year we'd probably "celebrate" as we usually did, and be sound asleep when the bells and whistles made all the noise!

Your mother called just to see how things were, and we talked a good while. She seems to be feeling good—we both did a lot of kidding about when Junior was coming. She'd told J. Ross that the whistle would blow at twelve and that he'd have to kiss someone so he said he guesses he'd kiss Thelma's baby. When asked if he wanted it to be a boy or a girl, he said, "a boy," and if it was a girl he would throw it away.

Well, sweetheart, tomorrow is the day and I am ready, but I don't think he or she is ready to come. I think I'd better tackle my hair problem right now, and then get to bed. Maybe I'll still be thinking of things to tell Poppy

*in the morning—the first day of 1945. If I do, you'll have
to take a day off from bridge to read this! Bye for now,
sweetheart.*

True to her word, Thelma struggled to get fully awake at eleven, even though Dimout was barking his fear of the wind howling outside. It had started at midnight and continued unabated until almost noon on New Year's Day.

Thelma began her first letter of 1945 after a cup of coffee and some corn flakes:

*Happy New Year, Sweetheart. Mother and I didn't get
to bed 'til about eleven. The wind blew hard all night—
reminded me of Big Spring. That reminds me, Norma
Jean Gatewood sent some photos of us with them at Big
Spring. I'll send them to you with the articles I've saved
about tomorrow's Rose Bowl. I'll wait till the Journal
comes in the morning so I can send you articles after the
game. I know you'll be listening to it so I'll listen too, then
I can feel closer to you. It's quite an honor for Tennessee
to get a Rose Bowl bid—but I think Southern Cal will win
handily.*

As Thelma had predicted, the USC Trojans walloped Tennessee 25-0 in front of 68,000 home team fans in Pasadena. Regardless of the lopsided loss, she knew Bud would want to read *Journal* sportswriter Tom Anderson's insightful account of the game. So Thelma set her alarm for an uncharacteristically early wake-up so she could have the articles about the Rose Bowl ready to send when the mailman made his morning pickup and delivery. She put them in a stamped envelope with only a quick note inside, *"Enjoy the articles about Tennessee's drubbing. I'll write more tonight. Love, Thelma."* A cold blast of air swept her breath away as she cracked the door, slipped the envelope into the wire rack that hung beneath the mailbox, and stepped back into the warmth of the living room.

Thelma spent the day finishing preparation for the long-awaited trip to the hospital. The birth was scheduled for New Year's Day, but it seemed Junior had not been informed of that schedule, so the wait would continue. She decided to wait until afternoon to traipse into town. After returning home and a light supper, she cleared off her normal writing place at the dining room table and began to scribble out another love letter.

Unfinished Letter from Thelma to Bud - January 2, 1945
Rosalind Perrin Davis Collection

A knock at the front door interrupted the silence of the early evening. "Thelma, can you get it?" her mother called. Dimout barked his concern about what or whom might be outside as he trotted dutifully to Thelma's side.

She pushed away from the table. "Coming," she called as she moved from the dining room and through the living room toward the door.

Unlatching the safety chain and twisting the doorknob, she opened the front door. Darkness came early to east Tennessee in January. But the almost-full moon of this clear evening framed the two men standing ramrod-straight on the small front porch. Through the screen, she could make out their military uniforms as they simultaneously removed their hats. "Mrs. Thelma M. Perrin?" the man on her right asked.

Only the icy air coming through the screen door kept her from dissolving into an instant puddle. She had long feared what she knew but didn't want to admit was happening. She grabbed the doorframe, her voice faltering out her response. "Ye—yes. Please come in." Her Southern gentility prevailed over the mounting fear that threatened to overcome her.

The men stepped inside and closed the door. Having heard the unfamiliar voice and the tone of her daughter's reply, Mrs. McGhee came to Thelma's side. She put her arm around her very pregnant daughter as the unsmiling men stood erect, each with his hat under his arm. The silence was shattered as one of the men handed Thelma an envelope containing a telegram. "Ma'am, it is our duty to inform you that your husband, Lt. Ross W. Perrin, Jr., has been reported as missing in action over Germany on December 11, 1944."

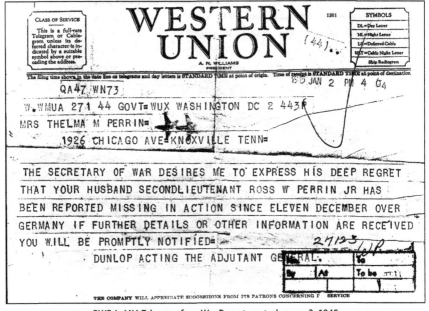

RWP Jr. MIA Telegram from War Department - January 2, 1945
Rosalind Perrin Davis Collection

Inside, Thelma was falling apart. But at that moment, her soft but stoic nature would not allow her fractured heart to show. With her mother's assistance, she sat down on the edge of the couch.

"We pray that the days ahead will bring the news that Lt. Perrin has been found safe. And good luck with your delivery," the second officer said as the men snapped a military turn and departed.

After closing the door behind the exiting officers, Mrs. McGhee sat beside her daughter, holding her close but saying nothing.

Emotion overtook Thelma, and she wept softly. After a few minutes, she pushed up from the couch. "I need to tell Mrs. Perrin," she said as she picked up the handset of the phone and began to dial the all-too- familiar number: 4–2–2–7–4.

"He said Bud was missing, not dead—." Mrs. McGhee stopped as she realized the word she had just spoken aloud. "Maude isn't well. Make sure you tell her he's just missing," she implored. Thelma, intent on her call, did not respond.

"Hello," came Leonard's voice on the other end of the line.

"May I please speak with Mrs. Perrin?"

When he heard Thelma's voice, Leonard immediately assumed her message must concern the impending birth of her baby. But hearing an unfamiliar intensity in her words, Leonard simply said, "Sure, just a minute."

In seconds, Bud's mother came on the line. "Thelma, how are you?"

Thelma paused, gained as much composure as she could, and plunged ahead. "Two servicemen just came to the door to tell me that Bud has been missing in action over Germany since the eleventh of December. They emphasized that he has only been reported as missing. I just know he'll be OK and coming home soon. I got a letter from him written on the evening of the tenth. I'll try to find out as much as I can tomorrow and let you know what I learn."

"Thank you, Thelma. Are you OK?" Mrs. Perrin's response hid a whelming tide of emotion. Before Thelma could respond, her mother-in-law blurted, "I have to go to the bathroom and pray." Consistent with her Baptist heritage, Maude Perrin was a prayer warrior. She took seriously the biblical injunction, "But when you pray, go into your room and shut the door and pray to your Father who is in secret. And your Father who sees in secret will reward you" (Matt. 6:6 RSV). Mrs. Perrin's prayer room was the small bathroom next to her bedroom.

On her way there, she relayed the stunning message to Leonard and Evelyn, her voice quivering and tears streaming. Realizing something was amiss, J. Ross frowned his concern as he interrupted, "Is my Palsy Walsy OK—is he coming home?"

"We hope so, son—soon," Leonard answered as he scooped up

the inquisitive almost-four-year-old and took him to the kitchen. Evelyn's tears, like Thelma's and her mother's, flowed from a broken heart.

On the following day, January 3, Thelma wired Alyce Vaughn about the telegram she received the previous day. The next month was tense, filled with tears, confusion, and mystery for Thelma and all connected to the crew and their families. Word of Bud's MIA status quickly made the rounds in Knoxville, and in time, leaked out to other areas.

Calls and letters of condolence began a steady flow to Thelma and the rest of Bud's family. Mothers of the crew members quickly coalesced around their common plight. Alicia Lauret, mother of ball turret gunner Lynn; Anna Collett, mother of navigator Jim; and Louise Belksis, mother of pilot Leo began an intense letter writing web to other crew contacts. Thelma and Alyce Vaughn, wife of copilot Glenn, shared a unique bond as wives and mothers, or, in Thelma's case, mother-to-be. They had written each other consistently since the crew was formed in the summer of 1944, so their bond had time to mature.

On the sixth, Thelma received a letter written on the fourth from Alyce that said, "*Guess you got my wire this morning. When I got the wire from you, I was glad because I had been debating whether or not I should wire you. I received my telegram from the War Department on the afternoon of the second. When I recovered from the shock, you were the first thing I thought about, but knowing your condition, I was afraid to wire.*"

Either from a lack of confidence in the message delivered by the War Department or an attempt to gather courage to ward off the inevitable, Alyce added:

> *As I told you in my wire, I am just as certain that they are alive as I am that I am writing this letter. I am not saying this just to make you or myself feel better. I can't do that. I never have been able to. I don't know much about Bud, but I do know Glenn and I know that if it is humanly possible, he will get through this thing. Either I feel something in my heart or I don't, and I feel they are not*

dead. And the War Dept. doesn't think so either because if they did, the telegram wouldn't have read as it did.

She further related what she had read in the *New York Times* about the mission and then added,

I was so thankful to know that the Luftwaffe didn't of-fer resistance because I know by that, that the ship was not shot down. Since there was some anti-aircraft fire, the ship may have been injured by flak so that they had to turn around and go back. You know B-17s—they are good ships, and they couldn't have been more than 100 miles from the Belgium line, or the French line. Unless they were badly injured, they could have gone a pretty good distance. But you know and I know that a million things could have happened. We can't dodge facts, but we can have faith. I've got it and I hope that you have. We will just have to keep it and hang on to it. It is our only hope. I don't mean to be preaching you a sermon; I am just pouring out my heart to you because I know that you can really understand how I feel. I can't find a place for war in religion. I can't understand that part about it, and I doubt if anybody really can. But, I firmly believe this; that if we really believe in God's power; if we leave it to Him; if we really have faith and trust Him to care for and look after Glenn and Bud; if we do the things—and I will—I have no doubt they will come to see us soon. Then we can have a Happy New Year!! And it will be a happy new year for you and me and our little Glenn and Bud! Just you wait and see!!!—Lots of love, Alyce

Alyce's well-articulated thoughts (or hopes) were shared by most of the women connected in this heart-wrenching vise of in-trigue and pain. Norma Gatewood, whose husband trained with Bud and Grover Blevins at Big Spring, had been shot down and was then imprisoned with Grover at Stallag Luft III, wrote to Thelma, *"Most likely at this very minute Grover and Gates are together worrying about you and having a reunion at the same time. Bud's safe and sound. Believe that, Thelma."*

On the ninth, Alicia Lauret wrote Thelma saying she was *"rather exuberant"* after hearing from Mrs. Suggs, mother of waist gunner Durward Suggs, that her son and McCoy, the other waist gunner, had been reported as German POWs. She added. *"Don't give an inch, pull all you can with our boys, they've got to come out."*

A few days later, Alicia Lauret wrote again:

> *Mrs. Vaughn's letter* [of the sixth, also sent to Mrs. Lauret] *follows precisely my own trend of thought and hopes. I also checked papers, maps, reports etc. and altho they are reported down in Germany, there's every possibility that they could get to Allied ground. 100 miles isn't too far to expect our B-17's to drift. And if the wind was blowing, you know it came from the north (during the blizzard) that should have helped some, even considering they bailed (is that correct?) before reaching Allied-held territory, and besides the help of the underground—and, best of all, every one of those boys was mentally alert, ingenuous, and resourceful. I have the outmost confidence that they will get out soon—those boys are safe and we'll get definite news soon. Sincerely, Alicia Lauret*

Mrs. Louise Belksis wrote, ". . . *the Suggs and McCoys have called—we're a happy bunch tonight."*

Anna Collett wrote a few days later and finished the letter with ". . . [My husband] *Jimmie and all the other boys and I really think they will be coming home to us, maybe not for a while, but one day—Love and best wishes—Mrs. Anna Collett."*

As she digested these various communications, Thelma's thoughts vacillated wildly. Her deep concern for Bud blended with the fact that "Junior" had seemingly decided to take up permanent residence inside her. Two weeks dragged on until at last, birth pangs heralded the impending arrival. On January 15 at St Mary's Hospital, Thelma gave birth to an eight-pound bouncing baby *girl*, just as she had always thought and Bud had frequently intimated.

Baby Girl Is Born to the Ross Perrins

A daughter, who has been named Rosalind Cannon, was born Monday at St. Mary's Hospital to Lt. and Mrs. Ross Perrin.

Lt. Perrin, a member of the Eighth Air Force, has been overseas since last August, and was reported missing in action following a mission on Dec. 11, according to word received recently by Mrs. Perrin from the War Department. He was formerly connected with the City Utilities Board.

Mrs. Perrin, the former Miss Thelma McGhee, makes her home with her parents, Mr. and Mrs. G. P. McGhee, 1926 Chicago Avenue. She is a copywriter in the advertising department of a local department store. Both she and Lt. Perrin are KHS graduates.

Rosalind Perrin Birth Announcement
Knoxville Sentinel - January 17, 1945
Rosalind Perrin Davis Collection

Rosalind Perrin aka "Junior"
February, 1945
Rosalind Perrin Davis Collection

She chose the name Rosalind Cannon Perrin for her new little one. "Rosalind" was as close as she could get to the name of her beloved husband, and "Cannon" was her mother's maiden name. But Glenn Vaughn's wife, Alyce, seemed intent on calling the Perrin baby "Rosebud," and no words to the contrary changed her mind.

In between feedings, Thelma had time to ponder the current situation. Before Rosalind's healthy delivery, Thelma had all the concerns that normally accompanied the birth of a child in that era. She recalled a letter from Bud in the late fall in which he mentioned a Knoxville boy named Cash, also a bombardier stationed at Ridgewell, with whom he had become close friends. On a hunch, Thelma wrote a note that was printed in Bert Vincent's "Strolling" column in the *Sentinel* on the evening of January 19.

It read:

THE KNOXVILLE NEWS SENTINEL
Friday, January 19, 1945

STROLLING   ***by Bert Vincent***

NOTE: If you know the family of Lt. C. D. Cash, B-17 bombardier, recently stationed at a bomber base in England, please get in touch with Mrs. Thelma McGhee Perrin, Tel. 3-2286. Mrs. Perrin's husband, Lt. Ross W. Perrin, is missing in action, and she thinks Lt. Cash may be able to tell her more about her husband than she has learned through the War Department.

Thelma's appeal for information in *News Sentinel* - January 19, 1945
Tennessee Historical Archives

That evening, Mrs. W. S. Cash in Oakdale, Tennessee, a rural mining town fifty miles west of Knoxville, read the appeal in the *Sentinel*. "This is Conan's friend that he has written so much about," Mrs. Cash said to her husband, her voice a mixture of sorrow and excitement. The next morning, she typed a tender message to Thelma:

Mrs Thelma MCGhee Perrin   Oakdale Tenn Jan 20 1945
1926 Chicago Ave,Knoxville Tenn

Dear Mrs Perrin :-

We are replying to your heart felt appeal in Last nights News-Sentinel. A chain of circumstances has gathered before us concerning your brave husband that is unfolding a human drama as we shall relate .

During november our son Lt.Conan D.Cash a member of the 532nd Bomb Sqdn 381st Bomb Group based in England,wrote in part""One of my friends whose home is in Knoxville is on a program that will be broadcast to the states tomorrow night and it will be carried by a Knoxville radio station, I ask him to say hello to Mom and Dad for me, I hope you are Listening in or some one near home will hear it and tell you.""

This program was to be broadcast in the early part of november but we didnot receive his Letter until near the end of november, Some time during the early part of december we read a news paper account of Lt. Ross Wallace Perrin of the 8th air force being missing in action and giving your and his mothers home address in Knoxville, We cut this article out of the paper and mailed it to our son with the uncanny knowledge that Lt Perrin surely is our sons Knoxville friend. And Last nights News Sentinel carried your appeal to us, ,confirming our belief throughout.

We have a Letter from our son dated december 19th and in one sentence he made this touching statement" I guess I will not see my friend again, he is not with us.

With a genuine duty bound feeling we send you the meager information we have of Lt Perrin and we are writing our son tonight via air mail an urgent request for him to collect and forward to you all the knowledge he has concerning your Dear Husband .

Lt Conan D.Cash 0-771896
532nd Bomb Sqdn 381st Bomb Group
APO 557 % PM. New York NY

Very Sincerily
Mr + Mrs W. S. Cash

Letter from Mrs. Cash to Thelma Perrin - January 20, 1945
Rosalind Perrin Davis Collection

This letter seemed to place a high degree of probability on the deaths of Bud and most of the crew. But Thelma chose not to share the information with the other women, at least not yet. She continued to receive hopeful correspondence from the crew families and hoped along with them for the safe return of Bud and the remaining men.

On January 27, Louise Belksis wrote, ". . . *a friend of Leo's was researching and was encouraged by what he had learned—Leo is competent and highly skilled in his duty which with the aid of each and every one of his intelligent crew members made it safe for them and all of us.*"

The next day, Alyce wrote that Walt, a friend of Glenn's, ". . . *talked to men at Ridgewell who said that ten chutes opened from the plane on the eleventh, so they all got out and that's one consolation—I have to believe that they are prisoners.*"

In the early morning on February 10, a knock sounded at Thelma's door. Her knees went rubbery as she again saw through the window two military men, framed in the sunlight of that clear but cold day. Home alone except for her baby, she carried three-week old Rosalind to the door and admitted her unwelcome visitors. They spoke a few words of condolence and presented her with the following telegram:

KIA Telegram from War Department - February 10, 1945
Rosalind Perrin Davis Collection

Was this the final news? She still didn't know, but her hopes were fading. On February 20, she received the promised letter, dated February 16, which confirmed the news contained in the earlier telegram.

Thelma continued to receive condolences along with glowing letters and calls about her husband and the respect so many had for him. Many were written in the past tense. Some continued to proffer hope of his survival. Thelma increasingly became resigned to the fact that Bud was not likely to return. But as late as April 30, 1945, she wrote to Alyce Vaughn, ". . . *'Rosebud' runs the house—I'm not giving up hope that my sweet Poppy will come back."* And Dorothy Pyles said in a June 28, 1945 letter, ". . . *I am as sure as you are that Bud is safe."*

Thelma took much comfort from the letters written by the group of friends they had met in the many stops since Bud entered the service. Jay Pyles, whom both Bud and Thelma had come to love, first sent a V-Mail on January 1, saying he had just missed seeing Bud when they were both in London the last of November. He didn't know of Bud's status at that time. Later, when he did, he told Thelma how much Bud had meant to him. Letters came almost every day through the spring of 1945 from Minnie Smith; Norma Gatewood; the Beazleys in Nebraska; Hack Wilson; Jimmie Hines; Lawrence Hill, Leonard's sister's husband, who was stationed at Great Ashfield only thirty miles from Ridgewell; Roy "Chappie" Chappell; Mrs. "Top" Toplinsky; Emma and Dusty Holder; the Chaddocks; and Evelyn Davis, whose husband Gene was killed in 1944 flying the hump in China, among many others.

In May, Evelyn revealed to Thelma that after months of trying, she was pregnant and due to deliver in late August or early September. Thelma expressed joy equal to that shown her the previous June when she wrote the thinly-veiled letter about the bundle of joy she and Bud expected sometime around New Year's.

The mighty 8th AF proved its mettle from its first flight over Europe on August 17, 1942 until the final mission to Pilsen, Czechoslovakia, on April 25, 1945. With the diminished capability of Nazi Germany, due in large part to the role of the Eighth, US and other Allied troops finally took France and moved East through Germany into Berlin. There they met Russian troops moving west. Hitler committed suicide on April 30 in his Fuehrer bunker, and one week later, the Reich fell. Germany surrendered on May 7, 1945, 146 days too late to have prevented the tragedy of December 11.

Almost two months after VE-Day, Thelma received a typed letter from Elvis McCoy, mailed from Miami, Oklahoma on June 29, 1945. It gave the first eyewitness account of what happened inside the fated B-17 on December 11:

> *I was in the radio room when the plane was hit and we had just released our bombs over Mannheim, Germany. The plane immediately caught on fire. Suggs and I think we were blown out when the plane exploded because neither one of us jumped. We were both in the waist of the plane. We were just getting our parachutes on and we didn't really know what happened. We were captured as soon as we hit the ground, and I did not see Suggs until three or four days after we were shot down. We had hopes of the other boys being in some other prison camp. I am very sorry I could not give you more information but it all happened so quickly that we really didn't know what took place. Yours very truly, Elvis A. McCoy*

Communication between the women of the Belksis crew continued throughout the summer of 1945. A few more details (or guesses) about the crew's fate came out, but nothing changed what now seemed to be the inevitable conclusion. Hope continued to spring up here and there and, in some hearts, was never doused.

Alyce, keeping up with the Perrin/Greene family, inquired if Evelyn's baby had been born. Thelma wrote that J. Ross's little brother, David Leonard Greene, had arrived on August 31, 1945, twenty-five days after Paul Tibbetts piloted the B-29 Enola Gay as it bombed Hiroshima. Japan capitulated after the bombing of Nagasaki three days later. And on the deck of the USS *Missouri* on September 2, 1945, General Douglas McArthur signed the documents confirming Japan's complete surrender. WWII was over at long last.

Thelma kept up her correspondence with the crew women,

especially Alyce Vaughn and Alicia Lauret and occasionally Dorothy Pyles and the Belksis sisters. As 1945 drew to a close, Christmas cards had largely replaced letters between the women. And by 1946, Thelma exchanged mail only with Alyce and Alicia.

In May of 1949, Bud's body was returned to E.B. Mann's Mortuary for a funeral service and burial at Lynnhurst Cemetery in north Knoxville. Over the ensuing years, the lives of the families of the Belksis crew, so inextricably entwined with the devastating effects of war and the loss of sons and husbands, may have returned to some degree of normalcy. However, the deaths of their loved ones left gaping holes in their hearts, lingering memories of what was, and continued grief over what might have been.

Although the story of the Belksis crew and Mission #222 from Ridgewell to Ludwigshafen-Mannheim on 11 December, 1944 lay dormant for decades, it was far from finished.

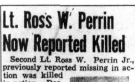

Lt. Ross W. Perrin Now Reported Killed

Second Lt. Ross W. Perrin Jr., previously reported missing in action was killed in action Dec. 11 over Germany, according to a War Department message received today by his wife.

The message read, "Report now received from the German government through the International Red Cross states that your husband, Second Lt. Ross W. Perrin Jr., who was previously reported missing in action, was killed in action on 11 December over Germany." The Secretary of War extends his deepest sympathy."

Lt. Perrin, bombardier of a B-17, had been stationed in England since last August. He was a KHS graduate. He was the only Knoxville member of his crew.

He was the husband of the former Miss Thelma McGhee, 1926 Chicago Avenue, and the son of Mrs. Maude F. Perrin, 9 Cherry Street. A daughter was born to Lt. and Mrs. Perrin several weeks ago.

Lt. Perrin

Ross W. Perrin Jr., KIA Article
-Knoxville News Sentinel -
February 1945
Greene Family Collection

(Note: the records of the 8thAAF differ slightly from those reported on the 12th by The New York Times and Stars & Stripes. Following is the data the 8th reported: Mission 746 was flown on December 11, 1944 with the largest number of bombers so far dispatched in WWII, 1,586, and 841 fighters were sent to hit rail targets and bridges in W. Germany using PFF means; 5 bombers and 2 fighters were lost: 171 of 182 B-17s hit bridges at Mannheim; 1 B-17 was lost and 18 damaged; 9 airmen are MIA. Escorting were 54 of 59 P-51s without loss. Source: WWII 8th AAF Combat Chronology-www.8thafhs.org.)

CHAPTER 23

A Renewed Search for Truth

Six Decades Later

USA and Europe: Spring 2009–Spring 2015

"HEY, ROZ." I SAW HER name come up on my phone display on that late May afternoon in 2009, so "hello" was inappropriate. I knew who was calling, and she knew that I knew.

"Roz" is Rosalind Perrin Davis, my cousin and only daughter of my Uncle Ross W. Perrin, Jr., for whom I am named. She lives in Ft. Lauderdale, Florida, with her husband, Arnold, whom she married in 1966. They have two children, Mary and Liz, and five grandchildren.

She and I were quite close growing up. "Rozzy," as we called her when she was younger, lived close by and spent a lot of time in our home, especially during the summers. For many reasons, my mother considered her as much a daughter as a niece. My brother, David (one of her high-school classmates); sister, Sally; and I also considered her a special part of the family.

Mom was devoted to her brother, Roz's father, and his untimely death in 1944 devastated her. She carried the scars of both his passing and her father's, only four years before Bud's, for the remainder of her life. I had many conversations with Mom about Uncle Bud over the years, including a long one only hours before she passed away on February 20, 2004. Over the past five-plus years, I've kicked myself for not asking her many of the questions to which I later struggled to find the answers.

Roz has spent all her married life in Florida. We kept in touch often over the years but saw each other infrequently. A call from her, however, was never unexpected and always a treat. And I know she looked upon mine the same way.

"Hey, J. Ross, how y'all doin'?" For Southerners, that's a common question, similar to "Y'all come and see us" or "How's ya momma 'n 'em?"

Roz's question was sincere; I knew so. Our infrequent contact was not because of any lack of love or interest but busy schedules and family responsibilities. At the time, my wife was suffering from persistent back pain, so our conversations always included questions about Lynne's condition. Roz and Lynne had been in a Young Life Bible study group together in high school, so they too had a great friendship.

"'Bout the same, still has pain, but keeps smilin' all the time," I responded. For a few minutes we got caught up on our families—spouses, kids, and grandkids.

Then Roz moved the conversation forward. "You know Mom's stroke's been difficult for all of us, and she's regressed over the past few months. So I thought I'd go to Knoxville and help Kathy and Patti pull her things together and clean up her house. Of course, Mom's housekeeping skills leave a lot to be desired, and she never throws anything away. Well—it's a good thing she's a pack-rat, because we found quite a collection of letters, newspaper clippings, and photos of my father that I think you'll be interested in."

Roz's mom, Thelma, remarried in the late forties to Bill Hancock, and they had a second family that included four more children. She had also returned to the work force and had an almost four-decade career in advertising and programming at WBIR-TV, the CBS affiliate in Knoxville. Her 2002 stroke resulted in a precipitous decline in her health in the years that followed.

"We found almost a thousand letters—a lot of 'em had references to you. Seems as though you were a little scamp," she said with her quiet but familiar laugh.

"*Were*. You mean I've changed?"

"No, you're right—still a scamp, just a little older one."

"Completely incorrigible," I confirmed.

"I'm going to send you a few of the ones that mention you, and a couple that you wrote to him."

"*I* wrote? You gotta be kidding."

"Yes. You sent him some Teaberry chewing gum in one and scribbled notes in a few others—you're gonna love seeing them."

I could hardly believe what I was hearing. *Sixty-five-year-old letters from my beloved uncle? Letters I wrote. Mentions of me. Photos of us that I had probably never seen.* I was beyond excited. "Send 'em FedEx—I'll pay for it," I said. *I don't want to run the risk of them getting lost. And I certainly don't want to wait even one more day.*

Over that evening and the next day, my interest escalated. I tried recalling the times I spent with Uncle Bud during 1943 and '44. I had a few vivid memories. Events and people had also added to my memory bank because of conversations over the years with my mother, daddy, and granny. These crept back into my thoughts as I awaited the arrival of the package from Roz. When it came, I tore into it with zeal.

As I read each of the dozen or so letters, I smiled—and yes, cried a little. Each one hooked me more. I called Roz to express my thanks and also to see how I could get the entire cache of documents scanned and sent to me. "I know that's a huge job. I'll be glad to have it done in my office or pay to have it done," I told her. Somehow, her sisters, Kathy and Patty, agreed to do the scanning, and in less than a month I had digital copies of everything, organized and dated. Little did I know how much the contents of those files would impact my life.

As I read the entire body of letters over the ensuing weeks, my connection with my larger-than-life childhood hero deepened. The letters revealed another side of him, one that let me see a young man with convictions, ethics, and dreams intersecting with fears, insecurities, and frustrations. The effects of war flowed through his words as he expressed veiled concerns over his future. Excitement over his soon-to-be born "Junior," who turned out to be a "Junior-ette" (Rosalind), filled almost every letter.

Years earlier, I had heard the recorded message my uncle made at the BBC in England that was broadcast over WROL in Knoxville on Thanksgiving 1944. The broadcast had been preserved for our family on a large black recording disc, the kind played from the spindle outward to the edge, unlike the 78-rpm records of the day. My grandmother kept the disc in a ragged, stained, brown padded envelope with an address sticker from her former employer,

J.C. Penney. This recording was almost like a shrine in our family. We listened to it infrequently, but it was often brought out and admired. In these letters, I read my uncle's thoughts about the broadcast, how it was made, and what he was able to say and not say, as well as the web of conversation the broadcast prompted. All of this gave the recording even more prominence in my thoughts.

Other memories came dribbling back, first shadowed, then vivid. I was traveling back in time. Not only could I visualize events, objects, and people, but I also felt the ambiance of those long-ago days. I savored the reverie, mysterious, warm, and comfortable all at once.

I recalled my grandmother taking out the round powder box in which she kept Uncle Bud's silver bombardier wings, shoulder chevrons, air medal, and uniform buttons. Once a week, she allowed me to look at his Purple Heart, his beautiful silver ID bracelet, and his watch, its hands fixed at 12:03. Back then, I had wondered about why the crystal was broken and the hands stopped. I would later learn the reason.

Ross W. Perrin Wings, buttons, medals and powder box
Photo by J. Ross Greene

As this Saturday-morning tradition with my Granny came to life again, I found the powder box, sequestered away in a drawer for years. Its smell was the same as I remembered. The look on my granny's face came back to me, and I could see the tears that would roll down her cheeks as she watched me place the chevrons, buttons, brass belt buckle, and wings on the kitchen table where I could see them better.

I remembered his body being returned in 1949 from its initial interment in Germany and then Avold, France, as well as the funeral at Mann's Mortuary in downtown Knoxville. I wasn't allowed to attend. At eight years old, I was considered too young, as was my four-year-old brother, David. "It might have disturbed you too much," our older relatives later told us. I always regretted that well-meaning but hurtful decision. To keep us occupied, our cousin, Buddy Green, himself a Navy veteran, walked us around downtown during the service.

Life went on. Time passed and memories faded—at least some of them. The letters I was devouring during the late spring of 2009 rekindled memories, some the clear recollection of specifics and others the vague remembrance of stories I had heard over the years. Everything I read helped me flesh out the character of the person who had lain dormant in my thinking for the previous sixty-five years. But none of this sated my appetite for knowing more than the letters revealed. In fact, what I learned only fed my hunger to know more. *But where do I begin?* I wondered.

Because of her stroke, Thelma had lost most of her ability to communicate. Both my parents had passed away, as had most everyone I knew of who had known Uncle Bud. *If only I had known of these letters years ago,* I thought. I remembered that my "Uncle Dick" Foster knew him well. *I'll start there.*

Uncle Bud's letters identified many people, both pre-war and during his military time. I recognized some of the names and had even known some of the people at one time, but most were new to me. The letters also identified dates, places, training sites, military group identifications, and activities. Roz was able to find her mother's date book for the year 1941. I slowly put together a rudimentary timeline and list of people I needed to seek out. I didn't know where this search might lead. I just wanted to take the journey.

I began my quest in Knoxville, where there were more people who had known my uncle than anywhere else. Aunt Thelma, Dick Foster, and Truji McCloud were the only ones from the September

1941 picnic who were still alive. I had remained in contact over the years with Uncle Dick, and my search gave me an added reason to spend time with him. He was able to give me some helpful first-hand background about Uncle Bud as well as some great family photos that I had never seen. "Bud was someone who was kind to everyone. Everybody liked him," Dick remembered. "I was younger and looked up to him. I always admired his confidence." But his information was limited to the years before they both entered the service.

Truji McCloud's health was fragile but her mind sharp. "Thelma sure fell hard for Bud. Once they found each other, no one else had a chance," she told me. "You know, Ty and I were responsible for getting them together. Thelma and I were on the *Blue and White* [the school newspaper at Knox Hi] staff together and also fellow thespians. Those were some wonderful days, and we were great friends." Truji tired quickly and I left, thrilled to have met her for the first time. She passed away a few months later.

My next stop was the Knoxville Utilities Board, formerly the Knoxville Electric Power and Water Board (KEP&WB). Jennifer Stooksbury in the Communications Department took much effort putting together the chronology of my Uncle Bud's time at KUB and located every mention of him in internal communication documents back into the late 1930s. In the August 2009 issue of the *Kilo-Water Account*, the KUB newsletter, she wrote a touching retrospective of my uncle that included a photo of his crew.

I started my search for Bud's fellow airmen with the names of his crew, two of whom survived the crash and seven of whom died. I decided to begin by trying to find the two who lived and served out the war as POWs, Suggs and McCoy. A Google search, a half-dozen calls, and a couple of days later, I was talking with Amanda Herd, the granddaughter of Elvis McCoy, one of the survivors of the December 11, 1944 mission. She told me several things about her grandfather, including his passing in 1988. She also provided a few candid photos of crew-members. I shared with her a letter her grandfather had written to my Aunt Thelma and some excerpts from other letters written by wives and mothers after the crash. That began what became my five-year exhaustive search for relatives of other crew members.

I soon learned that Durward Suggs had passed away at age eighty-four on March 24, 2004. Through a nephew of Leo Belskis, Dennis Winsky, I was able to communicate with two of the pilot's sisters, Katherine Feykes and Stella Koludrovic. They were able to give great insight into his family, life, and personality. Over this journey, I've been able to gather some information on all crew members, more on some and less on others.

The name Conan D. Cash appeared in many of my uncle's letters, so he was the person I sought out next. Again, Google came to the rescue, and after some searching I found a young (at eighty-six) Mr. Cash in Bartlett, Tennessee. Over the next four years, from our first conversation on the evening of June 8, 2009 until his death on March 4, 2013, I never talked with anyone who had contemporaneous knowledge of Ridgewell, the 381st Bomb Group, or my uncle who remembered more detail than C. D. Cash. He was incredible in the way he could take me on a verbal walk through Ridgewell, the small towns surrounding the base, and The Fox Pub. When on a couple of occasions later I spent days at Ridgewell, I felt almost as if I had been there before, all because of C.D. Cash's oral paintings on the canvas of my mind.

When my wife and I were in Memphis on August 20, 2010, preparing for one of her many back surgeries, I met with Mr. Cash and his son, Peter. (I have always had trouble calling these men who went through so much in WWII by their first names. Whether a result of my Dad's admonition to respect my elders, the genuine admiration I have for these true heroes, or both, I still call most of them "Mr.")

Over those two memorable hours, I shared with him his mother's January 20, 1945 letter to my aunt. He smiled as he looked at the end of the letter and said, "It's been a long time since I saw that signature, but it is my momma's." He gave me some photos of his crew and helped me identify people from an October 1944 photograph of all bombardiers and navigators then at Ridgewell. As he looked at these photos, he would tell little stories about how the boys got their nicknames, where they lived on base, and where they were from. In each of our numerous conversations over the years, I could hardly write or type fast enough to get down all the details he related. Invariably, I would have to call him back and go over my notes to make sure I hadn't made errors. I often did, but he never did. I treasure the picture I had taken with him in Memphis. I also treasure the friendship we were able to develop and how much he contributed to this story.

He was also the first to tell me about the 381st Bomb Group (H) Memorial Association reunion group and its president, Dr. Kevin Wilson. Only a few days after my initial conversation with Mr. Cash, I was able to make contact with Kevin. As we talked that evening, I realized that not only was he a plethora of knowledge on WWII and the 381st but also a gracious professional with a heart to help someone like me who possessed a weak accumulation of knowledge but a strong desire to learn. Soft-spoken and friendly, he was the consummate historian on the 381st. He provided me with details of both the 381st Bomb Group and the 8th Air Force, as well as a few of the many stories he would share with me over the next five years. Kevin's father, Howard E. Wilson, was an electrician in the 448th Sub Depot from before Ridgewell's opening until the completion of the war.

Over the course of that evening, Kevin further fueled my research machine with numerous sources: books, periodicals, and detailed information on museums, cemeteries, and people he suggested I contact. I worked until early the next morning organizing my notes and outlining my research schedule for the next weeks, which turned into years. I could barely sleep that night because of my desire to move forward on the project that was fast becoming a major effort. He suggested I might like to join the 381st Group and attend the reunion in Charleston, South Carolina in August, only two months ahead. I heartily accepted his gracious invitation.

I read in my uncle's letters that Bing Crosby had performed a concert at Ridgewell and asked Kevin what he knew about it. He e-mailed me a photo of the September 2 concert, and I found others elsewhere. The photos were classic, showing Crosby on stage and airmen literally hanging from the purlins and rafters in the hangar. I scoured the photos, looking in vain for my uncle in the small

segments of the crowd shown there. But I became intrigued (my
wife says obsessed) with finding out more about the concert. I researched newspapers in London and New York and found articles
about the Crosby stops on that September 1944 whirlwind tour of
the ETO and air bases. I broadened my research to include a search
for an audio of the concert. Two years later, I found a CD of one,
with the same cast of participants, which took place in London just
one week after the one at Ridgewell. With the same cast and performance length, I am confident it was exactly the one given to the
381st on September 2. It was an incredible find!

Much of what I was learning to that point included general information about people and places along with resources to further
expand that information. But I wanted to go deeper. I wanted to
know details of the explosion and crash that took my uncle's life. I
also wanted to find everything I could about his other missions. I
knew just a few hard facts, enough to whet my appetite but not even
a small part of what I wanted to know. I'm sure Kevin thought I was
already obsessed, but he didn't show it if he did. I suspected that
evening that the initial conversation would grow into a wonderful
friendship, and it has.

Kevin said I definitely needed to get a copy of the Missing Aircraft
Report (MACR) for the mission on which Uncle Bud was killed. In its
final form, the MACR is a combination of mission information from
two sources. It contains, first, data provided by the USAF about the
aircraft, crew, and witnesses leading up to the aircraft disappearing
or crashing. It goes on to share information from the German's KU
(*Kampfflugzeug*, combat aircraft) report that contains post-crash
facts and data, including conditions of airmen, burial information,
and personal items found by the German government.

Initially, Kevin obtained for me a few of the key pages from the
MACR #11341 report on my uncle's fatal mission. Concurrently, I
filed for a complete report from the Department of the Army under
the Freedom of Information Act. In addition, I filed for my uncle's
IDPF (Individual Deceased Personnel File), which was received
some months later. It contained virtually all records from his enlistment forward through the return of his remains from Europe. Even

his complete dental records were there, which I was able to link up with the various dental issues he mentioned in his letters.

Kevin also directed me to the 381st website from which I could research 1st Division, 1st Wing, and 381st BG diaries for daily, monthly, and specific mission reports. At that point, I believed I was on track for putting the puzzle together and that, while waiting for the Army reports to be delivered, I would continue on my people search. I was soon to learn, however, that the pieces of the puzzle would not easily fit together and some would be missing and difficult if not impossible to find.

The name Harvey Tidwell appeared throughout Uncle Bud's letters. My search for him proved a little more difficult, but in mid-June I was able to find him at his home outside of Houston. He insisted I call him "Harv." For a couple of hours, he regaled me with detailed stories of bridge and touch football games with my uncle, shenanigans on the base which Bud instigated or in which he participated, and the characters with whom Harv cavorted in England. Like Cash, Harv's memory was sharp and his storytelling spellbinding. He taught me things I had not and would not find in any book or article because he had lived the story.

In one of our conversations, I asked Harv's age. He responded, "My real age, or my Air Force age?" He went on to tell me that he was eighty-three, born in December of 1925. A judge in Gary, Indiana had provided him a birth certificate showing he was eighteen and not sixteen in the summer of 1942 when, as a headstrong teenager, he enlisted. Harv was the respected lead bombardier in the 532nd during my uncle's time at Ridgewell. Sadly, Harvey Gordon Tidwell died on May 29, 2010, before we were able to meet in person as planned. But on a few occasions, he helped me fill in gaps in my research and entertained me in the process.

Two other names received prominent mention in the letters from Uncle Bud: Grover Blevins and Bob Angevine. Flipping a mental coin, I opined that I had never heard the name Angevine anywhere else, so that might be the easier of the two to find. I hoped he was still living. A Google search provided the name of a Robert Angevine in Midland, Texas. *This has to be the same Bob*, I thought.

Within sixty seconds, my good fortune was confirmed. "Is this by chance the residence of Bob Angevine who served in the 381st Bomb Group in England in World War II?" I asked the woman who answered my phone call.

"Yes, it is."

I was so elated I could hardly respond. "May I speak with him?"

"I'm his wife, Bea, and I'll be glad to have him call you. He's not here right now, but I know he'd love to talk with you." He called in an hour or so, the wonderful beginning of what would turn into a cherished, warm, and valued friendship.

Over the ensuing years Bob graciously taught me much about his job as a navigator and Mickey Man on a Pathfinder ship from July 1944 through his 31st mission to Bordeaux, France, on April 14, 1945. We discussed his instruction of my uncle at bombardier training in Big Spring, Texas, not far from his current home. He asked me to come visit him so we could visit the Commemorative Air Power Heritage Museum in Midland and the training site in Big Spring. It took a couple of years for me to get there, but in August of 2013, I visited Bob and Bea and we took in both sites. I hung on his words as he recalled his instructional time at Big Spring.

Aunt Thelma spent the last month of Uncle Bud's bombardier training with him. She stayed the first week at the ornate and tall (for Big Spring) Settles Hotel. This iconic structure fell into disrepair and was closed for many years before being completely refurbished in 2013. As Bob and I strolled through its lobby, I could almost visualize the young couple's joy when, after five months of separation, they were reunited there on that April day in 1944.

On the evening of December 29, 2014, my good friend Robert H. "Bob" Angevine died peacefully in his sleep two days shy of his ninety-sixth birthday. I was privileged to count him and Bea, his second wife, who preceded him in death, as friends.

The many times Grover Blevins was mentioned in my uncle's correspondence confirmed the close friendship they forged, beginning even before their basic training in January of 1943. I had heard all my life of their relationship as well as the one between Thelma and Grover's wife, Henrietta. I was quite surprised to discover her alive, well, and living near St. Petersburg, Florida. I first reached her on July 3, 2009 and talked with this spry, spunky, but genteel lady numerous times before finally meeting her again after sixty-three years.

I didn't recall our initial encounter decades before, but she did. When she met me at the front door of her Seminole, Florida apartment on that blazing hot day in July of 2013, she said, "You look a lot older than you did in 1951." We both laughed. She shared many stories of "Cleve," as Bud called Grover Cleveland Blevins in many of his letters home.

I was also able to tell her a story of an encounter I had with her husband in the spring of 1951. After the war, Grover bought a grocery store at the corner of Magnolia and Olive Streets, a couple of blocks from my grammar school, Park City-Lowry. On my way home in the afternoon I would often stop in Blevins' Market to buy candy (Charms, the square version of Life Savers, and peanut butter logs). I knew Mr. Blevins had known my uncle—he mentioned him on occasion.

One day, I handed him twenty cents to purchase some candy. He returned change of a nickel and four pennies, which I stuck in my pocket. After walking outside, I realized that he had given me two pennies more than he should have. I walked back in, returned them, and said, "Mr. Blevins, you gave me too much change."

With a broad smile, he responded, "I know I did, J. Ross. I just wanted to see if you are the same kind of young man your uncle was." I've since told the story to my children and grandchildren to show them you never know who is watching and even testing you.

Henrietta shared many photos and documents from Grover's confinement in Stalag Luft III after he was shot down on his 5th mission in a B-24 out of Foggia, Italy on August, 23, 1944. He was ultimately liberated in April 1945 after taking part in the forced march from the POW Camp in Sagan to Spremberg. Many of these photos were published, with attribution, in Marilyn Jeffers Walton and Mike Eberhardt's 2014 book, *From Interrogation to Liberation: A Photographic Journey, Stalag Luft III—The Road to Freedom.*

In late July of 2009, I located Frank Vaughn, a younger brother and one of seven siblings of co-pilot Glenn Vaughn. Frank helped me get in touch with Glenn's wife, Alyce, on October 22, 2009. I was pleased to have a couple of warm conversations with her during

Marilyn J. Walton
and Edouard Reniere
8th Air Force Reunion - circa 2009
Marilyn Walton Collection

C. D. Cash and his son, Peter
Memphis, Tennessee - August 20, 2010
Photo by J. Ross Greene

Grover Blevins (L) at Liberation after
march from Stalag Luft III-April 1945
Blevins Family Collection

Ross Greene and Bob Angevine
Midland, Texas-August, 2013
Photo by Bea Angevine

Henrietta Blevins-
Summer 2013
J. Ross Greene

Howard E. Wilson; 448th Sub
Depot Electrician-1944
Dr. Kevin Wilson Collection

Marti Pieper, Editor of
A Fortress and a Legacy
Marti Pieper Website

which she revealed some of the emotions she had shared in letters to my aunt after Glenn's death. In the summer of 2012, I talked at length with their son, Glenn, Jr. Since then, we have exchanged information and photographs. Glenn also loaned me some correspondence between his mother and Thelma that helped immensely in my ability to chronicle the period in early 1945.

I followed Kevin Wilson's earlier advice and in August 2009 drove to Charleston for my first reunion of the 381st Bomb Group. I felt like a sponge, maybe even a pesky one, as I tried to pick the brains of the twenty-five or so veterans in attendance. One very memorable and poignant personal moment occurred at this reunion. At the memorial luncheon on the third day, Bob and Bea Angevine asked me to join them at their table. 381st veterans Dick Schneider and his wife, Barbara; Bill Palmer and his wife, Ellen; and Jack Lantz and his wife, Frankie, were also present. In his October 15, 1944 letter to Thelma, Bud said, *"I met Bob Angevine going in so we sat together and sang together. For once they sang a few songs I know. And I was able to carry a tune."* At the memorial service in 2009, song sheets were distributed to those present, and we sang "Amazing Grace." On that day, I shared my song sheet with Bob Angevine just as Uncle Bud did almost exactly sixty-five years earlier. Through tears, I shared the story and moment with Bob.

At the Charleston reunion, I heard numerous references to Ron MacKay. A prolific writer, Ron had authored twenty or so World War II books, many of which focused on the 8th AF. One of them, *Ridgewell's Flying Fortress: The 381st Bombardment Group (H) in World War II*, was considered the seminal work on the bomb group. Lynne and I took a trip to England later that fall, and on October 8, we met Ron at a restaurant along the M-40 Motorway north of London. It was easy to see why the veterans held Ron in such high esteem. He was and is more than willing to share his vast knowledge and expertise. This willingness coupled with his fast-paced speaking cadence made me feel like I was drinking from a fire hydrant.

Also on that trip, Ridgewell resident, Museum Historian and President, Dave Osborne gave us our first tour of what was left of the aerodrome and surrounding area. He and his wife, Joanne, graciously afforded us both time and information, adding much to my bank of knowledge.

In early January of 2010 I was able to fly in a B-17, the *Liberty Belle,* out of the airport adjacent to the Mighty Eighth Air Force Museum in Savannah. John Madden, father of a business associate, Dan Madden, had given me information about a WWII experience weekend conducted by Tim Shannon of WWII Adventures. I signed up right away and soon drove to Savannah for a weekend designed to reproduce, as much as possible, preparation for and implementation of a B-17 bombing mission.

Ridgewell Historian Dave Osborne - with WWII vintage bike, Ridgewell- Spring 2010
Photo by J. Ross Greene

To familiarize myself with the Fortress on the forty-minute flight portion of the weekend, I clambered from the bombardier's seat, back over the narrow ramp between the two sides of the bomb bay, around the ball turret, through the fuselage between the waist gunner positions and finally to the back side exit just short of the tail gunner position. As I traversed the length of the plane, slightly buffeted in flight, I understood the limited visibility the boys would have had during a mission. And that day, we were flying in clear conditions, not the intensity of battle. This personal experience in a B-17 was a great help when I wrote about conditions in the aircraft during battle and after being struck by enemy ordnance. This flight also shed light on the difficulty of getting consistent accounts of facts concerning the crash. In order to prepare a clear and credible report, I would have to seek other information to help clarify the differing versions of the final mission—if, in fact, it could be done.

By the middle of 2010, I was knee-deep in conflicting data as I attempted to put together the pieces of an increasingly fuzzy puzzle. Not surprisingly, the witness section of MACR #11341 did not line up with information from the War Diary accounts from each of the four 381st Bomb Squads. Did four men bail out of the plane, or was it two? One source said six. Another account said ten. *That can't be right*, I thought, *since the craft only carried a crew of nine.*

All the witnesses from that day were, themselves, well-engaged, trying to complete the bomb run amid exploding flak, close formations, and their specific responsibilities in their own planes. Limited visibility and changing sight lines as planes were buffeted about and turning also added to the conflict in the various accounts. All in all, such mixed reports were understandable but frustrating

Putting together an accurate list of my uncle's missions proved to be another obstacle-laden process. Crews were identified by the pilot's last name. For example, the Belskis crew flew on mission #222. However, airmen would occasionally move between crews and bombardiers and navigators were, because of their specific training, the most likely to be shuffled. So one could not be certain which airmen flew with Belskis on a specific flight just by looking at the flimsie or crew load list.

There were numerous reasons for alterations in crew composition. Mickey Men would replace a non-Pff trained navigator if the crew was placed in the lead position of an element. Also, training of navigators, after reaching the ETO, would remove them from flight status until certification was completed. This caused Bud to lose missions flown by the Belskis crew during October, and it was difficult to confirm that the other eight crew members actually flew a specific mission even though Leo was listed as the pilot on the flimsie and the crew load list.

Occasionally, sickness after arriving at the hardstand would require crew substitutions, thus altering the mission's crew-load list. But those alterations were not noted on the load list and, therefore, not a part of the available microfilm-data at Maxwell AFB. Adding to the confusion was the fact that September 1944 crew load lists for the 381st were lost in a fire at the repository in St Louis.

All this meant that creating an accurate mission list for anyone other than a pilot was an intricate challenge. Some of the puzzle pieces are lost forever. Some, however, fit snugly. Airmen were instructed not to convey details of missions; crew names, destination, results, injuries, and conditions, etc. Some violated this admonition. Bud did not. Not only was he one of the officers charged with

Above: Liberty Belle B-17G;
January, 2010
Photo by J. Ross Greene

Left: Ross looking out right waist position
of Liberty Belle talking with Rosalind-
January, 2010
Photo by Van "Gator" Robertson

Bob and Bea Angevine;
Bill and Ellen Palmer,
381st Reunion
September, 2009
Photo by J. Ross Greene

Left-Right: Ron MacKay, 381st Author and WWII Historian-Fall 2010; Kevin Wilson, Executive Secretary
of 381st BG Memorial Association-Fall 2012; Lt. Leonard Spivey-381st Navigator and SLII captive after
Schweinfurt Raid on 8/17/43; Capt. Sam Whitehead-381st Pilot-2013
Photos by J. Ross Greene

scrubbing letters of details that, if they got into enemy hands, could compromise the safety of airmen and the efficacy of missions, but he was also the consummate rule-follower. An overview of his letters did, however, reveal an embedded code phrase to indicate a mission flown: "Yesterday was a tough day." A search through 381st and 1st Wing War Diaries, mission flimsies (where available), and crew load lists almost always confirmed that Bud flew on the days he so designated. However, determining the crew with which he flew, his position in the crew (navigator or bombardier), and whether or not he was in a lead position proved a little more difficult.

This difficulty notwithstanding, the list I have been able to assimilate is, to the best of my exhaustive research and ability, "Ivory Snow" accurate—ninety-nine and forty-four one hundredths of a percent. To accomplish this, I started with Leo Belskis's missions list. I cross-referenced this with Bud's letters containing a reference to "a rough day," missions flimsies, crew load lists, and books written by other 381st airmen in which they listed crews for various missions.

(Note: In his book *Friendly and Enemy Skies*, Bob Armstrong wrote that Ross W. Perrin replaced his normal bombardier [Lt. White] on the September 28, 1944 Magdeburg mission. This confirmed Bud's position on another crew that flew on the same day the Belskis crew also flew. Without that information, I would have assumed that Bud flew with Belskis on that day, because the letter he wrote Thelma the next day only identified the day before as a "rough day.")

Somehow, I had to find European help to extend my search, but how? In 2002, I had a couple of consulting engagements for a multi-country European bank with dual management locations in Amsterdam and Frankfurt. The Frankfurt-based key executive and my client contact, Udo Cremer, was not only a business associate but had also become a friend. After I called him and explained my dilemma, he graciously put me in touch with one of his coworkers, Klaus Ulrich. Klaus lived in Mannheim-Neckarau, the final resting place of the B-17 from Mission #222. He had often played soccer on the field along the plane's suspected flight path. Klaus and his daughter spent a number of weekends trying, with significant success, to find information about the flight pattern and crash. He sought but was unable to find people who knew about the incident almost seven decades earlier. But in the months that followed, I would put the specific information he gained to good use.

During the fall of 2010, I advanced my circle of advisors and knowledgeable contacts. Lynne and I had told Ron MacKay to let us know if and when he came to the States. And in the summer of 2010, he did just that. Ron took to heart my casual invitation to "come see us," and I'm so glad he did. In early August he flew to Atlanta on a red-eye out of London. The following morning, we flew to Detroit where we met Kevin Wilson and attended the Thunder over Michigan Air Show concurrent with the 8th AF Reunion. There I also met Jim Tennet and his son Chris. Jim serves as Chairman of the Ridgewell Airfield Commemorative Association Museum. At the air show, eight operational B-17s flew in formation, a thunderous and impressive sight.

Folding tables laden with books covering various aspects of the air war were scattered throughout the reunion venue, their proud

Ron MacKay, Matt Wilson, Kevin Wilson, Chris Tennet and Jim Tennet-
Thunder over Michigan-August, 2010
Photo by J. Ross Greene

authors monitoring the sale of their works. At one of the tables, a soft-spoken, attractive lady offered her book entitled *Rhapsody in Junk: A Daughter's Return to Germany to Finish Her Father's Story*. We discussed her experiences, and I bought and later read her book. After I gave her a brief overview of what I was doing, she said, "I might be able to help you. If you'd like me to try, please give me a call."

Her words proved a clear understatement. Our phone call a few days later began not only a deeper understanding of the war, but also an incredible expansion in worldwide contacts and a resulting enhancement in my ability to accomplish my mission. It also initiated a significant and close friendship between the author, Marilyn Jeffers Walton, and her husband, John, with Lynne and me.

Ron, Kevin, and I drove from the Eighth Reunion in Detroit to Dayton constantly engaged in WWII conversation, which included plenty of Ron's expansive recounting of 8th AF details in his distinctive Scottish-British accent. After joining Jim and Chris Tennet, we spent two days exploring the National Museum of the US Air Force at the Wright-Patterson Air Force Base and clarifying information there at what is arguably the largest and most valuable display of aircraft in the world. Our WWII journey then carried us to the reunion of the 381st BG in Nashville. Throughout the ten-day sojourn, I enhanced my growing base of knowledge on the war and the operation based in Ridgewell.

Every contact provided specific facts, details, and information about the objectives of my search. But I wanted a much more expansive contextual understanding of all aspects of the period and the war itself. Early in the process, I became a compulsive consumer of World War II documentaries, books, and movies. With this broadening perspective, I was better able to frame my understanding of the vast amount of information coming my way. To this day, I'm constantly trying to rearrange storage for my growing cache of material.

At that point I had begun to clarify my specific desires for the finished book. With that evolving clarity, I formulated an initial outline. That outline and the accompanying first two chapters were soon quashed, along with my early visions of writing grandeur.

My first-level editor, who is also my wife, read what I had written and cautiously but clearly opined, "This is not your best work. It's uninteresting."

I knew she meant "this stinks." Smarting from that blow to my fragile ego, I crawled into the writing doghouse. While licking my wounds, I soon came to realize her loving but pointed critique was absolutely right. Undaunted, I threw away months of drudgery and again struck out with renewed vigor on the scribe's path to success. But this would not be the last jolt I would encounter along the bumpy literary road. Significant alterations were still on the horizon. I just didn't know how many and how extensive they would be or from where the initiative for the changes would come.

As a special gift for his daughter, I wanted the book to shine a bright light on Ross Perrin's life, cut short by the insidious war. My brother, David; sister, Sally; and I were so blessed to have known, learned from, and been loved by our father. Rosalind never had such an opportunity, and I wanted to do something to repair that loss. I also wanted my work to be as accurate as I could make it, incorporating historical fact while relating my uncle's story. Further, I wanted it to motivate readers to gain both knowledge and gratitude for the sacrifice paid by our soldiers of WWII. I would later add to these goals, but the initial tenets would remain.

In addition to informing me in 2010 of the B-17 flight opportunity, John Madden had also told me he and his wife, Mary, had lived in Mannheim, final resting place for the B17, for a period of time. While there, they had developed a friendship with a local resident, Ruth Reiss, and her husband, who had since passed away. John was sure she would be very interested in helping in my search, and when he contacted her, she confirmed his words.

The information Klaus Ulrich provided, along with the salient facts I had already gathered, gave Ruth a place to start. I remained perplexed about putting the puzzle pieces together and communicated my hope that she could help me. Through our stumbling efforts to communicate (she speaks slightly broken English, and I speak no German), I took delight in her excitement about assisting in the search. Her ardor was infectious, and she jumped headlong into the project. While she researched German libraries, museums, and periodicals, I continued my search on the US side of the pond.

As we conducted our independent research throughout 2010, I was making slow but sure progress in the now-arduous task of crafting the book. After earning both bachelor's and master's degrees in Civil Engineering, working toward a Ph.D, receiving certification as a professional engineer, changing careers and starting a financial consulting practice more than three decades earlier, I had conquered some pretty tough projects. But the one of writing a historically accurate book that also appealed to a reader's heart was kicking my butt, and I knew it. I got half-hearted encouragement from some family and friends and, no doubt, raucous, behind-my-back belly laughs from many others.

But everything I encountered, whether successes or impediments, only fueled my resolve to move ahead with dispatch. The book had moved from dream status through that of an exciting adventure on to the solving of a puzzle, and it had now become an albatross hanging from my neck. But things were about to change.

By late spring of 2011, Ruth Reiss had uncovered a resource containing a fairly comprehensive account of the last stages of the mission on December 11, 1944. *Neckaraurer Impressionen—1939-1945-Chronicle of 75 Years Mannheim AG Power Station* by Norbert Hasiba (Verein Geschichte Alt-Neckarau [Mannheim-Neckarau, Germany, 1996]) provided a much clearer description than I had ever seen of the final path of Uncle Bud's plane. It added significant detail about the crash location and what was affected on the ground during the plane's descent. But was it accurate? It was not exactly congruent with other information I had gathered. The author's sources were undefined in the book, and he died before I embarked on this project. Since this account was also somewhat in conflict with the MACR and KU reports, I knew that finding witnesses was important if it could occur. The English translation of the Hasiba account follows.

> On 11 December 1944, the North American 1st Bomb Division started attacking different targets in the Rhein-Main-Area with 171 bombers of type Fortress II

(B-17). At the same time, around 11.50 a.m., an adversary [or better hostile?] bomber was brought down by the German air raid defences over Neckarau. It came down in the back area of the restaurant "Zum Niederbrück" [former owner Otto Rühl, today Ristorante Sorrento—now in 2014 it is a doctor's office] at the Neckarauer Waldweg #33. This bomber must already have dismantled [in German aviator language, the word is *abmontieren*] during its fall, since parts of this brought-down bomber were found on the premises of the Rheinische Gummi-und Celluloid-Fabrik.

Eyewitnesses saw the bomber, which was hit by the flak, flying on an extremely low level. It flew from the extended Rheingoldstraße to the Paul-Billet-Platz (today Waldweg-Stadion) and managed to drop the bombs left on board. After that, the bomber changed its direction to Neckarau until it came down at the Neckarauer Waldweg. The bomber's level of height was so extremely low that the detonation of the dropped bombs catapulted four of the occupants out of the bomber. Their crashed bodies were found on the grassland next to the branch from the 3rd Aufeldweg into the Neckarauer Waldweg. One occupant, probably the sniper [Note: This comment probably refers to another part of the book], was found dead next to the bomber. The other three occupants who were still inside of the bomber fell victim to the heat of the burning bomber. Their bodies could only be saved charred.

The bombing caused another victim on the Paul-Billet-Platz. The Russian woman Anna Schewelkowa, born Pyrjukowa (21 September 1898, Wolkowa, district Smolensk) was an *Ostarbeiterin* [worker from the East] accommodated in Lager Ost I on the Paul-Billet-Platz. She was in a barrack that was built up there when the bombs were dropped nearby. Moreover, three other Russian women and one Russian man were hurt; they had to go to the Neckarauer *Rettungsstelle* [first-aid post] (see Aufnahme-Nr.

1036-1039 in the Aufnahmebuch of the first-aid post, page 126/127).

The supposedly last bomb dropped by the bomber de-stroyed the house Neckarauer Waldweg #67 completely. This house was near the Paul-Billet-Platz and Peter Zen-kert, a locksmith, used to own it. (Hasiba, *Neckaraurer Impressionen, 1939-1945,* translated from the German manuscript by Edouard Reniere.)

As she walked the neighborhood looking for information about the period of the war to supplement my research, Ruth Reiss had, almost a year earlier, found Ms. Waltraud Fleck outside her home at Neckarauer-Waldweg #144. She gave Ruth a sketchy account of a 1944 B-17 crash in the area. I was unsure whether the crash she remembered took place during a bombing on September 9, 1944, or if it was the one that took my uncle's life and that of six other airmen on Mission #222.

After hearing of Ruth's encounter, I began planning a trip to Ger-many to hear her eyewitness account myself. As far as I was con-cerned, I couldn't get there soon enough. In only three weeks of hectic co-ordination of schedules on both sides of the Pond, I was able to fly to Frankfurt, my first stop on the way to Mannheim.

Ruth was an incredibly gracious host. After she picked me up at the Frankfurt Airport, we headed to the Autobahn. That was not my first trip on this highway, famous for its unlimited speeds, but it was the most eventful. Before closing my eyes and gripping the armrest for what I just knew was an impending crash, I glanced at the speedometer. It registered 205. A quick calculation told me that the US equivalent of this metric speed was 127 miles per hour. The crash never occurred, and Ruth and I made it safely to her house in Bruehl, outside of Mannheim.

When I arrived, she placed a call to Ms. Fleck to confirm our meeting for the next afternoon. In spite of my limited (approaching non-existent) understanding of German, I could tell from Ruth's demeanor that there was some sort of problem. Ruth had said the day before that Ms. Fleck had cold feet because she couldn't understand why I wanted to come all the way to Germany and to her house. It seems that the older Germans, especially those in heavily bombed areas as Neckarau, are either very eager to talk about their experiences or totally non-communicative, with no in-between.

I feared that Ms. Fleck was concerned about my agenda and didn't want to be confronted in any way by an American on some sort of retributive mission. But as Ruth continued to speak with her, I could see by her softening expression and tone that the next day's meeting would take place after all. I was filled with relief—about three years', $5,000, and 10,000 round-trip miles' worth.

The next day, Ruth Reiss, her son Timo Sauer, and I drove up Neckarauer-Waldweg Road after leaving the Haus Niederbruck'l and an encouraging conversation with Annette Heizmann, a nurse in the medical office now occupying the historic structure. We came to Ms. Fleck's home, parked, and passed through the front gate protecting a pristine lawn. Lining the yard was a beautiful, variegated flower garden that spoke volumes about the home's occupant. Ms. Fleck later told us her house had belonged to her parents and she had lived there her entire life.

Our hostess met us on the walkway with an inviting smile and outstretched hand. I felt somewhat relieved but still anxious. Ms. Fleck was close to eighty, spry and sharp, with short, gray, tightly coiffed hair.

She invited us into her immaculate home and asked us to sit at the dining room table. On the table was a doily straight out of the 1940s or earlier. On top of it rested *Neckaurer Impressionen . . . 1939-1945* by Norbert Hasiba. Of course, I knew the book and had read excerpts from it detailing war life under intense Allied bombing in Mannheim-Neckarau. She told us she knew the author well and had contributed to his research almost two decades earlier (the book was published in 1996). I didn't tell her I had seen it before.

The book was open to page 124, where Hasiba had written comprehensive accounts of the crashes in Mannheim-Neckarau on both September 6, 1944, and December 11, 1944. Ms. Fleck quickly began to share her personal recollections. Timo and Ruth listened intently, and I searched for any words I understood. Timo would frequently break the conversation and give me a cryptic account of what was being said. I was on the edge of my seat both physically and emotionally. "I'll go over with you in detail what she says after we're done here," he told me at last.

Ms. Fleck often turned her face to her right to catch my eyes, obviously wanting me to know what she was saying. I began asking questions through Ruth and Timo, entering the discussion as best I could. Both my translators knew what I wanted to learn and did their best to communicate my inquiries.

The September crash seemed to be the most vivid in her mind. The plane came to rest in a field behind her house, but parts fell just ahead of her front gate.

The December crash in which my uncle died was, as she recalled, in the field behind the restaurant Zum Niederbruck'l that occupied the building at Neckarauer-Waldweg #33 at that time. This house/ restaurant was then owned by Otto Ruhl. She said that this structure, known by old-time residents as "Haus Niederbruck'l," had housed many businesses over the years and after the war became Restaurant Sorrento. (Note: I found and copied three photographs of the Restaurant Sorrento taken in 1960 in a case at the front of the now doctor's office, so the conversion had probably taken place a decade or so after the war.) Ms. Fleck said the house was owned by Ruhl's family and later became his. She thought he was about seventeen at the time of the war and was enlisted in the German army.

After the earlier crash in September, she told us, some families in the houses bordering hers left town because of the extensive damage to their homes. She and her mother stayed. She didn't see the final impact of my uncle's B-17, but her remembrances coupled with Hasiba's research confirm the final resting place of the Fortress behind Haus Niederbruck'l at Neckarauer-Waldweg #33. As the history-book account also relates, Neckarauer-Waldweg #67, then owned by locksmith Peter Zenkert, was completely destroyed by what was supposedly the last bomb dropped by the Belskis piloted B-17. The current house at that location was obviously of newer construction, confirming its earlier destruction.

I related to Ms. Fleck the differences between the American MACR containing the German KU and Hasiba's account of the crash. She lost no time in stressing that hers and Hasiba's accounts were factual. There is some evidence that the Fort piloted by 1st Lt. Leo Belskis had been diverted somewhat from the original target of the Mannheim-Ludwigshafen Bridge (now a widened and expanded structure named the Konrad-Adenaurer Bridge) connecting the marshalling yards at the Hauptbahnhauf-Mannheim with the BASF facilities across the Rhine.

As we talked, Ms. Fleck spoke of her father, Arthur. He died in the war, but the family never knew how or when. But three months earlier, in March of 2011, she had received a sudden notice from the German government stating he had died in a Russian prison in 1948, three years after the conclusion of the war. Born in 1914, the year WWI began, he was thirty-four years old at the time of his death. Her mother, Amelia, died in 1991 at approximately age eighty, without ever knowing the fate of her husband.

Arthur Fleck saw intense and varied service in the German army without injury. He first served in Norway as Hitler attempted to capture the Baltic region and then fought in France when the German blitz moved north to take Paris. He was next shipped to the eastern front as Hitler turned his wrath on Russia in June of 1941. In mid-1945, after the war, Arthur Fleck was marching back home when he was captured for unknown reasons in Czechoslovakia and shipped back to Russia where, three years later, he died of starvation.

Fighting back tears, Ms. Fleck said in halting words that her father had left for war when she was three years old, and she never saw him again. My own voice cracking and tears flowing, I told her of my uncle Bud's daughter, Rosalind, born thirty-five days after his death, and the love I had for my uncle whose name I carry. I also told her how my mother would help me grasp a pencil and write to my Palsy Walsy. In one of those letters, I wrote, *"For Christmas I want you to come home. When you do, I will never let you leave again."* Ross W. Perrin, Jr. died in a flak-impaled B-17 a mere tenth of a mile from where I was sitting without ever seeing either my letter or his daughter.

Ms. Fleck's mother, fearful of having her family imprisoned in a concentration camp, told her daughter that wars were conflicts between high-up politicians fought by other people who didn't hate each other at all. I showed her the picture of me, at age three and a half, saluting my Uncle Bud while he was on leave before going to England in the late summer of 1944. This picture was taken four days before Valkyrie, the unsuccessful attempt to kill Hitler at the Wolf's Lair (*Wolfsschanze*) on July 20, 1944. "If Klaus von Stauffenburg had been successful on that day," I told her, "perhaps neither my uncle nor your father would have died."

At that point, an elderly German lady who spoke not a word of English and lived sixty-eight years with the anxiety resulting from not knowing the time or condition of her father's death, and a not-quite-as-elderly Southerner with a three-word German vocabulary connected in a way only God could ordain. She placed her hand over mine, smiled through her tears, and said, "We each lost something very dear to us, didn't we?"

Through my own tears and a loving smile for my newfound friend, we embraced as I told her, "Yes, we did."

Ms. Fleck spoke with disdain about Hitler. I said that the Americans, many of whom were isolationists and others skeptical of the war, felt compelled to enter the war to aid Britain and all of Europe. Each of us understood the depth of the other's emotion.

Timo took some photos of Ms. Fleck and me as we connected and snapped a couple more as we walked toward the front gate. We again embraced and, through our interpreters, promised to keep in touch, which we still do.

As I paused to reflect on what had just happened, I took another picture of Ms. Fleck in front of her roses, smiling brightly and waving. That day, something happened in both our hearts.

Before driving back to the final resting place of the B-17, we stopped to take pictures of and from the soccer field, Waldweg-Stadion on Neckarauer-Waldweg, which was in 1944 the Paul-Billet-Platz. USAAC accounts of the flight indicated this as what might have been the plane's final resting place, in conflict with the Hasiba account.

Ruth and I then walked further along Neckarauer-Waldweg Road. The trek was both poignant and exciting as I saw the object of my search in real time while envisioning what it was like sixty-six years, six months, five days, and four hours earlier. After

Ms. Waltrud Fleck and
Ross Greene; Mannheim-
Neckarau–June, 2012
Photo by Timo Sauer

Kim Arends and Ruth Reiss–June, 2012   Timo Sauer–June, 2012
Photo by J. Ross Greene   *Photo by J. Ross Greene*

John Luke, Wycombe Abbey Burser and Pinetree historian–September, 2013
Photo by J. Ross Greene

searching for that setting since 2009, I hardly knew how to assimilate my thoughts. The small, peaceful, flower-laden hamlet before me seemed so unlike the war-scarred town where a half-destroyed bomber spent its last seconds aloft before careening to an explosive stop in a parking lot, killing seven boys barely out of their teens. But it was.

We then walked down one of the three *Aufeldwegs,* narrow paths that run perpendicular to the main road. The Hasiba account indicates that four crew members were blown from the plane and came to rest on the third of these roads leading to the power plant on the river.

Further down, we stood in front of a new structure at #67. A scraggly, shirtless man who looked to be in his seventies came toward us from his yard at #75, picking dead leaves from his flower garden as he trudged our way. I asked Timo to inquire if he had information about the area during the war. Timo told him of our mission and asked if he would read the flyer I had prepared. He refused. "I have bad memories of the war. It's in the past, and I don't want to try to remember it again."

We thanked him and left, knowing he held recollections in the recesses of his memory that he would carry to his grave. I wished I could have fished out a few, but that was not to be. In a later conversation, a female Mannheim resident deemed him "a bird," one who in her estimation had weird ideas and also still harbored Nazi views.

The next day, I was privileged to attend the wedding of Timo and Nina and to join Ruth's daughter, Kim Arends, and her husband, Mitch, at the post-wedding reception. After the reception, they took me on a motor tour of the bridges connecting Mannheim and the massive BASF complex west of the Rhine. As with other locations that had become so hallowed in my mind, crossing that bridge was both haunting and exhilarating.

I can't be a mere four hundred miles and six hours by train from Berlin without absorbing its aura and history, at least for a day or so, I thought. So the next morning, I boarded the ICE train that would take me north through Frankfurt and on to Berlin. The "Big B," as airmen referred to Berlin, was the heart of the Reich until

1945. Today, it's a bustling modern city with sometimes-obscure remembrances of the horrific period under Hitler.

On the comfortable trip, virtually alone in the first-class section, I reminisced, planned, and wrote, attempting to bring into concert the diverse emotions I had experienced since leaving Atlanta. Sadness, fear, anger, confusion, and joy swirled together as I reexamined the puzzle, now coming together at last.

I had a limited time—a day and a half—to take in as much visual history of Berlin as possible. Of course, the Reichstag and the Brandenburg Gate were on my list of must-sees as was the site of the 1936 Olympics, if possible. But at the top was the Bendlerblock, the current site of the memorial to Valkyrie. On July 20, 1944, it was the center of turmoil for the German Reich. The Bendlerblock is one of the obscure WWII sites in Berlin, overshadowed but not diminished by other, more renowned, points of interest. Across the street from its gated but open entrance was a hotel, on that night the site of a graduation party for an elite group of teenagers. I stood and watched as the revelers strutted and preened outside the venue. English is broadly spoken across the globe, so I thought I'd ask if any of the *jungens* (young people) knew the historical significance of the Bendlerblock. None with whom I spoke did. It was a sad moment,

Bendler Bloc; Berlin, Germany; Site of Valkyrie executions-7/20/1944
Photo by J. Ross Greene

although the dearth of knowledge or exposure to the vestiges of WWII is certainly not limited to this area.

I spent a quarter of an hour walking through the enclosed compound alone, trying to visualize its appearance amid the chaos following the ill-fated attempt on Hitler's life. Less than a mile away was the Reichstag. Undaunted by the Reichstag guard's insistence that one could only take a tour by going online and buying a pass weeks in advance, I pleaded my case. It didn't work, and I was turned away. For about fifteen minutes, I observed the ticketed tourists enter the building to see if I could crack the code of entrance without a ticket.

With renewed courage, I tried again. This time, my "I've come a long way. I'm just a dumb redneck from the South, and I have to go home tomorrow" appeal worked. Taking pity on me at last, the young guard, who luckily spoke better English than I, told me to stand aside for a minute. After a large group entered, he motioned me through the gate. In my two-hour stroll through this facility, I was struck by the complete lack of any mention of Hitler despite his devastating role in German and Reichstag history.

At an early-evening outdoor dinner at the Hotel Adlon Kepinski east of the Brandenburg Gate, I listened to the cheering of more than 250,000 German soccer enthusiasts. They were watching a key World Cup soccer match on wide-screen TV in the Tiergarten, a large garden similar to Central Park in New York, west of the gate.

As I took in the panorama, I pondered the dichotomies that comprised Berlin. Through the famous gate, *Brandenburger Tor*, and two blocks to the right stood the Reichstag. Only a short walk away was the Bendlerblock. Hitler's bunker, the location of his final days in April of 1945, lay less than a mile away to the south. Checkpoint Charlie, where Russian and American soldiers faced off for years during the Cold War, and a remaining portion of the Berlin Wall that separated East from West were only a few blocks to the east of the gate. Intense oppression by Hitler was followed by more of the same in the post-WWII years. In November of 1989, the wall came down, and freedom flowed forth.

The purge of the Third Reich from observable German history was clear but somewhat understandable. It was interesting to see the remnants of the Berlin Wall and the blocks in the street that replaced the wall and follow the path it covered until its destruction.

I'd been dating Lynne for a year when the Wall went up in August of 1961, and we're, at this writing, approaching our fiftieth wedding anniversary, I thought. (We have since celebrated our 50th Anniversary on May 16, 2014) After a walk along the remainder of the original wall and three hours in an adjacent WWII Museum where Hitler's despotic acts are on prominent but controlled display, my first trip to Berlin concluded. The flight home seemed to take not ten hours but ten minutes.

When I began the research for this book, I created a digital photo album of Uncle Bud and gave it to Aunt Thelma. "She can't speak, as you know," Rosalind told me. "But she smiles and makes loving sounds as she looks through the photos." I so hoped that I could finish this book in time for my aunt to see and possibly read parts of it. But she passed away peacefully on June 28, 2011, her ninety-second birthday.

In May of 2012, Kevin Wilson and I attended a reunion of the Stalag Luft III POWs held in Dayton, Ohio. It was a unique experience on a number of fronts. The firsthand experiences of men held captive in that infamous prison captivated me. Also, the documentary *The Lost Airmen of Buchenwald* debuted that week. I spoke with two of the airmen, Joe Moser and Ed Carter-Edwards, who served hard time as POWs in the Buchenwald concentration camp and were highlighted in the film. We also attended a tribute, highlighted by a B-25 flyover, for four of the then-remaining Doolittle Raiders who flew B-25s off of the carrier *Hornet* on its April 18, 1942, mission to bomb Japan. I was also able to speak with the woman who took Col. Doolittle into her home and fed him after his plane crashed in China after dropping his payload on Tokyo.

Back home, I continued writing and trying to sort through the conflicting information coming from my expanding research. In July of 2012, I was discussing the book project with family while on our annual vacation. Dan, one of our twin sons, asked me a question about the direction of the book. He should have warned me by saying "incoming," because his question was a grenade from which the pin had been extracted: "What would make a woman want to read your book?"

I had no answer, but I knew I needed to deal with his concern. Lynne, my most honest but loving critic, had questioned me earlier about the same issue. After much thought and discussion, I began formulating a plan to balance the work with an increased component of the love story between Bud and Thelma so poignantly portrayed in the letters.

At about the same time, I was also introduced to my editor, Marti Pieper, who gave this novice scribe some important tips about how to add interest to my work. After an initial conversation in which I related my story, I asked her, "Do I have a story worth telling, and if so, can you help me make it a good one?" She said yes to both. With this encouragement, I trudged forward with a renewed sense of purpose.

In the fall of 2012, the 381st Bomb Group Reunion returned to Dayton. A month after that, I was scheduled to take a tour which would begin in Normandy but could also include Bastogne, with a group from Focus on the Family, led by two great historians and guides, Ray and Cristy Pfeiffer of Euro Insights. I was conflicted. Both segments would provide tremendous learning experiences. The trip to Normandy was one I had long wanted to take. And an opportunity to continue on to Bastogne and Malmedy in Belgium, key sites in the month-long Battle of the Bulge that began five days after my uncle was killed, was an added bonus. I knew that the father of Willis Everette, my boss in my investment career's early years, was the assigned lead counsel in the defense of Joachim Peiper, Sepp Dietrich, and seventy-two other German officers tried and convicted of the atrocities in the Malmedy Massacre on December 17, 1944. This trip, too, was destined to be both exciting and informative.

However, I was still haunted by an unsated hunger to solve the mystery centered in Mannheim, and it was unlikely that either trip would nourish that hunger. They would, however, contribute significantly to my broader perspective of the war, and I knew that time with great friends Doug and Deb Birnie, Focus on the Family coordinators of the European trip, would be wonderful, so Lynne and I decided to go. As time drew near for the trip, Lynne's health

Focus on the Family Normandy Group, Bayeaux, France-September, 2012
FOF Group Collection

made it difficult for her to travel, so our daughter, Meredith, became my partner on this journey. What a blessing sharing the trip with her proved to be.

For at least two years, I had been writing museums, historical organizations, and the German government in an attempt to get information I hoped had been kept after the war. I had determined that to deem my search satisfactory, I needed to find three things.

First, I wanted to find witnesses to the crash. "Not likely," I was told. I knew that witnesses could, in 2012, be as young as their early seventies (four to five years old at the time of the crash) with no upper age limit.

Second, I wanted pictures of the crash site, plane, etc. I knew the Germans, with their leadership in photographic technology, had photographed everything. I also knew that silver, a component of film development, was in short supply during the war, but surely there would be a picture somewhere. But where?

Finally, I wanted a piece of the plane, a metal shard, a piece of a prop—anything. I think that, except for researchers who had similar goals and were able to reach them, everyone felt I had two chances to find what I wanted: slim and none.

I asked Marilyn how she thought I could break through these obstacles. Her suggestion was that we contact Ed Reniere, one of the leading researches and WWII historians in the world, for his advice and help. He and fellow historians Ed Zander and Herb Weber, had already assisted me in the previous few years. Ed Reniere in particular had been a constant source of information, analysis, advice, and direction. He suggested I send a letter to five potential resources in the Mannheim-Neckarau area. I composed the letter and asked Marilyn to suggest where I could have it professionally translated.

"I have a good source," Marilyn said. And she did. The translator she recommended was a most unlikely one, Hanns-Claudius Scharff. Scharff is the son of the late Hanns Joachim Scharff, the Master interrogator of Germany who interrogated Allied fighter pilots at the interrogation center in Oberursel, Germany. He, in fact, interrogated Marilyn's father, bombardier Lt. Thomas F. Jeffers, when his B-24 was shot down on June 18, 1944.

I quickly sent the letters to the five potential sources in Mannheim-Neckarau and waited. Then on Friday morning, September 14, a message popped up in my e-mail inbox. It follows.

On 9/14/12 5:24 AM, "Natalie Blaquiere" wrote:

Dear Ross Greene,

[Do] you speak only English or German, too? Well, I will try in German first. [She did so. What follows is a translation.]

I read your article in our newspaper here in Neckarau. My name is Natalie Blaquiere. I live right in Neckarau on the marketplace. If you don`t understand German, please let me know. They wrote your email wrong in the newspaper, so I hope this will be the right one.

I know how difficult it is to provide information about the past. I'm doing the same with my [personal] research in New Zealand. If you can get help on the spot, it is always great. There also seems to [be] some information in the archives in the city Mannheim, which I use myself [many] times.

[With] your time shift this [may] be a bit difficult. Surely there are records of this plane crash. I would love to help you. I then would need more information simply about

Lt. Ross W. Perrin—maybe birthdate, maybe load [take-off] *location in Ridgewell, Essex/UK. I would be very happy if I could help you. Take care and maybe you will give me an answer.*

Yours, Natalie—from Neckarau-Mannheim

I immediately contacted her by e-mail, got her phone number, and called her. Before calling, I had looked up her location and found that she lived only five short blocks from the place where Uncle Bud's plane came to rest. She said, "I go on-air [her term for riding her bike in the open air] almost every day on Neckarau-er-Waldweg Road."

I could tell from this first conversation that Natalie, a European championship skier, was a go-getter who would not be thwarted once she made her mind up to reach a goal. We connected immediately. Her energy level was palpable, and I sensed her desire—genuine and appreciated— to help in my search. I was excited about what we might accomplish. I sent her all the information I had: data, pictures, copies of key letters, the Hasiba account, the MACR and KU reports—everything.

Her idea was to write a follow-up letter to the *Mannheimer-Morgen*, the newspaper for which staffer Jan Cerny had written the article Natalie read the previous day. She was going to request anyone who had witnessed or knew anything about the crash to meet her mother, Helma Schafer, and her on the town square the following Saturday. Her letter was published, and on that Saturday, nine people showed up. Some were witnesses and their family members; others knew specific facts about the incident. Natalie emailed me about her success, and I was elated.

A week afterward, my daughter and I began our trip to Normandy. We traveled first to Paris on September 26 and then on to the Normandy coast for a memorable week of taking in the sights and stories of D-Day. Meredith returned home after this segment of our trip, and I went on to Bastogne. I was there on the next phase of the excursion when I got an e-mail from Natalie. She asked if I could come to Mannheim. She said that Helma had worked with the museum director, Mr. Christian Helmut Wetzel; and the Erster Burgermeister (First Mayor) of Mannheim, Mr. Christian Specht; to arrange a reception for me in the Mannheim Town Hall. Further, they wanted to assist in my ongoing research. They planned to invite Natalie's family, the witnesses she had found, newspaper officials, city dignitaries, and other interested parties. I called Lynne to tell her of the invitation and my desire to go. As always, she encouraged me to continue my obsessive quest.

Since I had brought no formal clothes on the Normandy tour, I hurried to the center of Bastogne in search of a suit or at least a blazer. I strode past the prominent statue of General Anthony McAuliffe, the man who uttered "Nuts" to the German request that his troops surrender to the surrounding Nazi forces, and continued down the main street. I didn't have as many purchasing options as I would have had back home in Atlanta, but I found a suit coat and tie.

I then arranged to take a train from Brussels through Cologne (Köln), on to Frankfurt and then to Mannheim. In the brief one-hour stop in Cologne's Bahnhoff, I was thrilled to see the adjacent cathedral that stood stately and undamaged throughout WWII even though almost all structures around it had been leveled by the bombing. Uncle Bud had flown a mission in the *Mizpah* to that city, bisected by the Rhine River, on October 14, 1944. *Everything I see makes me want to know more about this era*, I thought.

I first met Natalie face to face in the lobby of the Steubenhoff Hotel on Rheingoldstrasse in Mannheim in what by then felt like a family reunion. Exactly as I had anticipated, Natalie was a diminutive ball of fire—friendly, outgoing, and in charge. Her mother, Helma; father, Claus; husband, Alexander; daughter, Charly, and her daughter's boyfriend, Yannick; gathered with us, and we got acquainted over coffee in the lounge. Mr. Wetzel, the museum director, joined us later and discussed plans for the following day. Natalie's family and I had a great evening together. I was ecstatic about the day ahead, but even more so the next day, when I fully realized the extent of Mr. Wetzel's plans.

The next morning, Natalie and I drove to Mannheim-Neckarau City Hall, a concrete and brick building, circa the WWII era. It

Yannick Schally, Charly Blaquiere, Alexander Blaquiere, Helma Schafer, Ross Greene,
Natalie Blaquiere, Claus Schafer-Mannheim-Neckarau 2012
Greene Family Collection

American Flag flown over Mannheim - October 8, 2012
Claus Schafer, Charly Blaquiere, Helma Schafer , Ross Greene & Natalie Blaquiere
Greene Family Collection

seemed appropriate that the day's planned reception was held here. It represented a historic occasion, the meeting of descendants of two countries locked in battle more than six decades earlier. Tall windows framed by concrete block arches guarded a stately lower floor. Above, similar windows framed by red brick arches faced the front of the building. In the center of the second floor, a balcony jutted forward in front of glass doors opening onto it. Large concrete haunches (cantilevered pedestals) supported the balcony of this building that was clearly built to last.

We walked up a sturdy wide stairway to the second floor. As we entered the hall where the reception was to take place, I saw Mr. Wetzel out on the balcony working to hang what looked like flags. *One of them looks like "Old Glory,* I thought. *No way!*

"Come help me with the flag," he said, beckoning me to join him. Shocked and thrilled, I moved to assist him. On that day, October 8, 2012, the flag of the United States of America flew alongside the current German flag over the city of Mannheim. This occurred in honor of my search; my visit; and my uncle, who, almost sixty-eight years before, lost his life only a few blocks away.

After a few minutes, the invited guests began to gather. I was pleased to meet Mr. Jan Cerny, who had written the articles in the *Mannheimer-Morgen* and had helped me to find witnesses. I told him that without his articles, my search would have been more difficult at best and, at worst, stymied for years.

I met three of the witnesses who had come forward. A few others were not able to attend. Communication was good with each, some in English and others through interpreters. It was hard to tell who was more excited to discuss the incident, them or me.

Mrs. Irene Penn, a tall, trim lady with an ever-present smile, told me she was a sixteen-year-old girl when on December 11, 1944, she witnessed two US airmen parachute over the Power Plant on the Neckarau River and land in front of her home. After the reception, we drove to her childhood home at Aufeldstrasse #10, about one mile to the southeast of the crash site. We stood in the doorway of her home as she pointed to the window from which she witnessed the two *fleigers* (flyers) landing and then running in an unsuccessful attempt to escape capture. These two were Elvis McCoy and

Mrs. Irene Penn in front of #10 Aufeldstrasse from which she saw Suggs and McCoy descend in parachutes-10/8/2012

Karl and Christa Schmidt at Mannheim reception-10/8/2012

Mr. Gerhard Stoll-on site of crash of Mission #222-10/8/2012

Location where 2 bodies were found along Neckarau Waldweg Road in mid afternoon of December 11, 1944. Bud Perrin was, in all probability, one of those men who died here.-October 8, 2012

Ross Greene looking at the crash site of the B-17 on December 11, 1944. behind the Haus Neiderbruckl at #33 Neckarau Waldweg Road in Mannheim-Neckarau, Germany on October 8, 2012

Photos by J. Ross Greene

Durward Suggs of the 381st. They were both captured, one by the police and the other by townspeople, one in Käfertal and the other in Feudenheim. I do not yet know which was which. During that era, private citizens who captured downed airmen were notorious for being much more barbaric than the police. Nonetheless, the two Americans were interrogated separately and later reunited in a German stalag, where they were POWs for the remainder of the war.

Mr. Gerhard Stoll, a serious man in his late seventies, was ten years old in 1944. He was in the local bomb shelter on Steubenstrasse when the B-17 crashed on December 11. He related what he remembered after exiting the shelter some minutes after the crash. He said that what remained of the wreckage of the B-17 did not burn immediately but broke into flames some time afterward and was consumed.

Karl Wolfram Schmidt, a stocky, grey-haired gentleman, was joined by his wife, Christa. Her warm smile drew me to someone I knew must be a wonderfully kind lady. Separated by our mutual inability to converse in the other's native tongue, smiles and a hug connected us.

Mr. Schmidt, who lived at #89 Freidrichstrasse, had a vivid memory of bolting from the Steubenstrasse bomb shelter and racing toward the wreckage. He first saw it through a hedge that separated the Haus Neiderbruk'l from the street. As any inquisitive twelve-year-old boy would, he ran around the building and came closer to the plane. Smoke was rising from the wreckage and the remaining engines were still running, he remembered. His father entered the aircraft and saw lifeless bodies inside. Mr. Schmidt also told me someone took money and a metal box from bodies in the plane. That was foolhardy, for if the Gestapo found anyone with such contraband, they would be severely punished.

Mr. Schmidt added that the plane lay there smoldering for half an hour before exploding, causing thick black smoke from the burning tires to rise above the wreckage. After a few days, the authorities carted off the remains of the burned-out B-17. After the reception, we walked down to where he had seen the crash. With Natalie's translation help, Mr. Schmidt and I continued to discuss both his remembrances and answers to my plethora of questions.

Before we parted, I asked Mrs. Schmidt to send me some pictures of Mr. Schmidt when he was a young boy. After returning home, I received a letter from their daughter, Sabine Haug, with the requested pictures and the following comments.

> *My dad did not understand what happened around him during WWII and tries, until today, to find the explanations for his memories of his childhood—he spent about 2 years in France (Alsace) to escape from the Allied attacks on Mannheim. Immediately after his return to Mannheim in November 1944, he remembers the destroyed American Bomber B-17 in which your uncle lost his life— Dad's vitality reduces more and more, he went sapless [lost his strength] in the last month. So we, especially my mother [Christa], are so happy about his interest in your research. It really inspirits [raises his spirits] him. Both of my parents are fond of you and look forward to your next visit in Mannheim. Could you please send me a photo of you and my parents? My parents showed me the newspaper with your photo and an article about your concerns.*

Frau Steinkuhler, who lived (at the time of the interview) at #67 Freidrichstrasse atop the Stadt Stadtlohn Bank Building and only a few houses from Natalie's residence at #33, told Natalie that she was a young girl at the time of the crash. In an emotion-filled voice, she related that after learning of my coming to Mannheim, she told her husband, "I can finally talk about it. I have been dreaming about that horrible day for so long and couldn't talk about it—now I can." She remembered four bodies on the ground along the flight path on Neckarau-Waldweg. "Four bodies stuck in the ground—parachutes didn't open," she said. She also said the plane came in upside down. Accounts differed on that fact, although witnesses from the air said the plane flipped after being struck by flak.

At the beginning of the ceremony, Mr. Wetzel presented me with a copy of the Norbert Hasiba book, *Mannheim Impressions, 1939-1945*; a beautiful stein depicting the history of Neckarau; and

„Das ist ein glücklicher Tag für mich"

Neffe des abgestürzten US-Bomberpilotes kommt nach Neckarau

Bedrückende Eindrücke im Luftschutzkeller: Patricia Popp erklärt verschiedene Exponate.   Fotos: Meixner

NECKARAU. Die amerikanische Stars & Stripes-Flagge, die neben der deutschen, der Mannheim- und der Neckarau-Fahne am Neckarauer Rathaus wehte, kündigte einen besonderen Gast an, der auf den Spuren seines 1944 in Neckarau bei einem Flugzeugabschuss beim Niederbrückl- platz tödlich verunglückten Onkels an den Ort des dramatischen Geschehens kam: M. Ross Greene aus Georgia, USA, angesehener Geschäftsmann und Neffe des getöteten, damals 25-jährigen Rossvall Perrin, ließ es sich nicht nehmen, im Rahmen eines Geschäftstermins in Brüssel einen Abstecher nach Neckarau zu machen. Begleitet von seiner entfernten Verwandten, der stellv. BIG-Lindenhof-Vorsitzenden Helma Schäfer, die mit Ehemann und Tochter akribische Recherchen durchgeführt hatte (Die NAN berichteten), wurde er im Balkonzimmer von dem Vorsitzenden des Verein Geschichte Alt-Neckarau, Helmut Wetzel, in englischer Sprache herzlich begrüßt. Auch Bürgerdienstleiterin Patricia Popp und drei Zeitzeugen, Irene Penn, Gerhard Stall und Karl Schmidt, waren gekommen, um dem Gast die Geschehnisse aus ihrer Erinnerung zu berichten, nach der einer der aus dem Flugzeug herausgeschleuderten bzw. durch die Explosion verbrannten Soldaten Ross W. Perrin war.

Der Neffe zeigte sich tief bewegt und dankte für die Bemühungen der Neckarauer, ihn bei seiner Spurensuche zu unterstützen. „Hier habe ich meine neue Familie gefunden", umarmte er Familie Schäfer und zeigte Fotos seiner Familie in Atlanta. Über die tragischen Ereignisse und den Tod des Onkels in Neckarau schreibe er ein Buch, erklärte er; dies ganz besonders für dessen Tochter, seine Cousine, die einen Monat nach dem Tod ihres Vaters geboren wurde und ebenfalls den Wunsch habe, mehr über den Vater zu erfahren, den sie nie kennenlernen durfte. Er selbst habe dem Onkel als Vierjähriger zwei Kaugummis und einen Brief, bei dem ihm die Mutter die Hand führte, ins Kriegsge- biet geschickt, erinnerte sich Ross Greene und mahnte, aus der jüngsten Geschichte zu lernen und in Frieden miteinander zu leben.

Nach regem Austausch bei einem Gläschen Sekt gab es für den amerikanischen Gast als Geschenke ein Buch über den Bombenkrieg in Neckarau und einen Bierkrug mit einem Bild von der Schlacht 1799 auf der Gießenbrücke.

Anschließend war der Gast zur Besichtigung des original eingerichteten Luftschutzkellers im Keller des Rathauses eingeladen, bevor er zur Absturzstelle des Bombers beim heutigen Niederbrückl-Platz begleitet wurde. M. Greene kündigte für November Untersuchungen auf dem Gelände mit speziellen Metalldetektoren an, in der Hoffnung, noch Teile des Flugzeugs oder andere Hinweise auf das Geschehen vom 11. Dezember 1944 zu finden.   *cm*

Empfang im Neckarauer Rathaus mit neuen Verwandten und Zeitzeugen: der amerikanische Gast ist beeindruckt.

Article in Mannheimer Morgen-10/10/2012

vintage photos of Mannheim sites during WWII, including one of the Steubenstrasse bomb shelter. He had many kind comments about how the US and my uncle helped free their country.

I responded with my gratitude for the way my newfound German family had assisted me in my search. I expressed how blessed I felt for so many making that day possible and for flying the Stars and Stripes alongside those of Germany, Mannheim, and Neckarau. "I will certainly return, both to continue my search and to visit the friends I have made," I said .

Following the ceremony, those present took a tour of the bomb shelter in the basement of the Mannheim-Neckarau City Hall. I learned that this privilege was an infrequent honor and had, to the museum director and his staff's knowledge, never before been extended to an American. As we walked down the stairs to the underground bunker, Mr. Wetzel turned on the bomb alert siren used in WWII. Unannounced, loud, and shrill in that confined space, it created quite a stir. Once I recovered from the shock, I thought of the information in the Phol Diary giving the times of the sirens on December 11, 1944, indicating that citizens should take cover as there were incoming US bombers. Thoughts of what it must have felt like went through my head for those experiencing the day's events on both sides. It was a chilling moment.

After the tour, Natalie, her family, and I joined Mr. Wetzel; Patricia Popp; the assistant museum director, Jan Cerny from the Mannheimer Morgen; the Doerners; and a number of other guests at the crash site behind the Haus Niederbruk'l. We discussed the varying remembrances about the exact position of the plane after it came to rest and were able to reach a consensus, a difficult task after almost seven decades.

We then walked down Neckarauer-Waldweg Road, stopping at the place where Mr. Schmidt said two bodies lay after the crash across from #58. Mr. Stoll said he only remembered one body there. I asked Mr. Schmidt if any specific thing made him remember the scene so vividly. He recalled that one of the men had on a pair of nice brown shoes. "They were not burned," he stated emphatically.

I remembered that following one of his trips to London, Uncle Bud had written Thelma about the brown high-top shoes he had bought there. When I got back to the hotel that evening, I searched the cache of scanned letters on my computer and found the one written on October 11, 1944, that said; *". . . I bought another pair of shoes, since I sold my buckle ones to our radio man. They didn't fit me. I got a pair of brown high top English shoes. I like them a lot and they are okay for dress and work."*

That had to be him, I thought. *This couldn't be a coincidence— or could it?* I lay back on the bed, relieved that, quite possibly, a few of the previously non-fitting pieces to the elusive puzzle had been snapped together, but also horrified at the chilling realization of what my Palsy Walsy's final minutes must have been like. I lay in dark silence for what seemed like hours.

The next day, Natalie, her husband Alexander, and I had lunch along the east bank of the Rhine River and walked to Wald Park from where two bridges connecting the war-critical locations in Ludwigshafen and Mannheim are visible. One is the reconstruction of the steel frame one so thoroughly pummeled by Allied bombing during the war. The other is a more modern structure built alongside. This area along the Rhine is part of Natalie's periodic bike training regimen. Buildings of the giant industrial and chemical complex to the west of the bridge still loom silently over the trees lining the bank of the Rhine, unaware of their role as an important cog in the wartime machinery of the Reich. To the east, hidden by the trees of the park, lie the tracks of the Mannheim *Hauptbahnhof* (rail station), a marshalling yard for war materiel, also vital in Hitler's prosecution of WWII, now the locus for commerce and personal rail travel.

As we walked along the river, I reflected back on two trips I had taken years before. In 2002, after finishing a business assignment

Mannheim-Ludwigshafen (now the Conrad Adnauer Bridge) along bank of Rhine-2012
Photo by J. Ross Greene

Mrs. Irene Penn, Natalie Blaquiere, Karl Schmidt, and Ross Greene
October 8, 2012
Photo by J. Ross Greene

Helmut Wetzel and Ross Greene
October 8, 2012
Greene Family Collection

Left: Helmut Wetzel and
Helma Schafer
October 7, 2012
Greene Family Collection

Right: Jan Cerny-writer
Mannheimer Morgen
October 8, 2012
Photo by J. Ross Greene

Bomb Shelter on Steubenstrasse in Mannheim-Neckarau
German Motto "Victory at any Cost"-circa WWII
Stadtarchiv Mannheim

Bomb Shelter on
Steubenstrasse in Mannheim-
Neckarau-October, 2012
Photo by J. Ross Greene

in Frankfurt, I flew to Munich and from there took a bus to the WWII concentration camp at Dachau. Walking down the street leading to the site, I was taken by the chilling starkness of the death camp on one side and, only feet away on the other side, a neighborhood that could have easily been the backdrop for the 1950s TV show *Father Knows Best*.

How could that be? I questioned. The disquieting hours that followed as I walked through the camp in complete silence made an indelible impression on my mind and spirit.

As I was eating breakfast at the Munich hotel before my trip to Dachau, the elderly hostess had asked what I was planning for the day. My clothes and newspaper in English revealed my nationality. When I told her I was going to visit Dachau, she leaned down and whispered, "It never happened, you know."

I was so shocked that I had no reply. That moment has haunted me ever since. Eisenhower was right when he demanded that photos be taken of the impact of atrocities resulting from Hitler's reign so the world would never forget. But many like this woman, refuse to acknowledge their existence in the first place.

In November of 2007, following a financial consulting assignment in continental Europe, my close friend and business associate, Rick Tyler, and I made a whirlwind journey through Eastern Europe, including Krakow, Amsterdam, Prague, Salzburg, and Vienna. From Krakow, we took a one-day trip to Auschwitz. After a two-hour guided tour through the first of the Auschwitz camps, we drove across the rail tracks to Auschwitz-Birkenau, the most well-known concentration and extermination camp of the three that comprised Auschwitz. As we exited the bus in front of the guard gate at the end of the long rail track, so familiar from photos and documentaries, pelting snow stung our faces. We turned our backs to avoid the icy blasts of wind.

In a bizarre way, those conditions framed the experience much more accurately than a warm sunny day would have. Such weather ensured that we got a small glimpse of the true conditions in which those prisoners lived, or more accurately, existed. That day, I purposed to help our children and especially our grandchildren not be blindsided by attempts to mute the reality of Hitler's demonic reign. Little did I know at that time how experiencing Dachau and Auschwitz would fuel my future search and provide immeasurable background to this story.

In the fall of 2013, Lynne and I spent a month in England, primarily as an early celebration of our fiftieth anniversary the following May. But, as a secondary goal, I wanted to research a few background elements before completing the *Fortress* manuscript. After a week in London, Lynne and I headed north on the M40 toward the Cotswolds. Since talking with Leonard Spivey, a 381st navigator, about the trip he and Colonel Joseph Nazzaro took to the 8th AF preparation site for the first Schweinfurt raid in August of 1943, I had wanted to visit it myself. Pinetree, the code name for High Wycombe, central command for the Eighth, was located about an hour north of London, west of the M40. On our way north to the Cotswolds, we turned off at the appropriate exit off the M40 and after finally getting directions, headed up the hill to Wycombe Abbey.

We turned into the campus gate and stopped. I began snapping photos even before leaving the car, and a guard spread himself across my windshield, threatening my life if I did not put away my camera. Needless to say, we were turned away without getting through the gate.

That night, I wrote a lengthy letter to the school's bursar, Mr. John Luke, who invited Lynne and me back for a thorough tour. He graciously guided us through key locations in the nerve center for the Eighth's planning of bombing runs into the heart of the Reich. What we observed on the tour, coupled with Spivey's recollections, provided me with everything I needed to describe the critical site where planning of 8th AF missions took place.

A few days later, Jim, Chris and Jenny Tennet; along with Alan and Monica Steele; Michael Land; and Paul Bingley; hosted Lynne and me on a visit to the Ridgewell Museum. Alan, Jim, and Chris took me on an extended walking tour of the base grounds and what remains of the buildings on the site. James and Claudia Gray, who currently own and operate Allies Farm, a working farm that includes much of the original Ridgewell base property, graciously received us into their home. They allowed us to examine the officers' mess hall that now serves as a barn and grain storage building. I also saw the specific location of The Fox Pub in relation to the B-17 hardstands. We also saw the remains of base bomb shelters, latrine and shower facilities and the gymnasium/theater. The ability to visualize these locations, coupled with C.D. Cash's detailed remembrances, helped me provide accurate descriptions of Essex County places and events in my uncle's story.

The Grays are planning a WWII period dance for July of 2015 to celebrate James's fortieth birthday. It will be held in the former officers' mess hall. They plan to invite those interested in Ridgewell and its history, and I hope to attend.

Through this exhaustive search, I have come to a place of restful peace about the facts surrounding my uncle's death. After piecing together information from all of the interviews, letters, witness accounts, USAF diaries, published works, and background material I reviewed, I believe those final minutes of the flight of the plane in which Ross W. Perrin, Jr. was the bombardier occurred as follows:

The plane was struck in the #2 engine by flak from an emplacement in the Mannheim vicinity somewhere between the IP and the bridge over the Rhine from Ludwigshafen to Mannheim. Its course then changed abruptly, taking the ill-fated aircraft over the area southeast of Mannheim-Neckarau where, from her window at Aufeldstrasse #10, Ms. Penn sighted McCoy and Suggs descending in parachutes. The plane then turned west and north, continuing to descend along Neckarauer-Waldweg Road. A bomb or bombs dropped from the plane, destroying the house at #67.

At that point, two men either jumped or were thrown from the plane and landed on the road in front of # 53 Neckarauer-Waldweg. One was, in all probability, my Uncle Bud. The other may have been Jim Collett. Two other men came out in the same manner a short distance farther along the road. None of the four parachutes opened. The aircraft then crashed, probably upside down, in a vacant lot behind the Haus Niederbru'l at #33 Neckarauer-Waldweg Road. Three men, probably Leo Belskis, Glenn Vaughn, and Robert Rogers, remained in the plane, which subsequently caught fire.

A few of the myriad pieces to this mystifying puzzle are still missing and may well remain so. I still have no pictures of the crash aftermath. But I haven't given up on this search. The farmer whose

Jim and Chris Tennet-October 2013
Photo by J. Ross Greene

Museum Group-Alan Steele, Ross Greene, Lynne Greene, Monica
Steele & Jenny Tennet-October 2013
Greene Family Collection

381st Monument at Ridgewell
Museum-2013
Photo by J. Ross Greene

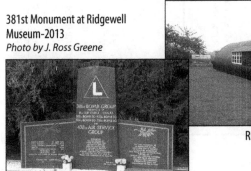

Ridgewell Airfield Commemorative Museum-
formerly base Hospital during WWII
Photo by J. Ross Greene

Below: Ridgewell Base WW2 Gymnasium/Theater & Chaplain Brown's Office-October 2013
Photo by J. Ross Greene

Ridgewell Base WW2 Shower &
Latrine-October 2013
Photo by J. Ross Greene

Ridgewell Base WW2 Bomb
Shelter-October 2013
Photo by J. Ross Greene

Ridgewell Base WW2 Allies Farm
Mess Hall during WWII-October
2013
Photo by J. Ross Greene

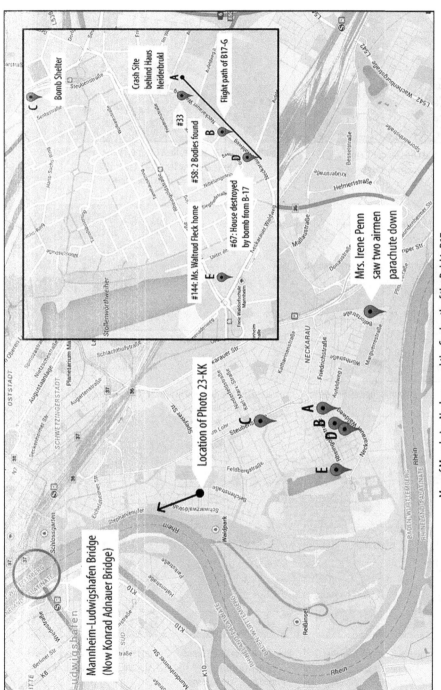

Map of Mannheim-Neckarau and the final path of the Belskis B17
Google Maps

ARNOLD AND ROSALIND PERRIN DAVIS FAMILY - 2012
L to R: Arnold Davis, Rosalind Perrin Davis, Katie Sickler, Rachael Sickler, (at time of pic, now Gagliardi),
Hannah Rosemary Park, Andy Park, Liz Davis Park, Daniel Elijah Park, Mary Davis Sickler
Rosalind Perrin Davis Collection

Roz 1948   Bud at age 28   Roz at age 28   Roz 2014
Rosalind Perrin Davis Collection

ROSS AND LYNNE GREENE FAMILY - JULY 2012
Children: Avery, David, Jr., and Lauren Greene; Perrin,
Griffin and Michael Sorrow; Jack (John Ross II) and Walker Greene.
Parents: Jackie and David Greene; Ross and Lynne Greene; Meredith Greene Sorrow,
and Michael Sorrow, Dan and Ginger Greene.
Greene Family Collection

property abutted the final resting place of the B-17G kept three pieces of the plane he found when he plowed his field in the spring of 1945. He gave them to Natalie, who is holding them for my next trip to Germany. It is possible that the city of Mannheim will excavate the crash site in the months ahead, to ensure that no latent ordnance remains on the site, in preparation for construction there. Nothing has been built there since that ominous day in 1944. Other items, photographs, and witnesses may crop up in the years ahead. But after six years of painstaking and exhaustive research, I have reached a place of intellectual and emotional quiet about my Uncle Bud's life and death.

To the best of my ability, I have accomplished my main goal for writing this book. I have given Ross Perrin's daughter, my cousin Rosalind, a clearer and more vibrant picture of her dad. I wanted her to read the unedited version of my manuscript with all its punctuation errors, improper sentence structure, and other flaws. Her responses as she read the work over the course of a week thrilled my heart and confirmed that I had reached my main goal.

This pursuit has invigorated me and satisfied my desire to share this compelling story. I hope I have told it well. I pray that my family and others who may read this book over the years will both enjoy and learn from the history embedded in this work. I also pray it will keep ever-burning the flame of heroism of my Uncle Bud; the 26,000 8th AF airmen who lost their lives in WWII; the other 400,000-plus Americans who died in the war; and the millions of other Americans and Allies who fought so valiantly to preserve our freedom. Long may their memories live.

Three children in the next generation carry either the name "Ross" or "Perrin."

Our son, Dan, named his first son John Ross Greene II. Our daughter, Meredith, named her daughter Perrin Lynne. Both honored these names and those who carried them before. My sister, Sally Kinder, named her first son, Ross, and my brother David's son Brady named his second son John Perrin—likewise continuing a cherished tradition. Hopefully others down the line will also deem these names worthy of preserving the legacy they embody.

CHAPTER 24

Acknowledgments and Thanks

A PROJECT SUCH AS *A Fortress and a Legacy* could not have been completed without the assistance of many kind and giving people. Some provided inspiration, some education, some information, some encouragement, some critique, and some even shared my intense dedication to this project that, for the past six years, has so captivated my interest and time. A few have participated in all of the above activities. Mere words cannot express my full gratitude. To each, I am eternally thankful for all you have contributed to this "baby of mine."

Trying to list everyone who has helped me carries with it the danger of leaving someone out. I am willing to take that risk, because to not do so would hide my deep gratitude to those who gave so much to help me make this a success (however that word is defined). Since this is my first attempt at a writing project with this degree of complexity, simply finishing this work serves as one simple measure of success. I leave others to my readers.

There are a few people without whom this project would have been impossible. I'll begin with them.

When I get to heaven, I'll be able to thank my **Uncle Bud, Ross W. Perrin, Jr.**, for his service to keep our nation free and for chronicling his life through his letters during this period. His written words allowed me to begin constructing this book. My **Aunt Thelma McGhee Perrin Hancock**, Bud's wife, was also faithful in writing to him as well as to the families of the other crew-members. I am also grateful she kept this correspondence—almost a thousand letters in all.

My mother, **Evelyn Perrin Greene**, and grandmother, **Maude Foster Perrin**, also wrote letters to Uncle Bud, many of which are a part of this cache. My mother also helped me write my love to my Palsy Walsy even before I was old enough to do so on my own. Thanks, Granny and Mom.

In the aggregate, these letters were the catalyst that precipitated this book. Without them, writing *Fortress* would have been virtually impossible. They provided the direction, facts, and insights that served as the road map, guiding the research and writing throughout the journey.

And to my dear cousin/sister **Rozzy (Rosalind Cannon Perrin Davis)**, thanks for much more than I can express. I have loved you as a sister from as far back as I can remember, and you made possible the transfer of the letters to me six years ago. You have always been my primary inspiration for this journey back in time. I pray it means as much to you as it does to me.

My muse, supporter, strength, encourager, and occasional expert critic is my wife, **Lynne Wheeler Hoover Greene**. She kept me going when I stalled and stopped me when I got so engrossed in the writing that I could think of nothing else. After more than fifty years of marriage, she often knows me better than I know myself, a scary but delightful truth. Thanks, my love, for encouraging me on this wonderful journey.

Without the willing assistance of Thelma's daughters, **Kathleen Hancock** and **Elizabeth Hancock LeMay**, who so diligently scanned and categorized these letters, I would have had a much more difficult time producing this work. Thanks, ladies, for your hard and valuable work.

Dr. Kevin E. Wilson, Ph.D., has not only been of immeasurable assistance in all aspects of my research but has also become a valued friend. As past president and current executive secretary of the 381st Bomb Group Association, he assisted me in immersing myself in the history and data of the people and missions of this WWII group. He also introduced me to key people, pointed me in the direction of needed data, and helped me gather the facts necessary to put together this most intricate puzzle. He has been gracious with his time, never seeking to elevate himself in the process and only seeking to help. I owe both him and his wife, Ellen, a great deal.

Marilyn Jeffers Walton's extensive knowledge of WWII and her contacts in the community of researchers and historians on the period have been and still are invaluable. Over the last five years, Marilyn and I have been in touch almost daily. She has been most gracious in helping me gather crucial elements of knowledge and contact key information sources all over the world. These include Edouard Reniere and Ed Zander, who provided much detail on the flight pattern and conditions of Mission #222. In the fall of 2013, Marilyn and her husband, John, joined Lynne and me in England where we explored WWII sites and museums. I am honored to call her my friend.

The detailed recollections of **Conan D. Cash**, a 532nd bombardier and close friend of my Uncle Bud, helped me bring many of the scenes in the book to life. Further, he and his mother, as the book explains, were key in helping Aunt Thelma confirm her husband's death. Years after the war, Mr. Cash worked on the refurbishing of the Memphis Belle when it was located in Memphis. That aircraft is currently under complete restoration at the National Museum of the United States Air Force in Dayton, Ohio. I am deeply grateful for his assistance prior to his passing on March 4, 2013.

Robert H. "Bob" Angevine became a close friend and incredible source of facts and background for *Fortress*. In addition, his daughters, Nancy and Janan, and his son, Terry, have been both helpful and kind as I sought to get his story right. My trip to Midland and Big Spring with Bob was an unforgettable experience. His second wife, Bea, passed away in 2013, but not before teaching me to make some delicious cookies made by freezing Ritz crackers that had been dipped in chocolate. I am thankful for Bob's influence on not only my uncle in 1944, but also me over the past five years. Sadly, he passed away on December 29, 2014.

Edouard Reniere was a vital link in making contacts in Mannheim who could assist my search. Without Ed's help, I might still be searching for the vast information and numerous contacts he helped me make. I cherish the friendship with this kind, resourceful friend and his wife Helena.

Ron Mackay, author of more than two-dozen books on various aspects of the air war in Europe, has been most gracious in sharing his vast reservoir of detailed information on the war. Affectionately dubbed "Ronnie Mac" by Kevin Wilson, Jim Tennet, and me, he has been most willing to relate stories and details that bring the period, aircraft and stories of the 381st Bomb Group and the 8th Air Force to life.

Mannheim resident **Ruth Reiss**, introduced to me by our mutual friend, John Madden and his son, Dan, was the first person I met in Germany to help me in my research. Ruth was key in my making the critical contact with Ms. Fleck, who was a link to the account of the crash found in the Hasiba book. I am eternally grateful for the help of Ruth and her family, Timo, Mitch and Kim.

The vast assistance of **Natalie Blaquiere** since the fall of 2012 is chronicled earlier in this book. In short, she took up my project as her very own. She is an incredible lady who possesses a big heart, unfathomable energy, a keen intellect, an indomitable spirit and "the eye of the tiger." Nothing has impeded her incredible desire to help, and she gets results. Thanks, Natalie, for who you are, all you continue to do, and all you mean to me. And to Natalie's mother, **Helma Schafer**, thanks for continuing to provide energy and wisdom in knowing how and what to do in continuing this pursuit.

I have been blessed to work with a wonderful editor, **Marti Pieper**. Early in the writing process, she gave me encouragement and some specific direction, and I took her valuable advice. In the ensuing two years, she has afforded me the benefit of her experience, skills, and editing abilities as we trudged through the crafting process of *Fortress*. Because of her honesty, diligence and desire for excellence, this work is significantly better than I could have imagined.

Many others played key roles in this journey, some large and some small, but all important. I list them in the various categories of their involvement.

September 1, 1941 Picnic Group

Most of those in attendance at the Labor Day picnic in 1941 were deceased when I began this journey in 2009. Over the years, my father, Leonard E. Greene, and mother, Evelyn, related volumes to me about Uncle Bud. Dad passed away at age eighty-four on November 10, 1996. Mother died on February 20, 2004 at age eighty-nine and was buried on my birthday two days later. My granny, Maude Perrin, also painted vivid pictures of my uncle even up to the week she died in late 1963. I am so grateful for those memories, continually rekindled as I wrote.

Grover Cleveland Blevins and his wife, Henrietta "Henry" Bowman Blevins, played an integral and intriguing part in the story woven throughout the pages of this book. Thanks, Henrietta, for your contribution to *Fortress*.

I was able to meet with Truji McCloud and her daughter, Maureen, and pick Truji's brain about her relationship with my uncle. I am grateful for her input and assistance.

Lynda and Joe Mucke were family friends with whom we spent many enjoyable hours. Joe died in 1989 and Lynda in 1987. Their daughter, Mary Evelyn, and I were childhood friends and graduated from high school together in 1958. She was very helpful in providing information about her parents and the photo included in the book. Our friendship continues today.

Walter Lee "Dusty" Holder and his wife, Emma Orben Holder, were close friends of my family, and I often heard about them over the years. "Little Dusty," as his nephew is known, and Kathy Holder Wolf provided me photos and information about their uncle and aunt. I was also able to talk with Dusty's second wife, Phyllis, whom he wed after Emma's death in 1977. Dusty died on December 7, 2000.

Dick Foster, whom I call "Uncle Dick" although he is actually my cousin, is a man I've always loved and admired. Our family spent many Sundays in the '50s with him, his wife, Mickey, and their family in Fountain City. Uncle Dick was most helpful in relating information about his service experiences and his recollections of my uncle.

Knoxville and Tennessee

The KUB (formerly the Knoxville Electric Power and Water Board) Communications Director, Jennifer Stooksbury, provided thorough research and encouragement early in my research.

Miss Jessie Lou Neubert taught my parents as well Bud and Thelma. Later, I was in her twelfth grade history class. Much to my later regret, I followed my uncle in a lack of attention to history during my high school years. During the research process for this book, I often chastised myself for this juvenile lack of foresight.

Tom Evans, son of Mr. W. E. Evans, helped by permitting me to access his cache of *Blue and White* newspapers.

Gifted historian and author Fred Brown, with the aid of Paul Efird, *News Sentinel* photographer, kindly used the story of my search and the life of Ross Perrin for an expansive article and pictorial in the May 27, 2012 edition of the Knoxville *News Sentinel*. The paper celebrated its centennial with an insert covering each of the ten decades of its existence. The focal point of the 1940 insert was Brown's article, "A Story of Sacrifice."

In June of 2014, Paul Efird put me in touch with Anita Coursey at the Tennessee Archives in Nashville. She graciously found for me my aunt's appeal for information about my uncle's death published in the January 19, 1944 issue of the *News Sentinel*.

John B. Romeiser, East Tennessee Veterans Memorial Association, added my uncle's name to the honor wall for WWII veterans located adjacent to the old L&N Rail Station. This means a great deal to our family.

Information and photos of Ridgewell airman Corky Moulton, later a POW as a result of being shot down on the first Schweinfurt raid, were supplied by his daughter, Mrs. Jan Moulton Jones, and niece, Jimmie Jane Moulton Ray.

Ann Davis Satterfield and Lib Davis Crossley, daughters of our Cherry Street next-door neighbors, John and Zettie Davis, provided information on their brother, Eugene "Gene" Davis. In turn, I was blessed to share with them an article they had never seen about the mission that resulted in his death in the Pacific on August 7, 1944.

My sixth-grade teacher, Thomas Raulston, was a private in the 101st and jumped into Normandy on D-Day. His wife, Rosie, and daughters, Suzanne and Rosie, provided photographs and information on his time in the service. In turn, I was glad to provide them with a photo of our class that they had never seen.

Training

Julius W. "Jay" Pyles was the closest friend Bud made during his training period. I am grateful for the insight that came from the numerous mentions and photos of him and his wife, Dorothy, in the letter cache. I wish I had been able to talk with him, but my research found that he and his wife had passed away earlier. Information about Vernon L. "Gate" Gatewood came from similar sources. In addition, his photo came from his daughter-in-law Betty's book about his POW days entitled *Kreige 7956, a WW2 Bombardier's Pursuit of Freedom*. Brief interviews of Arthur W. Schusseler; Amelia Ann, the wife of Arwyn Arnhart; and the son of John Spare provided additional background information about Bud's fellow trainees at Big Spring.

Belskis Crew

At the time I began this project, all of the Belskis crew had passed away. The two survivors died years after the crash: Elvis McCoy on August 1, 1988, and Durward Suggs on March 24, 2004. Two of Leo Belskis's sisters along with a nephew assisted me in my research: Katherine Belskis Feykes, Stella Belskis Koludrovic, and Dennis Winsky.

Glenn Vaughn's brother, Frank; son, Glenn Jr.; and wife, Alyce, were most helpful during our long discussions about Glenn. Glenn, Jr. also provided letters and photos valuable to the story. Alyce passed away at age ninety on October 25, 2012.

Elvis McCoy's granddaughter, Amanda Herd, provided candid photos of the crew from 1944 and some information on her grandfather.

Mr. Alfred S. Lauret, Jr., was able to provide extensive information on the Lauret family tree. Information on Durward Suggs, Walter Newman, Robert Rogers, and Jim Collett came primarily from numerous letters between the families. I am grateful to have had access to as many as I did.

381st Bomb Group

Discussions with 381st airmen during the reunions since 2009 have broadened and deepened my perspective of the period, airbase, and missions flown out of Ridgewell. I give a heartfelt thanks to all my fellow members of the mighty 381st.

Many "boys" from the 381st have written books about their experiences. Each has been helpful in providing context, including Ed Carr's *On Final Approach*, James F. "Jim" Grey's *Vanishing*

Contrails, Robert "Bob" Gilbert's *The View From the Bottom Up*, Theodore "Ted" Homdrom's *Mission Memories*, and Dave Osborne's *They Came From Over The Pond* and *Halstead and Colne Valley at War (1939-1945)*. Ted Homdrom also provided a photo of Roke Manor, where he, like my uncle, spent a week in R & R.

Robert "Bob" Armstrong wrote *Friendly and Enemy Skies*. His account of the Magdeburg mission on September 28, 1944 was critical to expanding the information provided by the war diary account of the day. Bob and his son Dan also allowed me to reproduce his extensive photo album for posting on my World War 2 Collection website (http://worldwar2collection.com/).

William L. "Bill" Palmer also permitted me to reproduce his extensive photo album and scrapbook for the website. Since Bill was at Ridgewell from its inception to war's end, his recollections added much to my research. He and his wife, Ellen, have also been personal and spiritual encouragers over these past five years.

In late summer of 1943, Lt. Leonard Spivey accompanied Ridgewell's first commanding officer, Colonel Joseph Nazzaro, to Pinetree-High Wycombe when the Eighth brass were planning the first Schweinfurt raid. Leonard's description of Pinetree (headquarters for the 8th AF) and its wartime operation provided tremendous insight into my description of this critical 8th AF location. Leonard's plane was shot down on the first Schweinfurt raid on August 17, 1943. He survived and was interred in the POW Camp, Stalag Luft III until the end of the war. Lt. Col Conway Hall led the 381st on this mission in which nine of the twenty B-17s from Ridgewell were lost.

In 2013, John Luke, Bursar of Wycombe Abbey School, graciously gave my wife and me an extensive tour and indoctrination on the use of the campus that was converted to Pinetree during the war.

Many others connected with the 381st have been most helpful during this sojourn, including Darrell Blizzard, Joseph "Joe" Waddell, Stuart Newman, Len Fahnstock, Ivory and Rick Wilson, Dick Schneider, Everett Worrell, Ray Hecker, Jack Lantz, Herb Kwart, Donald Wilson, Floyd Metts, Virgil Kline, Vernon Williams, Vinnie Perrone, and Lou Perrone, who at ninety can still get in and out of his ball turret gun position as he did seven decades ago.

Others also provided valuable information and items: Colonel Conway Hall (autographed photo), Mike Thomas (photo album of his grandfather), John Howland (mission stories), and Jerry Gerasko (movies his uncle made in 1944).

Sam Whitehead, still as ramrod-straight in 2013 as he was in the famous book cover photo from 1944, provided valuable and detailed information about missions, pre-flight preparation, and post-flight interrogation. His daughter, Rita, assisted with details she knew well from her many conversations with her dad.

Mrs. Thomas Sellers along with Ann Hodge, wife of Alpheus, who was part of the team producing information for the MACR of my uncle's fatal mission, were helpful in providing background information.

Ridgewell Base and Ridgewell Airfield Commemorative Association Museum

Author, historian, 381st member, museum president, and Ridgewell resident Dave Osborne and his gracious wife, Joanne, kindly gave me my first guided tour in 2010 of what is left of the aerodrome.

I also owe thanks to Jim, Chris, and Jenny Tennet (museum chairman), along with Alan and Monica Steele, Michael Land, and Paul Bingley, who hosted Lynne and me on a visit to the Ridgewell Museum. Further, their continued work for the benefit of veterans and those interested in Ridgewell is greatly appreciated.

James and Claudia Gray opened their property and home to Jim, Alan, Chris, and me at the end of our trek across their farm, originally a large part of the Ridgewell base. We are grateful.

Robert Roote, current owner of the portion of the property where the original entrance to the base and infirmary (Now the Nissen hut housing the museum) kindly allows the Ridgewell Memorial Association to maintain the property. Thanks, Robert, for your commitment to the preservation of this historic site.

United States

Many contacts in the US provided bits of information that, in the aggregate, helped me develop contextual background for the book.

Please forgive me for not listing each one. A few in particular bear mentioning:

Greg Powell, owner of Hambones BBQ in Hapeville, Georgia, allowed me to see the memorabilia, including the lock and key to his cell, from his father's confinement as a POW at Stalag III.

Al Pela, guide at the Mighty Eighth Museum in Pooler, Georgia, graciously provided background material used to educate visitors to the museum. This narrative helped greatly in developing a deeper understanding of the importance of the 8th AF in WWII.

In an incredible, extensive conversation arranged by his son, Doug, Wolfgang Otto helped me understand the mindset he had as a young member of the *Hitlerjugend* (Hitler Youth) during the early 1940s. The time Lynne and I spent with this committed Christian and his wife along with their son and his family was most captivating and educational.

Film and sound archivist Bradley Reeves, director of the Tennessee Archive of Moving Image and Sound, broadcast the BBC interview of my uncle on WDVX in November of 2012. Thanks for allowing many of Bud's fellow airmen to hear the re-broadcast on their computers across the country.

Bob Dukes has been a trusted friend, prayer partner, intercessor, and professional critic (the latter only when he allowed his wisdom and intellect to outweigh his kindness and empathy). Thanks for your encouragement and insight on this project.

Thanks to Tim Shannon, who masterminded a weekend B-17 WWII Adventure during which I was able to experience much of the flight operation of a B-17 mission. The flight on the B17-G *Liberty Belle* was a moving experience that I'll not forget. Unfortunately, on June 13, 2011, a fuel leak forced it to make an emergency landing in an Illinois cornfield where it was destroyed by the resulting fire.

Mannheim, Germany

When I began to search for help in locating people and crash-related sites in Mannheim, I turned to Udo Cremer, client, friend, and longtime resident of Frankfurt, Germany. Udo put me in touch with Mannheim resident Klaus Ulrich, who kindly searched records, maps, and locations to provide an initial road map for my search.

Ruth Reiss then located Ms. Waltraud Fleck, who lived along the mission #222 flight path in the fall of 1944. Ms. Fleck provided a shared moment of critical connection, a personal glimpse into the angst Hitler's diabolical mind and actions caused for the German people.

Natalie Blaquiere's research, contacts, and the articles written for the Mannheim morning newspaper, the *Mannheimer-Morgen*, culminated in a reception for me in the City Council's administrative offices. Mr. Christian Helmut Wetzel, museum director of Verein Geschichte Alt-Neckarau Mannheim, presided over the event. I am indebted to these individuals. In addition, I am grateful to Erster Burgermeister; Christian Specht; Ms. Patricia Popp, assistant museum director; Mr. Sommer, photographer; and especially to Mr. Jan Cerny, whose articles kept this story alive for Mannheim-Neckerau readers.

Witnesses to the Crash of Mission #222, Mannheim-Ludwigshafen

Finding people who actually witnessed parts of the pre- and post-crash elements of the B-17 crash in Mannheim was always a goal of my search. These kind people with such vivid memories have added so much to both this work and to my ability to bring more clarity to the final moments of the flight of my uncle's plane. Special thanks to Mr. Gerhard Stoll; Mr. and Mrs. Karl Wolfram Schmidt and their daughter, Sabine Haug, who helped me gather follow-up information and photographs from her father; Mrs. Irene Penn; Mr. Hubert Guthlein; and Frau Steinkueller.

Greene Consulting Associates

I work with some incredibly talented professionals in my primary business, Greene Consulting Associates. Without their help and guidance, I would have failed to pull this project together. I give heartfelt thanks to Cindy Byrd, for almost three decades a trusted and dear friend and consummate professional, always striving for excellence in everything she does; Rick Tyler, my dear friend, confidant, multi-faceted professional, sometime-editor, writing critic, and spiritual growth acolyte has been a consistent supporter of this project. Shawn and Faith Janes have graciously and vigorously applied their broad and unique skills and professionalism to my attempts at artistic expression. They have also guided me, both technically and emotionally, through the production process for this book, I also want to thank Patti Lee, who has continually helped with numerous details, including scanning, punctuation advice, and a myriad of administrative items; and Stephanie Urbas, who has worked tirelessly with me on my newfound professional ventures, websites and design, increasing her own professional skills in the process. She has also applied her considerable skills in taking my cover concept and making it come to life as she added important elements to it, making it a significantly better representation of the message within its pages.

Normandy Trip

The meaningful, educational 2012 trip to Normandy and Bastogne that my daughter Meredith and I took with a Focus on the Family tour group provided tremendous context and flavor for this project. I give a special thanks to Doug and Deb Birnie and Tom and Deb Minnery, who arranged the opportunity, and to our professional and engaging guides, Ray and Cristy Pfeiffer.

I hope the others who helped but remain unmentioned only due to my aging memory and not my lack of gratefulness will forgive me. Many thanks and God's richest blessings to all!

Bibliography

Multiple sources from numerous genres of information were used to provide both text and context in the writing of *A Fortress and a Legacy*. The following lists comprise many but not all of the sources used in developing this work.

Books

Armstrong, Robert, *Friendly And Enemy Skies* (Hutchinson, Kansas: Robert Armstrong, 2003).

Bebb, Russ, *The Big Orange: A Story of Tennessee Football* (Knoxville, Tennessee: Strode Publishing, 1973).

Bowman, Martin W., *Echoes of England—The 8th Air Force in the Second World War* (Stroud, Gloucestershire, United Kingdom: Tempus Publishing Limited, 2006).

Boyne, Walter J., *Clash of Wings: World War II in the Air* (New York: Simon and Schuster, 1994).

———, *The Influence of Air Power Upon History* (Gretna, Louisiana: Pelican Publishing Company, 2003).

Brown, James Good, *The Mighty Men of the 381st: Heroes All.* (Salt Lake City: Publishers Press, 1984).

Childers, Thomas, *Wings of Morning: The Story of the Last bomber Shot Down Over Germany in World War II* (Reading, Massachusetts: Addison-Wesley Publishing Company, 1995).

Carr, Edward C., *On Final Approach: Recollections of a WWII B-17 Air Crew* (Couperville, Washington: Edward C. Carr, 2002).

Comer, John, *Combat Crew: The Story of 25 Missions Over Europe from the Daily Journal of a B-17 Gunner* (United Kingdom: Sphere Publishing, 1988).

Denton, Helen, *World War II WAC* (Marietta, Georgia: Deeds Publishing, 2012).

Karen Farrington, *Handbook of World War II: An Illustrated*

Chronicle of the Struggle for Victory (London: Abbweydale Press, 2008).

Fletcher, Jesse C., *Bill Wallace of China* (Nashville: Broadman Press, 1963).

Flint, Lorna, *Wycombe Abbey School 1896-1986 Partial History* (United Kingdom: Wycombe Abbey School, Private Printing, 1989).

Freeman, Roger A. and Norman Ottaway, *The Mighty Eighth War Manual*. London: Cassell-Wellington House, 1984).

———, *The Mighty Eighth: A History of the US Army Air Force* (London: Jane's Publishing Company, 1986).

Freeman, Roger A. and David R. Osborne, *The B-17 Flying Fortress Story* (London: Arms & Armour, 1998, reissue ed.).

Freeman, Roger A. and David A. Anderton, *B-17 Fortress and B-29 Superfortress at War* (London: Bookmart Limited, 1996).

Freemont-Barnes, Gregory, *American Bomber Crewman 1941-1945* (Oxford, United Kingdom: Osprey Publishing, 2008).

Gilbert, Robert, *Neyland: The Gridiron General* (Savannah, Georgia: Golden Coast Publishing Company, 1990).

Gilbert, Bob, *The View From The Bottom Up: Growing Up Fast In World War II* (Bennington, Vermont: Merriam Press, 2012).

Lukacs, John, *The Duel: The Eighty Day Struggle Between Churchill and Hitler* (New York: Tickner & Fields, Houghton Mifflin Company, 1991.

———, *Five Days in London, May 1940* (New Haven, Connecticut: Yale University Press, 1999).

———, *The Legacy of the Second World War* (New Haven, Connecticut: Yale University Press, 2010).

———, *The Last European War, September 1939-December 1941* (New Haven, Connecticut: Yale University Press, 1976).

MacKay, Ron, *First In The Field: The First Air Division Over*

Europe In World War II (Atglen, Pennsylvania: Schiffer Publishing, Limited, 2006).

——, *Ridgewell's Flying Fortress: The 381st Bombardment Group (H) In World War II* (Atglen, Pennsylvania: Schiffer Publishing, Limited, 2000).

——, *The First Combat Wing In World War II* (Atglen, Pennsylvania: Schiffer Military History, 2014).

——, *381st Bomb Group* (Carrollton, Texas: Squadron/Signal Publications, 1994).

MacMillan, Margaret, *Paris 1919: Six Months that Changed the World* (New York: Random House Trade Paperbacks, 2003).

Metaxes, Eric, *Bonhoeffer: Pastor, Prophet, Martyr, Spy* (Nashville: Thomas Nelson, 2010).

Miller, Donald L., *Eighth Air Force: The American Bomber Crews in Britain* (London: Aurum Press Limited, 2007).

——, *Masters of the Air: America's Bomber Boys Who Fought the Air War Against Nazi Germany* (New York: Simon & Schuster, reprint edition, 2006).

Olson, Lynne, *Citizens of London: The Americans Who Stood with Britain in its Finest, Darkest Hour* (New York: Random House, 2011).

Osborne, Dave, *Halstead and the Colne Valley at War* (Halstead, Essex, United Kingdom: Halstead & District Local History Society, 1992).

Osborne, David R., *They Came From Over The Pond* (Oregon, Wisconsin: 381st Bomb Group Memorial Association, 1999).

Peck, Richard, *On the Wings of Heroes*. New York: Puffin, reprint ed., 2008).

Pitts, Jesse Richard, *Return To Base: Memoirs of a B-17 Copilot, Kimbolton, England, 1943-1944* (Stroud, Gloucestershire, United Kingdom: Tempus Publishing Ltd., 2004).

Schrecengost, Tammy Burrow, *Webb Air Force Base 1942-1977* (Big Spring, Texas: Tammy Burrow Schrecengost, 2002).

Serber, A. M., *Murrow: His Life and Times* (New York: Fordham University Press, 1999).

Smith, Graham, *Essex Airfields In The Second World War* (Newbury, Berkshire, United Kingdom: Countryside Books, 1996).

The Stars & Stripes: WWII Front Pages (Southport, Connecticut: Hugh Letter Levin Associates, 1985).

Stone, Ken, *Triumphant We Fly: A 381st Bomb Group Anthology 1943-1945* (Paducah, Kentucky: Turner Publishing Company, 1994).

US Army, *Instructions for American Servicemen in Britain* (London: US Army War Department, 1942).

US Army Air Force, *Target Germany: The U S Army Air Force's Official Story of the VIII Bomber Command's First Year Over Europe* (London: The Sun Engraving Company, 1944).

Ibid., *The Official Guide to the Army Air Forces* (New York: Simon & Schuster, 1944).

Walton, Marilyn Jeffers, *Rhapsody In Junk: A Daughter's Return To Germany To Finish Her Father's Story* (Bloomington, Indiana: Author House, 2007).

Whitman, Kenneth, *World War II: Saving The Reality, A Collector's Vault* (Whitman Publishing, 2009).

Willmott, H. P., *B-17 Flying Fortress.* (London: Bison Books Limited, 1980).

Winant, John Gilbert, *Letter from Grosvenor Square: An Account of a Stewardship, a Study of an Enduring Friendship of Men and of Nations* (Boston: Houghton Mifflin, 1947).

German Documents and Books

Hisaba, Norbert, *Neckarauer Impressionen 1939–1945: Chronicle of 75 years Mannheim AG Power Station*, (Mannheim, Germany, Mannheim AG Power Station, 1996).

Wolfe, Dieter, *Luftkriegsereignisse in Mannheim 1939-1945*, (Mannheim, Germany: Online-Publikationnen Des Stadtarchivs).

Keljer, Volker and Verlag, Wartberg *Mannheim im Bombenkrieg 1940-1945*, (Mannheim, Germany, GmbH & Co, KG).

Pohl, M.d., *Pohl Diary-Kreigs-Tagebuch Luftgefahr-Offentliche Luftwarnung-Fliegeralarm und Luftangriffe,sowie der hierdurch entstandene Personen-und Sachschaden in Mannheim*, Zusammengestellt und bearbeitet von M.d. SchP. Pohl, 23 and 174.

United States Government Records

The 381st War Diaries, www.381st.org. Each Bomb Group and Bomb Squad posted contemporaneous mission-related diaries. Also, each station posted numerous memos, directives, personnel information, and base-related activities communication. These records provided expansive information to enable the author to connect the letters with specific data and facts from the European Theater of Operation.

8th Air Force Records: Similar to the 381st records, the First Division and the First Wing created contemporaneous records of activities in the ETO. These records were the source of additional data for this book.

Office of Air Force History: Washington D.C.: afhso.research@pentagon.af.mil

Maxwell Air Force Base, Alabama: Expanded records for the 8th AF are available at Maxwell Air Force Base. These records provided data for this book.

National Archives: http://www.archives.gov/research/military/ww2/

Interviews

Multiple interviews of historians, authors, military personnel, and aviators from the 381st BG at Ridgewell, Essex, England.

Letters

Crew Family Letters: Fifty-six letters written between the wives, mothers, and family members of the nine crew members: Belskis, Perrin, Vaughn, Collett, Lauret, McCoy, Suggs, Rogers, and Newman from 1944 through 1947.

Family Letters: Seven hundred and twenty-seven letters written from late 1942 to December of 1944 by and between Ross W. "Bud" Perrin; his wife, Thelma McGhee Perrin; his sister, Evelyn Perrin Greene; his mother, Maude Foster Perrin; and his nephew, J. Ross Greene.

Friends' Letters: Sixty-one letters written by various friends and business associates to Bud and Thelma between 1943 and December of 1944.

Military Personnel Letters: Thirty-nine letters from military friends and acquaintances.

Movies

12 O'Clock High. Directed by Henry King. Twentieth Century Fox Film Corporation, 1949.

The Gathering Storm. Directed by Richard Loncraine. New York: Home Box Office Films, 2002.

The Great Escape. Directed by John Sturges. Hollywood: Metro-Goldwyyn-Mayer, 1963.

Ike: Countdown to D-Day. Directed by Robert Harmon. A & E Television Networks, 2004.

Into the Storm. Directed by Thaddeus O'Sullivan. New York: Home Box Office Films, 2009.

Sergeant York. Directed by Howard Hawks. Burbank, California: Warner Brothers, 1941.

The King's Speech. Directed by Tom Hooper. New York: The Weinstein Company and Momentum Films, 2010.

Memphis Belle. Directed by Michael Caton-Jones. Burbank, California: Warner Brothers, 1990.

Schindler's List. Directed by Steven Spielberg. Hollywood: Universal Pictures and Amblin Entertainment, 1993.

Shining Through. Directed by David Seltzer. Twentieth Century Fox Film Corporation, 1992.

Swing Kids. Directed by Thomas Carter. Hollywood: Hollywood Pictures, 1993.

Valkyrie. Directed by Brian Singer. Hollywood: Metro-Goldwyn-Mayer and United Artists, 2008.

Museums

CAF Airpower Museum, Midland, Texas: http://www.airpowermuseum.org/

Commemorative Air Force-Dixie Wing Museum, Peachtree City, Georgia: www.dixiewing.org

Hangar 25 Air Museum, Big Spring, Texas: https://www.facebook.com/pages/Hangar-25-Air-Museum/169080189279

Imperial War Museums-IWM Churchill War Rooms, London, United Kingdom: http://www.iwm.org.uk/visits/churchill-war-rooms

Imperial War Museums-IWM Duxford, Cambridge, United Kingdom: http://www.iwm.org.uk/visits/iwm-duxford

Imperial War Museums-IWM London, London, United Kingdom: http://www.iwm.org.uk/visits/iwm-london

Mannheim Archives Museum; https://www.stadtarchiv.mannheim.de/

Museum of World War II, Boston, Massachusetts: http://www.museumofworldwarii.com/

National Museum of the Mighty Eighth Air Force, Pooler, Georgia: http://mightyeighth.org/

National Museum of the US Air Force, Wright-Patterson Air Force Base, Ohio: http://www.nationalmuseum.af.mil/

Ridgewell Airfield Commemorative Museum, Ridgewell, Essex, England: http://www.381st.com/

The National WWII Museum–New Orleans, New Orleans, Louisiana: http://www.nationalww2museum.org/

United States Air Force Academy Museum, Colorado Springs, Colorado: http://www.usafa.af.mil/information/visitors/

Periodicals

After the Battle: High Wycombe Air Headquarters-Issue 87, Essex, England.

Brown, Fred, *A Story of Sacrifice*, (Knoxville, Tennessee: *Knoxville News Sentinel*, May 27, 2012).

Knoxville Journal, April 20, 1944 and other issues.

Knoxville News Sentinel, December 8, 1941 and other issues.

Life Magazine, Bombardier Cover, May 18, 1942.

Life Magazine, Battle of Midway Cover, August 31, 1942.

London Times: London, United Kingdom, various issues.

New York Times, December 12, 1944.

Stars & Stripes, daily publication during WWII, multiple issues.

World War II-Weider History Group, Inc., Leesburg, Virginia, multiple issues.

YANK Magazine, Weekly publication during WWII, multiple issues.

Television Documentaries

"The B-17 Flying Fortress," Original Training Films, 2005.

"B-17 Flying Fortress," Roaring Warbirds, 2007.

"Biography: FDR–Years of Crisis, Arts & Entertainment, 1994.

B-17 Flying Fortress–Roaring Warbirds, 2007.

"The Color of War (Five Volumes)," The History Channel, 2001.

"Decisions that Shook the World (Roosevelt), Starz/Anchor Bay, 2005.

"Lost Airmen of Buchenwald," Marauder-Michael Dorsey, 2012.

"Paris 1919," National Film Board of Canada, 2008.

"Target for Today: Eighth Air Force," First Motion Picture Unit, 1944.

"War Planes of World War II," The History Channel, 1998.

"Winston Churchill," The History Channel, 2003.

"The World at War (12 Volumes)," Arts & Entertainment, 1973.

"World War II in Color," The Discovery Channel, 2009.

"World War II from Space," The History Channel, 2014.

Websites

Knoxville Heritage, Knoxville, Tennessee and Atlanta, Georgia: http://knoxvilleheritage.com/

Military Factory, "Military Aircraft of the World": http://www.militaryfactory.com/aircraft/index.asp

YOUTUBE–Various film clips about Ridgewell and the 381st taken during WWII

Bing Crosby Visits Ridgewell Station 167– September 2, 1944 & Cynthia Burwell Christens Smashing Time–September 3, 1944; Film Courtesy of Jerry Gerasko: https://www.youtube.com/watch?v=U_OAaxdxpRs

————London 1944–Taken by 381s Airman; Film Courtesy of Jerry Gerasko: https://www.youtube.com/watch?v=fVfatuoM1-g

————Ridgewell - Mission #Mission 172 to Brest, Germany–August 11, 1944: https://www.youtube.com/watch?v=U_OAaxdxpRs

————Ridgewell - Mission #187 to Brux, Czechoslovakia - September 12, 1944: https://www.youtube.com/watch?v=Bhs5VOioK-w

————Ridgewell Airfield 1945 - Film by Dave Osborne: https://www.youtube.com/watch?v=sMbmrqTwbAU

World War II Collection, Atlanta, Georgia: http://worldwar2collection.com/

Photo Album of Ross W. Perrin, Jr., http://worldwar2collection.com/virtual-museum/photo-albums/

381st Bombardment Group (Heavy), http://www.381st.org/

Ridgewell Airfield Commemorative Association, Ridgewell, Essex County, England: http://www.381st.com/

Additional WWII Research Aids

381st Bomb Group Reunions: 2009, Charleston, South Carolina; 2010, Nashville, Tennessee; 2011, Colorado Springs, Colorado; 2012, Dayton, Ohio; 2013, San Antonio, Texas. http://www.381st.org/

Doolittle Raider Reunion, 2012, Dayton, Ohio.

Malmedy Massacre Trial documents, books, and documentaries.

Research on the 136 graduates of Knoxville High School who were killed in WWII.

Stalag Luft III Reunions: Dayton, Ohio, 2012; and Colorado Springs, Colorado, 2014.

Trip to Normandy, France, 2012, sponsored by Focus on the Family, Colorado Springs, Colorado.

ARMY AIR FORCE HISTORICAL ASSOCIATION: http://www.aafha.org/